The Political Economy of WTO Implementation and China's Approach to Litigation in the WTO

This research was sponsored by the China-EU School of Law (CESL) at the China University of Political Science and Law (CUPL) www.cesl.edu.cn. The activities of CESL at CUPL are supported by the European Union and the P.R. of China.

Authors' names are not in order of precedence but in alphabetical order.

The Political Economy of WTO Implementation and China's Approach to Litigation in the WTO

Yenkong Ngangjoh Hodu

Manchester University School of Law, UK

Zhang Qi

Associate Professor, Shanghai International Studies University, China

Cheltenham, UK • Northampton, MA, USA

Published by
Edward Elgar Publishing Limited
The Lypiatts
15 Lansdown Road
Cheltenham
Glos GL50 2JA
UK

Edward Elgar Publishing, Inc.
William Pratt House
9 Dewey Court
Northampton
Massachusetts 01060
USA

A catalogue record for this book
is available from the British Library

Library of Congress Control Number: 2015945459

This book is available electronically in the **Elgar**online
Law subject collection
DOI 10.4337/9781783473854

ISBN 978 1 78347 384 7 (cased)
ISBN 978 1 78347 385 4 (eBook)

Typeset by Servis Filmsetting Ltd, Stockport, Cheshire
Printed and bound in Great Britain by TJ International Ltd, Padstow

Contents

List of abbreviations   viii
Table of cases   xiii

Introduction   1

PART I   NORMATIVITY AND IMPLEMENTATION
         ISSUES IN THE WTO

1.   World trade law and changing fundamentals in the global
     architecture   7
2.   The evolution of the GATT/WTO dispute settlement system   16
     2.1   The relevance of dispute settlement mechanisms in trade
           agreements   16
     2.2   Resolving disputes 'the GATT way'   20
     2.3   Constructing a more legalistic dispute settlement method
           under the General Agreement   22
     2.4   The Uruguay Round package as agreed by WTO
           members   27
     2.5   The dispute settlement understanding as a rule-based
           system   30
     2.6   Greater use of the WTO dispute settlement mechanism by
           a broader WTO membership   32
     2.7   Controversies surrounding remedies for non-compliance
           with DSB rulings and recommendations   35
3.   Applicable law before the WTO disputes settlement body   41
     3.1   Introduction   41
     3.2   What are the purposes of the WTO dispute settlement
           system?   43
     3.3   Applicable law in dispute settlement   47
     3.4   The text of the WTO covered agreements: straightforward
           sources   49
     3.5   Customary international law as a source of WTO law   53
     3.6   General principles of law   57
     3.7   Brief concluding remarks   61

4.   Theorising the WTO implementation regime   63
      4.1   Trade liberalisation as limitation of the power of the
            nation-state   63
      4.2   World trade law compliance discourse and
            constructivism   72
      4.3   Reputation costs as essential tool to enhance compliance
            with international trade rules   81
      4.4   The nature of treaties and reputation costs   87

PART II   CHINA AND WTO RULES IMPLEMENTATION:
          CONTEMPORARY POLICY AND
          DIPLOMACY

5.   The Chinese approach to law   91
6.   China and WTO law: from accession negotiations to current
      commitments   95
      6.1   A brief history of China's accession to the WTO   95
      6.2   An assessment of China's accession to the WTO   101
            6.2.1   Response from international and national media 101
      6.3   Commitments of the Chinese government to fulfil
            China's obligations   106
7.   China and the WTO dispute settlement system   108
      7.1   Chinese practice within the WTO dispute settlement
            framework   108
            7.1.1   An astonishing beginning as a complainant   108
            7.1.2   A diplomat within the first five years   112
                    7.1.2.1   A predictable dispute   112
                    7.1.2.2   First outing as a respondent   119
                    7.1.2.3   Revisiting the issue of subsidies   125
                    7.1.2.4   WTO Chinese years   133
                    7.1.2.5   The challenge of compliance for China 153
      7.2   Perspectives on China and the WTO dispute settlement
            system   178
            7.2.1   The Chinese government's perspective   178
            7.2.2   Academic scholarship   186
                    7.2.2.1   The DSU introductory phase   186
                    7.2.2.2   The DSU deep study phase   188
                    7.2.2.3   The Chinese cases deep study phase   191
8.   Chinese Confucianism and compliance   194
      8.1   Chinese Confucianism in context   194
      8.2   Contemporary China and compliance   197
            8.2.1   From a bilateral perspective   198

8.2.2   From a multilateral perspective   198
8.2.3   From the WTO perspective   200
9.   Conclusion   202

References   206
Index   249

Abbreviations

1 COMMON ABBREVIATIONS USED IN THE TEXT

AB	Appellate Body of the World Trade Organization
ABA	American Bar Association
ACP	African, Caribbean and Pacific
AD	antidumping
ADR	Alternative Disputes Resolution
AFP	Agence France-Presse
APEC	Asia-Pacific Economic Cooperation Organization
AVHE	audio-visual home entertainment
BSID	GATT Basic Instruments and Selected Materials
BYBIL	British Yearbook of International Law
CAP	European Community Common Agricultural Policy
CCCME	China Chamber of Commerce for Machine and Electricity
CDs	compact disc
Cf./cf.	confer
CKD	complete knocked down
CPPCC	Chinese People's Political Consultative Conference
DG	Director General of the World Trade Organization
Doc.	Document
DSB	Dispute Settlement Body of the World Trade Organization
DSM	Dispute Settlement Mechanism of the World Trade Organization
DSS	Dispute Settlement System of the World Trade Organization
DSU	Dispute Settlement Understanding
DVD	digital video disk
EC	European Communities
ECHR	European Court of Human Rights
ECOSOC	Economic and Social Council
ed./eds	editor/s
EEC	European Economic Community

EFTA	European Free Trade Area
e.g.	exampli gratia (for example)
EPS	electronic payment services
et al.	et alii (and others)
ETS	European Treaty Series
et seq./et seqq.	et sequens (and the following)/et sequentia (and those that follow)
EU	European Union
fn.	footnote
FTAA	Free Trade Area of the Americas
FYBIL	Finnish Yearbook of International Law
FYROM	Former Yugoslav Republic of Macedonia
GATS	General Agreement on Trade in Services
GATT	General Agreement on Tariffs and Trade
GDP	gross domestic product
GNP	gross national product
GPA	Agreement on Government Procurement
GSP	Generalised System of Preference
GYBIL	German Yearbook of International Law
Ibid./ibid.	ibidem (in the same place)
ICJ	International Court of Justice
i.e.	id est (that is)
IIPA	International Intellectual Property Alliance
ILC	International Law Commission
ILM	International Law Materials
ILO	International Labour Organization
ILR	International Law Reports
IPR	intellectual property right
ITLOS	International Tribunal for the Law of the Sea
ITO	International Trade Organization
K.B.	Kings Bench, United Kingdom of Great Britain and Northern Ireland
MEA	Multilateral Environmental Agreement
MFA	Multi-Fibre Agreement
MFN	most favoured nation
MMPA	United States Marine Mammal Protection Act
MOFCOM	Ministry of Commerce (China)
MOFTEC	Ministry of Foreign Trade and Economic Cooperation (China)
MPYBUNL	Max Planck Yearbook of United Nations Law
MTN	multilateral trade negotiations
NAFTA	North American Free Trade Area

NATO	North Atlantic Treaty Organization
No./no.	number
NT	National Treatment
NYBIL	Netherlands Yearbook of International Law
OECD	Organisation for Economic Co-operation and Development
p./pp.	page/pages
PCIJ	Permanent Court of International Justice
PRC	People's Republic of China
RMB	Ren Ming Bi (Chinese currency)
S&D/SDT	Special and Differential Treatments
SAIL	Steel Authority of India Ltd
SCM	Subsidies and Countervailing Measures
SKD	semi knocked down
SMIC	Semiconductor Manufacturing International Corporation
SOE	state-owned enterprise
SPS	Sanitary and Phytosanitary Agreement
TBT	technical barriers to trade
TEU	Treaty on European Union
TMB	Textiles Monitoring Body
TPRM	Trade Policy Review Mechanism
TRIMS	Trade-Related Investment Measures
TRIPS	Agreement on Trade-Related Aspects of Intellectual Property Rights
UN	United Nations
UNCITL	United Nations Commissions on International Trade Law
UNCTAD	United Nations Conference on Trade and Development
UNIDROIT	International Institute for the Unification of Private Law
UNTS	United Nations Treaty Series
US	United States of America
USDOC	United States Department of Commerce
USITC	United States International Trade Commission
USTR	United States Trade Representative
VAT	value-added tax
VCLT	Vienna Convention on the Law of Treaties
WHO	World Health Organization
WIPO	World Intellectual Property Organization
WTO	World Trade Organization
YBILC	Yearbook of the International Law Commission

2 ABBREVIATIONS RELATING TO JOURNALS

AFDI	Annuaire Français de Droit International
AJCL	American Journal of Comparative Law
AJICL	Arizona Journal of International and Comparative Law
AJIL	American Journal of International Law
AJJ	American Journal of Jurisprudence
ARIA	American Review of International Arbitration
ARIEL	Austrian Review of International and European Law
ASIL	American Society of International Law
BCEALR	Boston College Environmental Affairs Law Review
BJIL	Brooklyn Journal of International Law
BMR	BRIDGES Monthly Review
CHJIL	Chicago Journal of International Law
CJTL	Columbia Journal of Transnational Law
CMLR	Common Market Law Review
ECJILTP	Estey Centre Journal of International Law and Trade Policy
EJIL	European Journal of International Law
EJPE	European Journal of Political Economy
FILJ	Fordham International Law Journal
GWILR	George Washington International Law Review
HICLR	Hastings International and Comparative Law Review
HILJ	Harvard International Law Journal
HJIL	Heidelberg Journal of International Law
HJLT	Harvard Journal of Law & Technology
HLJ	Hastings Law Journal
HLR	Harvard Law Review
ICLQ	International and Comparative Law Quarterly
ILTA	International Law and Trade Abstracts
IO	International Organisation
IRLE	International Review of Law and Economics
ITLO	International Trade Law and Organization
JIEL	Journal of International Economic Law
JLEO	Journal of Law and Economic Organisation
JLS	Journal of Legal Studies
JWIP	Journal of World Intellectual Property
JWIT	Journal of World Investment & Trade
JWT	Journal of World Trade
LIEI	Legal Issues of Economic Integration
LJIL	Leiden Journal of International Law
MIJIL	Michigan Journal of International Law

MJIEL	Manchester Journal of International Economic Law
MJIL	Minnesota Journal of International Law
NILR	Netherlands International Law Review
NJCL	Nordic Journal of Commercial Law
NJIL	Nordic Journal of International Law
NYLSJICL	New York Law School Journal of International and Comparative Law
OJ	Official Journal of the European Communities
PILR	Pace International Law Review
RES	Review of Economics Studies
RGIP	Review Générale de Droit International Public
SJIL	Stanford Journal of International Law
SMJ	St Mary's Journal
TICLJ	Temple International and Comparative Law Journal
VJIL	Virginia Journal of International Law
WTAM	World Trade and Arbitration Materials
WTR	World Trade Review
YJIL	Yale Journal of International Law
YLJ	Yale Law Journal
YLPR	Yale Law and Policy Review

Table of cases

PANEL REPORTS ISSUED UNDER ARTICLE XXIII GATT 1947 AND UNDER THE 1979 TOKYO ROUND AGREEMENT

All cases can be obtained from www.wto.org.

Cuba – Discriminatory Consular Taxes
Panel report GATT/CP.2/SR.11, (24 August 1948)   21
Australian – Subsidy on Ammonium Sulphate
Report Adopted by the Contracting Parties, GATT/CP.4/39, 11/188, (3 April 1950) 23
Treatment by Germany of Imports of Sardines
Report Adopted by the CONTRACTING PARTIES, G/26 – 1S/53, (31 October 1952)
Swedish Anti-Dumping Duties
Panel Report, L/328–3S/81, (26 February 1955)
European Communities – Refunds on Exports of Sugar
Panel Report, L/4833–26S/290, (6 November 1979)
New Zealand – Imports of Electrical Transformers from Finland
Reports of the Panel L/5814–32S/55, adopted 18 July 1985
United States – Taxes on Petroleum and certain Imported Substances
Complaint – Canada L/6085, dated 7 November 1986
Complaint – EEC L/6080, dated 30 October 1986
Complaint – Mexico L/6093, dated 10 November 1986
Reports of the Panel L/6175 – 34S/136, adopted 17 June 1987
Japan – Customs Duties, Taxes and Labelling Practices on Imported Wines and Alcohol Beverages
Complaint – EC L/6031, dated 22 July 1986
Panel Reports, 1 L/6216–34S/83, (10 November 1987)
Canadian – Imposition of Countervailing Duties on Imports of Manufacturing Beef from the EEC
Panel Report, SCM/85, (13 October 1987)
US – Custom User Fees
GATT Panel Report, L/6264–35S/245, (adopted 2 February 1988) 19
Japan – Trade in Semi-Conductors (Japan – Semi-Conductors)
Panel Report, BISD/116, (4 May 1988)
European Economic Community – Restrictions on imports of Dessert Apples
Complaint – Chile L/6329, dated 22 April 1988 and L/6929/Add.1, dated 3 May 1988 and L/6339, dated 2 May 1988
Panel Report, L/6491–36S/93, (22 June 1989)
Norway – Restriction on Apples and Pears from the United States

Panel Report, L/6474–36S/306, (22 June 1989)
European Economic Community – Payments and Subsidies paid to Producers and Processors of Oilseed and Related Animal-Feeds Proteins
Panel Report, L/6627–37S/86, (25 January 1990)
United States – Imposition of Antidumping Duties on Imports of Seamless Stainless Steel Hollow Products from Sweden
Panel Report, ADP/47, (20 August 1990)
United States – Restrictions on Importation of Sugar and Sugar-Containing Products Applied under the 1955 Waiver and under Headnote to the Schedule of Tariff Concessions (US – Agricultural Waiver)
Panel Report, 37S/228, (7 November 1990)
United States Countervailing – Duties on Fresh, Chilled and Frozen Pork from Canada
Panel Report, DS7/R – 38S/30, (11 July 1991)
Norway – Procurement of Toll Collection Equipment for the City of Trondheim (Trondheim case)
Panel Report, GPR/DS2/R, (13 May 1992)
United States – Antidumping Duties on Gray Portland Cement and Cement Clinker from Mexico
Panel Report, ADP/82, (7 September 1992)
United States – Restriction on the Imports of Tuna (both unadopted)
Complaint – Mexico 30ILM 1594, (1991)
Complaint – EC 33ILM 839, (1994)

WTO PANEL AND APPELLATE BODY REPORTS

All cases can be obtained from the WTO website at http://www.wto.org/english/tratop_e/dispu_e/distabase_wto_members4_e.htm   or   www.worldtradelaw.net (last visited 20.08.04).
United States – Standard for Reformulated and Conventional Gasoline
Panel Report, WT/DS2/R29, (20 May 1996)
Appellate Body Report, WT/DS2/AB/R, (29 April 1996).............................. 53, 55
Japan – Taxes on Alcoholic Beverages
Panel Reports, WT/DS8/11, WT/DS10/11, WT/DS11/8, (11 July 1996)
Appellate Body Reports, WT/DS8/AB/R, WT/DS10/AB/R, WT/DS11/AB/R, (4 October 1996) 55, 67
European Communities – Trade Description of Scallops
Panel Reports, (Peru and Chile Complaints) WT/DS12/R, WT/DS14/R, (mutually agreed solution, report circulated 5 August 1996)...................... 86–7
Panel Report, (Canada Complaint) WT/DS7/R, (mutually agreed solution 5 August 1996).. 86–7
Brazil – Measures Affecting Desiccated Coconut
Panel Report, WT/DS22/R, (17 October 1996) Appellate Body Report, WT/DS22/AB/R, (20 March 1997) 14, 52, 57
European Communities – Regime for the Importation, Sale and Distribution of Bananas (EC Bananas Case)
Panel Report, (US Complaint) WT/DS27/R/USA, (22 May 1997)
Panel Report, (Complaints by Guatemala and Honduras) WT/DS27/R/GTM WT/DS27/R/HND, (22 May 1997)

Appellate Body Report, WT/DS27/AB/R, (25 September 1997) 2, 11, 59, 82
Arbitration Report, WT/DS27/ARB, (19 April 1999) 37, 38, 71
Argentina – Measures Affecting Imports of Footwear, Textiles, Apparel and Other Items
Panel Report, (US Complaint) WT/DS56/R, (25 November 1997) 64
United States – Measures Affecting Imports of Woven Wool Shirts and Blouses from India
Panel Report, WT/DS33/R, (6 January 1997)
India – Patent Protection for Pharmaceutical and Agricultural Chemical Products (complaint by US)
Panel Reports, WT/DS50/R, (19 December 1997)
Appellate Body Reports, WT/DS50/AB/R, (16 January 1998)
European Communities – Measures concerning Meat and Meat Products (Hormones) (Hormones case)
Panel Reports, WT/DS26/R/USA, WT/DS48/R/CAN, (18 August 1997)
Appellate Body Reports, WT/DS26/AB/R, WT/DS48/AB/R, (13 February 1998)..................................... 14, 18, 33, 34, 35, 56, 60, 82
Japan – Measures Affecting Consumer Photographic Film and Paper
Panel Report, (US Complaint) WT/DS44/R, (25 March 1998)
Japan – Measures Affecting Consumer Photographic Film and Paper (Fuji-Kodak)
Panel Report, WT/DS44/R, (31 March 1998)
Argentina – Measures Affecting Imports of Footwear, Textiles, Apparel and Other Items
Panel Report, WT/DS56/R, (25 November 1997)
Appellate Body Reports, WT/DS56/AB/R, (22 April 1998)................................56
European Communities – Customs Classification of Certain Computer Equipment
Panel Reports, WT/DS62/R, WT/DS67/R, WT/DS68/R, (5 February 1998).......64
Appellate Body Reports, WT/DS62/AB/R, WT/DS67/AB/R, WT/DS68/AB/R, (22 June 1998)
European Communities – Measures Affecting Importation of Certain Poultry Products
Panel Report, (Brazil Complaint) WT/DS69/R, (12 March 1998)
Appellate Body Report, WT/DS58/AB/R, (23 July 1998)....................................56
Canada – Measures Affecting the Importation of Milk and the Exportation of Dairy Products
Panel Reports, WT/DS103/R, WT/DS113/R, (17 May 1999)
Indonesia – Measures Affecting the Automobile Industry
Panel Reports, WT/DS54/R, WT/DS55/R, WT/DS59/R, WT/DS64/R, (23 July 1998)
India – Patent Protection of Pharmaceutical and Agricultural Chemical Products (Complaint by EC)
Panel Reports, WT/DS79/R, (22 September 1998) 60
United States – Import Prohibition of certain Shrimp and Shrimp Products (Shrimp case)
Panel Report, WT/DS58/R, (15 May 1998)..49
Appellate Body Report, WT/DS58/AB/R, (6 November 1998) 65, 144
Australia – Measures Affecting Importation of Salmon
Panel Reports, WT/DS18/R, (12 June 1998)
Appellate Body Reports, WT/DS18/AB/R, (6 November 1998)
Korea – Taxes on Alcoholic Beverages
Panel Reports, WT/DS75/R, WT/DS84/R, (17 September 1998)

Appellate Body Reports, WT/DS75/AB/R, WT/DS84/AB/R, (17 February 1999)
United States – Anti-Dumping Duties on Dynamic Random Access Memory
    Semiconductors (DRAMS) of One Megabit or Above from Korea
Panel Reports, WT/DS99/R, (19 March 1999)
European Communities – Regime for the Importation, Sale and Distribution of
    Bananas, (Recourse by EC to Article 21.5 of the DSU)
Panel Reports, WT/DS27/RW/EEC, (12 April 1999)
European Communities - Regime for the Importation, Sale and Distribution of
    Bananas, (Second Recourse to Article 21.5 of the DSU by Ecuador /Recourse
    to Article 21.5 of the DSU by the United States)
Appellate Body Reports, WT/DS27/AB/RW2/ECU, WT/DS27/AB/RW/USA,
    (adopted 22 December 2008) 59
European Communities – Regime for the Importation, Sale and Distribution of
    Bananas, (Recourse by Ecuador to Article 21.5 of the DSU)
Panel Reports, WT/DS27/RW/ECU, (6 May 1999)
Australia – Subsidies Provided to Producers and Exporters of Automotive
    Leather
Panel Reports, WT/DS126/R, (16 June 1999)..40, 46
Brazil – Export Financing Programme for Aircraft
Panel Reports, WT/DS46/R, (14 April 1999)
Appellate Body Reports, WT/DS46/AB/R, (20 August 1999)
Canada – Measures Affecting the Export of Civilian Aircraft
Panel Reports, WT/DS70/R, (17 April 1999)
Appellate Body Reports, WT/DS70/AB/R, (20 August 1999)
Canada – Measures Affecting the Importation of Milk and the Exportation of
    Dairy Products
Panel Reports, WT/DS103/R, WT/DS113/R, (17 May 1999)
Appellate Body Reports, WT/DS103/AB/R, WT/DS113/AB/R, (27 October
    1999) 56
Turkey – Restrictions on Imports of Textile and Clothing Products
Panel Reports, WT/DS34/R, (31 May 1999)
Appellate Body Reports, WT/DS34/AB/R, (19 November 1999) 51
Chile – Taxes on Alcoholic Beverages
Panel Reports, WT/DS87/R, WT/DS110/R, (15 June 1999)
Appellate Body Reports, WT/DS87/AB/R, WT/DS110/AB/R, (12 January 2000)
United States – Sections 301–310 of the Trade Act of 1974
Panel Reports, WT/DS152/R, (27 January 2000)......................37, 68–9, 73, 82, 87
Australia – Subsidies Provided to Producers and Exporters of Automotive Leather
    (Recourse by the US to Article 21.5 of the DSU)
Panel Reports, WT/DS126/RW, (11 February 2000)
Mexico – Anti-Dumping Investigation of High Fructose Corn Syrup (HFCS)
    from the United States
Panel Reports, WT/DS132/R, (24 February 2000)
Canada – Patent Protection of Pharmaceutical Products (Canada – Patent
    protection case)
Panel Report, (EC and their Member States Complaint) WT/DS114/R, (17
    March 2000)
United States – Tax Treatment for "Foreign Sales Corporations" (FSC case)
Appellate Body Report, Second Recourse to Article 21.5 of the DSU by the
    European Communities, WT/DS108/ABRW2, (adopted 14 March 2006)

United States – Imposition of Countervailing Duties on Certain Hot-Rolled Lead and Bismuth Carbon Steel Products Originating in the United Kingdom (US – Hot-Rolled)
Panel Report, WT/DS138/R, (23 December 1999)
Appellate Body Reports, WT/DS108/AB/R, (20 March 2000)
Australia – Measures Affecting Importation of Salmon (Recourse by Canada to Article 21.5 of the DSU)
Panel Report, WT/DS18/RW, (20 March 2000)
Canada – Patent Protection of Pharmaceutical Products
Panel Report, WT/DS114/R, (7 April 2000)
Appellate Body Report, WT/DS138/AB/R, (7 June 2000) 33
Canada – Certain Measures Affecting the Automotive Industry
Panel Report, WT/DS139/R, WT/DS142/R, (11 February 2000)
Appellate Body Report, WT/DS139/AB/R, WT/DS142/AB/R, (19 June 2000)
Korea – Measures Affecting Government Procurement
Panel Report, WT/DS163/R, (19 June 2000) 14, 46, 50, 57
United States – Section 110(5) of the US Copyright Act
Panel Report, WT/DS160/R, (27 July 2000)
Brazil – Export Financing Programme for Aircraft (Recourse by Canada to Article 21.5 of the DSU)
Panel Report, WT/DS46/RW, (9 May 2000)
Appellate Body Report, WT/DS46/AB/RW, (4 August 2000)
Canada – Measures Affecting the Export of Civilian Aircraft (Recourse by Brazil to Article 21.5 of the DSU)
Panel Report, WT/DS70/RW, (9 May 2000)
Appellate Body Report, WT/DS70/AB/RW, (4 August 2000)
United States – Act of 1916
Panel Report, (EC), WT/DS136/R, (31 March 2000)
Panel Report, (Japan), WT/DS162/R, (29 May 2000)
Appellate Body Report, WT/DS136/AB/R, WT/DS162/AB/R, (26 September 2000) 60, 64
United States – Anti-Dumping on Dynamic Random Access Memory Semiconductors (DRAMS) of One Megabit or Above from Korea (Recourse to Article 21.5 of the DSU by Korea)
Panel Report, WT/DS99/RW, (7 November 2000)
United States – Import Measures on Certain Products from the European Communities
Panel Report, WT/DS165/R, (17 July 2000)
Appellate Body Report, WT/DS165/AB/R, (10 January 2001)
Korea – Measures Affecting Imports of Fresh, Chilled and Frozen Beef
Panel Report, WT/DS161/R, WT/DS169/R, (31 July 2000)
Appellate Body Report, WT/DS161/AB/R, WT/DS161/AB/R, (10 January 2001)
United States – Definitive Safeguard Measures on Imports of Wheat Gluten from the European Communities
Panel Report, WT/DS166/R, (31 July 2000)
Appellate Body Report, WT/DS166/AB, (19 January 2001)
Brazil – Measures Affecting Patent Protection (US–Brazil dispute) withdrawn
Request for the Establishment of the Panel by United States – WT/DS199/3 (9 January 2001)

European Communities – Anti-Dumping Duties on Imports of Cotton-Type Bed Linen from India
Panel Report, WT/DS141/R, (30 October 2000)
Appellate Body Report, WT/DS141/AB/R, (12 March 2001)
European Communities – Measures Affecting Asbestos and Asbestos-Containing Products
Panel Report, WT/DS135/R, (18 September 2000)
Appellate Body Report, WT/DS135/AB/R, (5 April 2001)............................ 79, 81
Thailand – Anti-Dumping Duties on Angles, Shapes and Sections of Iron or Non-Alloy Steel and H-Beans from Poland
Panel Report, WT/DS122/R, (28 September 2000)
Appellate Body Report, WT/DS122/AB/R, (5 April 2001)
United States – Anti-Dumping Measures on Certain Hot-Rolled Steel Products from Japan (US – Hot-Rolled Steel from Japan)
Panel Report, WT/DS184/R, (28 February 2001)
Appellate Body Report, WT/DS184/AB/R, (23 August 2001) 33, 78
Argentina – Definitive Anti-Dumping Measures on Imports of Ceramic Floor Tiles from Italy
Panel Report, WT/DS189/R, (5 November 2001)
United States – Import Prohibition of Certain Shrimp and Shrimp Products (Recourse to Article 21.5 of the DSU by Malaysia)
Panel Report, WT/DS58/RW, (15 June 2001)
Appellate Body Report, WT/DS58/AB/RW, (21 November 2001)
Mexico – Anti-Dumping Investigation of High Fructose Corn Syrup (HFCS) from the United States (Recourse to Article 21.5 of the DSU by the United States)
Panel Report, WT/DS132/RW, (22 June 2001)
Appellate Body Report, WT/DS132/AB/RW, (21 November 2001)
India – Measures Affecting the Automotive Sector, WT/DS146/R, WT/DS175/R (21 December 2001) 60
United States – Tax Treatment for "Foreign Sales Corporations" (FSC Case) (Recourse to Article 21.5 of the DSU by the EC)
Panel Report, WT/DS108/RW, (20 August 2001)
Appellate Body Report, WT/DS108/AB/RW, (29 January 2002) 86
United States – Section 211 Omnibus Appropriations Act of 1998 (US – Section 211)
Panel Report, WT/DS176/R, (6 August 2001)
Appellate Body Report, WT/DS176/AB/R, (1 February 2002)............................33
United States – Definitive Safeguard Measures on Imports of Circular Welded Carbon Quality Line Pipe from Korea
Panel Report, WT/DS202/R, (29 October 2001)
Appellate Body Report, WT/DS202/AB/R, (8 March 2002)......... 14, 33, 39, 56, 57
United States – Anti-Dumping and Countervailing Measures on Steel Plate from India
Panel Report, WT/DS206/R, (29 July 2002)..78
European Communities – Trade Description of Sardines (EC – Sardines)
Panel Report, WT/DS231/R, (29 May 2002)
Appellate Body Report, WT/DS231/AB/R, (23 October 2002) 50
United States – Preliminary Determinations of Softwood Lumber from Canada
Panel Report, WT/DS236/R, (1 November 2002)
United States – Countervailing Measures Concerning Certain Products from the European Communities

Panel Report, WT/DS212/R, (31 July 2002)
Appellate Body Report, WT/DS212/AB/R, (8 January 2003)
Canada Measures Affecting the Importation of Milk and the Exportation of Dairy Products (Second Recourse to Article 21.5 of the DSU by New Zealand and the United States)
Panel Reports, WT/DS103/RW2m, WT/DS113/RW2, (26 July 2002)
Appellate Body Report, WT/DS103/AB/RW2, WT/DS113/AB/RW2, (17 January 2003).. 74–6, 77
United States – Continued Dumping and Subsidy Offset Act of 2000 (Byrd Amendment)
Panel Report, WT/DS217/R, WT/DS234/R, (16 September 2002)
Appellate Body Report, WT/DS217/AB/R, WT/DS234/AB/R, (27 January 2003).. 49
European Communities – Anti-Dumping Duties on Imports of Cotton-Type Bed Linen from India (Recourse to Article 21.5 of the DSU by India)
Panel Report, WT/DS141/RW, (29 November 2002)
Appellate Body Report, WT/DS141/AB/RW, (24 April 2003)
United States – Tax Treatment for 'Foreign Sales Corporation', Recourse to Arbitration by the United States under DSU Article 22.6/SCM Agreement Article 4.11, paras 5.5–5.6 (Authorization to Suspend Concessions: 7 May 2003)...37, 50, 71
Panel Report, *Argentina – Definitive Anti-Dumping Duties on Poultry from Brazil*, WT/DS241/R, paras 7.45–7.47 (adopted 19 May 2003) 78
European Communities – Anti-Dumping Duties on Malleable Cast Iron Tube or Pipe Fittings from Brazil
Panel Report, WT/DS219/R, (7 March 2003)
Appellate Body Report, WT/DS219/AB/R, (18 August 2003)
United States – Definitive Safeguard Measures on Imports of Certain Steel Products (US Steel Case)
Panel Report, WT/DS248/R, WT/DS249/R, WT/DS251/R, WT/DS252/R, WT/DS253/R, WT/DS254/R, WT/DS258/R, WT/DS259/R, (11 July 2003)
Appellate Body Report, WT/DS248/AB/R, WT/DS249/AB/R, WT/DS251/AB/R, WT/DS253/AB/R, WT/DS254/AB/R, WT/DS258/AB/R, WT/DS259/AB/R, (10 December 2003)...86, 180, 181
United States – Sunset Review of Anti-Dumping Duties on Corrosion-Resistant Carbon Steel Flat Products from Japan
Panel Report, WT/DS244/R, (14 August 2003)
Appellate Body Report, WT/DS244/AB/R, (9 January 2004)........................ 49, 53
United States – Final Countervailing Duty Determination With Respect to Certain Softwood Lumber from Canada
Panel Report, WT/DS257/R, (29 August 2003)
Appellate Body Report, WT/DS257/AB/R, (17 February 2004)
European Communities – Conditions for the Granting of Tariff Preferences to Developing Countries
Panel Report, WT/DS246/R, (1 December 2003)
Appellate Body Report, WT/DS246/AB/R, (20 April 2004) 14, 56
United States – Investigation of the International Trade Commission in Softwood Lumber from Canada
Panel Report, WT/DS277/R, (26 April 2004)
Mexico – Measures Affecting Telecommunications Services
Panel Report, WT/DS204/R, (1 June 2004)

United States – Final Dumping Determination on Softwood Lumber from Canada
Panel Report, WT/DS264/R (13 April 2004)
Appellate Body Report, WT/DS264/AB/R (31 August 2004)
Canada – Measures Relating to Exports of Wheat and Treatment of Imported Grain
Panel Report, WT/DS276/R (26 April 2004)
Appellate Body Report, WT/DS276/AB/R (27 September 2004)
United States – Sunset Reviews of Anti-Dumping Measures on Oil Country Tubular Goods from Argentina
Panel Report, WT/DS268/R (16 July 2004)
Appellate Body Report, WT/DS268/AB/R, (17 December 2004)
United States – Subsidies on Upland Cotton
Panel Report, WT/DS267/R, (8 September 2004) 34
Appellate Body Report, WT/DS267/AB/R, (21 March 2005)..............................56
Korea – Measures Affecting Trade in Commercial Vessels
Panel Report, WT/DS273/R, (7 March 2005)
Appellate Body Report, WT/DS273/AB/R, (11 April 2005)
United States – Measures Affecting the Cross-Border Supply of Gambling and Betting Services
Panel Report, WT/DS285/R, (10 November 2004)
Appellate Body Report, WT/DS285/AB/R, (20 April 2005)
European Communities – Export Subsidies on Sugar
Panel Report, WT/DS266/R, WT/DS266/R, WT/DS283/R, (15 October 2004).
Appellate Body Report, WT/DS262/AB/R, WT/DS266/AB/R, WT/DS283/AB/R, (19 May 2005) 49, 58–9, 78
Appellate Body Report, *European Communities – Customs Classification of Frozen Boneless Chicken Cuts*, WT/DS DS269/AB/R, WT/DS286/AB/R (adopted 27 September 2005).. 53–4
Appellate Body Report, *Mexico – Tax Measures on Soft Drinks and Other Beverages*, WT/DS308/AB/R, (adopted 24 March 2006)...............................47
Appellate Body Report, *United States – Investigation of the International Trade Commission in Softwood Lumber from Canada (Recourse to Article 21.5 of the DSU by Canada)*, WT/DS277/AB/RW, (adopted 9 May 2006)
Appellate Body Report, *United States – Laws, Regulations and Methodology for Calculating Dumping Margins ("Zeroing")*, WT/DS294/AB/R, (adopted 9 May 2006)
Appellate Body Report, *United States – Final Dumping Determination on Softwood Lumber from Canada, (Recourse to Article 21.5 of the DSU by Canada)*, WT/264/AB/RW, (adopted 1 September 2006)...............................78
Appellate Body Report, *United States – Sunset Reviews of Anti-Dumping Measures on Oil Country Tubular Goods from Argentina (Recourse to Article 21.5 of the DSU by Argentina)*, WT/DS268/AB/RW, (adopted 11 May 2007)
Panel Report, *United States – Measures Affecting the Cross-Border Supply of Gambling and Betting Services (Recourse to Article 21.5 of the DSU by Antigua and Barbuda)*, WT/DS285/RW, (adopted 22 May 2007)
Appellate Body Report, *Brazil – Measures Affecting Imports of Retreaded Tyres*, WT/DS332/AB/R, (adopted 17 December 2007)..144
Appellate Body Report, *United States – Final Anti-Dumping Measures on Stainless Steel from Mexico*, WT/DS344/AB/R, (adopted 20 May 2008) .. 33, 62

Appellate Body Report, *United States – Subsidies on Upland Cotton (Recourse to Article 21.5 of the DSU by Brazil)*, WT/DS267/AB/RW, (adopted 20 June 2008)

Appellate Body Report, *United States – Measures Relating to Shrimp from Thailand (DS343)*, *United States – Customs Bond Directive for Merchandise Subject to Anti-Dumping/Countervailing Duties (DS345)*, (adopted 1 August 2008)

US – Continued Suspension / Canada – Continued Suspension, WT/DS320/AB/R, WT/DS321/AB/R (adopted 14 November 2008) 45, 61

Appellate Body Report, *India – Additional and Extra-Additional Duties on Imports from the United States*, WT/DS360/AB/R, (adopted 17 November 2008) 19

Appellate Body Reports, *China – Measures Affecting Imports of Automobile Parts*, WT/DS339, 340, 342/AB/R, (adopted 12 January 2009)

Appellate Body Report, *United States – Continued Existence and Application of Zeroing Methodology*, WT/DS350/AB/R, (adopted 19 February 2009) 79

Panel Report, *China – Measures Affecting the Protection and Enforcement of Intellectual Property Rights*, WT/DS362/R, (adopted 20 March 2009)

Panel Report, *Colombia – Indicative Prices and Restrictions on Ports of Entry*, WT/DS366/R, (adopted 20 May 2009)

Appellate Body Report, *United States – Laws, Regulations and Methodology for Calculating Dumping Margins ("Zeroing") (Recourse to Article 21.5 of the DSU by the European Communities)*, WT/DS294/AB/RW, (adopted 11 June 2009) 46

Appellate Body Report, *United States – Measures Relating to Zeroing and Sunset Reviews (Recourse to Article 21.5 of the DSU by Japan)*, WT/DS322/AB/RW, (adopted 31 August 2009)

Appellate Body Report, *China – Measures Affecting Trading Rights and Distribution Services for Certain Publications and Audiovisual Entertainment Products*, WT/DS363/AB/R, (adopted 19 January 2010) 60

Panel Report, *United States – Anti-Dumping Measures on Polyethylene Retail Carrier Bags from Thailand*, WT/DS383/R, (adopted 18 February 2010)

Panel Report, *United States – Certain Measures Affecting Imports of Poultry from China*, WT/DS392/R, (adopted 25 October 2010)

Appellate Body Report, *Australia – Measures Affecting the Importation of Apples from New Zealand*, WT/DS367/AB/R, (adopted 17 December 2010)

Appellate Body Report, *United States – Definitive Anti-Dumping and Countervailing Duties on Certain Products from China*, WT/DS379/AB/R, (adopted 25 March 2010) 14, 57

Appellate Body Report, *European Communities and Certain Member States – Measures Affecting Trade in Large Civil Aircraft*, WT/DS316/AB/R, (adopted 1 June 2011) 85

Panel Report, *United States – Anti-Dumping Administrative Reviews and Other Measures Related to Imports of Certain Orange Juice from Brazil*, WT/DS382/R, paras 7.126–7.129 (adopted 17 June 2011) 78

Appellate Body Report, *Thailand – Customs and Fiscal Measures on Cigarettes from the Philippines*, WT/DS371/AB/R, (adopted 15 July 2011)

Appellate Body Report, *European Communities – Definitive Anti-Dumping Measures on Certain Iron or Steel Fasteners from China*, WT/DS397/AB/R, (adopted 28 July 2011) 183

Appellate Body Report, *United States – Measures Affecting Imports of Certain Passenger Vehicle and Light Truck Tyres from China*, WT/DS399/AB/R, (adopted 5 October 2011)

Appellate Body Reports, *Philippines – Taxes on Distilled Spirits*, WT/DS396, 403/AB/R, (adopted 20 January 2012)

Appellate Body Report, *United States – Measures Affecting Trade in Large Civil Aircraft (Second Complaint)*, WT/DS353/AB/R, (adopted 23 March 2012) 85, 86

European Union and Certain Member States – Certain Measures Affecting the Renewable Energy Generation Sector, WT/DS452, (18 December 2012) 146

European Communities – Measures Prohibiting the Importation and Marketing of Seal Products, WT/DS401/9, (dated 9 January 2014) 34

Panel Reports, *United States – Certain Countries of Origin Labelling (COOL) Requirements*, recourse to Article 21.5 of the DSU by Canada and Mexico, WT/DS 384, 386/RW, (Notice of Appeal, 28 November 2014) 32

Panel Reports, *United States – Anti-Dumping Measures on Certain Shrimp from Viet Nam*, WT/DS429/R, (Notice of Appeal, 6 January 2015) 32

WTO CASES INVOLVING CHINA

United States – Definitive Safeguard Measures on Imports of Certain Steel Products – WT/DS252, (24 February 2010) 108–11, 180, 181

China – Value-Added Tax on Integrated Circuits – WT/DS309, (complaint by the US), Mutually Agreed Solution at Consultation Stage, (5 October 2005) 183

China – Value-Added Tax on Integrated Circuits – WT/DS309, (24 February 2010) 112–18, 131

China – Measures Affecting Imports of Automobile Parts – WT/DS339, (31 August 2009) 119, 182, 189

China – Measures Affecting Imports of Automobile Parts – WT/DS342, (24 February 2010) 120–21, 131, 132

China – Certain Measures Granting Refunds, Reductions or Exemptions from Taxes and Other Payments – WT/DS358, (24 February 2010) ... 125–8, 131, 132

China – Measures Affecting the Protection and Enforcement of Intellectual Property Rights – WT/DS362/R, Panel Report, (20 March 2009) 159

China – Measures Affecting the Protection and Enforcement of Intellectual Property Rights – WT/DS362, (26 May 2010) 154–9, 182

China – Measures Affecting Trading Rights and Distribution Services for Certain Publications and Audiovisual Entertainment Products – WT/DS363, (12 October 2012) 160–63, 178

China – Measures Affecting Financial Information Services and Foreign Financial Information Suppliers – WT/DS372, (24 February 2010) 133–6

China – Grants, Loans and Other Incentives – WT/DS387, (24 February 2010) 131, 132

China – Measures Related to the Exportation of Various Raw Materials – WT/DS394, (6 May 2013) 137–43, 178

China – Certain Measures Affecting Electronic Payment Services –WT/DS413, Panel Report, (adopted 31 August 2012) 172

China – Certain Measures Affecting Electronic Payment Services – WT/DS413, (30 September 2013) 168–73, 178

China – Countervailing and Anti-Dumping Duties on Grain Oriented Flat-rolled Electrical Steel – WT/DS414, (3 March 2014) 175–7

China – Measures Related to the Exportation of Rare Earths, Tungsten, and Molybdenum WT/DS431, 432, 433/AB/R, (adopted 29 August 2014) 35, 56, 178

CASES OF THE PERMANENT COURT OF INTERNATIONAL JUSTICE (PCIJ)

S.S. Wimbledon, UK, France, Italy, Japan v. Germany, PCIJ, (Series A. No 1, 21), (1923)

Responsibility of Germany for Damage Caused in the Portuguese Colonies in the South of Africa (Portugal v. Germany – Naulilaa Arbitration), 2 *R.I.A.A*, 1011 (1928)

Mavrommatis Palestine Concessions (Greece v. Great Britain), Judgment of 30 August 1924, 1924 PCIJ (Ser A) No. 2 ....16, 44

S.S. Lotus (France v. Turkey), PCIJ 1927 (ser. A) No. 10..........................78, 79–80

Chorzow Factory judgment, *(Germany v. Poland)* PCIJ, 1929, Series A, No. 8...39, 40, 57

Case Concerning Treatment of Polish Nationals in Danzig, PCIJ, Series A/B, No. 44, (1932)

Legal Status of Eastern Greenland: Judgment of 5 April 1933, PCIJ, Series A./B, No. 53.

CASES AND ADVISORY OPINION OF THE INTERNATIONAL COURT OF JUSTICE (ICJ)

All cases can be obtained from the ICJ homepage at www.icj-cij.org/www/idecisions.

Corfu Channel Case, (United Kingdom v. Albania), ICJ Report, (1949)....32, 39, 40

Interpretation of the Peace Treaties with Bulgaria, Hungary and Romania, Advisory Opinion of 30 March 1950 (first phase), 1950 *ICJ Rep*. 65 44

Anglo Norwegian Fisheries case (United Kingdom v. Norway), ICJ Reports 116, (18 December 1951) 54

Case Concerning Rights of Nationals of the United States of America in Morocco *(France v. United States – Merits)*, (27 August 1952)

Effect of Awards of Compensation Made by the United States Administrative Tribunal, Advisory Opinion, ICJ Reports, (13 July 1954)...............................58

Israel v. Bulgaria, ICJ, preliminary objection, (27 July 1955)

Barcelona Traction, Light and Power Company Limited, *(Belgium v. Spain)* ICJ Report, (1958–1960)

South West Africa Cases, *(Ethiopia v. South Africa, Liberia v. South Africa)*, Preliminary Objections, Judgment of 21 December 1962, ICJ Report, (1962)

Temple of Preah Vihear (*Cambodia v. Thailand*), (15 June 1962)...........................59
Republic of Cameroon v. United Kingdom, ICJ Judgment of 2 December 1963 ...60
South West Africa Cases, (*Ethiopia v. South Africa, Liberia v. South Africa*),
    Second Phase, Judgment of 18 July 1966, ICJ Report, (1966)
North Sea Continental Shelf (*Federal Republic of Germany v. Denmark/ Federal
    Republic of Germany v. Netherlands*), ICJ Report, (20 February 1969).... 53, 54,
                                                                                                79
Legal Consequences for States of the Continued Presence of South Africa in
    Namibia (South West Africa) notwithstanding Security Council Resolution
    276 (1970)
Nuclear Tests Cases (*New Zealand v. France*) ICJ Reports, (1974) 58, 60
*Texaco Overseas Petroleum Co. and California Asiatic Oil Co. v. The Government
    of Libyan Arab Republic*, 17 I.L.M. 1 (1978)
        Air Services Agreement Arbitration (*France v. United States*) (1978)
        XXVIII UNR.I.A.A.
        Continental Shelf Case, (*Tunisia/Libyan Arab Jamahiriya*) ICJ Report, (24
        February 1982)..77
Continental Shelf Case, (*Libyan Arab Jamahiriya/ Malta*), ICJ Report,
    (1985)
Military and Paramilitary in and Against Nicaragua, *(Republic of Nicaragua v.
    United States of America)* (27 June 1986) 39, 79
Frontier Dispute Case (*Burkina Faso v. Mali*) ICJ Reports, (1986).....................77
*Amoco International Finance Corporation v. The Government of the Islamic
    Republic of Iran*, Iran-U. S. C.T.R., Vol. 15 (1987) 39
East Timor Case, (*Portugal v. Australia*), ICJ Reports, (June 30, 1995)
*Request for an Examination of the Situation with Paragraph 63 of the Court's
    Judgment of 20 December 1974 in the Nuclear Tests* (*New Zealand v. France*)
    Case, Order of 22 September 1995, ICJ Reports, (1995)................................58
Legality of the Threat or Use of Nuclear Weapons, Advisory Opinion, ICJ
    Reports, (8 July 1996)..79
Gabcíkovo-Nagymaros Project (*Hungary/Slovakia*), General List No. 92, (25
    September 1997)
Land and Maritime Boundary between Cameroon and Nigeria (*Cameroon v.
    Nigeria*) (*Preliminary Objections*) ICJ Reports, (1998)....................................58
LaGrand (Germany v. United States of America), Judgment, I.C.J. Reports,
    (2001)..39
Ahmadou Sadio Diallo (*Guinea v. Democratic Republic of the Congo*), Preliminary
Objections, Judgment of 24 May 2007 54–5
Jurisdictional Immunities of State (*Germany v. Italy*, Greece intervening), ICJ
    Reports, (2012)...53

OTHERS

INTERNATION ARBITRATION

AMCO v. Indonesia 89 ILR 365 77
Rann of Kutch Arbitration 50 ILR (1968) 2 77

Permanent Court of Arbitration
North Atlantic Coast Fisheries Case (*United Kingdom v. United States*), 11 RIAA
(1910) 66–7
Island of Palmas Case (*The Netherlands v. United States*), II UNRIAA (1928) ... 67

EUROPEAN COURT OF HUMAN RIGHTS

Central London Property Trust Ltd. v. High Trees House Ltd. [1947] K.B. 130
Loizidou v. Turkey, European Court of Human Rights (ECHR), Series A.
Judgments and Decisions, Vol. 310, p. 29, (July 28, 1998) 59

INTERNATIONAL TRIBUNAL ON THE LAW OF THE SEA
Argentina v. Ghana, ITLOS (15 December 2012) 58

UNITED STATES
Planned Parenthood of Southeastern Pennsylvania v. Casey, 505 US 833 61

Introduction

As a multilateral institution with currently 161 members,[1] the WTO is somewhat the centre of the universe of major legal systems around the world. Apart from its developed members, there has been increased participation in the activities of the organisation, especially in its dispute settlement mechanism, by many of its emerging economies such as Brazil, China, India, and so on. For instance, since joining the WTO in December 2001, China has been party either as complainant or respondent to some 46 disputes.[2] These numbers are obviously staggering if we compare them with cases involving other emerging BRICS[3] economies or even some developed country members.[4] Because of the size of its economy and the fact that China acceded to the WTO under relatively less than favourable terms, this high number of cases was somehow not unpredicted.[5] Moreover, while many major economies in the last few years

---

[1] As of 26 April 2015, see https://www.wto.org/english/thewto_e/whatis_e/tif_e/org6_e.htm (last visited 18 May 2015).

[2] As of May 2015, China has been complainant in 13 cases, respondent in 33 cases and third party in 119 cases. See https://www.wto.org/english/thewto_e/countries_e/china_e.htm (last visited 18 May 2015).

[3] BRICS is an acronym for an association of five major emerging economies: Brazil, Russia, India, China and South Africa. Their sixth summit was held in Brazil in July 2014. See http://www.brics6.itamaraty.gov.br/ (last visited 19 May 2015).

[4] For instance, between 1995 and May 2015, India has been a party to a total of 43 cases while Brazil has been a party to 42 cases as complainant or respondent respectively. See https://www.wto.org/english/tratop_e/dispu_e/dispu_by_country_e.htm (last visited 18 May 2015).

[5] Many commentators usually see the terms of accession of China to the WTO as being more unfavourable than those under which many major WTO members assumed. On this see Robert Z. Lawrence, 'China and the Multilateral Trading System', *National Bureau of Economic Research (NBER) Working Paper* No. 12759 (2006), Xiaohui Wu, 'No Longer Outside, Not Yet Equal: Rethinking China's Membership in the World Trade Organization', *Chinese Journal of International Law (CJIL)*, Vol. 10, No. 2 (2011), pp. 227–70 and Pasha L. Hsieh, 'China's Development of International Economic Law and WTO Legal Capacity Building', *Journal of International Economic Law (JIEL)*, Vol. 13, No. 4 (2010), pp. 997–1036.

have witnessed reduction in their shares of world trade due to the 2008 financial crisis, China has become a holder of the world's largest foreign exchange reserves and has tremendously increased its share of world trade.[6] Membership of the WTO has undoubtedly been key to China's economic success in the last 14 years. While the process of internal economic liberalisation started long before China finally acceded to the WTO in 2001, the accession to the WTO was a catalyst for several regulatory and institutional reforms in China.[7]

Although China may be thought of as generally sceptical with regard to international law and tribunals, its integration into the rule-based global trading system requires a rethink of how it views the rule of law and compliance with those rules. In other words, as a rule-based multilateral trade organisation with members from varied legal traditions, the 161 WTO members are undoubtedly confronted with some interesting questions on the approach of each of the members to compliance and disputes resolution in the world trading system.[8] Consequently, a monograph that explores the operation of the WTO implementation regime in the context of international law theory of compliance while at the same time providing significant insights into China's view on the notion of 'compliance with public international law of trade' in its Confucian context is an absolute must-read. This is precisely what this monograph intends to do.

However, the concept of 'rule of law' has only recently begun to resonate in China, mainly through the country's agreement to settle disputes using the WTO dispute settlement mechanism. Confucian values, identified as the foundation of China's great cultural tradition, have controlled the social order and regulated people in all activities of Chinese daily lives, including the people's legal consciousness, expectations of justice and trust in law. Persuasion and negotiations are central tenets of Confucian

---

[6]   See International Monetary Fund (IMF), World Economic Outlook (April 2015) at http://www.imf.org/external/pubs/ft/weo/2015/01/index.htm (last visited 19 May 2015).

[7]   As was somehow expected, China's accession to the WTO meant that future economic reforms in China will be rooted within the core WTO disciplines. On this, see Julia Ya Qin, 'The Impact of WTO Accession on China's Legal System: Trade, Investment and Beyond', *Wayne State University Law School Research Paper* No. 07-15 (2007).

[8]   It is important to point out that with regard to complying with a particular panel or AB report, Article 21.6 of the DSU states that '[T]he issue of implementation of the recommendations or rulings may be raised at the DSB by any Member at any time following their adoption'. In the *EC – Bananas* case, the AB pointed out that WTO members have broad discretion in deciding whether to bring a case against another member under the DSU. WT/DS27/AB/R, paragraphs 88–9.

theory. The notion of law in Confucian tradition has over many centuries largely been seen in the context of 'penal and administrative law'.[9] Yet, the idea of rooting normativity in a formal structure condoning sanctions or retaliation as forms of remedies is alien to Confucian tradition.[10] This legal tradition is distinct from the common and civil law of the Western society rooted in normativity. This therefore means that with the changing fundamentals of global economic order, the notion of law in a Confucian tradition requires adaptation. This monograph aims partly at examining the conflicting and conciliating processes between the Chinese approach to litigation and the Western approach of legal orientation in the field of the WTO dispute settlement mechanism. This objective is achieved first by examining the normative framework of WTO rule implementation in a globalised international economic order and secondly by examining the notion of the rule of law in a Confucian system such as China and how it has interacted with a rule-based world trading system.

More precisely, in the first part of this volume, we provide fundamental insights into the law and policy of the WTO dispute settlement system. In order to contextualise the analysis, Part I also discusses the sources of law that may be applicable in a dispute brought before a WTO panel or appellate body (Chapter 3). We further employ two significant international relations theories, namely constructivism and reputation costs, to explain why and how WTO members behave *vis-à-vis* their international trade law obligations. Beyond the work of few academics that have largely explored China's participation in the world trading system in terms of its contributions to the development of international economic law,[11] very little has

---

[9] See H. Patrick Glenn, *Legal Traditions of the World* (OUP, 5th ed., 2014), p. 326.

[10] In this regard, Confucianism is in direct contrast to legal positivism. Anything appearing as a formal structure highly favoured by legal positivism is incongruous with Confucian values. The power of persuasion and reasons rather than strict obligations therefore becomes the modus operandi in Confucian society. On this see H. Patrick Glenn (2014), pp. 320–21.

[11] See for instance Donald C. Clarke, 'China's Legal System and the WTO: Prospects for Compliance', *Global Studies Review*, Vol. 2 (2003), pp. 97–120, Julia Ya Qin, 'The Impact of WTO Accession on China's Legal System: Trade, Investment and Beyond', *Wayne State University Law School Research Paper* No. 07-15 (2007), Henry S. Gao, 'China's Participation in the WTO: A Lawyer's Perspective', *Singapore Year Book of International Law*, Vol. 11 (2007), pp. 1–34. Pasha L. Hsieh, 'China's Development of International Economic Law and WTO Legal Capacity Building', *Journal of International Economic Law* (*JIEL*), Vol. 13, No. 4 (2010), pp. 997–1036, Xiaohui Wu, 'No Longer Outside, Not Yet Equal: Rethinking China's Membership in the World Trade Organization', *Chinese Journal of International Law* (*CJIL*), Vol. 10, No. 2 (2011), pp. 227–70.

been written on Confucianism and the rule of law and how the Chinese government has conducted the whole WTO implementation process. As a consequence, Part II of this volume focuses on the concept of law in Chinese culture and how this fits into China's reading of its international law commitments since its accession to the WTO in 2001. In this regard, it discusses the approach of China in the litigation of trade disputes in the WTO. The section discusses China's relations with the multilateral trading system from the days of the General Agreement on Tariffs and Trade (GATT) to the WTO. Further, it discusses briefly law and Confucianism and the challenges faced by China with regard to compliance with WTO rules. We argue here that in an interconnected world, reputation costs have played an important role in the way China – as well as some WTO members – goes about implementing WTO rules.

PART I

NORMATIVITY AND IMPLEMENTATION ISSUES IN THE WTO

1. World trade law and changing fundamentals in the global architecture

In recent decades, international law, and in particular international economic law, has been greatly impacted by globalisation and the emergence of global governance. Unlike other processes of norm-making in international economic law, the influence of globalisation on international trade law is sometimes very subtle but also very far-reaching and usually goes unnoticed. The World Trade Organization (WTO) is an engine for trade liberalisation and the promotion of economic growth, and is therefore considered to be firmly rooted in the idea of globalisation and interconnectivity. While the notion of globalisation is not new, the increasing integration of commodity, capital and labour markets has undoubtedly altered the landscape of the global trading system over the past few decades.[1] Globalisation is a multidimensional construct whose meaning largely depends on the context in which it is discussed. While it is viewed in this volume in the light of greater economic integration of the different factors of production, academic scholarship has also approached it from other perspectives. Joseph Stiglitz, winner of the 2001 Nobel Prize in economics for his outstanding work on the 'theory of market with asymmetric information', described the concept of globalisation in his seminal work entitled *Globalization and its Discontents* (2002) as 'the closer integration of the countries and peoples of the world which has been brought about by the enormous reduction of costs of transportation and communication, and the breaking down of artificial barriers to the

---

[1] Some of these analyses are very much reflected in Ngangjoh-Hodu, *Theories and Practices of Compliance with WTO Law* (Kluwer, 2012) (hereinafter 'Ngangjoh-Hodu (2012)'). There is no universally agreed definition of globalisation. However, international integration in labour, commodity and capital markets is usually used by economists to mean globalisation. On this, see Michael D. Bordo, Antu Panini Murshid, 'Globalization and Changing Patterns in the International Transmission of Shocks in Financial Markets', *Journal of International Money and Finance (JIMF)*, Vol. 25 (2006), pp. 655–74.

flow of goods, services, capital, knowledge, and (to a lesser extent) people across borders'.[2]

Given the continuous connectivity of global activities to the fabric of our different municipal societies, we cannot overestimate the rate at which international economic law has become enmeshed in our national legal systems. While international economic lawyers need to familiarise themselves with certain domestic concepts to be able to conduct their day-to-day activities, domestic lawyers would hardly be capable of engaging in litigation on a sound basis without knowledge of key aspects of international law. In other words, the international law of trade is becoming more important than ever before in the municipal systems of the 160 WTO members. Despite the fact that the discourse on globalisation and its effects on our day-to-day lives depends on the perspective from which one conceptualises this relationship, the nexus between the WTO and globalisation is to a great extent no longer in dispute. For international traders in goods and services, the notion of economic globalisation implies better market access for their products to more competitive foreign markets. From the standpoint of everyday consumers of goods and services, economic globalisation implies the easy availability of competitive foreign products as well as cheaper domestic products as a consequence of the competition that accompanies trade liberalisation.

Although the effects of globalisation are sometimes exaggerated, it is nevertheless clear that it has facilitated the distribution of goods and services on the international markets. Yet, as with all engagements, it is in the interest of the community of nations who are parties to the global trade project to cultivate an attitude of compliance with these international law obligations. As international trade norms evolve, so too does the way in which private actors and governments view the remedies that accompany those norms. The notion of remedies as a traditional fall-back option for non-compliance with international obligations is germane to our understanding of how international trade rules have been influenced by globalisation. This is so despite the increasing difficulties involved in achieving 'hard law' in international trade norm-making as opposed to the soft law which has typified most of the debates and trade negotiations in recent years.

Some 12 years ago, Supachai Panitchpakdi, the then WTO Director General, selected a group of eight persons, mostly from the private sector,

---

[2]   See Joseph Stiglitz, *Globalization and its Discontents* (Pengiun Books, 2002), p. 9. See also an earlier work on globalisation by Thomas Friedmas, *The Lexus and the Olive Tree: Understanding Globalisation* (First Anchor Books, 2nd ed., 2000).

to examine some key institutional challenges facing the world trading system and make proposals on how to improve it. Many, if not all, of the challenges facing the WTO in 2005 when the consultative team carried out its tasks are as relevant today as they were then. Apart from the Bali 2013 Package,[3] no conclusion has been reached on any of the issues under the Doha trade talks agenda. Although two such requests for outside help had been made under the troubled GATT (1948–1994), this was the first time since the establishment of the WTO in 1995 that the institution had established an external board to examine and provide input on how to shape the WTO to meet the challenges of the twenty-first century.[4] The first group, appointed by the GATT contracting parties in 1947, consisted of three experts (and later four), and was chaired by Professor Gottfried Haberler, an economist from Harvard University. Their report, commonly referred to as the 'Haberler Report', appeared in 1958. Their mandate included, among other things, assessing the reasons why less-developed countries' trade had failed to develop as rapidly as that of the industrialised countries. About 25 years later, Director General Arthur Dunkel requested another group of independent experts to study and report on the problems facing the international trading system. This group comprised seven members and was chaired by Fritz Leutwiler. The 2003 consultative board was made up of renowned personalities from different parts of the world and was largely representative of the WTO membership.[5] On 17 January 2005 it issued its long-awaited report,

---

[3]   Consistent with the WTO Ministerial Decision of December 2013 in Bali, the members of the WTO on 27 November 2014 adopted a Protocol of Amendment to incorporate the Bali Trade Facilitation Agreement into Annex 1A of the Marrakesh Agreement Establishing the WTO. In this regard the Trade Facilitation Agreement will enter into force once a two-thirds majority of WTO members have ratified it domestically. The agreement is available at https://www.wto.org/english/tratop_e/tradfa_e/tradfa_e.htm (last visited 11 May 2015).

[4]   The Leutwiler Report offered 15 recommendations, which were lauded for giving perspectives to negotiators during the 1986 launching of the Uruguay Round.

[5]   The board members were as follows: Peter Sutherland (former Director General of the GATT and the WTO between 1993 and 1995), who chaired the group, Jagdish Bagwati (Professor, Columbia University), Kwesi Botchwey (Executive Chairman, African Development Policy Ownership Initiative), Niall FitzGerald (Chairman, Reuters), Koichi Hamada (Professor, Yale University), John H. Jackson (Professor, Georgetown University), Celso Lafer (Professor, University of São Paulo), Thierry de Montbrial (President and Founder, French Institute of International Relations). However, there has been some criticism as to the board members chosen. In this regard, see Armin von Bogdandy and Markus Wagner, 'The "Sutherland Report" on WTO Reform – A Critical Appraisal',

entitled *The Future of the WTO: Addressing Institutional Challenges in the New Millennium.*[6]

Since the launch of the Sunderland Report published at the tenth anniversary of the WTO, it has been difficult to identify any major normative change in respect of some of the key difficulties that led to the establishment of the consultative board, let alone the implementation of the recommendations made in the Sutherland Report. Despite persistent efforts by many WTO members to address key institutional and normative challenges facing the world trading system, 'constructive ambiguity' continues to be the modus operandi in WTO negotiations. Notwithstanding the December 2013 Bali Package on trade facilitation and food security, the so-called Doha Development Round remains far from concluded almost 15 years from being launched.[7] As a consequence of the consensus and single undertaking principles used in decision-making at the WTO, everyone must be on board for a decision to be considered as approved in the context of the Doha Development trade talks. In other words, 'nothing is agreed until everything is agreed'.[8] Therefore, the promised reform to clarify and amend some of the provisions of the WTO Dispute Settlement Understanding (DSU) as part of the Doha Development Round of trade negotiations has failed to move forward as originally agreed by members.[9] The circumstances leading to the establishment

---

World Trade Review, Vol. 4, No. 3, pp. 439–47 (2005) (hereinafter, 'von Bogdandy and Markus Wagner').

[6] Chapter 6 of the report contains an 11-page document dealing with dispute settlement reform. The report is available at: http://www.wto.org/english/thewto_e/10anniv_e/future_wto_e.pdf (last visited 5 September 2014).

[7] The euphoria that followed the signing of the Bali Package on trade facilitation and food security seems to have faded away as WTO members could not agree on the required protocol by the 31 July 2014 deadline to adopt it in WTO legal text. See the December 2013 WTO Ninth Ministerial Conference Decision in WTO Document, WT/MIN(13)/36 (December 2013).

[8] The Punta Del Este Declaration, which launched the Uruguay Round of trade talks, directed the contracting parties to treat the conduct of the negotiations, and their conclusion, as a single process – in other words, to consider any agreement arrived at as a single undertaking as opposed to the obligations under the GATT. Currently, the term 'single undertaking' is understood as a requirement that WTO members must join all the agreements administered by it, except for the plurilateral agreements on Civil Aircraft and Government Procurement. The Doha Ministerial Declaration also directs members to factor in the single undertaking principle in the negotiations. See para. 47 of the Doha Ministerial Declaration, WT/MIN(01)/DEC/1, adopted on 14 November 2001.

[9] Doha WTO Ministerial 2001: Ministerial Declaration, WT/MIN(01)/DEC/1, 20 November 2001, para. 30. See also para. 34 of the Hong Kong Ministerial Declaration (adopted 18 December 2005).

of the consultative board were neither unique nor new. When the new dispute settlement system was established to replace the troubled GATT dispute settlement structure in 1994, some fundamental questions still remained to be answered as to how the new two-tier system was going to operate in practice. In view of the fact that it was likely that certain changes might be introduced on the strength of the experience acquired, ministers undertook at the conclusion of the Uruguay Round in 1995 to 'complete a full review of dispute settlement rules and procedures within four years after the entry into force of the Agreement Establishing the WTO, and to take a decision on the occasion of its first meeting after the completion of the review, whether to continue, modify or terminate such dispute settlement rules and procedure'.[10]

In spite of the very broad and unhindered mandate and lack of sensitive issues in the negotiations between 1995 and 1999, members were unable to meet either the January 1999 or the extended July 1999 deadline to complete preliminary negotiations on amendment of the DSU. While remedies, remand, amicus briefs and precedent had already started emerging as issues of potential concern in the WTO dispute settlement system, the issue of sequencing[11] with regard to Articles 2.15 (compliance panel) and 22.6 (arbitration procedures) of the DSU almost provoked a major crisis in the system[12] because of the peculiarity of the ongoing cases at the time.[13] The sequencing issue was further considered by a group of countries spearheaded by Japan, and was resubmitted to the members as the so-called Suzuki Text[14] in November 1999, before the failed Seattle Ministerial Conference in December 1999, and thereafter to the General Council in

---

[10]   Third tier of the Decision on the Application and Review of the Understanding on Rules and Procedures Governing the Settlement of Disputes, *The Legal Texts: The Results of the Uruguay Round of Multilateral Trade Negotiations* (Cambridge University Press, 2002), p. 408.

[11]   As a result of the *EC – Bananas* saga, there were sharp differences between the two major users, the European Communities and the United States, on the question of whether the procedures under Article 21.5 of the DSU should be exhausted if there is disagreement as to the measures taken by the losing party to comply with the recommendations and rulings of the DSB before recourse may be made to Article 22 of the DSU.

[12]   Article 21.5 (compliance panel) was initiated for the first time in late 1998 in the *Bananas* case. The EC and the US were very much in disagreement in this case as to whether a request for authorisation to suspend concession should take priority over a request for the establishment of a compliance panel to assess whether the measures the EC had put in place sufficiently met the DSB's recommendations.

[13]   See for instance the comments of members in the minutes of the Meeting of Special Session of the DSB, 22 October 2004, TN/DS/M/20.

[14]   See WT/MIN(99)/8; 22 November 1999.

September 2000.[15] Throughout the negotiations, until 2001 (when the Doha Ministerial Conference was launched) and beyond, the question of remedies for continuous non-compliance with an adopted Dispute Settlement Body (DSB) report appeared to be one of the issues most likely to cause divisions among members. The reason for this may be linked to what some consider the 'revolutionary' aspects of the proposals, the changing fundamentals of the international financial system and lack of political will on the part of negotiators to 'rock the boat'. There have been disagreements among members as regards proposals such as early determination of injuries once nullification and impairment have been established, negotiable remedies, preventive measures, collective countermeasures, and so on.

Although there is broad consensus on the importance of the WTO dispute settlement system, and the mandate accorded by ministers to negotiators in November 2001 to continue the negotiations on the 'improvements and clarifications' of the DSU was relatively uncomplicated, constructive ambiguity continues to impede progress in the negotiations on amendment and clarifications of the DSU pursuant to paragraph 30 of the Doha Ministerial Declaration.[16] Even though more than 13 years had elapsed since the launch of the Round, ministers meeting in Geneva in December 2011 during the eighth WTO Ministerial Conference barely discussed issues relating to WTO disputes settlement reforms at all.[17] As mentioned above, even the work of the independent experts appointed to establish a proper framework on dealing with institutional challenges affecting the future of the WTO has been criticised for having not added very much, in the domain of remedies for non-compliance, to the existing work of international economic lawyers such as John Jackson who sat on the panel.[18] Yet, with

---

[15] Proposal to Amend Certain Provisions of the Understanding on Rules and Procedures Governing the Settlement of Disputes (DSU) Pursuant to Article X of the Marrakesh Agreement Establishing the World Trade Organization, WT/GC/W/410, 29 September 2000 and Rev.1.

[16] Paragraph 30 of the Doha Declaration states 'members agree to negotiations on improvements and clarifications of the Dispute Settlement Understanding'.

[17] The WTO Eighth Ministerial Conference took place in Geneva from 15–17 December 2011. See www.wto.org/english/thewto_e/minist_e/min11_e/min11_e.htm (last visited 30 December 2011). Most WTO members, especially the small, vulnerable economies, regretted the outcome of the conference. See, for instance, the interview with the representative of the Solomon Islands in one of their local newspapers (the *Solomon Star*) at www.solomonstarnews.com/news/national/13273-we-are-all-losers-today-sisilo-tells-wto-ministerial-conference (last visited 30 December 2011).

[18] See von Bogdandy and Markus Wagner, p. 442. But there are also some positive appraisals of the way in which the report dealt overall with the issues

respect to dispute settlement, one must admit that the Sutherland Report to some extent provides useful comments on some relevant legal issues which have always been contested by academics. Such topics include questions relating to precedents,[19] standard of review (that is, *de novo* review or total deference) and deference by panels and the AB, amicus briefs[20] and some of the conceptual comments on DSU reform proposals put forward by WTO members in the context of the Doha trade talks.[21]

However, the consultative board's report failed to sufficiently respond to some fundamental international economic law questions that have for a long time been the subject of vigorous debate within international legal scholarship. The report admits the already widely accepted view that other international law has relevance in the WTO jurisprudence. However, in doing so, it cautions against pushing such a view too far without actually delving further into the extent to which international law should be seen as part of the WTO system of law. Given that various remedies exist for breach of an international obligation under general international law, the issue of international law's place in the WTO *acquis* remains very relevant to the debate on compliance with WTO law.[22] This is the more so because we have witnessed in recent years growing intercourse between WTO rules and other international law rules. In a number of cases the panels and the

---

entrusted to it. On this point, see Richard Blackhurst, 'The Future of the WTO: Some comments on the Sutherland Report', *World Trade Review*, Vol. 4, No. 3 (2005), pp. 378–89; and Niall Meagher, 'So far, so good: but what next? The Sutherland Report and WTO dispute settlement', *World Trade Review*, Vol. 4, No. 3 (2005), pp. 409–17.

[19]   The report rightly pointed out that although the strictest type of precedent as utilised in many common law jurisdictions may not be applicable in international proceedings like the WTO dispute settlement system, 'it is quite clear that some degree of "precedent" concepts motivates the WTO dispute settlement processes'. See para. 231 of the Sutherland Report.

[20]   As the report pointed out, through jurisprudential progressivism, the panels and the AB have followed the procedure laid down in Article 13 of the DSU and also regulated the issue of *amicus curiae* briefs on a case-by-case basis. Nonetheless, it is important, as the Sutherland Report notes, for WTO members to 'develop a general criteria and procedures, at both levels to fairly and adequately handle amicus submissions' (para. 260 of the Report).

[21]   Sutherland Report, pp. 51 and 56–9.

[22]   The link between the WTO and other rules of international law has traditionally been provided by Article 3.2 of the DSU on customary rules of interpretation. Articles 31 and 32, in particular Article 31.3(c), of the VCLT have always been viewed by the DSB as a codification of the customary rules of interpretation and are, as such, the centre of the universe as far as this debate is concerned. Obviously, specific WTO-covered agreements, such as TRIPS, TBT, SPS, etc., contain specific references to other international rules outside the WTO treaty provisions.

Appellate Body (AB) have referred to other international law practices unrelated to treaty interpretation. These include *locus standi*,[23] the precautionary principle,[24] *jura novit curia*,[25] no retroactive application of treaties[26] and manifest error in the formation of a treaty, and so on.[27] Moreover, both the WTO members[28] and the AB have also referred to certain of the international law concepts ingrained in the law of state responsibility.[29]

Further, while recognising the development of a vast amount of jurisprudence in the WTO, the Report also elaborates on the nature of the WTO DSU remedies regime under Articles 21 and 22 of the DSU as a *lex specialis* or confined regime. In circumscribing the remedies regime as one different from conceptual international law remedies, the report fails to deal with the issue of *restitutio in integrum*, which has been vigorously debated over the past years. Although rationality would lead one to assume that the maxim *ubi jus, ibi remedium*[30] applies, there seems to be a lack of realisation of the role third parties/participants and other non-

---

[23] See *European Communities – Regime for the Importation, Sale and Distribution of Bananas (EC – Bananas)*, WT/DS27/R, para. 133 (27 September 1997). It is also important to note in this context that the panel and the AB in the *Bananas* case went so far as to utilise the Lomé Convention, which is not part of general international law.

[24] Appellate Body Report, *EC – Hormones* case, paras. 123–4.

[25] Appellate Body Report, *EC – Tariff Preferences*, para. 105.

[26] Appellate Body Report, *Brazil – Desiccated Coconut*, pp. 15 and 167 at paras. 179–80.

[27] In dealing with the issue of error in treaty formation, under the concept of non-violation complaint, the panel in *Korea – Measures Affecting Government Procurement*, WT/DS163/R (May 2000) resorted to customary international law practice (from the Permanent Court of International Justice (PCIJ) and the International Court of Justice (ICJ)), as codified in Article 48 of the VCLT 48. See panel report, paras. 7.120–7.123.

[28] See, for instance, more recently China's arguments in *US – Antidumping and Countervailing Duties (China)*, Appellate Body Report, *United States – Definitive Anti-Dumping and Countervailing Duties on Certain Products from China*, WT/DS379/AB/R (adopted 25 March 2011), paras. 22, 36–41 and 305.

[29] See, for instance, para. 259 of the Appellate Body Report, *US – Line Pipe* on the principle of proportionality of countermeasures. Moreover, in para. 20 of *US – Cotton Yarn* (Appellate Body Report, *United States – Transitional Safeguard Measure On Combed Cotton Yarn from Pakistan*, WT/DS192/AB/R (adopted 5 November 2001)) the AB stated: 'Our view is supported further by the rules of general international law on state responsibility, which require that countermeasures in response to breaches by states of their international obligations be commensurate with the injury suffered.'

[30] A Latin maxim, which means 'where there is law, there is remedy'. See *The Code of Justinian*, 'Corpus Juris Civilis', *The Attorney's Pocket Dictionary* (Oxford University Press, 2001), pp. 527–65.

disputing parties may play in effecting compliance with WTO obligations. In view of the fact that the WTO may be seen as an organisation based on trade-related agreements, one would have expected an approach to handling some of the twenty-first-century challenges facing the world trading system to also look closely into situations where some remedies for breaches of these agreements are somewhat systemic in nature.

In view of some of the issues highlighted above, we hope in this volume to further explore issues of compliance with WTO law. The volume employs some key international relation theories to conceptualise the arguments on how and why states comply or fail to comply with WTO rules. While the first few chapters deal with the general evolution of WTO dispute settlement and perspectives on different theories of compliance with international law, the second part focuses more on China and the WTO. The lack of progress in the Doha trade negotiations provides a compelling rationale for such an exercise. Moreover, apart from offering insights into the remedies available for non-compliance with legal obligations in WTO law, the book provides a systematic account of how the issue of rule of law and compliance with international trade rules have interacted with Chinese Confucian theory.

In view of the foregoing, as a multilateral institution which, as of May 2015, has 161 members, the WTO is something of a focal point for the major legal systems around the world. In addition to its developed members, emerging economies such as Brazil, China, India and Mexico have increasingly participated in the organisation's activities, especially in respect of its dispute settlement mechanism. For instance, since joining the WTO in 2001, China has been party either as complainant or respondent to more than 58 disputes.[31] This therefore begs some interesting questions on the approach taken by each member to compliance and dispute resolution in the world trading system. Confucian values, identified as the foundation of China's great cultural tradition, have controlled the social order and regulated people in all activities of Chinese daily lives including the people's legal consciousness, expectations of justice and trust in law. This legal tradition is distinct from the common and civil law of Western society. This book accordingly examines the conflicting and conciliating processes between the Chinese approach to litigation and the Western, legally oriented, approach in the field of the WTO dispute settlement mechanism. In so doing, the evolution of the WTO dispute settlement system is traced.

---

[31]   As of May 2015.

2. The evolution of the GATT/WTO dispute settlement system

2.1 THE RELEVANCE OF DISPUTE SETTLEMENT MECHANISMS IN TRADE AGREEMENTS

In the light of the nexus that exists between institutional dispute settlement and the debate on compliance, this section discusses the relevance of introducing dispute settlement provisions in international economic agreements. The proliferation of international trade and investment agreements in recent decades has led to a series of fragmented dispute resolution facilities. Although almost all regional, bilateral or multilateral agreements, whatever their nature, endorse peaceful settlement of disputes as an important aspect of the agreement in question, the true meaning of what constitutes a dispute for the purpose of dispute settlement has been subject to disagreement. The first very general definition of dispute in this field is to be found in the *Mavrommatis Palestine Concessions* case where the Permanent Court of International Justice (PCIJ) stated that '[a] dispute is a disagreement on a point of law or fact, a conflict of legal views or of interests between two persons'.[1] And 26 years later the International Court of Justice (ICJ) defined a dispute as 'a situation in which the two sides held clearly opposite views concerning the question of the performance or non-performance of certain treaty obligations'.[2] Consequently, determination of the existence of a dispute is important in the delimitation of the contours of the application of a particular dispute settlement mechanism. A dispute arising from an international instrument is, therefore, generally seen as a disagreement between two or more entities – typically, but not exclusively, states – over the interpretation and application of the international instrument in question.[3]

---

[1]   Mavrommatis Palestine Concessions (*Greece v. Great Britain*), Judgment of 30 August 1924, 1924 PCIJ (Ser A) No. 2, p.11.
[2]   Interpretation of the Peace Treaties with Bulgaria, Hungary and Romania, Advisory Opinion of 30 March 1950 (first phase), 1950 ICJ Reports 65, at 74.
[3]   On this issue, see John Merills, 'The Means of Dispute Settlement', in Malcolm D. Evans (ed.), *International Law* (Oxford University Press, 4th ed., 2014), pp. 563–88.

However, the landscape of these fragmented dispute settlement facilities has radically shifted so that the proliferation of these bodies has been seen by some academics as the 'single most important development of the post-Cold War' era.[4] Dispute settlement is at the heart of events in inter-state cooperation and recent international economic institutions have placed emphasis 'on dispute-settlement mechanisms and on institutions to support compliance with those mechanisms'.[5] For example, since the establishment of the WTO in 1995, one of the most recognised and functional aspects of the organisation is its two-tier dispute settlement mechanism. This is something of a novelty compared with what existed under GATT 1947, the predecessor of the WTO. From a regional perspective, when the North American Free Trade Agreement (NAFTA) was established, the three contracting parties instituted an elaborate dispute settlement mechanism for trade and investment disputes. The same holds for the Association of South East Asian Countries (ASEAN), which has been working to improve its dispute settlement mechanism with the introduction of the 2004 Enhanced Dispute Settlement Mechanism and the 2010 Protocol on Dispute Settlement.[6]

Introducing dispute settlement provisions in inter-state agreements is consistent with the general notion that those agreements are the constituent elements of binding international law requiring good faith compliance

---

[4]   See Cesare P.R. Romano, 'The Proliferation of International Judicial Bodies: The Pieces of the Puzzle', *New York University Journal of International Law and Politics (NYUJILP)*, Vol. 31, (1999), pp. 723–28, in Robert O. Keohane, Andrew Moravcsik and Anne-Marie Slaughter, 'Legalized Dispute Resolution: Interstate and Transnational', *International Organisation*, Vol. 54, No. 3 (2000), pp. 457–88. The assessment of these authors, made over ten years ago, was that the continuous fragmentation of the international legal order has led to a corresponding increase in the numbers of international courts and tribunals. There are now almost a hundred international tribunals and courts around the world.

[5]   Beth V. Yarbrough and Robert M. Yarbrough, in Edward D. Mansfield and Helen V. Milner (eds), *The Political Economy of Regionalism* (Columbia University Press, 1997), p. 138.

[6]   See the 2004 ASEAN Protocol on Enhanced Dispute Settlement Mechanism, Adopted by the Economic Ministers at the 10th ASEAN Summit in Vientiane, Laos (29 November 2004), available at http://cil.nus.edu.sg/rp/pdf/2004%20ASEAN%20Protocol%20on%20Enhanced%20Dispute%20Settlement%20Mechanism-pdf.pdf and the April 2010 Protocol to the ASEAN Charter on Dispute Settlement Mechanisms at http://cil.nus.edu.sg/rp/pdf/2010%20Protocol%20to%20the%20ASEAN%20Charter%20on%20Dispute%20Settlement%20Mechanisms-pdf.pdf (last visited 20 June 2014).

by states.[7] Typically, dispute settlement may serve as a tool to ensure compliance with agreed results of prolonged negotiations by states. And because it is inconceivable after a prolonged negotiation to draft an agreement in a manner that will be explicit enough to cover all future eventualities, dispute settlement may also be seen more as an essential instrument to make sense of the concluded deal, thereby enhancing the security and predictability of the concluded treaty.[8]

In spite of the generally accepted role dispute settlement plays in international trade and investment agreements, as sketched above, there is ongoing debate as to its future role in respect of trade and investment agreements, especially in the context of the WTO. Firstly, one school of thought holds that dispute settlement under the WTO should be strictly limited to clarifying the provisions of the Marrakesh Agreement Establishing the World Trade Organization (the 'WTO Agreement') and its covered agreements consistent with the common intentions of WTO members.[9] The interpretation of such common intentions is also strongly disputed. In other words, the interpretation of international treaties is riddled with inconsistencies. For instance, despite the impressive jurisprudence of the WTO dispute settlement system (the WTO DSS), the question of consistency of approach in interpreting Article XX of GATT as well as the manner in which the AB allocates burden of proof remain far from settled in the eyes of many international economic lawyers.[10] For instance,

---

[7] See Article 26 of the VCLT.

[8] It is important to note that the texts of most, if not all, international agreements do not indicate that dispute settlement mechanisms have the capacity to add to or diminish the contracting parties' negotiated rights and obligations. See, for instance, Articles 3.2 and 19.2 of the WTO DSU.

[9] In this regard, strictly adhering to what they regard as the spirit of Articles 3.2 and 19.2 of the DSU.

[10] See Michelle T. Grando, 'Allocating the Burden of Proof in WTO Disputes: A Critical Analysis', *Journal of International Economic Law (JIEL)*, Vol. 9, No. 3 (2006), pp. 615–56; Federico Ortino, 'Treaty Interpretation and the WTO Appellate Body Report in US – Gambling: A Critique', *JIEL*, Vol. 9, No. 1 (2006), pp. 117–45; Tomer Broude, 'Genetically Modified Rules: The Awkward Rule–Exception–Right distinction in EC–Biotech', *World Trade Review*, Vol. 6, No. 2 (2007), pp. 215–31. Boude in the latter piece systematically identifies cases where the WTO DSB has not been consistent in drawing a distinction between a positive rule and an exception. In addition to the inconsistency of approach in *EC – Biotech*, the author discusses the reading of Articles 3.1, 3.3 and 5.1 of the SPS Agreement in the *EC – Hormones* case. It is also important to note that even the WTO AB does not in principle have a final say on how a provision of a WTO covered agreement should be interpreted. In fact, pursuant to Article IX.2 of the WTO Charter, this power lies with the Ministerial Conference and the General

a GATT panel in *US – Custom User Fees*,[11] for the purpose of allocating burden of proof, interpreted Article II.2(c) of GATT as an exception, while the panel and the AB dealing with similar issues in a subsequent case did not exactly reach the same conclusion.[12] Secondly, a more radical school of thought views the dispute settlement system more through the prism of an activist court whose role is to make sense of relevant agreements, fill gaps where necessary and eventually set precedent for future rulings.[13] This view is mostly held by economists who employ contract law theory to analyse the WTO dispute settlement system. Proponents of this approach further contend that dispute settlement may also serve as a mechanism to complete 'an incomplete contract' previously negotiated by nation-states.[14]

International economic disputes, especially in the trade field, may arise for a number of reasons, including anticipation of a likely breach of a treaty by the respondent[15] or an actual breach of a treaty obligation. With this in mind, the purpose of dispute settlement will be to strike a careful balance between the rights and obligations of the parties consistent with the origi-

---

Council, but has in practice never been resorted to. On this issue, see Clause-Dieter Ehlermann and Lothar Ehring, 'The Authoritative Interpretation Under Article IX:2 of the Agreement Establishing the World Trade Organization: Current Law, Practice and Possible Improvements', *JIEL*, Vol. 8, No. 4 (2005), pp. 803–24.

[11]   GATT panel report, *United States Custom User Fees*, L/6264-35S/245 (adopted 2 February 1988) para. 84.

[12]   See Appellate Body Report, *India – Additional and Extra-Additional Duties on Imports from the United States*, WT/DS360/AB/R (adopted 17 November 2008), at paras. 188–93. For comprehensive comments on this, see Paola Conconi and Jan Wouters, 'Appellate Body Report, *India – Additional and Extra-Additional Duties on Imports from the United States* (WT/DS360/AB/R, adopted on 17 November 2008)', *World Trade Review*, Vol. 9, Issue 1 (2010), pp. 239–63.

[13]   Making an economic analysis of the role dispute settlement should play in trade agreements, Maggi and Staiger see dispute settlement under the WTO as being more about 'filling gaps in the agreement where it is silent than about enforcing clearly-stated obligations'. Giovanni Maggi and Robert W. Staiger, 'The Role of Dispute Settlement Procedures in International Trade Agreements', *Quarterly Journal of Economics* (*QJE*), Vol. 126 (2011), p.475. The latter view is clearly inconsistent with the general understanding (Articles 3.2 and 19.2 of the DSU) that panels and AB rulings and recommendations are not to be seen as adding to or diminishing members' obligations.

[14]   Giovanni Maggi and Robert W. Staiger, 'The Role of Dispute Settlement Procedures in International Trade Agreements', *QJE*, Vol. 126 (2011), p.476.

[15]   This is the case in the area of antidumping and subsidies and countervailing measures under the WTO. See in this regard Article VI:1 of GATT 1994, Article 3.7 of the Antidumping Agreement and Article 15.7 of the Agreement on Subsidies and Countervailing Measures.

nal negotiated commitments. In some cases, no actual violation occurs, but the dispute settlement process is needed in order to provide redress for the loss of a legitimate expectation. This may take place through a third party adjudicatory body, as in the WTO, or through a more diplomatic process such as consultation, negotiation, conciliation and mediation.[16] This was the approach taken by the contracting parties to GATT 1947 in resolving their trade differences. Whether contracting parties to international agreements decide to opt for a more diplomatic or a more legalistic dispute settlement mechanism, this volume views dispute settlement in trade and investment agreements as a mechanism to preserve the rights and obligations of the parties to such agreements. In this regard, the dispute settlement processes provided for in many international agreements should aim at providing positive solutions to disputes between the parties.[17]

2.2   RESOLVING DISPUTES 'THE GATT WAY'

As discussed above, institutionalising dispute settlement in an international agreement serves to demonstrate the contracting parties' willingness to ensure that the rights and obligations emanating from the agreement are respected. Dispute settlement, therefore, lies at the heart of the international law compliance debate. Although there are many reasons, going beyond the fear of retaliation, as to why states respect their international commitments, the inclusion of a comprehensive dispute settlement provision helps to demonstrate good faith and honesty on the part of the contracting parties. In this regard, it is incumbent upon contracting parties to international trade agreements to decide either to rely on informal diplomatic methods or to establish a legalistic third-party dispute settlement mechanism to deal with complaints regarding breaches of international trade law obligations by its members. When so doing, states are also required to specify in advance certain general procedural rules to be followed by the parties to such disputes. They may either try to re-introduce the types of remedies put forward by legal positivist scholars,[18] or rely on

---

[16]   This is the case with situation and non-violation complaints in the WTO dispute settlement system.

[17]   See Article 3.7 of the DSU.

[18]   For instance, in his 1832 English legal classic, *The Province of Jurisprudence Determined*, Austin viewed 'law', as distinct from opinions or mores, as command from the sovereign that must be enforceable through sanctions administered by the sovereign. Here, Austin could not agree with any remedial action that was not in the form of punishment. See John Austin, *The Province of Jurisprudence*

each state party's good faith to provide compensation for non-compliance, or perhaps even rely on unilateral countermeasures to discourage or stop such violation. In making a decision on any of these means of enforcement, thought must be given to such questions as when to seek remedies in respect of a breach, against whom to seek them, and whether the chosen remedies suffice to discourage or prevent violations.

Contracting states to an international treaty may also avail themselves of the right to veto the setting-up of bodies to resolve disputes or even prevent the adoption of the reports made by such bodies once they have been set up. This was one of the features of GATT 1947. In its first 35 years, the modus operandi under the GATT 1947 (which came into existence in lieu of a failed attempt to create an International Trade Organization) was pragmatism and the avoidance of legalism. With Geneva as its de facto seat, GATT problems were resolved through ad hoc solutions and provisional measures. There was, however, no clear provision in the GATT 1947 on the legal method to be used to settle disputes, nor was there any explicit provision on recourse to the ICJ for the settlement of disputes arising from non-compliance with GATT rules. As a consequence, there was a great deal of uncertainty on the part of the complainants in the very first cases under GATT as to whether to address their case to the GATT working parties or to the chairman. In *Cuba – Discriminatory Consular Taxes*, the Netherlands did not directly address the matter before the Second GATT Working Session.[19] Instead of directly addressing the inconsistency of the Cuban discriminatory measures with GATT, the Netherlands requested a ruling from the chairman on whether Article I of GATT (Most-Favoured-Nation obligation) applied to consular taxes. Without further discussion of the topic, the chairman ruled that it did. The same situation came up in the *Discriminatory Administration of India's export tax rebates Against Pakistan*. Though India reserved its position and the case had to be pushed forward to the next session, the chairman still ruled that Article I of GATT 1947 applied to tax rebates.[20] By way of a move in the direction of a more

---

Determined (Cambridge Texts in the History of Political Thought), Lecture V (Cambridge University Press, 1995). An insight into this view was well articulated by another legal positivist, H.L.A Hart, in *The Concept of Law* (Oxford, first published in 1961 and republished in 1994), p. 209 (hereinafter, 'Hart (1994)').

[19]   GATT/CP.2/SR.11 (24 August 1948).

[20]   GATT Panel Report, *Discriminatory Administration of India's export tax rebates Against Pakistan*, BISD 11/18/ (24 August 1948). A comprehensive analysis of this case is given in Robert E. Hudec, *The GATT Legal System and World Trade Diplomacy* (Butterworth Legal Publisher, 1990) (hereinafter, 'Hudec (1990)'), pp. 113–22.

legalistic style of dispute settlement, the contracting parties appointed a small working party to handle the emergency trade barriers request made by Cuba. Unsurprisingly, the working party was not able to deal with the factual issues relating to the dispute.

2.3   CONSTRUCTING A MORE LEGALISTIC DISPUTE SETTLEMENT METHOD UNDER THE GENERAL AGREEMENT

The first few decades of the existence of GATT 1947 were characterised, among other things, by the lack of a proper and reliable dispute settlement structure.[21] The underlying issue here was that of whether to approach dispute settlement from a more legalistic manner or rather to rely on a diplomacy-oriented approach.[22] The diplomatic means of settling disputes was characterised by flexibility, control over the dispute by the parties, avoidance of 'winner–loser situations', with the political weight of the disputing parties playing a significant role in the eventual settlement. However, the legal-oriented approach involved the parties wishing to achieve rule-based and binding decisions in conformity with negotiated long-term agreed rights and obligations through third-party adjudication, with power politics having no influence on the end results. The types of remedies available to a successful party to a dispute was an important issue in the process. This was all the more the case because it was an issue which was never clearly dealt with by the GATT contracting parties.

But above and beyond the achievements of any system, dispute settle-

---

[21]   As is well known, some of the reasons for this stemmed from the ease with which contracting parties unhappy with a request to establish dispute settlement panels could block such a request. Moreover, once established it was never easy to get the report of the panel adopted because of the contracting parties' ability to block it. For the challenges and controversies facing the GATT dispute resolution, see Hudec (1990); Ernst-Ulrich Petersmann, *The GATT/WTO Dispute Settlement System: International Organizations and Dispute Settlement* (Kluwer, 1997) (hereinafter, 'Petersmann (1997)'); and John H. Jackson, *The World Trade Organization: Constitution and Jurisprudence* (Chatham House Papers, 1998) (hereinafter, 'Jackson, *World Trade Organization* (1998)'), pp. 64–81.

[22]   The idea that this kind of diplomatic approach is a cornerstone in GATT practice was also greatly felt in the overall GATT decision-making processes. For the debate on rule-making under GATT, see Armin von Bogdandy, 'Law and Politics in the WTO – Strategies to Cope with a Deficient Relationship', in *Max Planck Yearbook of United Nations Law* (MPYBUNL) (2001) Vol. 5, pp. 609–74. See also another thesis on this issue by Frieder Roessler, 'The Competence of GATT', *Journal of World Trade Law (JWTL)* (1987), pp. 21, 73 et seq.

ment is essential for the implementation of any rights and obligations. In the municipal as well as in the international arena, it may be supposed that the strength of rules derives from the fact that lack of good faith adherence to the agreed rights and obligations will be more costly than respecting them.[23] Because the issues constantly addressed in the context of international trade are often politically sensitive, politicians occasionally prefer to employ rather more protectionist policies as quid pro quo for political support from rent-seeking interest groups. Yet, the consumer interest in such protectionist market policy may be far from being symmetrical (at least in the long run) to those of the rent-seeking interest groups reaping the short-term benefits of non-liberal trade policies. Consumers and citizens with overarching interests in a liberal trade policy are, thus, unaware of the numerous tariff categories in respect of trade in both goods and services and lack essential organisation to influence government policies which may be largely discretional.

Pressure from trade protectionist interest groups characterised the first two decades of GATT's existence, as a result of which there were frequent violations of contracting parties' rights and obligations under GATT 1947. As has been pointed out by Robert Hudec, the differences in approaches to trade policymaking also influenced GATT diplomats' 'jurisprudence' and led to poorly argued cases, which were consequently blocked at the adoption stage by the contracting parties. Article XXIII of GATT in effect provided for regular consultations, where contracting parties' representatives met with one another to address issues affecting the operation of GATT commitments. Pursuant to the provisions of Article XXIII, the contracting parties had the possibility to make investigations and seek rulings on a particular GATT violation or non-violation complaint brought forward by another contracting party. Originally, the key to invoking the GATT dispute settlement mechanism rested on 'nullification or impairment'; a relatively ambiguous phrase which might still connote a power-oriented approach.[24] But the general posture of the

---

[23]   This theory is well formulated in the writings of legal theoreticians, such as in the work of Austin, Lecture V (1995); Hart (1994), pp. 50–78.

[24]   This ambiguous phrase was taken up in the *Australian Ammonium Sulphate* (*Australia Subsidy*). In this case, the working party opened its discussion by defining nullification or impairment as including actions by a contracting party that harmed the trade of another and which 'could not reasonably have been anticipated' by the other at the time it negotiated for a concession. By implication, the basis was a contract-type theory of 'reasonable expectation'. For a succinct analysis of the case, see Hudec (1990), pp. 159–68. For the facts of the case, see GATT, BISD (Vol. II) (1952), p. 188.

GATT structure favours the view of Palmeter and Mavroidis that 'GATT diplomats for many years were decidedly averse to the very notion of turning conciliation into a legal proceeding'.[25] This was because there was a general belief that any dispute settlement structure under GATT should be structured primarily to achieve a mutually agreeable solution to the disputing parties rather than producing a decision based on a point of law. Therefore, legal principles in the context of GATT dispute settlement were seen as asymmetrical to the common intention of the contracting parties.[26] As a consequence, the responsibility to ensure compliance with any panel report remained in the hands of the parties to the dispute and nothing could be done if compliance was not forthcoming.

Nonetheless, as evading GATT obligations by contracting parties progressively became the norm rather than the exception, there was ambivalence on how to construct a functioning dispute settlement system to deal with the problems that continued to emerge. As discussed in the foregoing section, there was a stark divide among those involved in GATT. One side of the divide favoured the continuation of a diplomatic-oriented approach to dispute settlement; while those on the other took the view that there was a need to move away from the weaknesses of a diplomatic approach to dispute settlement to a more legalistic system where a neutral third party adjudicator would decide on cases on the basis of legal principles.[27] As the 'power-oriented technique' of modern diplomacy[28] continued to guide the GATT dispute settlement system, by the late 1970s and early 1980s there was an

---

[25]   David Palmeter and Petros C. Mavroidis, *Dispute Settlement in the World Trade Organization: Practice and Procedure* (Springer Publishing, 1999), p. 50; Matthias Oesch, *Standards of Review in WTO Dispute Resolution* (Oxford University Press, 2003), pp. 4–5. See also Michael J. Trebilcock and Robert Howse, *The Regulation of International Trade* (Routledge, 3rd ed., 2005).

[26]   It is also submitted that the lack of procedural rules on the settlement of disputes in GATT 1947 was largely due to the general anticipation that the failed International Trade Organization (ITO), in respect of which detailed procedural rules on the settlement of disputes had been drafted, would soon come into being. See Palmeter and Mavroidis (1999), p. 7. See also Jackson, *World Trade Organization* (1998), p. 65.

[27]   As Jackson has pointed out, the rule-oriented approach was necessary, since it made it easier to predict what an impartial tribunal might conclude in respect of a particular GATT violation, nullification or impairment. This in turn had the advantage of making the contracting parties pay closer attention to the GATT rules. See Jackson, *World Trade Organization* (1998), pp. 60–61.

[28]   See John H. Jackson, *The World Trading System, Law and Policy of International Economic Relations* (MIT Press, 2nd ed., 1997), p. 109; Robert E. Hudec, 'The GATT Legal System: A Diplomat's Jurisprudence', *Journal of World Trade (JWT)*, Vol. 4 (1970), p. 615.

emerging enthusiasm on the part of the contracting parties for a paradigm shift from diplomacy to a more legalistic dispute resolution system.[29]

Consequently, with the conclusion in 1979 of the Tokyo Round of multi-lateral trade talks there was lingering optimism prompted by a move toward a more legalistic approach to international trade rules.[30] The codification and the development of GATT dispute settlement 'customary practice' in the 1979 'Understanding Regarding Notification, Consultation, Dispute Settlement and Surveillance' represented a significant shift away from a system that had since its inception been guided by diplomacy in the field of dispute settlement. The outcome of the Tokyo Ministerial Conference was a significant improvement to the GATT rules on dispute resolution. Many of the fragmented codes agreed upon contained their own rules on dispute settlement as well as specific deadlines for dealing with cases and provision for resort to dispute settlement as of right.

One unambiguous aspect of the GATT rules that was not altered by the Tokyo Round Code was the remedy of last resort in case of nullification or impairment of benefits as provided for under Article XXIII of GATT. There was no prescription in the 1979 Tokyo Round Code that allowed for the goalposts to be moved beyond the possibility to unilaterally suspend the application of concessions and other obligations on a discriminatory basis *vis-à-vis* the party that effected the nullification or impairment. However, suspensions of concessions could not happen without the authorisation of the contracting parties,[31] which had to decide whether to authorise or not by consensus.[32] This, comparatively speaking, broad mandate for resorting to the suspension of concessions and other obligations in case of unilateral trade restrictive practices appears to have

---

[29] This enthusiasm can be identified in the critical views of many contracting parties in respect of the prolonged period of mediation in some GATT disputes. See for instance, Jackson, *World Trade Organization* (1998), p. 67.

[30] The Tokyo Round Agreement supplemented GATT law with half a dozen multilateral agreements encompassing non-tariff measures, three sectoral agreements on civil aircraft, bovine meat and dairy products, and by various additional framework agreements, 'understandings' and 'decisions' by the GATT contracting parties.

[31] BISD 26 S/216.

[32] The key elements of the GATT dispute resolution mechanism were the following three features: (1) nullification or impairment and not violation formed the basis for the invocation of GATT dispute settlement; (2) the fact that the contracting parties were vested with the sole power not only to investigate and make recommendations, but also to rule on any particular complaint; and (3) the contracting parties also had the sole right to authorise the suspension of GATT obligations against a contracting party or parties in appropriately serious cases.

been formally applied only once throughout the lifespan of GATT 1947.[33] In this single case, the contracting parties did not authorise an equivalent suspension of concessions and other obligations (as provided for under Article XXIII of GATT), but instead made an authorisation limited to what they considered sufficiently appropriate to compel the US, which was the respondent in this case, to bring its measures in line with GATT obligations. It was not surprising that the authorisation eventually had no real effect. In subsequent cases individual contracting parties decided to unilaterally suspend concessions and other obligations without necessarily seeking authorisation to do so from the other contracting parties.

Despite these unilateral actions by some contracting parties, Article XXIII.2 of GATT 1947 clearly required authorisation by the contracting parties before a contracting party could take retaliatory measures. Article XXIII.2 was very much drafted with the very objective of GATT in mind, i.e. to limit unauthorised unilateral economic sanctions which had previously led to international disorder. The suspension of the concession regime under GATT was an unambiguous move against the kind of multilateral retaliation seemingly suggested under general international law as codified under Article 60 of the Vienna Convention on the Law of Treaties (VCLT).[34] However, because unilateral action was somewhat frequently taken by contracting parties whose dispute settlement reports were blocked (especially but not limited to the US, the European Communities and Canada),[35] there was growing concern about the future of GATT and how it would continue to serve its original purpose. Moreover, with increasing numbers and diversity of contracting parties to GATT, cases became more complex and difficult to resolve. The underlining weaknesses of the

---

[33] This concerned a case brought by the Netherlands against the US in respect of its continuous infringement of Article XI. For the complete facts of the case and the nature of the GATT retaliatory regime, see Robert E. Hudec, *The GATT Legal System and World Trade Diplomacy* (New York, 1975), pp. 165–84; John H. Jackson, *World Trade and the Law of GATT* (Indianapolis in Bobbs Merrill), p. 185. See also Petersmann (1997).

[34] Article 60 of the VCLT allows contracting parties to a multilateral treaty to suspend in part or in whole the application of the treaty as against the offending party. See Article 60.2 of the VCLT, adopted on 22 May and opened for signatures on 23 May 1969 by the United Nations Conference on the Law of Treaties. *United Nations Treaty Series (UNTS)*, Vol. 1155, 331.

[35] Another area of concern had to do with the lack of transparency in GATT dispute settlement and delay in both the establishment of panels and adoption of the panel reports. Regarding various weaknesses in the GATT 1947 dispute settlement mechanism, see Robert E. Hudec, *Enforcing International Trade Law: The Evolution of the Modern GATT Legal System* (London, 1993) (hereinafter, 'Hudec (1993)'), pp. 354–5; and Petersmann (1997), pp. 90–91.

substantive and procedural GATT rules on dispute settlement became more evident. As a consequence, one of the fundamental issues on the agenda at the end of the eighth Ministerial Conference in Uruguay was to finalise a comprehensive DSU. As was agreed, these comprehensive rules and procedure for settling multilateral trade disputes are now enshrined in Annex 2 of the WTO Charter.[36] Despite the fact that some observers and academics opine that the picture in terms of GATT compliance was better than it has generally been portrayed as being,[37] many GATT contracting parties were undoubtedly convinced that there was a need to revamp the multilateral trade dispute settlement process so as to remedy the shortcomings of GATT. In this regard, it was clear that for a dispute resolution process to function properly, it was imperative that access to such a process should be more automatic in nature. Therefore, before discussing the issue of implementation which lies at the heart of this volume, it is important to offer an overview of some of the important items in the Uruguay Package.

2.4   THE URUGUAY ROUND PACKAGE AS AGREED BY WTO MEMBERS

As one of the newest multilateral economic institutions, the WTO was established in 1995 to succeed the GATT, which had been marred by many different challenges. As stated by Peter Sutherland et al. in an edited volume in 2001, '[t]he Multilateral Trading System with the World Trade Organization (WTO) at its centre, is the most important tool for global economic management and development we possess'.[38] Unlike GATT,

---

[36]   Or as it is known, the 'Marrakesh Agreement Establishing the World Trade Organization'.

[37]   See Hudec (1993). However, it may also be submitted that this generally positive picture of compliance with the GATT on the part of the contracting parties was either a function of reputation cost, or a general reason why nations obey international law. In the same vein, the lack of effective participation by developing countries in the whole GATT process, as contrasted with the post-1994 WTO era, may also have contributed to this positive picture of compliance within GATT. The reason for this is that most of the GATT participants had enough market power to make credible a threat of unilateral suspension of concessions. For reasons as to why nations respect international law, see, for instance, Louis Henkin, *How Nations Behave: Law and Foreign Policy* (Frederick A. Praeger, 1968).

[38]   See Peter Sutherland, John Sewell and David Weiner, 'Challenges facing the WTO and Policies to Address Global Governance', in Gary P. Sampson (ed.), *The Role of the World Trade Organization in Global Governance* (UN University Press, 2001), p. 81.

the WTO provides a legal and institutional framework for the multilateral trading system. The WTO Agreement put in place an organisation with a legal personality in contrast to GATT, which was merely a set of agreements. With a legal personality[39] similar to those of other multilateral organisations like the International Monetary Fund, the World Bank and the United Nations, the WTO and its staff enjoy immunity from the jurisdiction of municipal courts.[40] While the immunity of states is generally grounded on the principle of *par in parem non habet imperium*,[41] the immunity of an international organisation such as the WTO is based on the idea of functional necessity. In other words, immunity is seen as essential to the proper functioning of the international organisation in question and may only be waived by those organisations in very rare situations. In this regard, relying on the relevant elements of the WTO Agreement, the WTO Headquarters Agreement,[42] and to a certain extent customary international law, courts will have little hesitation in granting immunity from jurisdiction to the WTO.[43] It is essentially for this reason that Article VIII of the WTO Agreement is unambiguous about the legal nature of the WTO as an institution. With regard to membership, the WTO was

---

[39] Article VII.1 of the WTO Charter states: 'The WTO shall have legal personality, and shall be accorded by each of its members such legal capacity as may be necessary for the exercise of its functions.'

[40] From the 1940s to the present date, largely for functional reasons, the rules on immunity of international organisation have been progressively codified. On the immunities of international organisations and their staff, see Niels Blokker, 'International Organisation: the Untouchable', *International Organisation Law Review*, Vol. 10 (2013), pp. 259–75; Johan G. Lammers, 'Immunity of International Organisation: The Work of the International Law Commission', *International Organisation Law Review*, Vol. 10 (2013), pp. 276–86.

[41] This is a principle in public international law which prohibits one sovereign power from exercising jurisdiction over another sovereign power. It is a principle of equality of states and the basis of the doctrine of sovereign immunity.

[42] Committee on Budget and Finance, Agreement between the Swiss Confederation and the World Trade Organization on the Long-Term Housing Needs of the WTO, WT/BFA/W/170 (26 May 2008).

[43] It is also important to note that the staff of the organisation also benefit from diplomatic immunity in relation to the activities of the WTO. For more on the immunity of international organisations, see Emmanuel Gaillard and Isabelle Pingel-Lenuzza, 'International Organisation and Immunity from Jurisdiction: To Respect or to Bypass', *International & Comparative Law Quarterly (ICLQ)*, Vol. 51, No. 1 (2002), pp. 1–15; and August Reinisch, 'The Immunity of International Organisations and the Jurisdiction of their Administrative Tribunals', *Chinese Journal of International Law (CJIL)*, Vol. 7, No. 2 (2008), pp. 285–306.

originally negotiated by some 124 members, but this has now increased to a current total of 160 independent states and separate territories.[44]

The substantive parts of the WTO include the WTO Charter and four separate annexes. More specifically, Annex 1 contains three subparts. Subpart A (Annex 1A), contains 14 separate agreements[45] dealing with trade in goods; with the first of the 14 separate agreements being GATT 1947 and the other decisions of the contracting parties which entered the WTO *acquis* in 1995. Annex 1A also includes six separate interpretative understandings and an implementing protocol also concluded at Marrakesh. The next two subparts of Annex 1 contain the trade in services (GATS) and trade in intellectual property (TRIPS) agreements, which together with the Agreement on Agriculture (AG) were newly introduced into the WTO in 1995. Although GATT had always been formally applied to trade in agriculture, this sector had for one reason or another largely escaped GATT discipline.[46]

Furthermore, the Understanding on the Rules and Procedures Governing the Settlement of Disputes (DSU), which is the focal point of discussion in this volume, is contained in Annex 2 of the WTO Agreement. Some of the WTO covered agreements contain specific provisions on dispute settlement. These include: the Antidumping Agreement, the Agreement on the Application of Sanitary and Phytosanitary Measures, the Agreement on Safeguards, the Agreement on Technical Barriers to Trade, and the Agreement on Trade-Related Intellectual Property Rights, etc.[47] It is, however, important to note that the jurisdiction of the DSU

---

[44]   At least, as of 29 July 2014. Yemen's accession was approved during the December 2013 Bali Ministerial Conference, and it became the 160th member 30 days after notification to the WTO of the ratification of the agreement. On the state of accession of other countries, see http://www.wto.org/english/thewto_e/acc_e/acc_e.htm (last visited 21 May 2014). See also Article XII of the WTO Charter on the criteria for membership of the WTO.

[45]   The WTO Agreement on Trade Facilitation signed at the 8th WTO Ministerial Conference in December 2013 in Bali and the subsequent Protocol adopted almost a year later by the WTO members brings the number of Annex IA agreements on trade in goods to 14. See Ministerial Decision of 7 December 2013, WT/MIN(13)/36, WT/L/911, Agreement on Trade Facilitation, and subsequently the Decision of the General Council of 27 November 2014 on Agreement on Trade Facilitation: Protocol Amending the Marrakesh Agreement Establishing the WTO in document WT/PCTF/W/28.

[46]   It is worth pointing out here that prior to the Uruguay Round trade talks, attempts to bring it into the GATT discipline had been unsuccessful in the two preceding rounds (i.e., the Kennedy Round of 1962–67 and the Tokyo Round of 1973–79).

[47]   Pursuant to Article 1.2 of the DSU, the rules and procedures covered in the DSU shall apply to the extent that there is no conflict between those rules and

in terms of subject matter extends to any dispute arising out of any of the WTO agreements. The rules on trade policy review (Trade Policy Review Mechanism – TPRM) are contained in Annex 3; while those on the remaining two functional plurilateral trade agreements, being the Agreement on Government Procurement and the Agreement on Trade in Civil Aircraft, are contained in Annex 4.[48]

2.5   THE DISPUTE SETTLEMENT UNDERSTANDING AS A RULE-BASED SYSTEM

In spite of various changes that led to GATT 1947[49] being credited with a shift away from traditional diplomacy-based dispute settlement towards a more legalistic approach,[50] it largely fell short of the type of institutional and jurisdictional model of dispute resolution established by the DSU. By introducing the current two-tier WTO dispute settlement mechanism in 1995, WTO members began the move away from the 'institutionalised bargaining'[51] that reigned during the GATT 1947 era. The DSU established a compulsory dispute settlement system covering all of the agreements annexed to the WTO Agreement. It encompasses the relevant procedural rules and guidelines, with the main purpose of enhancing a secured and

---

'such special or additional rules and procedures on dispute settlement contained in the covered agreements as are identified in Appendix 2' of the DSU.

[48]   These plurilateral agreements are the only 'pick and choose' or 'à la carte' agreements under the WTO system. This means that WTO members may either choose to join or not to join these two agreements. The other plurilateral agreements – the International Dairy Agreement and the International Bovine Meat Agreement – were phased out as of 1 January 1998: WT/L/251, 17 December 1997, and WT/L/252, 16 December 1997. For the legal texts of the WTO, see *World Trade Organization: The Legal Texts, The Results of the Uruguay Round of Multilateral Trade Negotiations* (Cambridge, 2002). This may also be obtained from the WTO website at www.wto.org. For a description of the WTO, see Bernard Hoekman and Michael Kostecki, *The Political Economy of the World Trading System: From GATT to the WTO* (Oxford University Press, 1995). See also Jackson, *The World Trade Organization* (1998).

[49]   Now known as GATT 1994.

[50]   Jackson, *The World Trade Organization* (1998), pp. 59–91; Hudec (1993); Claus-Dieter Ehlermann, 'Tensions between the Dispute Settlement Process and the Diplomatic and Treaty-Making Activities of the WTO', *World Trade Review* (*WTR*), Vol. 1, No. 3 (2002), pp. 301–8.

[51]   A phrase used by Keohane et al. at the beginning of the twenty-first century to describe a more diplomatic and flexible type of dispute resolution mechanism. See Robert O. Keohane et al., *International Organization* (2000), p. 457.

predictable global trading system.[52] Moreover, the rules provided in the DSU also function as a central element in preserving the balance of rights and obligations of WTO members.[53]

The pursuit of these goals means that WTO members attach great importance to the maintenance of a cohesive and stable trading system in which the application of, and compliance with, established WTO norms is carried out in an even-handed manner among the members. In turn, these defining objectives reflect the level of priority of any dispute brought before the panel or the AB.[54] Accordingly, the WTO dispute resolution mechanism is guided *mutatis mutandis* by the provisions of GATT 1994 (Articles XXII and XXIII) as elaborated and applied in the DSU.

However, the centrepiece of the DSU, which distinguishes it from other third-party inter-state adjudicatory bodies as well as the kind of political flexibility exhibited in the earlier GATT dispute resolution system,[55] lies in the fact that members are endowed with an automatic right to resort to the panel process when consultation has failed.[56] Another core feature of the DSU, as distinct from the GATT practice, is founded on the premise of the appeal stage of disputes, which permits members dissatisfied with the panel examination of a particular issue of law to appeal to the AB. This to some extent replaces some of the procedures previously used, which required GATT Council approval.[57] Thus, the stage-one rulings and rec-ommendations issued by the panel will be deemed adopted by the DSB, except where there is a consensus to the contrary or one of the disputing

---

[52]   In respect of the issue of jurisdiction *materae*, Appendix 2 of the DSU enumerates other special and additional rules and procedures contained in various covered agreements. Where there is a conflict between the special rules and the DSU, the former shall prevail (Article 1.2 of the DSU). For the DSU's function as a cornerstone for the maintenance of security and predictability within the multi-lateral trading system, see Article 3.2 of the DSU.

[53]   See Article 3.2 of the DSU.

[54]   See Articles 3.7 and 3.10 of the DSU.

[55]   It is submitted that the political flexibility that defined the GATT was buried upon the coming into place of the DSU. See Steve Charnovitz, 'Rethinking WTO Trade Sanctions', *American Journal of International Law (AJIL)*, Vol. 95 (2001), pp. 792–832 at p. 803.

[56]   See Articles 4 and 6 of the DSU.

[57]   See Article 17 of the DSU regarding Appellate Review and Procedure. For the scope of standard of review, see Matthias Oesch, *Standard of Review in WTO Dispute Resolution* (Oxford University Press, 2003); Claus-Dieter Ehlermann and Nicolas Lockhart, 'Standard of Review in WTO Law', *JIEL*, Vol. 7, No. 3 (2004), pp. 491–521. For a survey of WTO dispute settlement in its first few years, see Peter Van den Bossche, 'World Trade Organization Dispute Settlement in 1997 (part I and II)', *JIEL*, Vol. 1 (1998), pp. 161–71 and 479–90.

parties appeals.[58] Apart from these procedural distinctions, Article 19.1, Article 21 and Article 22 of the DSU are also very important in the domain of remedies.[59] The controversy surrounding the issue of remedies in WTO dispute settlement is covered below after the section that discusses why WTO members have made such extensive use of the WTO appeal system.

2.6   GREATER USE OF THE WTO DISPUTE SETTLEMENT MECHANISM BY A BROADER WTO MEMBERSHIP

The elaborate rules and procedures enshrined in the DSU[60] have led to an overwhelming number of cases, from both developed and developing countries, successfully going through the new dispute settlement structure. Roughly 30 per cent of panel reports have been appealed.[61] This is a far higher proportion than have gone through many third-party inter-state adjudicatory bodies, and is even more impressive when compared with the number of cases that have been heard by the ICJ over its entire lifespan of more than 65 years.[62] It is thus important to identify why so many appeals have been made by WTO members.

---

[58]   This means that the winning party will also vote against such adoption. As regards the adoption of the panel and AB reports, see Article 16 and Article 17.14 of the DSU.

[59]   As regards dispute relating to a prohibited subsidy, as provided for under the Agreement on Subsidies and Countervailing Measures (SCM), Article 3, Articles 4.7, 4.10 and 4.11 of this Agreement, further amplify the provisions relating to remedies contained in the DSU. On dispute settlement in the WTO and the distinctive features of the DSB, see, for instance, Peter Van Den Bossche, *The Law and Policy of the World Trade Organization: Text, Cases and Materials* (Cambridge University Press, 2nd ed., 2008), pp. 168–319.

[60]   Including Articles XXII and XXIII of GATT as well as provisions in different covered agreements dealing with dispute settlement.

[61]   From 1996, when the first WTO Appellate Body Report was issued, until 20 January 2015, 116 Appellate Body Reports had been adopted, with one appeal in progress and one Article 21.5 appeal in progress. The two cases currently under review are Panel Reports, *United States – Certain Country of Origin Labelling (COOL) Requirements*, recourse to Article 21.5 of the DSU by Canada and Mexico, WT/DS384, 386/RW (Notice of Appeal, 28 November 2014); and Panel Reports, *United States – Anti-Dumping Measures on Certain Shrimp from Viet Nam*, WT/DS429/R (Notice of Appeal, 6 January 2015).

[62]   Between 22 May 1947, when the Corfu Channel case (*UK v. Albania*), the first registered ICJ case, was heard, and 20 May 2014, 160 cases were registered in the general ICJ list of contentious cases. The most recent case was an application instituting proceedings against the United Kingdom of Great Britain and

As noted above, an appeal can only be based on an issue of law and the AB may 'uphold, modify, or reverse the legal findings and conclusions of the panel'.[63] The DSU provides no explanation as to why only issues of law, not issues of facts, may be appealed. However, the jurisprudence of the AB shows that it has interpreted Article 17.6 of the DSU to mean that factual findings, as opposed to 'legal interpretations or legal conclusions, made by the panel are, in principle, not subject to review by the Appellate Body'.[64] For instance, '[t]he determination of whether or not a certain event did occur in time and space is typically a question of fact'.[65] Although matters relating to a member's domestic law are usually issues of fact in respect of a review before the AB, the assessment of such law to determine whether it complies with a particular provision of the WTO Agreement is 'a legal characterisation'.[66] In this regard, most of the WTO covered agreements have been the subject of appeals.[67]

Although it is well known that a large number of WTO cases involve private companies that seek help from their governments to resolve specific problems relating to export destinations,[68] the number of appealed cases does not only reflect the AB system's effectiveness but also the trust WTO members have in it.[69] On average an appeal before the WTO takes

---

Northern Ireland by the Republic of the Marshall Islands (22 April 2014). For an up-to-date list of ICJ cases, see http://www.icj-cij.org/docket/index.php?p1=3 (last visited 21 May 2014).

[63] See Articles 17.6 and 17.13 of the DSU respectively.

[64] Appellate Body Report, *EC Measures Concerning Meat and Meat Products (Hormones)*, para. 132.

[65] Ibid. para. 132. For a discussion of the distinction between issue of facts and issue of law, see Tania Voon and Alan Yanovich, 'The Facts Aside: The Limitations of WTO Appeals to Issues of Law', *Journal of World Trade (JWT)*, Vol. 40, No. 2 (2006), pp. 239–58; Simon Lester, 'The Development of Standards of Appellate Review for Factual, Legal and Law Application Questions in WTO Dispute Settlement', *Trade Law & Development*, Vol. 4, No. 1 (2012), pp. 125–49. See also the Appellate Body Report in *US – Section 211 Appropriations Act*, paras. 105–6, *US – Line Pipe*, para. 158.

[66] See Appellate Body Reports *US – Section 211 Appropriations Act*, paras. 105–6, *US – Hot-Rolled Steel*, para. 200 (Appellate Body Report, *United States – Anti-Dumping Measures on Certain Hot-Rolled Steel Products from Japan*, WT/DS184/AB/R/ (adopted 23 August 2001)).

[67] For a complete list of the cases and agreements involved, see www.worldtradelaw.net.

[68] This takes account of the fact that cases may also be filed based on 'threat of injury' under the WTO Antidumping Agreement (including Article VI of GATT 1994) and the Agreement on Subsidies and Countervailing Measures.

[69] This was noted to some extent by the AB in *US – Stainless Steel (Mexico)*, paras. 156–8, 160–62.

three to four months,[70] as compared with an average of four years before the ICJ or two years before the Court of Justice of the European Union. A dispute heard pursuant to Chapter 20 of NAFTA typically takes three years, while an investment dispute under Chapter 11 typically takes five years.[71] An ICSID tribunal may take on average three and a half years to resolve a dispute.[72] Moreover, appealing a panel report sometimes makes economic sense to a party against whom a panel report has found a challenged measure inconsistent with WTO law, since remedies are not retroactive under the WTO DSS.[73] Furthermore, the large number of appeals is partly due to the fact that many appellants have interpreted the panel's obligations under Article 11 of the DSU very broadly. This means that many instances where panels have exercised judicial economy[74] with regard to claims made by either of the parties have faced close scrutiny.[75]

---

[70]   Even when one adds this time period to the average of 11 months that it takes to complete a panel report, the WTO's two-tier system still appears very effective.

[71]   On NAFTA, see Armand de Mestral, 'NAFTA Dispute Settlement: Creative Experiment or Confusion?' in Bartel et al. (eds) *Regional Trade Agreements and the WTO Legal System* (Oxford University Press, 2006), pp. 359–81; David Quayat, 'The Forest for the Trees: A Roadmap to Canada's Litigation Experience in Lumber IV', *JIEL*, Vol. 12, No. 1 (2009), pp. 115–51.

[72]   For an update on ICSID cases, see ICSID website at https://icsid.worldbank. org/apps/ICSIDWEB/cases/Pages/AdvancedSearch.aspx (last visited 12 January 2015).

[73]   See, in particular, Ngangjoh Hodu and Roberto Rios, *Manchester Journal of International Economic Law (MJIEL)* (2004); and more recently, Ngangjoh Hodu, *Theories and Practices of Compliance with WTO Law* (Kluwer, 2012).

[74]   On when the panel can exercise judicial economy, see *US – Upland Cotton*, para. 732, See also Appellate Body Report, *Canada – Measures Relating to the Feed-in Tariff Program*, WT/DS426/AB/R (adopted 24 May 2013), paras. 5.33–5.35.

[75]   As pointed out by the AB in a number of WTO cases, including *US – Cotton Yarn*, para. 68, and Appellate Body Report, *US – Countervailing Duty Investigation on Dynamic Random Access Memory Semiconductors (DRAMS) from Korea*, WT/DS296/AB/R (adopted 20 July 2005), para. 182, a claim relating to non-fulfilment by the panel of the objectivity requirement under Article 11 of the DSU involves not only 'an error of judgment in the appreciation of evidence' but an 'egregious error that calls into question the good faith of a panel'. See Appellate Body Report, *EC Measures Concerning Meat and Meat Products (Hormones)*, paras. 132–3. See also *European Communities – Measures Prohibiting the Importation and Marketing of Seal Products*, where in its notice of appeal, Norway claimed that the panel had failed 'to make an objective assessment of the facts as required under Article 11 of the DSU, when it found that the objectives of the EU Seal Regime *do not* include protecting the interests of indigenous communities ('IC')', WT/DS401/9 (dated 9 January 2014), para. 5. While finding that

Appeals may also be brought for more systemic reasons or to seek further clarification on points of law not satisfactorily explained by a panel in its report. If such issues are not clarified by the AB, more measures inconsistent with WTO law may appear in the future.[76] The fact that dissents are rare at the WTO AB means that there is a great deal of confidence in the system and a high degree of predictability in the AB's jurisprudential progressivism.

2.7 CONTROVERSIES SURROUNDING REMEDIES FOR NON-COMPLIANCE WITH DSB RULINGS AND RECOMMENDATIONS

One of the most controversial topics in international law discourse over the years has been that of the provision of remedies for a breach of an international law obligation by a recalcitrant state or a non-state actor. The debate on the sufficiency of a remedy for a particular breach has even led to others questioning the legality of international law in their practice of law within their domestic jurisdictions.[77] Although the exact function of remedies is debatable, they drive home a simple message that violation will be taken seriously by those who are endowed with overseeing the implementation of agreed obligations. Chief Justice Oliver Wendell Holmes Jr once stated that, 'obligations that exist, but cannot be enforced, are ghosts that are seen in the law but are elusive to the grasp'.[78] Consequently, one would hardly celebrate the existence of a right without a remedy. As is the

---

there had been a violation of Article 11 of the DSU in *US – Carbon Steel*, the AB stated, 'not every error allegedly committed by a panel amounts to a violation of Article 11 of the DSU (footnote omitted), but only those that are so material that, taken together or singly, they undermine the objectivity of the panel's assessment of the matter before it (footnote omitted)', Appellate Body Report *United States – Countervailing Measures on Certain Hot-Rolled Carbon Steel Flat Products from India* WT/DS436/AB/R (adopted 19 December 2014), para. 4.447 and para. 4.456. See also Appellate Body Report *China – Measures Related to the Exportation of Rare Earths, Tungsten, and Molybdenum* WT/DS431, 432, 433/AB/R (adopted 29 August 2014), para. 5.228.

[76]   Some examples of these kinds of appeals include the *EC – Hormones* and *Canada – Feed-in Tariffs* cases.

[77]   See John R. Bolton, 'Is there Really "Law" in International Affairs?', *Transnational Law and Contemporary Problems*, Vol. 10, No. 1 (2000), p. 1, citing Robert Bork, *The Limits of International Law* (Winter 1989–90), p. 3.

[78]   A.R. Gubbay, 'Human Rights in Criminal Justice Proceedings: The Zimbabwean Experience', in Cherif Bassiouni and Ziyad Motala (eds), *The Protection of Human Rights in African Criminal Proceedings* (Kluwer, 1995), p. 307.

case with other areas of international law, the controversy surrounding the remedy for breach of international trade rules has polarised academic scholarship ever since the entry into force of the WTO Agreement.[79]

Although the entry into force of the WTO Agreement and its elaborate rules and procedures enshrined in the DSU[80] to govern the settlement of disputes has led to an increased participation in dispute settlement by a broad array of WTO members, some of the controversies that haunted the flawed GATT system of remedies are still very much visible in the WTO. As was the situation under GATT, the DSU generally provides for 'compensation and suspension of concessions or other obligations' as the only remedies for failure to comply with a particular ruling and recommendation by the DSB. In the WTO, compensation typically takes the form of the losing member being obliged to provide tariff reductions or reductions in other trade barriers in favour of the winning member (this may also be done on a most favoured nations – MFN – basis). In practical terms, the suspension of concessions or other obligations means the imposition of discriminatory tariffs or other trade barriers by the winning member against the losing party. The DSU clearly requires that any measure taken as a consequence of non-compliance should only be of a temporary nature pending compliance.[81] Compliance is, therefore, the ultimate goal of the WTO DSS.

From an economic standpoint, compensation may appear preferable to suspension of concessions or other obligations because it concerns trade liberalisation, which is the core objective of the WTO. However, it is neither the best solution for the complainant nor for a losing respondent, as the case may be. From the perspective of the complainant, compensation in the form of market access in a completely different sector from that which was the subject of the dispute does no good to the private sectors suffering from a particular violation. Moreover, because compensation is normally awarded on an MFN basis, a member which has succeeded in a case at the WTO would generally require a higher degree of market

---

[79] See, for instance, John Jackson, 'The WTO Dispute Settlement Understanding – Misunderstandings on the Nature of Legal Obligation', *AJIL*, Vol. 91, No. 1 (1997), pp. 60–64; Ngangjoh Hodu and Roberto Rios, *MJIEL* (2004); Marco Bronckers and Naboth van den Broek, 'Financial Compensation in the WTO Improving the Remedies of WTO Dispute Settlement', *JIEL*, Vol. 8, No. 1 (2005), pp. 101–26; Bagwell et al., 'The Case for Tradable Remedies in WTO Dispute Settlement', in Simon Evenett and Bernard Hoekman (eds), *Economic Development and Multilateral Trade Cooperation* (Palgrave and the World Bank, 2006), pp. 395–413 etc.

[80] Including Articles XXII and XXIII of GATT.

[81] Article 22.1 of the DSU.

access than that provided on a discriminatory basis.[82] In a similar vein, the non-complying respondent may find it daunting to liberalise a different sector of its economy in lieu of a sector of its economy that actually benefitted from particular trade restrictive measures.[83] All these issues explain why compensation is not usually awarded in the WTO DSS.

The notion of suspension of concessions or other obligations (used interchangeably in this writing with retaliation and countermeasures) and how it is seen in the context of the WTO has many weaknesses that undermine its ability to work as a credible remedy. Although the notion of retaliation was not unknown in GATT practice,[84] its application in the WTO seems largely incongruous with the WTO's overarching objectives and principles.[85] The former aim to provide an effective safeguard for compliance, and the latter to defend global welfare interests through a liberalised global market. Not surprisingly, in restating these objectives, panels and arbitrators have also reiterated their importance. In establishing the common ground as to how the principle of good faith may guide members in achieving a number of the objectives of the DSU and the WTO as a whole, the *US – Section 301* panel held that 'the most relevant in

---

[82] This is the case notwithstanding the fact that from the perspective of standard gains-from-trade theory, global welfare as a whole would be improved. Conversely, since compensation is voluntary (Article 22.1 of the DSU), the losing member may have greater control over the process and could even terminate it at any time when cosmetic measures are taken to obliterate the WTO-inconsistent measures.

[83] This seems to go against the notion of administrative justice, because private sectors which are not the focus of the proceedings will have to pay for governmental failure to respect international obligations by way of being opened up to foreign competition in favour of other sectors of the economy. Compensation in this form goes against what may be termed in French as *égalité devant les charges publique* (contextually interpreted as equality of citizens before the State when imposing any financial burden).

[84] It was rarely used because of the positive consensus-based decision-making under GATT.

[85] Article 22.8 of the DSU et seq. states the objective of retaliation. This was expanded upon by the arbitrators in the *EC – Bananas* case. See Article 22.6 of the Arbitration Decision, *European Communities – Regime for the Importation, Sale and Distribution of Bananas (EC – Bananas)*, Recourse to Arbitration by the European Communities, para. 6.3 (Authorization to Suspend Concessions: 19 April 1999). Though in the context of the SCM Agreement Article 3 prohibited subsidies, this objective was also reconfirmed in the *US – FSC* case. See Article 22.6/4.11 Arbitration Decision, *United States – Tax Treatment for 'Foreign Sales Corporation'*, Recourse to Arbitration by the United States under DSU Article 22.6/SCM Agreement Article 4.11, paras. 5.5–5.6 (Authorization to Suspend Concessions: 7 May 2003).

our view are those which relate to the creation of market conditions conducive to individual economic activity in national and global markets and
to the provision of a secure and predictable multilateral trading system'.[86]

In the light of this, unlike other international treaties, the WTO does not
allow for reservation to any of its instruments.[87] Consequently, in order to
ensure that the WTO and its covered agreements remain predictable both
for its members and for exporters/importers, '[e]ach Member shall ensure
the conformity of its laws, regulations and administrative procedures with
its obligations as provided in the Annexed agreements'.[88]

While international lawyers are to a large extent clear that governments
have a duty to take responsibility for damage caused by their action or
inaction,[89] economists have linked respect for international norms to
incentives that would make abiding by such rules rational.[90] Similarly,
an established tradition in political philosophy advocated by Immanuel
Kant as well as by certain economists, such as David Ricardo and Adam
Smith, emphasises that the mutual gains from international trade and
division of labour based on free market policies, represent important tools
to overcome the 'Hobbesian war of everybody against everybody else' by

---

[86]   Panel Report, *United States – Sections 301–310 of Trade Act of 1974 (US –
Section 301)*, WT/DS152/R, para. 7.71 and paras. 73–5 (adopted 27 January 2000).
Similarly, in the *EC – Bananas* case (WT/DS27/ARB) the arbitrators held that,
'[w]hile it may be necessary to develop more sophisticated rules in this regard in
the future, we believe that the line we have drawn is appropriate in this particular
case, which involves the suspension of concessions. We imply no limitations on
the extent of WTO obligations for this or other cases by this decision.' Para. 6.18.
[87]   See Article XVI:5 of the WTO Charter.
[88]   See Article XVI:4 of the WTO Charter.
[89]   The very first article of the International Law Commission Articles on
the Responsibility of State for Internationally Wrongful Acts is unequivocal
on this issue. It states: 'Every internationally wrongful act of a State entails the
international responsibility of that State.' See Report of the International Law
Commission on the work of its fifty-third session (A/56/10), Yearbook of the
ILC (2001). See also James Crawford, Jacqueline Peel, Simon Olleson, 'The
ILC's Articles on Responsibility of States for Internationally Wrongful Acts:
Completion of the Second Reading', *European Journal of International Law
(EJIL)*, Vol. 12, No. 5 (2001), pp. 963–91.
[90]   Some writers have used game theory to explain this strategic mode of
behaviour. On this point, see Monika Bütler and Heinz Hauser, 'The WTO
Dispute Settlement System: A First Assessment from an Economic Perspective',
Journal of Law, Economics & Organization (JLEO), Vol. 16, No. 2 (2000)
(hereinafter 'Bütler and Hauser (2000)'). And for the role played by game
theory in contractual relationships, see Avinash K. Dixit and Barry J. Nalebuff,
*Thinking Strategically: The Competitive Edge in Business, Politics, and Everyday
Life* (W.W. Norton & Co., 1993).

means of peaceful co-existence.[91] On the other hand, from the standpoint of legal positivist scholarship,[92] the rulings and recommendations of an adjudicating body such as that of the WTO DSB would be more likely to be respected if accompanied by a credible threat of sanctions.[93] This latter view may also be worthy of consideration for other reasons, if not for the strict positivist definition of what should be seen as legal rules that would warrant respect by WTO members in the context of the rulings and recommendations of WTO panels and the AB.

However, the central elements of these arguments may be identified from a variety of perspectives. The first perspective may support the classical thesis on the notion of reparation in public international law. To establish the background to this approach, it is important to revisit the principle in the context of the PCIJ's judgment in the landmark *Factory of Chorzow* case as developed in recent codification and applied in subsequent cases.[94] Viewed through the lens of the PCIJ's judgment,

---

[91]   On this issue, Petersmann adopts a more human rights-based approach in seeking to understand the economic logic of international trade. The institution of the open market is regarded as an indispensable complement of human rights for promoting individual autonomy. See Ernst-Petersmann, *The GATT/WTO Dispute Settlement System*, (Kluwer Law International, 1997), pp. 2–3 and his response to critics in Ernst-Ulrich Petersmann, 'Taking Human Dignity, Poverty and Empowerment of Individuals More Seriously: Rejoinder to Alston', *EJIL*, Vol. 13, No. 4 (2002), pp. 845–53.

[92]   Although positivism can be seen as a very old-fashioned and conservative method of looking at law, it can also be viewed in international law terms as a way of enhancing legal pluralism. See for instance, Bruno Simma and Andreas Paulus, 'The Responsibility of Individuals for Human Rights Abuses in Internal Conflicts – A Positivist View', *AJIL*, Vol. 93, 302 (1999), p. 302. See more recently, Jean D'Aspremont and Jörg Kammerhofer (eds), *International Legal Positivism in a Post-Modern World* (Cambridge University Press, 2014).

[93]   This explains why, in his book, John Austin was of the view that law or 'command' is habitually obeyed because of the threat of punishment and a sense of the legitimacy of the sovereign from which the 'command' emanates. For another impressive contribution on this topic, see Hart (1994). Also of importance here are the ideas encapsulated in the writings of Hans Kelsen in his *General Theory of Law and State* (Cambridge University Press, 1999). However, although Kelsen's argument is very relevant, in order to narrow the scope somewhat, the references in this chapter have been restricted to the works of Austin and Hart.

[94]   See the ICJ's reference to this decision in *LaGrand (Germany v. United States of America)*, Judgment, ICJ Reports (2001), p. 485, para. 48. See also the following earlier cases: *Amoco International Finance Corporation v. The Government of the Islamic Republic of Iran*, Iran-U.S. C.T.R., Vol. 15 (1987), p. 189, para. 192; *Corfu Channel, Merits,* Judgment, ICJ Reports (1949), p. 4, at para. 23; *Military and Paramilitary Activities in and against Nicaragua (Nicaragua v. United States*

the challenges yet to be met in the WTO stem from the fact that the DSU remedies fall short of the kind of retroactivity that would be warranted by this codification and by certain developments in case law relating to third-party adjudication.[95] Conversely, it may undoubtedly be posited with some degree of certainty that seeking to trace the progressive development of WTO jurisprudence purely on the basis of the DSU is likely to lead one to conclude that a remedy *ex nunc* may lie outside the *acquis* of the WTO. However, a different conclusion may be reached by examining this issue in the broader framework of other WTO covered agreements.[96] Secondly, states' insistence on respect for international obligations may, in the absence of meaningful incentives not to deviate from WTO obligations, gain support from the principle of *pacta sunt servanda*. The impact of this important principle of international law on the interaction between different WTO members has so far been relatively small when considered as a counterweight to offset the incentives not to comply with specific WTO obligations. Some of the disturbing challenges relating to why some WTO members may continue to lack incentives to comply with their WTO obligations are grounded on the notion of diminishing reputation cost for non-compliance, especially when short-term domestic interests clash with international obligations. Moreover, one could also argue that one aspect of WTO practice that may improve the compliance regime would be for any party participating in the dispute, regardless of their status, to have some ability to influence compliance.

---

of America), Merits, Judgment, ICJ Reports (1986), p. 142, para. 283. And with regard to the application of criteria for reparation under the law of state responsibility, see generally Appellate Body Report in *US – Cotton Yarn*, WT/DS192/AB/R, paras. 119–20; *US – Line Pipe*, WT/DS202/AB/R, para. 259.

[95]   On this issue, see the *Factory of Chorzow* dispute, PCIJ (Ser. A) No. 17, pp. 47–8. See also the rulings of the ICJ in the *Corfu Channel* case where the United Kingdom was awarded damages as compensation for injury incurred (ICJ Report at 4). However, the compensation was only paid after the change of regime in Albania. Cf. Rosenne Shabtai, *The World Court: What it is and How it Works* (Martinus Nijhoff, Dordrecht, 1995), p. 44. In the domain of codification, the provisions that give most support to the concept of reparation are to be found in Article 31 et seq. of the 2001 report of the International Law Commission (ILC), on the *Responsibility of States for Internationally Wrongful Acts*, UN Doc. A/RES/56/83, of 28 January 2002.

[96]   Despite the criticisms of the panel rulings in the *Australia – Leather* case, the rulings represent a historical step in the discourse on retroactivity of WTO dispute settlement remedies. See Panel Report, *Australia – Subsidies Provided to Producers and Exporters of Automotive Leather (Australia – Leather)*, Recourse by the United States to Article 21.5 of the DSU, WT/DS126/RW (adopted 11 February 2000).

3. Applicable law before the WTO disputes settlement body

3.1 INTRODUCTION

As with other areas of international law, the public international law of trade is derived from a variety of sources that are not all of equal significance. In other words, the body of rules that may be regarded as sources by a WTO panel or AB are not hierarchically of equal significance when it comes to practical application. While municipal law is principally produced by national parliaments, the same does not apply at international level because there is no international parliament. Due to this lack of a centrally elected international legislator, the international legal system is a decentralised structure. As noted by Charles Rousseau almost a century ago, the law governing the activities of nation-states is one of cooperation and not of subordination.[1] While the sources of municipal law may be straightforward, discovering where a particular rule of international law is to be found or whether a particular rule forms part of international law is not that straightforward.[2] As is true of other inter-governmental organisations, the WTO is a member-driven organisation and only WTO members, as subjects of international law, may design and agree on the body of rules that will govern their activities and relationships with one another. In other words, consent is a key element in the formation of WTO law. With

---

[1]   Charles Rousseau, 'De la Compatibilité des normes juridiques contradictoires dans l'ordre international', *Revue General de Droit International Public*, Vol. 39, No. 133 (1932), pp. 150–51.

[2]   There is an avalanche of academic scholarship on sources, including the following: James Crawford, *Brownlie's Principles of International Law* (Oxford University Press, 8th ed., 2012), pp. 20–47; Hugh Thirlway, *The Sources of International Law* (Oxford University Press, 2014); Malcolm N. Shaw, *International Law* (Cambridge University Press, 7th ed., 2014), pp. 49–91. On the theory of sources, see for instance, Jean D'Aspremont, 'The Idea of "Rules" in Sources of International Law', *British Yearbook of International Law*, Vol. 84 (2014), pp. 1–31; Martti Koskenniemi, *From Apology to Utopia: The Structure of International Legal Argument* (Cambridge University Press, 2005) (hereinafter, 'Koskenniemi (2005)'), pp. 303–87 etc.

the exception of rules having the status of *jus cogens*, from which no derogation is permissible.[3] WTO members are completely autonomous when it
comes to rules that would apply to them. However, despite 'the anarchic
nature of world affairs and the clash of competing sovereignties',[4] there is
a body of rules which WTO adjudicatory bodies may undoubtedly rely on
when hearing a case.

Apart from the fact that the notion of sources has always been less
visible when WTO members are engaged in the different rounds of trade
talks, no clear specification of the sources of WTO law is to be found in
any of the WTO's legal texts.[5] This phenomenon is certainly not uncommon in international law, of which the WTO law is clearly an integral
part.[6] Although it is a highly debatable and strongly contested subject in
international law, the concept of sources is dynamic and is continuously
shaped and reshaped by international legal scholarship.[7] This continuous
debate about the notion of sources is not so clearly visible at the domestic
level, although naturally municipal courts must be able to determine the
applicable law when hearing cases.

However, the term 'sources', as used in this chapter, means the law that
can be invoked by a WTO panel or AB in a case brought before it by any
of the subjects of that law – that is, by a WTO member. In other words, this
chapter does not contain an abstract analysis of the theory of sources of

---

[3]   The relevant part of Article 53 of the VCLT states: 'A treaty is void
if, at the time of its conclusion, it conflicts with a peremptory norm of
general international law.' See UN Treaty Series (1980), No. 18232, Vol. 1155,
1-18232.

[4]   Malcolm Shaw (2014) p. 50.

[5]   Article II of the WTO Charter refers only to the constituent elements of
'WTO law' without mentioning the term 'sources of WTO law'. On the other hand,
Article 3.2 of the DSU only talks about how the panels and AB should interpret
different WTO provisions.

[6]   A great deal has been written on the nexus between WTO law and other
types of international law and this is no longer a subject of much debate. Works
on this topic include the following: Donald McRea, 'The WTO in International
Law: Tradition Continued or New Frontier?' *JIEL*, Vol. 3, No. 1 (2000),
pp. 27–41; Joost Pauwelyn, 'The Role of Public International Law in the WTO:
How Far Can We Go?' *AJIL*, Vol. 95, No. 3 (2001), pp. 535–78; Joost Pauwelyn,
*Conflict of Norms in Public International Law: How WTO Law Relates to other
Rules of International Law* (Cambridge University Press, 2003); John H. Jackson,
'International Law Status of WTO Dispute Settlement Reports: Obligation to
Comply or Option to "Buy Out"?', *AJIL*, Vol. 98, No. 1 (2004), pp. 109–25; Anja
Linderoos and Michael Mehling, 'Dispelling the Chimera of "Self-Contained
Regimes"', International Law and the WTO, *EJIL*, Vol. 16, No. 5 (2006),
pp. 857–77 etc.

[7]   See D'Aspremont (2014); Koskenniemi (2005), pp. 303–87 etc.

WTO law.[8] The reason for this is not because the theory of sources debate is irrelevant or has been settled once and for all in legal scholarship – far from it. It is rather that a discourse on the applicable law before the WTO adjudicatory body in the context of a debate on the subject of compliance ought to be in some way linked to the actual behaviour of WTO members.[9] Although changes in the fundamental nature of international rule-making have diminished the persuasiveness of mainstream arguments that profess absolute state consent as the basis of sources of international law, WTO members, as the subjects of WTO law, do to a large extent have autonomy over the rules that bind them. Despite the fact that aspects of international law derived from a variety of sources are subject to the conflict rules under Articles 3.2 and 19.2 of the DSU and may in principle be invoked before a WTO panel or AB, a proper analysis of the behaviour of WTO members in relation to the compliance debate ought to be carried out with the concreteness of WTO rules in mind.[10] Before turning our attention to discussing specific sources as generally understood and applied by the WTO panels and the AB, it is important to briefly discuss the purpose of the WTO DSS.

3.2 WHAT ARE THE PURPOSES OF THE WTO DISPUTE SETTLEMENT SYSTEM?

Dispute settlement lies at the heart of inter-state cooperation and recent international economic institutions have placed emphasis 'on dispute-settlement mechanisms and on institutions to support compliance with those mechanisms'.[11] For example, since the establishment of the WTO in

---

[8] On theories relating to the sources of international law, see D'Aspremont (2014); Koskenniemi (2005), pp. 303–87; and D'Aspremont, *Formalism and the Sources of International Law: A Theory of the Ascertainment of Legal Rules* (Oxford University Press, 2011).

[9] This of course takes into account the persistent argument that 'only a limited part of the exercise of public authority at the international level nowadays materialises itself in the creation of norms which can be considered international legal rules according to classical understanding of international law'. See D'Aspremont (Oxford University Press, 2011), p. 2.

[10] While this chapter hinges more on the actual commitments of WTO members under primary rules, the discourse on theory of sources in general seems to be more about secondary international rules. Of course, the approach taken in this chapter also recognises the point of agreement between the different schools of theory of sources which sees justice as emerging 'with consent to create a norm which would be both concrete and normative'. On this issue, see Koskenniemi (2005), p. 309.

[11] Beth V. Yarbrough and Robert M. Yarbrough, in Edward D. Mansfield

1995, one of the most recognised and functional aspects of the organisation is its two-tier dispute settlement mechanism. To date, WTO members have initiated over 470 disputes, underscoring the central role the dispute settlement system plays in the multilateral trading system.[12] Yet, although almost all international regimes, whatever their nature, endorse the peaceful settlement of disputes as an important aspect in their founding treaties, the true meaning of what constitutes a dispute for the purpose of dispute settlement was once a divisive issue. The very first case where the issue arose was that of *Mavrommatis Palestine Concessions*, where the PCIJ stated that '[a] dispute is a disagreement on a point of law or fact, a conflict of legal views or of interests between two persons'.[13] Twenty-six years later, the ICJ defined a dispute as 'a situation in which the two sides held clearly opposite views concerning the question of the performance or non-performance of certain treaty obligations'.[14]

Consequently, determination of the existence of a dispute is important for the delimitation of the sources of law that may be applicable before the dispute settlement mechanism involved. A dispute arising from noncompliance with an international instrument is, therefore, generally seen as a disagreement between two or more, typically but not exclusively, states as to the interpretation and application of that instrument.[15] In the context of the WTO, a dispute is said to arise 'when a member government believes another member government is violating an agreement or a commitment that it has made in the WTO'.[16] More specifically, a dispute may arise when there is 'a violation of obligations or other nullification or impairment of benefits under the covered agreements or [when there is] an impediment to the attainment of any objective of the covered agreements'.[17]

---

et al. (eds), *The Political Economy of Regionalism* (Columbia University Press, 1997), p. 138.

[12]   As of December 2014. See the WTO website at www.wto.org.

[13]   *Mavrommatis Palestine Concessions* (*Greece v. Great Britain*), judgment of 30 August 1924, 1924 PCIJ (Ser. A) No. 2, p. 11.

[14]   Interpretation of the Peace Treaties with Bulgaria, Hungary and Romania, Advisory Opinion of 30 March 1950 (first phase), 1950 *ICJ Rep.* 65, at 74.

[15]   On this, see John Merills, *The Means of Dispute Settlement*, in Malcolm D. Evans, *International Law* (Oxford University Press, 4th ed., 2014), pp. 563–88.

[16]   See http://www.wto.org/english/tratop_e/dispu_e/dispu_e.htm.

[17]   See Article 23.1 of the DSU. In this regard, the three different types of complaint that exist in the WTO are violation, non-violation and situation complaints. See also Article 26 of the DSU as well as GATT 1994 Article XXIII. A great deal has been written about the types of complaints in the WTO dispute settlement system. For instance, see John H. Jackson, 'The WTO Dispute Settlement Understanding – Misunderstandings on the Nature of Legal Obligation', *AJIL*, Vol. 91, No. 1 (1997), pp. 60–64; Ngangjoh Hodu, '*Pacta sunt servanda* and

Therefore, the introduction of dispute settlement provisions in inter-state agreements is consistent with the general notion that those agreements are the constituent elements of binding international law requiring good faith compliance by states.[18] Typically, dispute settlement may serve as a tool to ensure compliance with the agreed results of protracted negotiations by states. And because it is inconceivable after prolonged negotiation to draft an agreement in a manner that will be explicit enough to cover all future eventualities, dispute settlement may also be seen more as an essential instrument to make sense of the concluded deal, thereby enhancing the security and predictability of the concluded treaty.[19] As stated in Article 3:2 of the WTO DSU, the dispute settlement system is:

> a central element in providing security and predictability to the multilateral trading system. The members recognize that it serves to preserve the rights and obligations of members under the covered agreements, and to clarify the existing provisions of those agreements in accordance with customary rules of interpretation of public international law.

In spite of the general acceptance of the role played by the dispute settlement mechanism in respect of international agreements, as sketched above, there is ongoing debate as to the future role of dispute settlement in trade and investment agreements at both regional and multilateral levels. In the context of the WTO, for instance, one school of thought holds that dispute settlement under the WTO should be strictly limited to clarifying the provisions of the WTO Agreement and its covered agreements consistent with the common intentions of WTO members.[20] On the other hand, a more radical school of thought views the dispute settlement system as playing the role of an activist court with the role of making sense of the relevant agreements, filling gaps where necessary and

---

Complaints in the WTO Dispute Settlement', *MJIEL*, Vol. 1, No. 2 (2004); Frieder Roessler and Petina Gappah, 'A Re-appraisal of Non-Violation Complaints Under the WTO Dispute Settlement Procedures' in Patrick F.J. Macrory et al. (eds), *The World Trade Organization: Legal, Economic and Political Analysis* (Springer, 2005), pp. 1371–87. On the interpretation of Article 23 of the DSU, see the Appellate Body Report in *US – Continued Suspension / Canada – Continued Suspension*, WT/DS320/AB/R, WT/DS321/AB/R, (adopted 14 November 2008), paras. 371–3.

[18] See Article 26 of the VCLT.

[19] It is important to note that most if not all international agreements do not treat dispute settlement mechanisms as being able to add or diminish the negotiated rights and obligations of contracting parties. See, for instance, Articles 3.2 and 19.2 of the DSU.

[20] In this regard, strictly adhering to what they see as the spirits of Articles 3.2 and 19.2 of the DSU.

setting precedents for future rulings.[21] This view, mostly held by economists who employ contract theory to analyse the WTO dispute settlement system, also involves the idea that dispute settlement may also serve as a mechanism to complete 'an incomplete contract' previously negotiated by nation-states.[22] This assertion, however, seems incongruous with the texts of Articles 3.2 and 19.2 of the DSU as well as the view that 'the aim of the dispute settlement mechanism is to secure a positive solution to a dispute'.[23] The WTO members, whether complainants or respondents in a particular case, are generally not at ease with any interpretation that deviates from this approach.[24] In this regard, dispute settlement under the DSU, as is the case for many international agreements, should aim at providing a positive solution to a dispute between the parties. Consequently, in order to perform their duties under the relevant provisions of the DSU, panels and the AB are afforded somewhat broad latitude as to the sources of law they can rely on in resolving a particular dispute.[25]

---

[21] Making an economic analysis of the role dispute settlement should play in trade agreement, Maggi and Staiger see dispute settlement under the WTO to be more about 'filling gaps in the agreement where it is silent than about enforcing clearly-stated obligations'. Giovanni Maggi and Robert W. Staiger, 'The Role of Dispute Settlement Procedures in International Trade Agreement', *QJE*, Vol. 126 (2011), p. 475. The latter view is clearly inconsistent with the general understanding (Articles 3.2 and 19.2 of the DSU) that panels and AB rulings and recommendations are not to be seen as adding to or reducing members' obligations.

[22] Giovanni Maggi and Robert W. Staiger (2011), p. 476.

[23] See Article 3.7 of the DSU.

[24] In a rather lengthy statement at the DSB meeting in which the compliance panel report in *Australia – Automotive* (*Australia – Subsidies Provided to Producers and Exporters of Automotive Leather*, Recourse by the United States to Article 21.5 of the DSU, WT/DS126/RW) was adopted, Australia criticised the panel's reasoning as being at odds with WTO jurisprudence and against democratic governance and economic reality. Along with other implementing members, Australia also unsuccessfully called for WTO members not to adopt the panel report; WT/DSB/M/75 (11 February 2000), pp. 5–7.

[25] See Panel Report in *Korea – Measures Affecting Government Procurement*, where it was stated that: 'We take note that Article 3.2 of the DSU requires that we seek within the context of a particular dispute to clarify the existing provisions of the WTO agreements in accordance with customary rules of interpretation of public international law.' This observation is supplemented by a footnote, which states that 'we should also note that we can see no basis here for *a contrario* implications that rules of international law order rules of interpretation do not apply' in WTO dispute settlement. See WT/DS163/R (adopted 19 June 2000), para. 7.96 and footnote 753 respectively. See also Appellate Body Report in *US – Zeroing Methodology (EC)*, paras. 133–4.

3.3 APPLICABLE LAW IN DISPUTE SETTLEMENT

From a traditional international law perspective, a discussion on sources of public international law of trade would normally start with Article 38(1) of the Statute of the ICJ, which is largely seen as a statement on the sources of international law.[26] It is of course important to point out that Article 38(1) relates only to sources and not to the subject matter of a dispute that can be brought before the WTO adjudicatory body. The jurisdiction of the WTO DSB is described in the relevant part of Article 1.1 of the DSU as follows:

> The rules and procedures of this Understanding shall apply to disputes brought pursuant to the consultation and dispute settlement rules and procedures of the agreements listed in Appendix 1 to this Understanding (referred to in this Understanding as the 'covered agreement').

Furthermore, the WTO DSB does not adjudicate on non-WTO issues. In this regard, the AB held in the *Mexico – Soft Drinks* case that:

> We see no basis in the DSU for panels and the Appellate Body to adjudicate non-WTO disputes. Article 3.2 of the DSU states that the WTO dispute settlement system "serves to preserve the rights and obligations of members under the *covered agreements*, and to clarify the existing provisions of *those agreements*".[27]

In view of this prescribed jurisdiction, WTO members normally bring claims when they consider a particular measure to amount to nullification and impairment of benefits accruing to them by another WTO member. The WTO also offers a unique opportunity for members to bring cases on the basis of 'non-violation' or 'situation' complaints.[28] Although the dispute settlement system under both GATT and the WTO has handled

---

[26] Note that the Statute of the ICJ has no relevance before the WTO panels and AB. The only rules that impose obligations on independent states and customs territories that hold WTO membership are those enshrined in the WTO Charter and its annexed agreements as well as those that have evolved from subsequent negotiations. Articles 3.2 and 19.2 of the DSU are also clear on the nature of panel and AB reports.

[27] Appellate Body Report, *Mexico – Taxes on Soft Drinks*, WT/DS308/AB/R, paras. 55–6 and footnote 115.

[28] Article 26(2) of the DSU sets out rules that apply to 'situation' complaints of the type described in para. 1(c) of Article XXIII of GATT (BISD 36S/61-67). For a discussion on situation and non-violation complaints, see Ngangjoh-Hodu, '*Pacta sunt servanda* and Complaints in the WTO Dispute Settlement', *MJIEL*, Vol.1. No. 2 (2004), pp. 76–96.

very few disputes relating to non-violation or situation complaints, these two forms of complaint give WTO members broad scope to initiate proceedings regardless of whether a particular measure conflicts with the WTO Agreement or not.

However, with regard to specific sources, Article 38(1) of the Statute of the ICJ identifies the following sources of international law:

> a. International conventions . . . establishing rules expressly recognized by the contesting states;
> b. international custom, as evidence of a general practice accepted as law;
> c. the general principles of law . . .;
> d. . . . judicial decisions and the teachings of the most highly qualified publicists of the various nations, as subsidiary means for the determination of rules of law.

Similarly, in the area of the law of the sea, under the United Nations Convention on the Law of the Sea (UNCLOS),[29] the International Tribunal for the Law of the Sea (ITLOS), the ICJ or an arbitral tribunal[30] having jurisdiction over a particular subject matter is directed to apply the rules of UNCLOS 'and other rules of international law not incompatible with' UNCLOS.[31] In this regard, the sources of law to be applied by ITLOS, the ICJ as well as the other arbitral tribunals are very clear and also broader. The language of Article 1.1 of the DSU is slightly different from that of Article 293(1) of UNCLOS. Article 1.1 of the DSU states:

> The rules and procedures of this Understanding shall apply to disputes brought pursuant to the consultation and dispute settlement provisions of

---

[29]   On the law of the sea and dispute settlement, see Xavier Furtado, 'International Law and the Dispute over the Spratly Islands: Whither UNCLOS?', *Contemporary Southeast Asia*, Vol. 21, No. 3 (1999), pp. 386–404; Alan Boyle, 'Further Development of the Law of the Sea Convention: Mechanisms for Change', *ICLQ*, Vol. 54, No. 3 (2005), pp. 563–84; Natalie Klein, *Dispute Settlement in the UN Convention on the Law of the Sea* (Cambridge University Press, 2009); Donald Rothwell and T. Stephens, *The International Law of the Sea* (Hart Publishing, 2010); Hong Nong, *UNCLOS and Ocean Dispute Settlement: Law and Politics in the South China Sea* (Routledge, 2012).

[30]   Pursuant to Article 287 of UNCLOS, each state party may opt for one or more of the following jurisdictions for the resolution of disputes concerning the interpretation and application of UNCLOS: ITLOS, the ICJ, an arbitral tribunal constituted in accordance with Annex VII and a special tribunal constituted in accordance with Annex VIII of UNCLOS.

[31]   See Article 293(1) of UNCLOS, entitled 'Applicable Law', available at http://www.un.org/depts/los/convention_agreements/texts/unclos/UNCLOS-TOC.htm (last visited 3 February 2015).

the agreements listed in Appendix 1 to this Understanding (referred to in this Understanding as the "covered agreements"). The rules and procedures of this Understanding shall also apply to consultations and the settlement of disputes between Members concerning their rights and obligations under the provisions of the Agreement Establishing the World Trade Organization (referred to in this Understanding as the "WTO Agreement") and of this Understanding taken in isolation or in combination with any other covered agreement.[32]

Article 3.2 of the DSU on applicable law with regard to interpretation of the different covered agreement may be seen as somewhat complementary to Article 1.1. However, it is obvious from these two WTO provisions that, contrary to the position under UNCLOS, WTO members have not relinquished jurisdiction on the settlement of trade disputes to any tribunals or courts outside the WTO DSS.

3.4 THE TEXT OF THE WTO COVERED AGREEMENTS: STRAIGHTFORWARD SOURCES

As primary rules that effectively emerged as a consequence of the consent of WTO members, the treaty text of GATT/WTO is above all the primary source of WTO law. The international law principle of *pacta sunt servanda* requires WTO members to observe their WTO treaty obligations in good faith.[33] Although the text of Article 1.1 of the DSU indicates that the

---

[32] Article 1.2 of the DSU deals with conflict resolution where there is a conflict between the provisions of the DSU and provisions contained in additional rules and procedures on dispute settlement under Appendix 2 of the DSU. The WTO AB has particularly addressed this issue in a number of cases, including Appellate Body Report, *US – Corrosion-Resistant Steel Sunset Review*, WT/DS244/AB/R, footnote 82 to para. 83; Appellate Body Report, *EC – Export Subsidies on Sugar*, WT/DS265/AB/R, WT/DS266/AB/R, WT/DS283/AB/R, paras. 333–5.

[33] Article 26 of the VCLT entitled *Pacta Sunt Servanda* states that '[e]very treaty in force is binding upon the parties to it and must be performed by them in good faith'. This is a familiar principle which has been repeatedly relied on by WTO panels and the AB. For instance in the Byrd Amendment case the AB stated: 'Article 26 of the VCLT, entitled *Pacta Sunt Servanda*, to which several appellees referred in their submissions (footnote omitted), provides that "[e]very treaty in force is binding upon the parties to it and must be enforced by them in good faith" (footnote omitted). Clearly therefore, there is a basis for a dispute settlement panel to determine, in an appropriate case whether a member has not acted in good faith.' Appellate Body Report, *United States – Continued Dumping and Subsidy Offset Act of 2000*, WT/DS217/AB/R, WT/DS234/AB/R (adopted 27 January 2003), paras. 296–7. See also Appellate Body Reports in *US – Shrimp*,

jurisdiction of the WTO DSS is restricted to issues arising from violation of GATT/WTO rules,[34] panels and the AB are not entirely restricted in terms of the laws which they may apply to resolve disputes. The terms of reference for panels under Article 7.1 of the DSU as well as their defined mandate under Article 11 can hardly be interpreted as precluding panels from considering issues of international law relevant to a particular case.[35] The reference in Article 38.1(a) of the ICJ Statute above to 'international conventions' may be to bilateral, plurilateral or multilateral treaties. Where the agreement in question is between states it may also be regarded as a convention for this purpose.[36] As previously noted, with the exception of rules that have the status of *jus cogens* from which no derogation is permitted,[37] there is generally no hierarchy between either of these trea-

---

para. 158, *US – FSC*, para. 166, *EC – Sardines*, para. 278 etc. *Pacta sunt servanda* is now seen as being more important than the notion of consent with regard to treaty obligations. On this point, see Jonathan Charney, 'Universal International Law', *AJIL*, Vol. 87, No. 4 (1993), pp. 529–51. On *pacta sunt servanda* and WTO law, see Ngangjoh-Hodu, *MJIEL* (2004).

[34]   The relevant part of Article 1.1 of the DSU states '[t]he rules and procedure of this understanding shall apply to disputes brought pursuant to the consultation and dispute settlement provisions of the agreements listed in Appendix 1 to this Understanding . . . as well as the settlement of disputes between members concerning their rights and obligations under the provisions of . . . WTO Agreement'. See *WTO Legal Text* (Cambridge University Press, 2002), p. 354.

[35]   This is the case bearing in mind the authority invested in the DSB under Article 3.2 of the DSU. This issue was clarified earlier on in *Korea – Government Procurement*, where the panel concluded as follows: 'The purpose of the terms of reference is to properly identify the claims of the party and therefore the scope of a panel's review. We do not see any basis for arguing that the terms of reference are meant to *exclude* reference to the broader rules of customary international law in interpreting a claim properly before the Panel.' Panel Report, *Korea – Measures Affecting Government Procurement*, WT/DS163/R (adopted 19 June 2000), para. 7.101, footnote 755.

[36]   With regard to the appellation of agreements signed between states, see Anthony Aust, *Modern Treaty Law and Practice* (Cambridge University Press, 3rd ed., 2013), p. 364.

[37]   For instance, by way of illustration, in spite of the obligations under Article III of GATT, a WTO member can discriminatorily prevent the circulation of imported materials within its territory on the basis of their anti-Semitic or racist contents. In this regard, a defence of *jus cogens* may be invoked by the respondent. *Jus cogens* is seen as very peculiar in terms of the sources of international law. It challenges the notion of voluntarism and consent-based sources of international law. On the nature of *jus cogens*, see Alfred Verdross, 'Forbidden Treaties in International Law', *AJIL*, Vol. 31 (1937), pp. 571–92; Mark Janis, 'Nature of *jus cogens*', *Connecticut Journal of International Law*, Vol. 3 (1988), pp. 359–63; Gennady M. Danilenko, 'International *Jus Cogens*: Issues of Law-Making', *EJIL*,

ties.[38] Therefore, the GATT/WTO rules are exceptions to this general rule in the sense that by joining the WTO, each country or separate custom territory agrees not to enter into a preferential trade regime that is inconsistent with GATT/WTO rules.[39] In other words, by joining the WTO, members not only agree to treat the citizens of each other as they treat theirs,[40] but also accept the general notion of treating each other equally.[41]

Thus, except in accordance with the basic requirements on free trade agreements (FTAs), customs unions and common markets, panels and the AB are mandated to declare whether measures or other agreements entered into by WTO members are consistent with these primary obligations.[42] It

---

Vol. 2, No. 1 (1991); Ulf Linderfalk, 'The Source of *Jus Cogens* Obligations – How Legal Positivism Copes with Peremptory International Law', *Nordic Journal of International Law (NJIL)*, Vol. 82, No. 3 (2013), pp. 369–89.

[38] Hierarchy may only occur in exceptional situations such as the case of the WTO where one treaty puts one above another, otherwise the general rules on conflict resolution will apply; i.e. *lex posterior* and *lex specialis/lex generalis* rules.

[39] Such other international trade agreements must conform to the requirements of Article XXIV of GATT 1994 or Article V of GATS. The same is true for preferential trade regimes with LDCs and developing countries notified to the WTO on the basis of the Enabling Clause. For rules on conflict resolution in relation to the WTO, see Joost Pauwelyn, *Conflict of Norms in Public International Law: How WTO Law Relates to other Rules of International Law* (Cambridge University Press, 2003).

[40] On the basis of the National Treatment Principle littered around different GATT/WTO provisions.

[41] On the basis of the MFN principle.

[42] Of course, there is ongoing debate as to whether such mandate lies with the Committee on Regional Trade Agreement (CRTA) – the political arm of the organisation – or with the adjudicatory arm. In the *Turkey – Textiles* case, the AB had to reverse a panel finding that the authority to rule on the consistency of a customs union with GATT/WTO rules lies with the CRTA and not with WTO panels or the AB. In so doing, the AB clearly stated that not only do panels have the jurisdiction to pronounce on the consistency of a specific agreement with Article XXIV of GATT, but they are indeed 'expected' to do so. See Appellate Body Report, *Turkey – Restrictions on Imports of Textile and Clothing Products* (adopted 19 November 1999), para. 59. There is extensive academic scholarship on this issue. See, for instance, Frieder Roessler, 'The Institutional Balance between the Judicial and Political Organs of the WTO', in *New Directions in International Economic Law* (Marco Bronckers and R. Quick, eds) (Kluwer, 2000); Gabriella Marceau and Reiman, 'When and How Is a Regional Trade Agreement Compatible with the WTO?', *Legal Issues of Economic Integration*, Vol. 28, No. 3 (2001), pp. 297–336; James Mathis, *Regional Trade Agreements in the GATT/WTO: Article XXIV and the International Trade Requirement* (Kluwer, 2002); Matthew Schaefer, 'Ensuring That Regional Trade Agreements Complement the WTO System: US Unilateralism a Supplement to WTO Initiative?', *JIEL*, Vol. 10, No. 3 (2007), pp. 585–603; Ngangjoh-Hodu, 'Regionalism in the WTO and

is therefore obvious from the above that the primary sources of WTO law are those agreements specified in Appendix 1[43] of the DSU.[44] In other words, the texts of the WTO agreements form the primary sources of WTO law which the WTO panels and AB must first and foremost consider when resolving trade disputes. Those covered agreements specified under Appendix 1 contain extensive references to other rules of international law outside the WTO[45] as well as references to the decision-making powers of organs[46] of the WTO which can be seen as potential sources of WTO law. Consequently, by acceding to the WTO, members automatically grant the WTO dispute settlement organs the power to make sense of or interpret their obligations under any of its covered agreements in accordance with the DSU[47] taking into account any other special or additional rules and procedures contained in any of those agreements.[48] Despite the significant

---

the Legal Status of a Development Agenda in the EU/ACP Economic Partnership Agreement', *NJIL*, Vol. 78, No. 2 (2009), pp. 225–48.

[43]   As well as Appendix 4 for those countries that are parties to the Agreement on Government Procurement and the Agreement on Civil Aircraft.

[44]   International Conventions in the wording of Article 38(1a) of the Statute of the ICJ.

[45]   See Article 1.3 and Article 9 of the Agreement on Trade Related Intellectual Property Rights (TRIPS), Annex I(k) of the Agreement on Subsidies and Countervailing Measures, Articles XV.6 and XXI(c) of GATT 1994, Article XIV *bis* of GATS, Articles 10.3(3) and 13.1(5) of the Agreement on Trade Facilitation as well as Article XXIX of GATT 1994 referring to the Havana Charter which is currently inoperative. For the Agreement on Trade Facilitation, see http://www.wto.org/english/tratop_e/tradfa_e/tradfa_e.htm.

[46]   See Article IX of the WTO Charter regarding the possibility for authoritative interpretation of WTO Agreements by a Ministerial Conference/General Council. The relevant part of Article IX:2 states that '[t]he Ministerial Conference and the General Council shall have the exclusive authority to adopt interpretations of this Agreement and of the Multilateral Trade Agreements'. World Trade Organization, *The Legal Texts: The Results of the Uruguay Round of Multilateral Trade Negotiations* (Cambridge University Press, 2002), p. 9. See also Article X of the WTO Charter on the authority to amend any of the WTO agreements.

[47]   See Article 3.2 of the DSU. Moreover, in *Brazil – Desiccated Coconut*, the AB stated that 'the DSU establishes an integrated dispute settlement system which applies to all the "covered agreements", allowing all the provisions of the WTO Agreement relevant to a particular dispute to be examined in one proceeding'. Appellate Body Report, *Brazil – Measures Affecting Desiccated Coconut*, WT/DS22/AB/R, p. 18.

[48]   Appendix 2 of the DSU. As a routine practice, the DSU covers all the cases brought pursuant to any GATT/WTO rules. However, as the AB pointed out, 'it is only where the provisions of the DSU and the special or additional rules and procedures of a covered agreement *cannot* be read as *complementing* each other that the special or additional provisions are to *prevail*'. See *Guatemala – Cement*

codification of different aspects of customary international law that has taken place, treaties remain the only sources of WTO law in which one can identify clear and unequivocal obligations.

3.5 CUSTOMARY INTERNATIONAL LAW AS A SOURCE OF WTO LAW

It is generally understood that an international norm is created if states act in conformity with that norm and the community of nations recognises it as creating international obligations. However, such a development is neither a one-off nor does it require a specific length of time in order for it to be elevated to the level of customary international law.[49] The only essential ingredients are that it should be a product of state practice and *opinio juris sive necessitatis* (or in short, *opinio juris*).[50] Whereas the ICJ has consistently stressed the importance of these two ingredients for the identification of customary international law,[51] the WTO DSB has largely taken the existence of customary international law as a given with respect to treaty interpretation.[52] Acceptance of a particular practice may sometimes only be established by acquiescence or inaction.[53] Because

---

I, Appellate Body Report, *Guatemala – Anti-Dumping Investigation Regarding Portland Cement from Mexico*, WT/DS60/AB/R (adopted 25 November 1998), para. 65 as well as Appellate Body Report *US – Corrosion-Resistant Steel Sunset Review*, footnote 82 to para. 83.

[49]   See the Second Report of the International Law Commission by Sir Michael Wood, Special Rapporteur on the Identification of Customary International Law, UN General Assembly, A/CN.4/672 (22 May 2014).

[50]   See ICJ report, *North Sea Continental Shelf* cases (*Federal Republic of Germany v. Denmark / Federal Republic of Germany v. Netherlands*) (20 February 1969). In a more recent case, the ICJ noted in relation to customary international law that 'there should be "a settled practice" together with *opinio juris*'. See *Jurisdictional Immunities of the State* (*Germany v. Italy*, Greece intervening), ICJ Reports (2012), p. 99, at p. 122, para. 55.

[51]   The ICJ has pointed out that 'the existence of a rule of customary international law requires that there be "a settled practice" together with *opinio juris*'. See for instance, *Jurisdictional Immunities of State* (*Germany v. Italy*, Greece intervening), ICJ Reports (2012) p. 99, at p. 122, para. 55.

[52]   Since the *US – Gasoline* case, largely with the acquiescence of WTO members, subsequent panels and the AB have taken customary rules of interpretation under Article 3.2 of the DSU as referring to those rules of interpretation under the VCLT.

[53]   Under current international law, lack of protest by states or negative action by a state is only seen as acquiescence if such inaction directly or indirectly affects an essential interest of a state. On this view, see Gennady M. Danilenko,

the views of states are essential in the development of norms, customary international law will hardly be established if states persistently object to a particular practice.[54] It is noteworthy that the persistent objector principle may only be valid in the process of formation of customary international law. Customary international law may of course emerge but will be of no consequence to a state that had persistently objected to such practice.[55]

Unlike GATT 1947, the WTO Agreement is *par excellence* an international treaty largely seen as an 'interdependence' regime under which members have a legitimate expectation that rights and obligations will be legally protected.[56] The notion of market opening emerging from the multilateral trading system has steadily evolved over the years as customary practice in international economic relations.[57] Although the content

---

Law-Making in the International Community (Martinus Nijhoff, 1993), p. 108. In pronouncing on this in *EC – Chicken Cuts*, the AB stated that 'in specific situations, the "lack of reaction" or silence by a particular treaty party may, in the light of attendant circumstances, be understood as acceptance of the practice of other treaty parties. Such situations may occur when a party that has not engaged in a practice has become or has been made aware of the practice of other parties . . . but does not react to it' (footnote omitted), Appellate Body Report, *European Communities – Customs Classification of Frozen Boneless Chicken Cuts*, WT/DS DS269/AB/R, WT/DS286/AB/R (adopted 27 September 2005).

[54]　There must be clear evidence of such objection. In spite of the controversy/ disagreement as to when and how the persistent objector principle can be validly invoked, it 'reinforces' the notion of 'state consent' in the formation of customary international law. See James Crawford, *Brownlie's Principles of Public International Law* (Oxford University Press, 8th ed., 2012), p. 28.

[55]　Since the *Anglo Norwegian Fisheries* case, where the ICJ dismissed the UK's argument as to the applicability of the ten-mile rule with regard to Norway, international courts and mainstream international scholarship have taken it as a given that an established rule of customary international law will be inapplicable against a state that has persistently protested against the creation of such practice. See *Anglo Norwegian Fisheries* case (*United Kingdom v. Norway*), ICJ Reports 116 (18 December 1951). See also the opinion of Judge Ammoun in *North Sea Continental Shelf*, ICJ Reports, 1969, pp. 3, 26–7; *Asylum Case Colombia/Peru*, ICJ Reports (20 November 1950); Andrew T. Guzman, *How International Law Works* (Oxford University Press, 2008); Lau Holning, 'Rethinking the Persistent Objector Doctrine in International Human Rights Law', *Chicago Journal of International Law*, Vol. 6 (2005) p. 495; Joel P. Trachtman, 'Persistent Objectors, Cooperation, and the Utility of Customary International Law', *Duke Journal of Comparative and International Law*, Vol. 21 (2010), pp. 221–33; James Crawford, *Brownlie's Principles of Public International Law* (2012), pp. 28–9.

[56]　Chios Carmody, 'WTO Obligations as Collective', *EJIL*, Vol. 17, No. 2 (2006), pp. 433–4.

[57]　One might regard the concept of trade liberalisation, which has evolved since the inception of the WTO, as somewhat customary in the practice of states in

of hundreds of existing FTAs are not exactly the same, it is not entirely accurate to see the 'spaghetti bowl'[58] of FTAs and custom unions as creating *lex specialis* rules that have nothing to do with countries outside those regimes. Trade liberalisation and the notion of MFN are elements which are somewhat constant and uniform in state practice in this area. There are, nonetheless, relatively few customs clearly in operation in the area of trade law. There is, however, a custom that the WTO DSB must adhere to rules of treaty interpretation that have evolved over the years through state practice and *opinio juris*.[59] Therefore, customary international law is central to the interpretation of WTO agreements as well as to the jurisprudential progressivism of the WTO DSB.[60] Beyond what is clearly mentioned under the rules of interpretation as codified in the VCLT lies the customary international law principle *ut res magis valeat quam pareat*,[61] to which panels and the AB have repeatedly referred.[62]

---

an era of steady globalisation. As was pointed out by the ICJ in *Ahmadou Diallo*, it is of course also true that absent *opinio juris*, such practice can hardly be regarded as an emerging aspect of customary international law. See the statement of the ICJ on this in *Ahmadou Sadio Diallo* (*Guinea v. Democratic Republic of the Congo*), Preliminary Objections, Judgment of 24 May 2007, p. 615, para. 90 of the Reports.

[58] The 'spaghetti-bowl effect' is a term that was first used by Jagdish Bhagwati to describe different complex trade rules that have emerged as a consequence of the proliferation of trade agreements. See Walter Goode, *Dictionary of Trade Policy Terms* (WTO and Cambridge University Press Publication, 4th ed., 2002), p. 322.

[59] Article 3.2 of the DSU.

[60] Some commentators originally saw the practice of taking the VCLT as expressing customary international law as problematic because not all WTO members are parties to the VCLT. However, this view was rebuffed in *Japan – Alcoholic Beverages*, in which the AB concluded that as a codification of customary international law in the area of interpretation, all WTO members are bound by customary international law. See *Japan – Taxes on Alcoholic Beverages*, p. 10, as well as *US – Gasoline*. For recent critical comment on customary international law, see Joel P. Trachtman, 'The Obsolescence of Customary International Law', *Tufts University Working Paper Series* (21 October 2014), available SSRN: http://ssrn.com/abstract=2512757 (last visited 17 February 2015).

[61] This Latin expression is loosely translated as things ought to have effect than being destroyed.

[62] The import of this maxim is that interpretation should be done in a holistic manner so that no phrase or provision would be rendered redundant. This principle was invoked in *United States – Standard for Reformulated and Conventional Gasoline* (*United States – Gasoline*), WT/DS2/AB/R (adopted 20 May 1996), p. 23; and subsequently in *Japan – Taxes on Alcoholic Beverages*, WT/DS8/AB/R, WT/DS10/AB/R and WT/DS11/AB/R (adopted 1 November 1996), p. 12. In both cases, the AB noted that: 'One of the corollaries of the "general rule of interpretation" in the Vienna Convention is that interpretation must give meaning and effect to all the terms of a treaty. An interpreter is not free to adopt a reading that would result

However, informed commentators have debated the nexus between the WTO law and international law over the years.[63] This debate has largely hinged on the application of customary international law by WTO panels and the AB. As limited as its application may be, customary international law in the area of remedies has also been recognised by the WTO DSB. In *US – Line Pipe*, the AB stated as follows:

> We note as well the customary international law rules on state responsibility, to which we also referred in *US – Cotton Yarn* (footnote omitted). We recalled there that the rules of general international law on state responsibility require that countermeasures in response to breaches by States of their international obligations be proportionate to such breaches. Article 51 of the International Law Commission's Draft Articles on Responsibility of States for Internationally Wrongful Acts provides that "countermeasures must be commensurate with the injury suffered, taking into account the gravity of the internationally wrongful act and the rights in question".[64]

Moreover, the panels and the AB have in a number of cases referred to other customary international law rules unrelated to treaty interpretation. These include *locus standi*,[65] the precautionary principle,[66] *jura novit curia*,[67] successive treaties,[68] no retroactive application of

---

in reducing whole clauses or paragraphs of a treaty to redundancy or inutility.' See also Appellate Body Reports in *Canada – Dairy*, para. 133; *Argentina – Footwear (EC)*, para. 81, *US – Upland Cotton*, para. 549 etc. See more recently China Appellant Submission in Appellate Body Report, *China – Measures Related to the Exportation of Rare Earths, Tungsten, and Molybdenum*, WT/DS431,-433/AB/R (adopted 29 August 2014), paras 2.13 and 2.20.

63   See Joost Pauwelyn, 'The Role of Public International Law in the WTO: How Far Can We Go?', *AJIL*, Vol. 95, No. 3 (2001), pp. 535–78; Lorand Bartels, 'Applicable Law in WTO Dispute Settlement Proceedings', *JWT*, Vol. 35, No. 3 (2001), pp. 499–519; James Cameron and Kevin Gray, 'Principles of International Law in the WTO Dispute Settlement Body', *ICLQ*, Vol. 50 (2001) (hereinafter, 'Cameron and Gray (2001)'), pp. 248–98; John H. Jackson, 'International Law Status of WTO Dispute Settlement Reports: Obligation to Comply or Option to "Buy Out"?', *AJIL*, Vol. 98 (2004), pp. 109–25; Andrew D. Mitchell, 'Proportionalities and Remedies in WTO Disputes', *EJIL*, Vol. 17, No. 5 (2007), pp. 985–1008; Chios Carmody, 'A Theory of WTO Law', *JIEL*, Vol. 11, No. 3 (2008), pp. 527–57.

64   Appellate Body Report, *United States – Definitive Safeguard Measures on Imports of Circular Welded Carbon Quality Line Pipe from Korea*, WT/DS202/AB/R (adopted 8 March 2002), para. 259.

65   See *European Communities – Regime for the Importation, Sale and Distribution of Bananas (EC – Bananas)*, WT/DS27/R, para. 133 (27 September 1997).

66   Appellate Body Report, *EC – Hormones* case, paras. 123–4.

67   Appellate Body Report, *EC – Tariff Preferences*, para. 105.

68   Appellate Body Report, *European Communities – Measures Affecting the Importation of Certain Poultry Products*, WTO Doc WT/DS69/AB/R (adopted 23 July 1998), para. 79.

treaties[69] and manifest error in the formation of a treaty, etc.[70] Similarly, both WTO members[71] and the AB have also recognised the existence of other customary international law principles in their submissions before the WTO DSB.[72] Thus, except where WTO members expressly opt out of an emerging principle of customary international law, such customary law would normally be seen as relevant to the WTO's *acquis*.[73] In whichever respect the panels and AB view customary international law as being of practical relevance to a case before them, it is important to note that, aside from rules of interpretation, the application of customary international law in WTO case law remains somewhat undeveloped. Members have, of course, not hesitated to rely on different aspects of customary international law when making submissions before panels and the AB.

3.6   GENERAL PRINCIPLES OF LAW

The existence of general principles as a source of law has been accepted by international courts since the *Factory of Chorzow* case.[74] However,

---

[69]   Appellate Body Report, *Brazil – Desiccated Coconut*, pp. 15 and 167 at paras. 179–80.

[70]   In dealing with the issue of error in treaty formation, under the concept of non-violation complaint, in *Korea – Measures Affecting Government Procurement*, WT/DS163/R (May 2000) the panel resorted to customary international law practice (from the PCIJ and the ICJ), as codified in Article 48 of the VCLT. See panel report, paras. 7.120–7.123.

[71]   See, for instance, China's arguments in *US – Antidumping and Countervailing Duties (China)*, Appellate Body Report, *United States – Definitive Anti-Dumping and Countervailing Duties on Certain Products from China*, WT/DS379/AB/R (adopted 25 March 2011), paras. 22, 36–41 and 305.

[72]   Appellate Body Report, *US – Line Pipe*, para. 259 on the principle of proportionality of countermeasures. Moreover, the principle of *in dubio mitius* which is not part of the VCLT has widely been invoked by the AB in the context of supplementary means of interpretation. On international law principles in WTO dispute settlement, see Cameron and Gray (2001); Joost Pauwelyn, 'The Role of Public International Law in the WTO: How Far Can we Go?', *AJIL*, Vol. 95 (2001), pp. 535–78; Donald McRae, 'What is the Future of WTO Dispute Settlement', *JIEL*, Vol. 7, No. 1 (2004), pp. 3–21; Andrew D. Mitchell, *Legal Principles in WTO Disputes* (Cambridge University Press, 2011) etc.

[73]   See Panel Report in *Korea – Government Procurement*, para. 7.96.

[74]   PCIJ, Series A, No. 9, No. 13 (1928), p. 29. Here the PCIJ stated that '[i]t is a principle of international law and even a general conception of law that the breach of an engagement involves an obligation to make reparation in an adequate form ... Reparation therefore is the indispensable component of a failure to apply a convention and there is no necessity for this to be stated in the convention itself.'

general principles of law have always been seen as secondary sources of international law since they can hardly be regarded as a stand-alone source of international law. In other words, general principles will only be applied where the case at hand cannot be settled either by reference to a treaty or to customary international law. They are of use where there is a *lacuna* in the primary rules and there is no established precedent or jurisprudence on the issue.[75] Even when a general principle is applied by the WTO DSB or any other international courts[76] or tribunals,[77] this cannot be done to the detriment of rights and obligations properly established in a treaty instrument. Because of the marked risk of over-reliance on general principles, Scharzenberger, as far back as 1966, sounded a note of warning on when they may be accepted as sources of law in the international arena.[78] Thus, the AB has concluded with respect to the invocation of the principle of estoppel, as an example of a general principle, that:

> the notion of estoppel . . . would appear to inhibit the ability of WTO Members to initiate a WTO dispute settlement proceeding. We see little in the DSU that explicitly limits the rights of WTO Members to bring an action; WTO Members must exercise their "judgement as to whether action under these procedures would be fruitful", by virtue of Article 3.7 of the DSU, and they must engage

---

Furthermore, with reference to *res judicata*, another general principle of law, the ICJ in 1954 stated, 'according to a well-established and generally recognized principle of law, a judgment rendered by such a judicial body is *res judicata* and has binding force between the parties to the dispute'. *Effect of Awards of Compensation Made by the United Nations Administrative Tribunal*, Advisory Opinion, ICJ Reports (13 July 1954).

[75] On this, see Malcolm N. Shaw, *International Law* (Cambridge University Press, 7th ed., 2014), pp. 69–77.

[76] See ICJ Reports in the *Nuclear Tests* Cases (*New Zealand v. France*) (1974), pp. 253, 267 as well as subsequent dissenting opinion of Judge Weeramantry in the ICJ Reports on the *Request for an Examination of the Situation with Paragraph 63 of the Court's Judgment of 20 December 1974 in the Nuclear Tests* (*New Zealand v. France*) Case, Order of 22 September 1995. See also ICJ Reports in *Land and Maritime Boundary between Cameroon and Nigeria (Cameroon v. Nigeria) (Preliminary Objections)* (1998), pp. 275, 303. In the latter case, the ICJ stated that 'estoppel would only arise if by its acts or declarations Cameroon had consistently made it fully clear that it had agreed to settle the boundary dispute submitted to the Court by bilateral avenues alone'.

[77] See the case of *Argentina v. Ghana*, ITLOS (15 December 2012).

[78] See Asif Qureshi and Andreas Ziegler, *International Economic Law* (Sweet & Maxwell, 2nd ed., 2007), p. 28, citing Georg Scharzenberger, *Principles and Standard of International Economic Law* (I Recueil Des Cours, 1966).

in dispute settlement procedures in good faith, by virtue of Article 3.10 of the DSU ... Thus, even assuming *arguendo* that the principle of estoppel could apply in the WTO, its application would fall within these narrow parameters set out in the DSU.[79]

Estoppel is a general principle of international law, resting on the principle of good faith and consistency.[80] However, few general principles, including the principle of estoppel,[81] have been seen as relevant in WTO case law. In spite of the caution exercised by WTO panels and the AB when invoking general principles as a source of law, the principle of estoppel undoubtedly has some relevance in WTO *acquis*. For instance, in the *EC – Subsidies on Sugar*, the AB noted that 'it is reasonable for a panel to examine estoppel in the context of determining whether a Member has engaged "in these procedures in good faith", as required under Article 3.10 of the DSU'.[82] It is fair to conclude from the WTO's jurisprudence that the key to the application of estoppel in respect of WTO dispute settlement lies in Articles 3.7 and 3.10 of the DSU, according to which WTO members must act in good faith when initiating a complaint.[83] Beyond this provision, it is hard to see that estoppel plays any role in WTO case law.

Unlike estoppel, the WTO panels and the AB have responded fairly positively to other general principles. They have not totally rejected

---

[79] Appellate Body Report, *European Communities – Export Subsidies on Sugar*, WT/DS265/AB/R, WT/DS266/AB/R, WT/DS/283/AB/R (adopted 19 May 2005), para. 312.

[80] See the comments of judges Alfaro and Fitzmaurice in the *Case Concerning the Temple of Preah Vihear (Cambodia v. Thailand)*, ICJ Reports (1962), pp. 39–51; Ian Brownlie, *Principles of Public International Law* (Oxford University Press, 7th ed., 2008) (hereinafter, 'Brownlie (2008)'), pp. 644–5; and Elisabeth Zoller, *La Bonne Foi en Droit International Public* (Pedone, 1977), pp. 155–8.

[81] See the Compliance Panel Report in *EC – Bananas III (Article 21.5 – Ecuador II) / EC – Bananas III (Article 21.5 – US)*, para. 228. Though objected to in some legal systems, promissory estoppel, which is one form of estoppel (the others being equitable, property and collateral estoppel), has been widely used in the contract law of England and Wales. Promissory estoppel was developed by Lord Denning in the case of *Central London Property Trust Ltd. v. High Trees House Ltd. [1947]* K.B. 130.

[82] Appellate Body Report, *EC – Export Subsidies on Sugar*, paras. 307 and 310. See also Appellate Body Reports, *European Communities – Regime for the Importation, Sale and Distribution of Bananas* Second Recourse to Article 21.5 of the DSU by Ecuador / Recourse to Article 21.5 of the DSU by the United States, WT/DS27/AB/RW2/ECU, WT/DS27/AB/RW/USA (adopted 22 December 2008), para. 228.

[83] See Appellate Body Report in *EC – Sugar*, para. 312.

the application of principles such as *in dubio mitius*,[84] *res judicata*[85] and, more importantly, good faith,[86] in WTO dispute settlement procedures. However, the relevance of general principles as sources of WTO law cannot be overemphasised. General principles are sources of law that contain significant weaknesses, although in many cases they are directly linked to state practice.[87]

Although WTO jurisprudence is inconclusive on the application of general principles as sources of WTO law, the argument often raised in the context of compliance discourse that these principles have no place at all in WTO cases is untenable. Indeed, the inherent power[88] that panels and the AB are endowed with undoubtedly allows them to cautiously apply these principles when necessary. Moreover, the principle of *competence de la compétence* permits panels and the AB to exercise maximum independence in considering a particular matter brought before them.[89] This independence is only subject to the requirements of

---

[84]   Appellate Body Report, *EC Measures Concerning Meat and Meat Products (Hormones)*, WT/DS26/AB/R, WT/DS48/AB/R (adopted 13 February, 1998), para. 165; Appellate Body Report, *China – Measures Affecting Trading Rights and Distribution Services for Certain Publications and Audio-visual Entertainment Products*, WT/DS363/AB/R (adopted 19 January 2010), paras. 410–11.

[85]   *Res judicata* was raised by India in *India – Patents (EC)*, WT/DS79/R and was also extensively considered by the panel in *India – Measures Affecting the Automotive Sector*, WT/DS146/R, WT/DS175/R (21 December 2001), paras. 7.55–7.66 (this report was appealed but was withdrawn prior to the oral hearing). This principle of municipal law ensures that an issue that has already been litigated is not re-litigated. In other words, there can be no further proceedings on a matter that has already been heard. See Vaughan Lowe, 'Overlapping Jurisdiction in International Tribunals', *Australian Year Book of International Law*, Vol. 20 (1999), p. 191.

[86]   The principle of good faith is raised in one way or another in almost all WTO cases, as a general principle of international law, regarding compliance with WTO obligations.

[87]   Brownlie (2008), p. 19.

[88]   In *Nuclear Tests (Judgment)*, ICJ Reports 253, 259–60, referring to the *Northern Cameroons (Cameroon v. United Kingdom) (Preliminary Objections)* (1963) ICJ Reports 15, 29, the ICJ unambiguously held that the Court does have 'an inherent jurisdiction enabling it to take such action as may be required . . . to provide for the orderly settlement of all matters in dispute'.

[89]   In *United States – Act of 1916*, the AB emphatically pointed out that an international tribunal has the mandate to exercise independence in considering whether it has jurisdiction to rule on a particular issue before it. In considering this, the AB referred to a number of cases from the PCIJ and the ICJ; see WT/DS136/AB/R, WT/DS162/AB/R (adopted 26 September 2000), para. 54, note 30. It is also worth noting here that the principle of *juria novit curia*, discussed above, prima facie permits the panels and the AB, with respect to questions of law, to

Articles 3.2 and 19.2 of the DSU regarding the rights and obligations of members, which cannot be altered or modified by the reports of panels and the AB.

3.7 BRIEF CONCLUDING REMARKS

This chapter has discussed the commonly invoked sources of WTO law. While the jurisprudence of the WTO panels and the AB may certainly be seen in the light of sources, we have deliberately avoided discussion of *stare rationibus decidendis* (or simply, *stare decisis*) in the WTO. There are two reasons for this. First, in many parts of this volume the legal consequences of adopted panel and AB reports are discussed, albeit indirectly. Second, while the panels and the AB do not totally ignore the *ratio decidendi* of previous reports, these cannot be seen as sources of law in the common law sense of setting a precedent.[90] For instance, the Supreme Court of the United States will frown at any decision that undermines the *ratio decidendi* of one of its previous cases.[91]And in the UK as well as in other common law jurisdictions, the previous decisions of a superior court create a binding precedent that is to be followed by courts of equal or lower status unless such decision can be legally or factually distinguished.[92] But an adopted panel or AB report binds only the parties

---

decide on particular issues on their own initiative. See also Appellate Body Report, *US – Continued Suspension / Canada – Continued Suspension*, WT/DS320/AB/R, WT/DS321/AB/R, paras. 3–10.

[90] There has been quite an animated debate on the notion of precedent in the WTO DSS. See for instance, Raj Bhala, 'The Power of the Past: Towards De Jure Stare Decisis in WTO Adjudication (Part Three of a Trilogy)', *George Washington International Law Review*, Vol. 33 (2001), pp. 873–978; Giorgio Sarcedoti, 'Precedent in the Settlement of International Economic Disputes: The WTO and Investment Arbitration Models', Bocconi Legal Research Paper No. 1931560 (2011); Anton Strezhnev, 'Using Latent Space Models to Study International Legal Precedent: An Application to the WTO Dispute Settlement Body', APSA 2014 Annual Meeting Paper (2014).

[91] Almost a century ago the US Supreme Court held that 'the very concept of the rule of law underlying our Constitution requires such continuity over time that a respect for precedent is, by definition, indispensable'. See *Planned Parenthood of Southeastern Pennsylvania v. Casey*, 505 US 833, pp. 854 and 864, referring to B. Cardozo, *The Nature of the Judicial Process* 149 (1921).

[92] In the case of the UK, see the 1966 Practice Statement on Judicial Precedent [1966] 3 All ER 77, [1966] 1 WLR 1234. On the simplification of the application of precedent in England and Wales, see James Holland and Julian Webb, *Learning Legal Rules* (Oxford University Press, 7th ed., 2010).

and impacts only their relationship *inter se*.[93] Although Article XVI.1 of the WTO Charter as well as some adopted panel and AB reports suggest continuity in the decision-making process of the WTO, '[i]t is well settled that Appellate Body reports are not binding, except with respect to resolving the particular dispute between the parties'.[94]

In view of the sources discussed in this chapter, it is important to note that while the DSU is generally silent as to the sources of law that the panels and the AB can rely on when reviewing a case, they have so far exercised great pragmatism in dealing with situations in respect of which no straightforward answer as to the applicable law can be found in the DSU. Consistent with practice of other international courts and tribunals, the panels and the AB have resolved conflicting obligations or dealt with ambiguities in respect of the applicable law by invoking international law and to some extent municipal law concepts which may not readily be found in WTO covered agreements. Therefore, the debate surrounding the exact sources of law to which the panels and the AB should revert when reviewing an allegedly WTO-inconsistent measure in a case is arguably academic in nature. This is the case for the reasons provided above and also because many, if not all, WTO members only expect the panels and the AB to ensure that the WTO dispute settlement mechanism aims at securing 'a positive solution to the dispute'.[95]

---

[93]   While many WTO members hesitate to call the DSB WTO 'courts', the ICJ is well recognised as the World Court. However, as stated in Article 59 of the ICJ Statute, its judgments cannot be seen as creating law.

[94]   See Appellate Body Report, *United States – Final Anti-Dumping Measures on Stainless Steel from Mexico*, WT/DS344/AB/R (adopted 20 May 2008), para. 158 and footnote 308. The issue of precedent is a sensitive one among some WTO members, although in this case the AB was 'deeply concerned about the Panel's decision to depart from well-established Appellate Body jurisprudence clarifying the interpretation of the same legal issues'. See Appellate Body Report, para. 162. On this, see also John Jackson, *Sovereignty, the WTO, and Changing Fundamentals of International Law* (Cambridge University Press, 2009), pp. 173–82.

[95]   See Article 3.7 of the DSU.

4. Theorising the WTO implementation regime

4.1 TRADE LIBERALISATION AS LIMITATION OF THE POWER OF THE NATION-STATE

The changing fundamentals in international economic law, especially in the area of world trade, have drastically altered the province of influence of nation-states within and beyond national frontiers.[1] Trade policy is no longer formulated without considering whether it is consistent with the international obligations of the state in question. Some observers even worry that the rate at which WTO members are becoming amenable to trade openness puts traditional state sovereignty at risk. Consequently, globalisation and trade liberalisation have drastically reshaped the conceptual approach taken in respect of governance within nation-states.[2] Similarly, because of the interconnectivity of the global economic order, it is certainly difficult nowadays to delink the activities of different international economic institutions. In view of this interconnectivity, in respect of many of its activities the WTO would hardly be able to operate in isolation from institutions such as the International Monetary Fund, the World Bank, the Bank of International Settlement, United Nations Conference on Trade and Development, and so on.[3] The notion of governance within

---

[1] With regard to the notion of sovereignty, Kelsen regarded international law as a mechanism for determining the sphere of the validity of municipal law. See Hans Kelsen, *General Theory of Law and State* (Harvard University Press, 1945) as translated and reprinted by Anders Wedberg (1999).

[2] Almost all international organisations advocating economic liberalism collaborate with each other. For instance, the World Bank Group and the WTO collaborate in different aspects of their activities. For more analyses on such collaborative activities, see Ludo Cuyvers and Stijn Verherstraeten, *The Network of Interlocking Directorates between International Economic Organisation*, Department of International Economics, International Management and Diplomacy working paper (University of Antwerp, Issue 024, 2004), available at http://ideas.repec.org/p/ant/wpaper/2005024.html (last visited 16 March 2015).

[3] Article XV of GATT clearly provides for such collaboration. With regard to exchange arrangement, Article XV.4 states: 'Contracting Parties shall not,

the community of nations cannot be regarded as inseparable from factors beyond national borders. In other words, 'the inter-dependent regulation of trade and other fields that are deemed to have an impact on trade has been a powerful principle for the expansion of WTO regulation and the single undertaking has, so far, served as the vector to implement linkage'.[4]

As indicated above in Chapter 3, although it is clear in the DSU and relevant WTO covered agreements that the WTO dispute settlement system does not have jurisdiction beyond the agreement of trade-related issues by WTO members, the law to be applied in resolving disputes arising from those covered agreements is to a large extent without such limitation.[5] As discussed at greater length in the previous chapter, different WTO covered agreements are also littered with references to other international treaties outside the GATT/WTO rules.

However, the euphoria that greeted the entry into force of the WTO and its comprehensive dispute settlement mechanism seems to have largely diminished in the last decade. The optimism generated in the first few years of the operation of the trading system seems to have been a consequence of the fact that the first few cases that went through the system were uncontroversial and largely remnants of GATT dispute settlement cases. Therefore, as new and complicated cases started emerging, the issue of compliance resurfaced as a major issue of concern in the world trading

---

by exchange action, frustrate the intent of the provision of this Agreement, nor, by trade action, the intent of the provisions of the Articles of Agreement of the International Monetary Fund.' Dispute settlement is one of the areas where such collaboration is most visible. For instance, in *Argentina – Textiles and Apparel*, the AB stated as follows in respect of Article XV:2 '[it] *requires* the WTO to consult with the IMF when dealing with "problems concerning monetary reserves, balances of payments or foreign exchange arrangements"'. See WT/DS56/AB/R, paras. 84–85. And in *EC – Computer Equipment*, the AB stated that 'we consider that in interpreting the tariff concessions in Schedule LXXX, decisions of the WCO may be relevant'. See *EC – Computer Equipment*, para. 90.

[4] Sonia E. Rolland, 'Redesigning the Negotiation Process at the WTO', *JIEL*, Vol. 13, No. 1 (2010), p. 65.

[5] This view of course takes into account that the principle of *compétence de la compétence* is very much grounded in the WTO dispute resolution mechanism. See in this regard, the Appellate Body Report in *United States – Anti Dumping Act of 1916*, WT/DS136/AB/R (2000), at para. 54, note 30. In relation to the appeal made by the US on the grounds that the panel had erred in finding that it had jurisdiction to consider the claims that the 1916 Act as such is inconsistent with Article VI of GATT 1994 and the *Anti-Dumping* case, the AB stated that '[w]e note that it is a widely accepted rule that an international tribunal is entitled to consider the issue of its own jurisdiction on its own initiative, and to satisfy itself that it has jurisdiction in any case that comes before it.'

system.[6] Informed observers and some domestic constituencies constantly question the extent to which trade liberalisation and the normative framework that accompanies it will continue to shape nation-states' economic sovereignty.[7]

The concept of sovereignty is one of the most strongly contested concepts in both the policy world and academic scholarship.[8] Academic scholarship on the subject tends to be very critical of the traditional notion of sovereignty and at times even lacks coherence.[9] In the traditional notion of the concept, which is grounded on the 1948 Treaty of Westphalia, nation-states are seen as possessing unquestionable authority

---

[6] One of the most informative pieces on this issue is that by Clause-Dieter Ehlermann, 'Tensions between the Dispute Settlement Process and the Diplomatic and Treaty-Making Activities of the WTO', *WTR*, Vol. 1, No. 3 (2002), pp. 301–8.

[7] Economic sovereignty here refers to the 'juridical independence from the authority of other participants in international economic relations' to design and implement economic policies. On this issue, see Qureshi and Ziegler, *International Economic Law* (Sweet & Maxwell, 2007), pp. 44–5.

[8] Examples of this literature include: Robert E. Hudec, 'Free Trade, Sovereignty, Democracy: The Future of the World Trade Organization', *WTR*, Vol. 1, No. 2 (2002), pp. 211–22; Matthew Schaefer, 'Sovereignty, Influence, Realpolitik and the World Trade Organization', *Hastings International and Comparative Law Review (HICLR)*, Vol. 25, No. 3 (2002), pp. 341–69; Stephen D. Krasner, *Sovereignty: Organized Hypocrisy* (Princeton University Press, 1999); Michael Ross Fowler and Julie Marie Bunck, *Law, Power, and the Sovereign State* (The Pennsylvania State University Press, 1995).

[9] The issue of sovereignty here is important because of its connection with the sources of international law which may be considered by a panel or the AB. If sovereignty means that there is no higher authority than the nation-state, it may be argued that no international law norm is valid without the consent of the state. Of course, in a broader sense, the application of treaties or conventions is almost always founded on the legitimate consent of states. But this strict view may, in every case, generate a number of important questions, especially when a treaty-based international system evolves over time, and the institutions contained in the system purport to have the power to prescribe obligations to the signatories. For instance, in the *US – Shrimp* case, the AB held that: 'From the perspective embodied in the preamble of the WTO Agreement, we note that the generic term "natural resources" in Article XX(g) is not "static" in its content or reference but is rather "by definition, evolutionary".' See *United States – Import Prohibition of Shrimp and Shrimp Products*, Appellate Body Report, WT/DS58/AB/R, para. 130 (adopted 6 November 1998). For a view on the sovereignty question, see John H. Jackson, 'Sovereignty Modern: A New Approach to an Outdated Concept', *AJIL* (2003), pp. 782–802; and a later article by the same author, 'The Changing Fundamentals of International Law and Ten Years of the WTO', *JIEL*, Vol. 8, No. 1 (2005), pp. 3–15. For a discussion on the evolving concept of sovereignty, see Gerard Kreijen et al. (eds), *State Sovereignty, and International Governance* (Oxford University Press, 2002), pp. 282–3.

over their territories as well as over the policies relating to the running of these territories. The following quotes from a previous work capture some of the difficulties and challenges facing reliance on the traditional notion of sovereignty:

> To concur with the Westphalian notion of sovereignty, which has been described as 'organized hypocrisy'[10] is largely to concur with the 128-clause Westphalian document with minute details on how to end 30 years of primitive warring. As it is well understood, one of the important implications of the Treaty of Westphalia was the transfer of properties to various feudal lords and a solemn promise by the contracting parties not to intervene with the rule of certain feudal lords within their territories.[11]

Despite the apparent intention of giving meaning to the notion of a nation-state, the legacy of the Westphalian project of sovereignty can hardly be seen nowadays as anything other than a peace treaty to end a brutal thirty-year war. Sovereignty is an evolving concept, and there is, therefore, no fixed definition of what it should amount to.[12] Regardless of the varying views as to the content of the concept, the notion of independence and the ability to determine one's future are germane to the definition of sovereignty in contemporary scholarship.[13] In the early twentieth century, Oppenheim defined sovereignty by making a distinction between internal and external sovereignty.[14] More recently, Brownlie opined that, '[t]he term "sovereignty" may be used as a synonym for independence, an important element in statehood'.[15]

The debates surrounding the true meaning of the concept of sovereignty have neither died down nor been settled by international courts and tribunals. For instance, in the *North Atlantic Coast Fisheries Case (United Kingdom v. United States)*, the Permanent Court of Arbitration held that 'one of the essential elements of sovereignty is that it is to be exercised within territorial limits, and that, failing proof to the contrary,

---

[10]   Stephen Krasner, *Sovereignty: Organized Hypocrisy* (Princeton University Press, 1999).

[11]   See Ngangjoh-Hodu (2012), p. 23.

[12]   The various ways in which sovereignty is contested are discussed in detail in Jens Bartelson, 'The Concept of Sovereignty Revisited', *EJIL*, Vol. 17, No. 2 (2006), pp. 463–74; Kal Raustiala, 'Rethinking the Sovereignty Debate in International Economic Law', *JIEL*, Vol. 6, No. 4 (2003), pp. 481–878.

[13]   See James Crawford, *Brownlie's Principles of Public International Law* (Oxford University Press, 2012), pp. 204–12; Ngangjoh-Hodu (2012), p. 23.

[14]   For a critical discussion on this, see Lassa Oppenheim, *International Law: volume i, Peace* (1905), pp. 113–15.

[15]   Brownlie (2008), p. 76.

the territory is co-terminous with sovereignty'.[16] In the early part of the twentieth century, Judge Huber in the *Island of Palmas Case* (1928) concluded that 'sovereignty in the relations between States signifies independence. Independence in regard to a portion of the globe is the right to exercise therein, to the exclusion of any other State, the functions of a State'.[17] More recently, in the case of *Right of Passage over Indian Territory* (*Portugal v. India*), Portugal claimed it had the right to transport military equipment through India to and from the Portuguese territory of Damao, an enclave deep inside the territory of India. Although a local custom existed regarding transportation of goods and persons through India to and from Damao, it was clear that no such custom existed with regard to the transportation of military equipment as claimed by Portugal. With regard to the question of sovereignty, Portugal submitted before the ICJ that the rights of passage through Damao were a logical necessity grounded in the notion of 'sovereignty'.[18] The issue of sovereignty was alluded to in one of the very first cases brought before the WTO. In *Japan – Alcoholic Beverages*, the AB noted that:

> The *WTO Agreement* is a treaty – the international equivalent of a contract. It is self-evident that in an exercise of their sovereignty, and in pursuit of their own respective national interests, the members of the WTO have made a bargain. In exchange for the benefits they expect to derive as members of the WTO, they have agreed to exercise their sovereignty according to the commitments they have made in the *WTO Agreement*.[19]

However, it is becoming clearer now than ever before that as a consequence of globalisation the traditional conception of sovereignty is no longer tenable.[20]

In a speech to the School of Foreign Service and the Mortara Center for International Studies at Georgetown University in Washington, DC,

---

[16] See *North Atlantic Coast Fisheries* Case (*United Kingdom v. United States*), 11 RIAA(1910) 167, p. 180. See further, Dixon and McCorquodale, *Cases and Materials on International Law* (Oxford University Press, 2011), p. 239.

[17] See *Island of Palmas Case* (*The Netherlands v. United States*), II UNRIAA, p. 829.

[18] ICJ, *Right of Passage over Indian Territory* (*Portugal v. India*), ICJ Report, 12 April 1960, Pleadings, 1, pp. 6 and 26.

[19] Appellate Body Report, *Japan – Alcoholic Beverages*, p. 15.

[20] According to Allott, Westphalian sovereignty has lost its relevance as 'alternative sovereignties' are developing. Philipp Allott, *Eunomia: New Order for a New World* (Oxford University Press, 1990), pp. 329–30.

in January 2003, Ambassador Haass summarised the discontent with the Westphalian concept of sovereignty as follows:

> Historically, sovereignty has been associated with four main characteristics: First, a sovereign state is one that enjoys supreme political authority and a monopoly over the legitimate use of force within its territory. Second, it is capable of regulating movements across its borders. Third, it can make its foreign policy choices freely. Finally, it is recognized by other governments as an independent entity entitled to freedom from external intervention. These components of sovereignty were never absolute, but together they offered a predictable foundation for world order. What is significant today is that each of these components – internal authority, border control, policy autonomy, and non-intervention – is being challenged in unprecedented ways.[21, 22]

While the conclusion of the global trade project was seen as a victory around the world, many national constituencies, including the US, viewed the unfolding of events in 1994 with great dismay. For many, 1994 was a year when individual governments were encouraged to limit the extent to which sovereign economic powers were to be relinquished to a supranational institution such as the newly born WTO. For instance, in 1994, various government officials in the US argued that 'no international body could require the United States (not even in the loose sense of an international law norm) to do anything'. Similarly, the United States Congress made it clear that the so-called Section 301 was here to stay and that the negotiation position of the Executive would be consistent with this position.[23] Section 301 was a provision of US legislation permitting the United States Trade Representative (USTR) to unilaterally take certain retaliatory measures, without going through any dispute settlement process, in response to restrictive trade measures imposed by other trading nations. The legislation in its entirety spans sections 301–310 of the Trade Act of

---

[21]   Richard N. Haass, *Sovereignty: Existing Rights, Evolving Responsibilities*, Remarks at the School of Foreign Service and the Mortara Center for International Studies at Georgetown University in Washington, DC, on 14 January 2003, available at www.iwar.org.uk/news-archive/2003/01-15.htm (last visited 20 May 2011).

[22]   See Ngangjoh-Hodu (2012), p. 24.

[23]   In view of the animated debate on this, see John H. Jackson, 'The Great 1994 Sovereignty Debate: United States Acceptance and Implementation of the Uruguay Round Results', *Columbia Journal of Transnational Law (CJTL)*, Vol. 36 (1997), pp. 157–88; and John H. Jackson, *Sovereignty, the WTO, and Changing Fundamentals of International Law, Lauterpacht Memorial Lectures* (Cambridge University Press, 2009), pp. 57–78. See also Dan Sarooshi, 'Sovereignty, Economic Autonomy, the United States, and International Trading System: Representations of a Relationship', *EJIL*, Vol. 15, No. 4 (2004), pp. 651–76.

1974 (codified at 19 USC §2411 et seq.).[24] The European Communities claimed that this legislation amounted to a violation on the part of the US of its obligations under the DSU in general and in particular under Article 23, which unequivocally requires WTO members to refrain from unilateral actions. Article 23 states:

> When Members seek the redress of a violation of obligations or other nullification or impairment of benefit under the covered agreements or an impediment to the attainment of any objective of the covered agreements, they shall have recourse to, and abide by, the rules and procedures of this Understanding.[25]

In this case, the EC alleged that by enacting the legislation in question, the US had acted inconsistently with its DSU obligation not to engage in unilateral action against another WTO member. Further, the EC claimed that the 1974 Trade Act violates Articles I, II, III, VIII and XI of GATT. While noting that the US legislation in question was an issue of fact not warranting interpretation by the panel, the panel considered it necessary to defer to that member's interpretation of its own laws.[26] It was not persuaded by the arguments put forward in support of the EC's claim, and accordingly rejected it under Article 23 of the DSU and the relevant GATT 1994 provisions on the basis of insufficient substantiation.[27] In this case, the burden of proof was on the EC, but it seems to have failed to adduce enough evidence to succeed with its claim.

In spite of the claim made by many observers and, indeed, some academics that the WTO is an integral part of the globalisation project because of 'its intrusion' into sectors that once represented the cornerstones of state sovereignty, many other critiques see the WTO as lacking openness and transparency.[28] Therefore, insofar as these challenges and the incentives

---

[24]   The EC challenged aspects of this measure before the WTO. See Panel Report, *United States – Sections 301–310 of the Trade Act of 1974*, WT/DS152/R (adopted 27 January 2000). For further analysis of this case, see Seung Wha Chang, 'Taming Unilateralism Under the Multilateral Trading System: Unfinished Job in the WTO Panel Rulings on U.S. Sections 301–310 of the Trade Act of 1974', *Law and Policy in International Business*, Vol. 31, 1151 (2000); Yoshiko Naiki, 'The Mandatory/Discriminatory Doctrine in WTO Law: The *US – Section 301* Case and its Aftermath', *JIEL*, Vol. 7, No. 1 (2004), pp. 32–72.

[25]   Article 23.1 of the DSU.

[26]   See the panel report, para. 7.20.

[27]   Panel report, paras. 7.187–7.189.

[28]   On the topic of transparency in the WTO, see Gabrielle Marceau and Peter Pedersen, 'Is the WTO Open and Transparent? Non-governmental Organisation and Civil Society's Claims for more Transparency and Public Participation', *JWT*, Vol. 33, No. 1 (1999), pp. 5–49; Thomas Cottier, 'Preparing for Structural Reform

to take measures that are inconsistent with the spirit of the WTO agreements continue to exist, theorising the compliance regime in the context of the founding principles of the legal system of a major WTO member like China remains highly relevant in contemporary debates.

Over the years, informed observers have come up with various critical analyses relating to the debate on implementation in the GATT/WTO system. Some of these writings poignantly paint a picture of a world trade dispute settlement system that sometimes struggles to get WTO members to comply with their international commitments.[29] This volume has to a large extent moved away from a discourse that hinges only on identifying cases where implementation has not happened or has happened half-heartedly to a discourse on the theoretical logic of implementation which at the same time focuses on Confucian theory as the foundation of the Chinese legal tradition. Because Confucian tradition seeks more to persuade than to oblige, this volume identifies the points of potential conflict that may exist between China's legal system and systems founded on Western legal traditions when discussing compliance with WTO treaty norms.[30] While the concept of *pacta sunt servanda* has sometimes been the cornerstone of the discussion on compliance with WTO rules, compliance in the context of the Confucian legal tradition is largely discussed without excessive emphasis on normativity.[31]

---

in the WTO', *JIEL*, Vol. 10, No. 3 (2008), pp. 497–508; Padideh Ala'i, 'From the Periphery to the Center? The Evolving WTO Jurisprudence on Transparency and Good Governance', *JIEL*, Vol. 11, No. 4 (2008), pp. 779–802; Ljiljana Biukovic, 'Selective Adaptation of WTO Transparency Norms and Local Practices in China and Japan', *JIEL*, Vol. 11, No. 4 (2008), pp. 803–25.

[29]   See David Palmeter and Petros Mavroidis, *Dispute Settlement in the World Trade Organization: Practice and Procedure* (Cambridge University Press, 2004); Petersmann (1997); Jackson, *The World Trade Organization* (1998); and in the context of GATT, see Hudec (1990).

[30]   Gilbert Rozman (ed.), *The East Asian Region: Confucian Heritage and its Modern Adaptation* (Princeton University Press, 1991); Heriyanto Yang and Yogyakarta, 'The History and Legal Position of Confucianism in Post-independence Indonesia', *Marburg Journal of Religion*, Vol. 10, No. 1 (2005); H. Patrick Glenn, *Legal Traditions of the World* (Cambridge University Press, 5th ed., 2014), pp. 319–56.

[31]   Confucian thinking is also notably in stark contrast to views appealing to legal positivism. The underlining tenet of legal positivism is that any piece of rules worth the name 'law' or norm can only be seen as valid if it possesses a formal legal status and not on the basis of its relationship to external validating factors. However, see here the critique of legal positivism in Bruno Simma and Andreas Paulus, 'The Responsibility of Individuals for Human Rights Abuses in Internal Conflicts – A Positivist View', *AJIL*, Vol. 93, No. 302 (1999) at p. 302; H.L.A. Hart, *The Concept of Law* (Oxford University Press, 2nd ed., 1994). Also of relevance

Persuasive conceptual arguments have been put forward in recent years in academic scholarship as to the need to ensure that there is sufficient nexus between international obligations of nation-states and the basic social reality in those states.[32] Although specific exceptions may exist, the fashioning of municipal legislation does not usually provide answers to problems relating to societal values or offer means of resolving conflicts.

International trade law scholarship seems to put forward separate lines of arguments from the foregoing. In this regard, it has been argued as follows:

> the central issue about the debates may be conceived on the premise that the independence of any particular rules in the objective resolution of actual disputes may only be contextually determined. The essential elements of pre-dictability and security essential in the WTO dispute settlement mechanism follow from this: it is hard to deny the fact that DSU represents a core pillar of the World Trading System and a sophisticated, but closely watched project of contemporary international law.[33]

Although there is arguably a consensus among both critics and admirers of the Uruguay Round project that the ability of the WTO adjudicating body to successfully settle disputes has been impressive, there has been no such consensus when it comes to unilateralism and mercantilism since the advent of the world trading system in 1995. While the Westphalian conception of sovereignty is highly incongruous with many of the reports of the WTO adjudicating body, the arbitrators in the *EC – Bananas* and *US – FSC* cases,[34] in particular, seem to have largely adhered to the notion that from its inception all members of the WTO adhered to the 'underlining principle of "mutual disarmament"'[35] in trade. In this regard, whatever remedy was available for non-compliance in the WTO was intended

---

here is the work of Hans Kelsen in his *General Theory of Law and State*, translated and republished by (Cambridge University Press, 1999).

[32] From the point of view of this scholarship, this argument supports the idealistic view that international law must not be disconnected from existing international challenges. This approach must also take into consideration the historical context. Koskenniemi, for instance, finds it necessary 'to read the law "backward" in order to reveal the interpretation which it carries of the world we live in'. See Koskenniemi (2005), p. 422 et seq.

[33] On this, see Ngangjoh-Hodu (2012), p. 26.

[34] See *EC – Bananas* Arbitration Report, WT/DS27/ARB/ECU, para. 76; and *US – FSC*, WT/DS108/ARB, paras. 5.5–5.6 (Authorization to Suspend Concessions, 7 May 2003).

[35] See Pascal Lamy, 'The World Trade Organisation: New Issues, New Challenges', *En Temps Réel* (4 September 2014), p. 5.

neither to be a permanent solution nor to be a substitute for compliance with an adopted DSB report. *A contrario*, because of the inherent defect in this remedial structure, individual domestic interests have largely been stumbling blocks to the realisation of the original objective of remedial functions.[36]

4.2   WORLD TRADE LAW COMPLIANCE DISCOURSE AND CONSTRUCTIVISM

For several years, constructivism has been the exclusive province of international relations scholarship.[37] Although the creation of norms and the interactions of those norms with the society within which they are created is one of the cornerstones of constructivist discourse, constructivism as a theory has only marginally caught the attention of international economic lawyers. While there are many variants within constructivist discourse, constructivism views international institutional regimes as important forums in which the legitimate expectations of actors converge.[38] Constructivism stresses the importance to the proper functioning of international relations of building institutional blocs like the WTO and other international economic organisations. As a key pillar of the contemporary international system, since its establishment in 1995, the WTO has over the last two decades championed the course of international legal system in generating a standard of behaviour that has created significant mutual and legitimate expectations between its main actors. In view of the fact that these mutual expectations are founded on the effectiveness of normative existence, constructivism is arguably an important theoretical

---

[36]   For a succinct discussion of the challenges facing WTO dispute settlement remedies, see Marco Bronckers and Neboth van den Broek, 'Financial Compensation in the WTO: Improving the Remedies of WTO Dispute Settlement', *JIEL*, Vol. 8, No. 1 (2005), pp. 101–26.

[37]   It has recently been argued that because of the inability of neorealism and institutionalism to explain or predict the peaceful evaporation of the Soviet bloc, '[t]he hope associated with constructivism derives from its emergence just as the Cold War was ending and the future of East-West Relationships was being reconsidered'. See Jutta Brunnée and Stephen Toope, 'Constructivism and International Law', in Jeffrey L. Dunoff and Mark Pollack (eds), *Interdisciplinary Perspectives on International Law and International Relations: The State of the Art* (Cambridge University Press, 2012).

[38]   See Andrew Lang, 'Reconstructing Embedded Liberalism: John Gerard Ruggie and Constructivist Approaches to the Study of the International Trade Regime', *JIEL*, Vol. 9, No. 1 (2006) (hereinafter, 'Lang (2006)'), p. 81.

framework to explain the discourse on states' behaviour towards each other and compliance with international trade rules.

Constructivist thinking in respect of trade law and trade regimes involves viewing the world trading system as an instrument or structure to enhance interdependence between its different actors as well as facilitating the legitimate expectations of those actors, which in this case are WTO members. It has been argued that the global trading system as a regime, 'consists in part of a set of collectively agreed answers to questions about why the [trade] regime itself exists' and the objectives members should be pursuing.[39] Although many international lawyers have not directly confronted constructivist discourse in trade law, it is not uncommon that in trying to make sense of the corpus of WTO law, those same lawyers may make an appeal to constructivist considerations. More precisely, it is all too easy to appeal to the 'spirit of the system'[40] without directly dealing with key contemporary theoretical and practical challenges. In fact, the world trade regime is arguably guided by the spirit of 'creation of market conditions conducive to individual economic activity in national and global market places'.[41] Therefore, in dealing with compliance and other key issues plaguing the regime, it is commonplace to argue in favour of answers that rise above 'abstract presumption'[42] in order to arrive at mutually supportive solutions to at least the core established objects and purposes of the regime. In contrast to the liberal school of thought,[43] in which utilitarianism is the essence of international relations, constructivism regards the identity of actors, rather than individual interests, as forming the guiding principle of inter-state interactions. More important

---

[39]   Lang (2006), p. 104.

[40]   Gerald Fitzmaurice, 'The General Principles of International Law Considered from the Standpoint of the Rule of Law', 92 RCADI 1957/II p. 51, in Koskenniemi (2005), p. 258.

[41]   This was highlighted by the Panel in *United States – Sections 301–310 of the Trade Act of 1974*, WT/DS152/R, para. 7.73 (27 January 2000). In this case, the panel observed that these goals, including the security and predictability of the multilateral trading system, are the most important objectives of the WTO.

[42]   Koskenniemi (2005), p. 259.

[43]   In an influential article that appeared in 1982, John Gerard Ruggie introduced the notion of 'embedded liberalism' in the context of international trade and the integration of the world economy in general. Various scholars have been persuaded by Ruggie's account of post-war trade liberalisation in 'International Regimes, Transactions, and Change: Embedded Liberalism in the Postwar Economic Order', *International Organisation*, Vol. 36 (1982), p. 379, which 'provides a useful introduction to the central elements of constructivist thinking about international relations and . . . expand our understanding of trade regime and of trade law'. See Lang (2006), p. 81.

to constructivism is the notion of 'collective legitimisation . . . that challenges or place limits on instrumental behaviour, rather than eliminating such behaviour wholesale'.[44] Language, 'norms and rules' in international relations[45] are therefore essential components of constructivist discourse.

The scholarship of Lon Fuller is highly recognisable to constructivists. In this context, law is seen in constructivist terms as a mutual construction of agents and structures in which the society operates. Contextually, and reading into the constructivist story, the behaviour of WTO members as key actors in the multilateral trading system is arguably 'shaped and reshaped by actions within the structure'.[46] As opposed to neorealists, who 'treat states as if they were individuals who try to maximise their ultimate aim of survival . . . constructivists focus more on the norms and shared understanding of legitimate behaviour'.[47] Moreover, constructivism in principle 'has more flexible assumptions that allow it . . . to more accurately describe state behaviour'.[48] It would be incongruous with constructivism to conclude that states' behaviour is usually formed before their interaction with each other, as most international relations scholarship seems to suggest. In constructivist thinking, the adoption of positions and the formation of identities only occurs in the course of interaction between states.[49]

Because ideas and norms appear to have more influence in international relations in constructivist thinking, one could explore this approach in the context of the WTO's system of adjudication by reference to previous compliance panel reports in *Canada – Dairy (Article 21.5 – New Zealand and US)*.[50] In this case, the parties had agreed that 31 January 2001 would

---

[44]   Jeffrey Lewis, 'Institutional Environment and Everyday EU Decision Making: Rationalist or Constructivist?', *Comparative Political Studies*, Vol. 36, No. 1/2 (February–March 2003), p. 106.

[45]   See K.M. Fierke, 'Constructivism', in Tim Dunne et al. (eds), *International Relations Theories: Discipline and Diversity* (Oxford University Press, 2007), pp. 167–9 (hereinafter, 'Fierke (2007)').

[46]   Jutta Brunnée and Stephen Toope, 'International Law and Constructivism: Elements of an Interactional Theory of International Law', *Columbia Journal of Transnational Law*, Vol. 39 (2000), p. 30.

[47]   Fierke (2007), pp. 169–70; cf. Hans J. Morgenthau, *Politics Among Nations: The Struggle for Power and Peace* (New York, Alfred A. Knopf, 6th ed., 1985); Claire R. Kelley, 'Realist Theory and Real Constraints', *Virginia Journal of International Law*, Vol. 44 (Winter 2004), pp. 545–636.

[48]   Andrew Guzman, *How International Law Works: A Rational Choice Theory* (Oxford University Press, 2008), p. 20.

[49]   Ian Hurd, 'Constructivism', in Christian Reus-Smit (ed.), *The Oxford Handbook of International Relations* (Oxford University Press, 2008), pp. 298–316.

[50]   Appellate Body Report, *Canada – Measures Affecting the Importation*

be the end date of a reasonable period of time allowed in order to comply with the DSB report. When this deadline was reached, both New Zealand and the US were unhappy with the measures Canada had taken to comply with the original report. Accordingly, on 25 March 1998, the DSB established a joint panel to hear a complaint from the US and New Zealand regarding Canada's alleged illegal subsidies for domestic milk production, as well as its tariff rate quota system for fluid milk importation. In this regard, the complainants alleged that Canada's Special Milk Scheme (Special Classes 5(d) and 5(e)) amounted to export subsidies within the meaning of Articles 9.1(a) and 9.1(c) of the Agreement on Agriculture and were therefore inconsistent with its obligations under Articles 3.3 and 10.1 of that Agreement.[51] Moreover, the US claimed that the tariff rates quota scheme violated Article II.I(b) of GATT 1994. On the issue of conveying a benefit, the panel concluded that there were indeed subsidies within the meaning of Article 9.1(a) and 'financed by virtue of governmental action' within the meaning of Article 9.1(c). In conclusion, the panel found that Canada's measures were inconsistent with its commitments under the relevant provisions of the Agreement on Agriculture and in particular Article 3.3 and Article 8 and, alternatively, Article 10.1. The panel further concluded that Canada's tariff rate quota was inconsistent with Article II.1 of GATT 1994. On appeal, the AB upheld most of the panel's findings.[52]

By the end of the reasonable period of time, New Zealand and the US were not satisfied with the measures taken by Canada to comply with the DSB's recommendations. Consequently, both complainants requested the establishment of an Article 21.5 compliance panel. Canada subsequently appealed the panel's findings.[53] In its report, the AB upheld most of the compliance panel's findings although it reversed its interpretation of Article 10.3 of the Agreement on Agriculture.

With regard to the findings under Article 9.1(c) of the Agreement on Agriculture, there were no straightforward rules that could be seen as an express identification of a particular standard or benchmark to determine whether the measure in question involved 'payment'. Determination of

---

of Milk and the Exportation of Dairy Products, First and Second Recourse to Article 21.5 of the DSU by New Zealand and the United States (adopted 18 December 2001 and 17 January 2003 respectively).

[51]   See US complaint in document WT/DS103/4 and New Zealand's complaint in document WT/DS113/4.

[52]   Appellate Body Report *Canada – Measures Affecting the Importation of Milk and the Exportation of Dairy Products,* WT/DS103, 113/AB/R (adopted 27 October 1999), para. 143.

[53]   WTO document WT/DSB/M/116 (dated 31 January 2002).

this point was necessary in order to decide whether any WTO-inconsistent agricultural subsidies had been granted by the Canadian authorities. Nonetheless, the first compliance panel was of the view that:

> Article 9.1(c) of the *Agreement on Agriculture* does not expressly identify any standard for determining when a measure involves 'payments' in the form of payments-in-kind. The absence of an express standard in Article 9.1(c) may be contrasted with several other provisions involving export subsidies which do provide an express standard.[54]

Although Article 9.1(c) of the Agreement on Agriculture clearly lacked a detailed standard by which to determine 'when a measure involves "payments" in the form of payment in kind', Canada could not rely on what may be regarded as a 'liberty principle' that would favour the free market principle in setting the prices of commercial export milk. In this case, the Article 21.5 panel went ahead to construct the applicable standard by reading Article 9.1(c) in the light of other relevant provisions of the same agreement. A lacuna was thus avoided by adopting a balanced approach to the interpretation of the Agreement on Agriculture. Canada's submission regarding the non-regulation of export prices as justification for the alleged illegal subsidies was unsuccessful. In this regard Canada was unable to demonstrate that, pursuant to the provision of Article 9.1(c), payments were not made to its domestic farmers.[55]

In constructivist terms, the specific provisions of the Agreement on Agriculture at issue in this case clearly gave rise to expectations that both the complainants and the respondent had relied upon. As framed by constructivism, ideas and norms remain the *modus operandi* in interstate intercourse, inasmuch as there continue to be difficulties in creating a comprehensive international agreement able to respond to every type of situation. In this regard, constructivist discourse may arguably be an appropriate approach to situations where states are confronted with a conflict of liberties. It has been strenuously argued that constructivism may, in general terms, provide a clearer understanding of pertinent international relations issues, such as conflict arising from individual state interests and power.[56] Constructivism provides an important means of clarifying

---

[54]   See *Canada – Measures Affecting the Importation of Milk and the Exportation of Dairy Products*, WT/DS103/AB/RW, WT/DS113/AB/RW, at para. 75.
[55]   Ibid., paras. 12–24.
[56]   On this issue, see an earlier writing by Ted Hopf, 'The Promise of Constructivism in International Relations Theory', *International Security (IS)*, Vol. 23, No. 1 (1998), pp. 171–200. See also Jutta Brunnée and Stephen Toope, 'International Law and Constructivism: Elements of an Interactional Theory of

the link between individual vested interests and power. This clarification is a linchpin in the discussion on international institutional norms and compliance. As can be deduced from the compliance panel report in the *Canada – Dairy* case discussed above, international courts and tribunals have largely been in favour of this constructivist approach. The rights and obligations of states are, arguably, not determined from abstract presumptions based on traditional sovereignty but rather by equitable balancing.

This approach is not unique to the WTO DSB. For instance, in responding to a request by Libya and Tunisia on the international law principles applicable to the delimitation of maritime boundaries, the ICJ in the *Tunisia – Libya* case observed that '[the Court] . . . is bound to apply equitable principles as part of international law, and to balance up the various considerations which it regards as relevant in order to produce an equitable result'.[57] This same approach can be seen in cases going beyond maritime boundary delimitation as was reiterated by the ICJ in the frontier dispute between Burkina Faso and Mali.[58] The *Rann of Kutch Arbitration* also confirmed that equity is an element of international law that parties may rely on in their relations with one another.[59] Furthermore, in international trade law phrases such as 'equitable competition'[60] and 'equitable share of the market'[61] are commonly used.

International Law', *CJTL*, Vol. 39 No. 1 (2000); Zehfuss Maja, *Constructivism in International Relations: The Politics of Reality* (Cambridge University Press, 2002).

[57] Continental Shelf Case (*Tunisia v. Libya*), ICJ Reports 1982, 18. The ICJ further observed here that '[t]he result of the application of equitable principles must be equitable . . . The equitableness of a principle must be assessed in the light of its usefulness for the purpose of arriving at an equitable result.' ICJ Reports 1982, p. 59.

[58] Frontier dispute case (*Burkina Faso v. Mali*) ICJ Reports 1986, pp. 567–568. In this case, the Chamber of the ICJ concur that the application of equity *infra legem* is not only limited to cases involving maritime delimitation but may also be applied with regard to other kinds of dispute including terrestrial disputes.

[59] *Rann of Kutch Arbitration* 50 ILR (1968) 2. However, an international tribunal will have a wider power to adjudicate *ex aequo et bono* where such power has been conferred on it by agreement between the disputing parties. See in this regard the views of the arbitrators in *AMCO v. Indonesia* 89 ILR 365.

[60] This phrase is used in connection with the freedom of competition of firms based on 'international harmonisation' of standards that would normally affect/influence the cost of production. See Walter Goode, *Dictionary of Trade Policy Terms* (Cambridge University Press, 4th ed., 2003), p. 122.

[61] This phrase is used in WTO law in connection with the level of subsidies to primary products that is legally permitted. Article XVI:3 of GATT defines the condition on which such subsidies is acceptable. See *ibid.*, p. 123 and Article XVI:3 of GATT. The notion of equity is sometimes used in combination with the doctrine of estoppel (equitable estoppel). However, it is important to point out here that the

Further use of the 'liberty principle'[62] may be illustrated by reference to the law of the WTO. The WTO Agreement on Antidumping (the 'AD Agreement') is a case in point here. It amounts to a sort of scheme of deference to WTO members. This is evidenced by the fact that its Article 17.6(ii) does not require WTO members to put in place a specific and identical antidumping mechanism but makes it incumbent upon each state to 'adopt the principles which it regards as best and most suitable'[63] to comply with its international obligations stemming from the AD Agreement.

It is possible to identify two interpretative methodologies at work in the AB's case law with respect to the rights conveyed by the AD Agreement. The rights of national authorities under its Article 17.6(ii) are of particular relevance here. In *US – Hot-Rolled Steel*, the AB stated that:

> [the] second sentence of Article 17.6(ii) *presupposes* that application of the rules of treaty interpretation in Articles 31 and 32 of the *Vienna Convention* could give rise to, at least, two interpretations of some provisions of the *Anti-dumping Agreement*, which, under that Convention, would both be '*permissible* interpretations'. In that event, a measure is deemed to be in conformity with the *Anti-Dumping Agreement* 'if it rests upon one of those permissible interpretations'.[64]

It is clear from the AB's review here that the choice of the applicable interpretative methodology rests upon whether such an approach is in line with Articles 31 and 32 of the VCLT. Consequently, if the text as required by Article 31 of the VCLT does not rule out a particular interpretative methodology, the national authorities arguably have the discretion to use it.[65] A great deal of controversy surrounds the meaning of Article

---

AB has rejected estoppel as a principle applicable in WTO law. See, for instance, the Appellate Body Report in *EC – Export Subsidies on Sugar*, paras. 310 and 312.

[62]   On this issue, see Koskenniemi (2005), pp. 258–272, in the context of international law generally.

[63]   See the PCIJ's decision in the *Lotus* case, PCIJ 1927 (Ser. A) No. 10, p. 18.

[64]   Appellate Body Report, *United States – Anti-Dumping Measures on Certain Hot-Rolled Steel Products from Japan*, WT/DS184/AB/R, para. 59 (adopted 23 August 2001). See also Panel Report, *United States – Anti-Dumping and Countervailing Measures on Steel Plate from India*, WT/DS206/R, para. 7.5-6 (adopted 29 July 2002); Panel Report, *Argentina – Definitive Anti-Dumping Duties on Poultry from Brazil*, WT/DS241/R, paras. 7.45–7.47 (adopted 19 May 2003); Appellate Body Report, *United States – Final Dumping Determination on Softwood Lumber from Canada*, Recourse to Article 21.5 of the DSU by Canada, WT/DS264/AB/RW, para. 123 (adopted 1 September 2006); Panel Report, *United States – Anti-Dumping Administrative Reviews and Other Measures Related to Imports of Certain Orange Juice from Brazil*, WT/DS382/R, paras. 7.126–7.129 (adopted 17 June 2011).

[65]   However, strict application of the principle of effective interpretation leads

17.6(ii) of the AD Agreement. However, it is worth mentioning that despite the divergence of opinion[66] as to the interpretation and the object of Article 17.6(ii), its second sentence[67] requires panels to demonstrate sufficient deference to the decisions of national authorities.

In spite of some very critical views,[68] the special standard of review for antidumping measures implies that national authorities may adopt either of the two interpretative methodologies so long as such interpretation is in line with customary rules of interpretation and remains consistent with the text of Article 17.6(ii). This approach appears to be in line with the case law of the PCIJ[69] and to some extent, contrary to that of the ICJ.[70] With regard to the former, in the *S.S. Lotus* case[71] the PCIJ took an interpretative approach which has divided academic scholarship over the years.[72] It

---

to a slightly different conclusion. On this issue, see the Appellate Body Report in *EC – Asbestos*, WT/135/AB/R, para. 115. Referring to Article 17.6(ii) of the AD Agreement, the AB observed as follows: 'The principles of interpretation that are set out in Articles 31 and 32 are to be followed in a holistic fashion. The interpretative exercise is engaged so as to yield an interpretation that is harmonious and coherent and fits comfortably in the treaty as a whole so as to render the treaty provision legally effective.' Appellate Body Report *United States – Continued Existence and Application of Zeroing Methodology*, WT/DS350/AB/R, para. 268 (adopted 19 February 2009).

[66]   See, for instance, James P. Durling, 'Deference, But Only When Due: WTO Review of Anti-Dumping Measures', *JIEL*, Vol. 7, No. 1 (2003), pp. 125–53; John Greenwald, 'WTO Dispute Settlement: an Exercise in Trade Law Legislation?', *JIEL*, Vol. 7, No.1 (2003), pp. 113–24.

[67]   It reads as follows: 'Where the panel finds that a relevant provision of the Agreement admits of more than one permissible interpretation, the panel shall find the authorities' measure to be in conformity with the Agreement if it rests upon one of those permissible interpretations'. In 2002, the US Senate Finance Committee accused the WTO panels of 'ignoring their obligation to afford an appropriate level of deference to national authorities'. See the Bipartisan Trade Promotion Authority Act of 2002 Report, Senate Finance Committee, S. Rep. No. 107-139, at section III.1 (2002).

[68]   See in this case Daniel K. Tarullo, 'The Hidden Costs of International Dispute Settlement: WTO Review of Domestic Anti-Dumping Decisions', *Law and Policy in International Business*, Vol. 34, 109, 118 (2002).

[69]   The most important of which being the PCIJ report in the *S.S. Lotus* case.

[70]   See for instance the ICJ report in the *Legality of the Threat or Use of Nuclear Weapons*, Advisory Opinion, 1996 ICJ 226, 238–39 (8 July); Military and Paramilitary Activities (*Nicaragua v. United States*), 1986 ICJ, 14, 24 (27 June); North Sea Continental Shelf (*Federal Republic of Germany v. Denmark, Federal Republic of Germany v. The Netherlands*), 1969 ICJ. 3, 44 (20 February 1969).

[71]   S.S. Lotus (*France v. Turkey*), 1927 PCIJ (ser. A) No. 10 (7 September 1927).

[72]   For instance, Henkin has termed the PCIJ's judgment in the *Lotus* case 'one

observed that '[r]estrictions upon the independence of States cannot . . . be presumed . . . [in this regard], the first and foremost restriction imposed by international law upon a state is that – failing the existence of a permissive rule to the contrary – it may not exercise its power in any form'[73] within the jurisdiction of another state.

Some international law scholars have taken this principle to mean that everything that is not prohibited by an express international rule is permitted.[74] In the context of WTO law, this interpretation assumes that if any of the WTO covered agreements, such as the Agreement on Agriculture or the AD Agreement, appears open on a particular issue, policy choices on those issues 'remain available to Member States'[75] to enhance national trade subject to express textual constraints. While this approach appeals to the admirers of the *Lotus* principle, it is, however, inconsistent with conventional practice on the basis of excessive reliance on states' discretion.

Nevertheless, if we subscribe to the view that the paradigms in international relations shift over time, it is inconceivable to imagine that any international trade agreement will be comprehensive enough to cover the least foreseeable trade issues.[76] Because of the principle of non-violation and situation complaints ingrained in the WTO treaty system, WTO members may only have limited choices to impose certain trade restrictive measures in a justifiable manner not contrary to the text of the treaty.

It can be seen from the examples discussed above that conflict between

---

of the landmarks of twentieth-century jurisprudence', Louis Henkin, 'International Law: Politics, Values and Functions', *Recueil des Cours*, 216, 9 (1989 IV), p. 278. And in Lauterpacht's view, the decision 'forms a mind of valuable material upon the subject of Jurisdiction', 1 *Oppenheim's International Law*, p. 270, footnote 2 (Hersch Lauterpacht edition, 1937). See also Bin Cheng, *General Principles of Law as Applied by International Courts and Tribunals*, 29 (1953). On the other hand, in disapproving the decision in the *Lotus* case, Ian Brownlie observed that '[i]n most respects the judgment of the Court is unhelpful in its approach to the principles of jurisdiction, and its pronouncements are characterized by vagueness and generality'. Brownlie (2008), p. 302.

[73]   PCIJ 1927 (Ser. A) No. 10, p. 18.

[74]   On this view, see Roger P. Alford, 'Reflections on *US – Zeroing*: A Study in Judicial Overreaching by the WTO Appellate Body', *Columbia Journal of Transnational Law*, Vol. 45 (2006), pp. 196, 203; Yuval Shany, 'Toward a General Margin of Appreciation Doctrine in International Law?', *EJIL*, Vol. 16 (2005), pp. 907, 912.

[75]   Ibid., p. 202.

[76]   For a note on the changing fundamentals of international law, see Jackson, 'State of International Economic Law – 2005: The Changing Fundamentals of International Law and Ten Years of the WTO', *JIEL*, Vol. 8, No. 1 (2005), pp. 3–15.

the multiple liberties of states may be better resolved by invoking the constructivist principle. For example, while Article XX of GATT clearly permits WTO members to deviate from general obligations arising from their market access commitments under the WTO treaty, such measures must not unnecessarily infringe the rights of other WTO members. In other words, the measure at issue must be necessary to achieve a particular legitimate objective. And, a measure may only be considered as 'necessary' when it is beyond any stretch of imagination that the defending member may achieve the same objective using a measure that is either consistent with GATT or at least less restrictive in scope.[77] In this respect, if conventional norms lack clarity, both parties may interpret them as being either permissible or prohibitory. Thus, only a balancing approach, as suggested by constructivism, can clearly determine the rights and duties of the disputing states. In international relations, it is arguably not sovereignty alone that determines the rights and duties of states, but it is those rights and duties that determine the extent of state sovereignty.

4.3 REPUTATION COSTS AS ESSENTIAL TOOL TO ENHANCE COMPLIANCE WITH INTERNATIONAL TRADE RULES

Because of the scepticism with the effectiveness of formal remedies in international conventions, a growing number of international relations and legal scholarships have for a long time seen reputation cost as germane in how a country behaves *vis-à-vis* its international obligations.[78] The fear of exclusion from future treaties as a price a state pays for non-compliance according to rational choice theory will be enough to deter a state from violating its international obligations. Moreover, reputation cost is an important instrument in ensuring the legitimacy of behaviour or actions of nation-states at the international arena.

---

[77] See Appellate Body Report in *EC – Asbestos*, paras. 171–2.
[78] See Robert E. Keohane, 'International Relation and International Law: Interests, Reputation, Institutions, American Society of International Law', *ASIL* (1999), pp. 375–9; George W. Downs and Michael A. Jones, 'Reputation, Compliance and International Law', *Journal of Legal Studies (JLS)*, Vol. XXXI (2002), pp. 95–114; Jack L. Goldsmith and Eric A. Posner, *The Limits of International Law* (Oxford University Press, 2005); Andrew T. Guzman, 'Reputation and International Law', *Georgia Journal of International and Comparative Law*, Vol. 34 (2006), pp. 379–92; Andrew T. Guzman, *How International Law Works* (Oxford University Press, 2008); Kristina Daugirdas, 'Reputation and the Responsibility of International Organizations', *EJIL*, Vol. 25, No. 4 (2015), pp. 991–1018.

In the context of the WTO, the importance of reputation costs as instruments to enhance compliance cannot be underestimated. The effects of a particular non-compliance with obligations under the WTO may from the outset be seen as only detrimental to the interests of a particular respondent(s) in a case. However, in spite of the fact that a particular dispute in question concerns only two genuine players – complainant(s) and respondent(s) – the overall effect of non-compliance by either of the two parties on the legitimacy of the WTO as a regime is very important.[79] Moreover, unlike other international law obligations of states, the effects of a violation of particular WTO rules are felt by individuals as well as business enterprises in members' jurisdictions.[80] At present, the fact that remedies are prospective in nature creates an incentive to delay compliance by inventing circumstances that will encourage a member against whom non-compliance is effected to go for panel or AB Article 21.5 compliance proceedings. In situations where a threat of retaliation fails to induce compliance, countermeasures will be seen more as a status quo rather than the remedy of last resort. This is, indeed, notwithstanding the fact that the primary aim of remedies under the WTO is to ensure compliance.[81]

Although countermeasures from a rational point of view may be seen as instruments more effective when applied by a more developed economy against a developing country, countermeasures have also in the past proven to be very ineffective between two developed countries.[82] As a consequence, in considering how to enhance the compliance regime of the WTO, it is necessary to assess the relevance of reputation costs as instruments to induce compliance with international trade rules. This chapter is, therefore,

---

[79]   On this, see Carmody ibid. See also Joost Pauwelyn, 'Enforcement and Countermeasures in the WTO: Rules are Rules – Toward a More Collective Approach', 94 *AJIL* (2000), pp. 335–47.

[80]   This concern was raised by a WTO Panel in the first decade of the WTO. In *United States – Sections 301–310 of the Trade Act of 1974*, the panel stated that 'Many of the benefits to Members which are meant to flow as a result of the acceptance of various disciplines under the GATT/WTO depend on the activity of individual economic operators in the national and global market places. The purpose of many of these disciplines, indeed one of the primary objects of the GATT/WTO as a whole, is to produce certain market conditions which would allow this individual activity to flourish'. Panel Report, *United States – Sections 301–310 of the Trade Act of 1974*, WT/DS152/R (adopted 27 January 2000), para. 7.73.

[81]   This is why this volume argues in favour of retroactive calculation of injury and increasing retaliation over time.

[82]   The *EC – Bananas*, the *EC – Hormones* and the *US – FSC* cases are glaring examples where countermeasures have been largely ineffective between two major players.

preoccupied with the value of reputation costs as incentives for compliance with WTO rules. The chapter argues that reputation costs will depend on the following: the size of a state, the way it presents itself in public discourse and the expectations of other WTO members arising from being parties to the WTO agreements. In this regard, it is suggested that even in those situations where respondents/non-compliant WTO members eventually implement an adopted panel or AB report as a consequence of retaliation/threat thereof, reputation costs are still relevant in such compliance. The analyses in this chapter on reputation costs as instruments to improve compliance are innovative in their approach. The analyses differ from previous scholarships on reputation costs because of its focus on the compliance regime of the WTO rather than on the impacts of reputation cost on compliance with international security law or general international law.[83]

From the standpoint of game theory, an international actor's reputation may be viewed in light of its opponent's or adversary's thinking or beliefs about the actor's strategy for compliance in connection with its obligations.[84] The higher the opponent's expectation that the state in question will conform with its obligation arising from international conventions, the greater that state's reputation, and vice versa. In his 1985 seminal work on inter-state cooperation, Joel Sobel discussed in great details the nexus between reliability and reputation costs.[85] We can conceptualise from Sobel's work that because 'reliability can only be communicated through action',[86] it pays for actors to always endeavour

---

[83] On this, see Joel Sobel, 'A Theory of Credibility', *Review of Economics Studies* (RES), Vol. 52, No. 4 (1985), pp. 557–73; Abram Chayes and Antonia Handler Chayes, *The New Sovereignty: Compliance with International Regulatory Agreement* (Cambridge: Harvard University Press, 1995); Thomas M. Frank, *Fairness in International Law and Institutions* (Oxford: Clarendon Press, 1995); Robert E. Keohane, 'International Relation and International Law: Interests, Reputation, Institutions, American Society of International Law', *ASIL* (1999), pp. 375–9; George W. Downs and Michael A. Jones, 'Reputation, Compliance and International Law', *Journal of Legal Studies (JLS)*, Vol. XXXI (2002), pp. 95–114; Jack L. Goldsmith and Eric A. Posner, *The Limits of International Law* (Oxford University Press, 2005); Andrew T. Guzman, 'Reputation and International Law', *Georgia Journal of International and Comparative Law*, Vol. 34 (2006), pp. 379–92; Andrew T. Guzman, *How International Law Works* (Oxford University Press, 2008); Kristina Daugirdas, 'Reputation and the Responsibility of International Organizations', *EJIL*, Vol. 25, No. 4 (2015), pp. 991–1018.
[84] See for instance, Allan Pierre, *Game Theory and International Relations: Preferences, Information and Empirical Evidence* (Aldershot, 1994).
[85] Joel Sobel, 'A Theory of Credibility', *Review of Economics Studies* (RES), Vol. 52, No. 4 (1985), pp. 557–73.
[86] Sobel (1985), p. 557.

to behave in a reliable manner. Reputation is therefore constructed on the basis of consistent reliable behaviour. From this perspective, stakeholders and international actors with a high degree of reliability will arguably be more concerned about their present actions on future behaviour of their opponents. In other words, the more reliable policy- or decision-makers are, the more concerned they will be about the so-called 'shadow of the future'.[87]

With regard to international conventions, the debate on reputation may be carried out from different viewpoints. With regard to the discourse on compliance with international obligations, two significant viewpoints can be vividly identified. In the first place, reputation may be employed by individual governments as a tool to exercise pressure on smaller or less powerful states to obtain compliance. In this respect, reputation will serve more as an instrument to bully weaker international actors. Secondly, reputation may be seen more as a guarantor of compliance with international law. While states may at some points revise their estimates of their opponents' reputation as a response to inconsistent actions of those opponents, reputation in this second instance is continuously seen as an instrument to guarantee compliance with institutional norms. Because reputation which is normally debated at inter-state levels is usually tilted in favour of respecting institutional norms, this approach has been given more emphasis in this book. In spite of the foregoing, reputation costs cannot be considered in isolation from other areas on inter-state relations. For instance, a well-constructed reputation in international trade law will have implications on a particular state's reputation in the area of human rights law, environmental law or law of the sea.[88]

Although it may be very tempting for egoistic states to shy away from their international obligations, reputation costs may hinder such states from acting contrary to an established international law. Such compliance may still happen even when myopic self-interest will advise them to break such international rules.[89] Reputation at the level of world trade law highly depends on a number of factors. Some of these factors include: the political structure of the WTO member involved in the case, the sensitivity and

---

[87]   The so-called shadow of the future was explained by Robert Axelrod in *The Evolution of Cooperation* (New York, 1984).

[88]   This may sound like a deviation from the main thesis advanced here, but on the strength of the argument that China lacks a good human rights record, the US periodically threatened to block its accession to the WTO. This by implication means that in most cases reputation costs rarely exist in isolation.

[89]   Robert Keohane, *After Hegemony: Cooperation and Discord in the World Political Economy* (Princeton University Press, 1984), pp. 106 and 108.

the size of the case in question.[90] Sensitivity sometimes goes with the size of the dispute. A larger case in financial terms tends to be the one with high sensitivity. The combination of size and sensitivity is likely to translate into higher reputation costs for the non-complying WTO member, at least domestically. The level of sensitivity here also depends on the exact nature of the interest groups affected by a particular violation in question – in other words, the importance of the interest group benefitting from continuous non-compliance in relation to, for instance, the future re-election prospects of the government then in power. For instance, in the *US – FSC* case, the US somehow failed to fully implement the DSB report although the level of suspension of concessions was calculated at \$4 billion while the WTO inconsistent measures would only generate about \$2–3 billion in permanent tax savings annually for US exporters.[91] A similar conclusion may be drawn with regard to the *US – Aircraft* dispute.[92]

Nonetheless, it is worth noting that the US took positive steps to comply with the rulings and recommendations of the DSB once the second report

---

[90] Bütler and Hauser's arguments in this direction support the fact that the importance of interest groups and concerns about re-election constitute useful instruments in determining reputation payoffs. See Bütler and Hauser (2000), pp. 509–14.

[91] DSU Article 26/SCM Agreement Article 4.11 Arbitration report, WT/DS108/ARB, paragraph 8.1. See also DSU Article 21.5 report, WT/DS108/RW2 (final report circulated 30 September 2005). Here the panel still found that 'to the extent that the United States, by enacting Section 101 of the Jobs Act, maintains prohibited FSC and ETI subsidies through the transition and grandfathering measures at issue, it continues to fail to implement the operative DSB recommendations and rulings', para. 7.65. The likely explanation for non-implementation here may well be connected to the nature of the interest group supporting the measures taken by the US. This view is also expressed in Bütler and Hauser (2000).

[92] The panel report in this case was circulated on 31 March 2011, and the notice of appeal was filed on 1 April 2011. At the time of writing, the appeal is still ongoing. *United States – Measures Affecting Trade in Large Civil Aircraft (Second Complaint)*, WT/DS353/R. See also Appellate Body Report, *European Communities and Certain Member States – Measures Affecting Trade in Large Civil Aircraft*, WT/DS316/AB/R (adopted 1 June 2011). However, on 1 December 2011 the EU announced its intention to comply with the AB Report in the latter case. See 'statement on the EU compliance report in the WTO Airbus case, by EU Trade Spokesman John Clancy' on the European Commission website at http://ec.europa.eu/trade/news-and-events/news-archive (last visited 20 December 2011). The EU's decision to comply with the AB Report was notified to the WTO on 19 December 2011. See 'EU informs the WTO of its implementation of Airbus rulings' at www.wto.org/english/news_e/news11_e/dsb_19dec11_e.htm (last visited 21 December 2011). The US has, however, made known its lack of satisfaction with the measures taken by the EU to comply with the DSB report.

of Article 21.5 compliance panel was issued.[93] In other words, because there were no immediate elections in prospect,[94] there appears to be very little incentive politically to continue to defend WTO inconsistent measures that were at issue in this case. Although not an exhaustive reason, the administration of the day was in its last term of office at this stage in the case. In this regard, reputation costs internationally were higher than political costs domestically.[95] Moreover, the importance of this reputation cost in the *US – FSC* dispute is demonstrated by the fact that the first appeal against the findings of the panel was withdrawn by the US just before the WTO Ministerial in 1999 in Seattle. Interestingly, when public attention shifted away from the US after the ministerial conference, it reinstated the appeal against the original panel rulings and recommendations. Consequently, the only conclusion we can draw from the action of the US in this case is that given the high public attention on the activities of the US *vis-à-vis* its WTO obligations prior to the Seattle ministerial conference, the reputation cost of maintaining WTO inconsistent measures was higher before the conference and lower after the ministerial conference.

Moreover, it is important to note other aspects in the WTO dispute settlement system that may arguably support our arguments on the relevance of reputation costs to the discourse on compliance with WTO rules. With this in mind, the number of co-complainants or even third parties/participants in a particular case will most likely influence the value of reputation costs in a particular case. The more the number of complainants/co-complainants and third parties/participants in a case, the higher the reputation costs in that particular case.[96] The fact that major

---

[93]   See Appellate Body Report, *United States – Tax Treatment for 'Foreign Sales Corporations'* Second Recourse to Article 21.5 of the DSU by the European Communities, WT/DS108/ABRW2 (adopted 14 March 2006).

[94]   Only the presidential election is referred to in this case.

[95]   This logic may also apply in the context of *United States – Measures Affecting Trade in Large Civil Aircraft (Second Complaint)* WT/DS353/AB/R (adopted 23 March 2012).

[96]   For instance, in *United States – Steel Safeguards*, where there were eight appellants/appellees (Brazil, China, the EC, Japan, Korea, New Zealand, Norway and Switzerland) and seven third participants (Canada, Chinese Taipei, Cuba, Mexico, Thailand, Turkey and Venezuela), the US announced the termination of the WTO inconsistent safeguard measures before the AB Report was even adopted. President Bush announced the withdrawal of the measures on 4 December 2003, while the AB Report was adopted on 10 December 2003. See *United States – Safeguard Measures on Imports of Certain Steel Products*, WT/DS248, 249, 251, 252, 253, 254, 258, 259/AB/R (10 December 2003). The same situation may also hold good in relation to *European Communities – Trade Description of Scallops (EC – Scallops)* where the EC withdrew its measures even before the

economies such as the US, the EU, China, India, and so on, comply with the rulings and recommendations of the DSB without bothering to go through DSU Article 21.5 or 22.6 procedures provides useful justification for this particular reputational costs argument. As has been vividly captured by one of the most informed international economic lawyers, 'even the most powerful entities in the world find it difficult diplomatically to ignore the results of the dispute settlement process, although in some sense, they could get away with it'.[97] The key therefore to this particular reputation cost is the effect non-compliance will have on the member's diplomatic relations.

4.4   THE NATURE OF TREATIES AND REPUTATION COSTS

It is now generally accepted that with regard to reputation costs, signatories to international conventions will normally act differently from non-parties to such conventions. With easy flow of information and public discussion surrounding any multilateral treaty before its entry into force, individuals within domestic constituencies are more likely to oppose any domestic action that would jeopardise the implementation of any such treaty. In other words, by publicising and embedding treaties in core domestic discourse, the reputation costs of any violation are increasingly becoming higher than ever before. Despite scepticism in some academic discourse on the value of reputation costs in sustaining international law, the growing importance of the rules of the global trading system and the nature of non-state actors affected by any breach of WTO rules[98] continue to support the arguments that reputation cost is an essential tool

---

issue of the final reports of the panel. In this case, there were three complainants and six third parties.

[97]   Jackson, *The World Trading System: Law and Policy of International Economic Relations* (Cambridge, 2nd ed., 1997), p. 170.

[98]   See the recognition of this importance by the Panel in *US – Sections 301–310 of the Trade Act of 1974*. In this dispute the panel stated: 'Trade is conducted most often and increasingly by private operators. It is through improved conditions for these private operators that members benefit from WTO disciplines. The denial of benefits to a member which flows from a breach is often indirect and results from the impact of the breach on the market place and the activities of individuals within it. Sections 301–310 themselves recognize this nexus. One of the principal triggers for US action to vindicate US rights under covered agreements is the impact alleged breaches have had on, and the complaint emanating from, individual economic operators,' Panel report para. 7.77. On the link between the WTO

in enhancing compliance with WTO law.[99] As is the general pattern with reputational concern, the agreements that get the most reputational help are those that states value most.[100] As indicated above, multilateral treaties, especially those dealing with issues very sensitive to domestic as well as international audiences, are more valuable in terms of reputation costs than those that are bilateral in nature and contain less sensitive issues. In other words, reputation cost as an instrument to ensure compliance would normally work better in a multilateral treaty such as the WTO than in a bilateral free trade agreement. The simple reason for this is that there are usually more parties in a multilateral treaty and therefore more publicity of a violation of a multilateral treaty than those containing fewer parties.[101] From this analogy, in a majority of cases, one could arguably conclude that the more information citizens[102] have about a particular treaty, the higher the reputation cost for violating such treaty. In view of the foregoing analyses, reputation will continue to be a cornerstone in the global trade rules compliance debate. This is even truer if we factor in the theory of Confucianism as the 'greatest source of normativity'[103] in the way China approaches its WTO obligations.

---

and individual companies in the area of services, see Rolf Adlung, Public Services and the GATS, WTO Secretariat Working paper No. ERSD-2005-03 (July 2005).

[99]   In rather varied perspectives, Qureshi has portrayed the deepening effects of international economic law in different national policies. See Asif H. Qureshi, *Perspectives in International Economic Law* (Kluwer Law International, 2002). On scepticism with the value of reputation costs, see George W. Downs and Michael A. Jones, *JLS* (2002), pp. 94–114; Andrew T. Guzman, *How International Law Works: A Rational Choice Theory* (Oxford University Press, 2008).

[100]   Though often working from different perspectives, some political scientists have tried to put forward this argument in various contexts. See in this case Robert O. Keohane, 'International Relations and International Law: Interests, Reputations and Institutions', *American Society of International Law* (1999), pp. 375–9; George W. Downs and Michael A. Jones, *JLS* (2002), pp. 95–114.

[101]   For further discussion on this, see Andrew Gruzman (Oxford University Press, 2008), p. 72. In line with this reasoning, Gruzman argues that because '[r]etaliation in multilateral agreements often suffers from significant free-rider problems', reputation is even more relevant as an instrument to induce compliance. Ibid., pp. 71–2.

[102]   By citizens here, we mean nationally and internationally.

[103]   See H. Patrick Glenn, *Legal Traditions of the World* (OUP, 5th ed., 2014), p. 320.

PART II

CHINA AND WTO RULES IMPLEMENTATION: CONTEMPORARY POLICY AND DIPLOMACY

5. The Chinese approach to law

The concept of the 'rule of law' has only recently begun to resonate in China, mainly through the country's agreement to settle disputes using the WTO dispute settlement mechanism. Confucian values, identified as the foundation of China's great cultural tradition, have controlled the social order and regulated people in all activities of Chinese daily lives, including the people's legal consciousness, expectations of justice and trust in law. Persuasion and negotiations are a central tenet of Confucian theory. The notion of law in Confucian tradition has over many centuries largely been seen in the context of 'penal and administrative law'.[1] This legal tradition is distinct from the common and civil law of the Western society. This therefore means that with the changing fundamentals of global economic order, the notion of law in a Confucian tradition requires adaptation.

In the eyes of the Chinese and most Asians, 'globalisation' implies the dominance of Western economic and cultural interests over the rest of the world. In the name of globalisation, economic development has reconstructed traditional social norms. Although Western legal systems and thoughts have greatly influenced China, fundamental differences remain. The WTO's dispute settlement system, which is based on the rule of law and can be characterised as rule-oriented, challenges traditional Chinese beliefs. The dispute settlement mechanism under the old GATT regime, which aimed at lowering tensions and defusing conflicts and had a diplomatic orientation, was consistent with the spirit of Chinese culture.

Legalisation has had an impact on the development of the WTO, and also influences the improvement of the WTO's Dispute Settlement Understanding (DSU). At the same time, it presents challenges to the domestic legal systems, social life, cultures and beliefs of some members. China, which has been overwhelmingly influenced by Confucianism for thousands of years, is a good example of this.

From the perspective of legal culture, the trend towards legalism within the WTO means the systemisation of Western ideologies, especially those of the United States. The Chinese regard the US as a litigious society – one

---

[1] See H. Patrick Glenn, *Legal Traditions of the World* (OUP, 5th ed., 2014), p. 326.

that has too many lawyers and pays too much attention to legalism. This legalistic approach is the opposite of the traditional Chinese approach to resolving disputes.[2]

Confucianism provides the basis for the norms of Chinese behaviour, emphasising virtue, modal behaviour, reason, education and the rule of law. The bible of Confucianism, called *Analects*, claims that the ultimate political goal is to create great harmony, where all people behave as brothers. Confucian values, identified as the foundation of China's great cultural tradition, have controlled the social order and regulated people in all their daily activities, including their legal consciousness, expectations of justice and trust in law.[3]

Confucianism emerged more than 2550 years ago,[4] but the idea of law appeared long before that in China. The earliest law dates back to more than 4000 years ago, during the Xia Dynasty, which was the first dynasty in Chinese history. The Chinese legal tradition is distinct from the common law and civil law traditions of the West.[5] The Chinese view the purpose of law as being that of punishment rather than regulation. In ancient time Chinese law primarily meant criminal law. The emphasis on the penal code in Chinese law indicates that civil matters were either ignored entirely or were included in the criminal codes. Ancient Chinese civil codes were few in number, and were not independent of the criminal code.

Confucius's followers regard law as being for uneducated people and not for Confucians.[6] The thinking behind this is that law is unnecessary because traditional Chinese behave themselves properly and preserve social harmony. A well-known proverb describes law as something meant for an ordinary person, but not for a gentleman. A classic saying of Confucius is that a gentleman understands righteousness; an educated

---

[2]   Shin-yi Peng, 'The WTO Legalistic Approach and East Asia: from the Legal Culture Perspective', *Asian-Pacific Law & Policy Journal*, Vol. 13, No. 1 (2000); Perry Keller (ed.), *Chinese Law and Legal Theory* (Ashgate, 2001) 10; Xingzhong Yu, 'Legal Pragmatism in the People's Republic of China', *Journal of Chinese Law*, Vol. 2, No. 3 (1989); Guiguo Wang, *Chinese Law* (Kluwer Law International, 1999); Guiguo Wang, *Law and Punishment: the Western and the Traditional Chinese 'Legal Mind'* (Clarendon Press, 1986).

[3]   Confucius edition, *Analects* (ancient poetry website): http://www.gushiwen. org/guwen/lunyu.aspx (last visited 29 November 2014) (available in Chinese only, author's translation); Brian McKnight, *Law and Order in Sung China* (Cambridge University Press, 1992).

[4]   Wang (1999), p. 11.

[5]   The legal system of China excludes the common law legal system of the Hong Kong Special Administrative Region and the civil legal system of Taiwan.

[6]   Wang (1999), pp. 2–34.

man understands profit. For example, if a party is believed to be in the right, it is better for him to show mercy to the party in the wrong and suffer a little himself. Forbearance is respected in Chinese society and such behaviour was highly praised by Confucius.

Confucians believe that effective management is best achieved through education.[7] They also follow the precept that education prevents bad consequences that might otherwise be inevitable, while law ameliorates what has already happened. Law is an instrument of last resort. The ancient Chinese considered an ideal society to be one that did not require extensive legislation or litigation because traditional Chinese morals were embodied in the ruler, who had responsibility for maintaining this harmony. The term 'a country of rite' originally derives from this belief.

If disputes arose, the granting of mutual concessions by means of consultation or mediation was always encouraged, on the basis that disputes should be dissolved rather than resolved.[8] In China failure to compromise resulted in a lawsuit, which caused both sides to lose and ruined one person's reputation in society. The winning party lost by bringing a lawsuit against the other party for his individual profit, as social harmony should prevail over individual profit. Law is viewed negatively because it is not virtuous to challenge another's rights. This is in sharp contrast to Roman law, the foundation of modern Western law, which regulated the private and economic rights and duties of the individual.

Law meant evil in ancient Chinese.[9] Since ancient China only established criminal law in people's minds, commoners feared law and legal institutions, which were used by their emperors solely to maintain the hierarchical order by punishing criminals and deterring common people from crime. In their view when they violated law, they would be punished by this evil thing. They never thought law could protect their civil interests. Therefore, the modern attitude of subordination and deference to law was unknown in ancient China. Taking this point of view into account makes it easy to appreciate that society was ruled by law rather than existing under the rule of law.

Deep-rooted attitudes to the concept of law in China influenced attitudes towards dispute settlement. Since conflicts are treated as being disruptive to social harmony, Chinese people prefer to resolve their

---

[7] In *Analects* the first thing is to learn. Everything is inferior, but good education is superior. This dominates the ideology of most Chinese people.
[8] Yu (1989), p. 29.
[9] Wang (1999) and (1986).

disputes outside the system of formal justice in order to better preserve social harmony.

As noted above, law was formerly considered as purely punitive in nature, was applied in relation to crime and litigation was regarded as a humiliating process. Because of this legal tradition, most Chinese people still prefer to settle disputes through a flexible, informal, moderate and less confrontational process, by which parties can maintain an amicable relationship.[10]

This unique phenomenon is at the heart of this great oriental civilisation, which has existed for thousands of years. Its utopian-style society has proven attractive to many Asian countries and has served as a standard model to shape oriental culture.

Modern Chinese people still prioritise conflict-free, group-based social interrelationships.[11] Although social and economic changes have been a shock to traditional Chinese perceptions, the 'Great Wall' of Chinese ideology has gained favour among Western countries, particularly after China's entry into the WTO and the dramatic improvement of the Chinese economy. For traditional reasons, China should push for improvement of the rule of law; on the other hand, it should seek to influence the WTO's dispute settlement mechanism through its own unique legal culture, the essence of which is to respect the spirit of legal rulings.

---

[10]   The Chinese social order is renowned for its relationship-driven structure. Confucianism stresses kinship and family. For example, the obligation to support aged or ill parents was a factor taken into account in deciding whether to grant immunity or suspend a sentence in both capital and non-capital cases. An offender's execution could be suspended until after his parents' death if he was their only son. China has been a most family-oriented society throughout its history, and the family is the principal unit of the social and political community. In China the family supports the individual and at the same time the behaviour of individual family members determines the fate of the family. The family's obligations to the individual and the individual's obligations to the family are interdependent, and these mutual obligations serve as an agent of social control.

[11]   Keller (2001).

6. China and WTO law: from accession negotiations to current commitments

6.1 A BRIEF HISTORY OF CHINA'S ACCESSION TO THE WTO[1]

In this section, we discuss the sequence of events with regard to China's bid to join the WTO. The analyses capture the history of China's interaction with the ill-fated ITO and how it sought participation in the GATT and eventual accession to the WTO in 2001. More crucial here is the challenges that China has faced while seeking membership of the WTO.[2] Obviously, these challenges have also shaped the thinking of China on compliance with the global trade rules.

After the Second World War, the United Kingdom and the United States submitted proposals to the Economic and Social Council (ECOSOC) of the United Nations (UN) regarding the establishment of an international trade body that was to be named the International Trade Organization (ITO). In 1946, ECOSOC convened the UN Conference on Trade and Employment to consider the UK and US proposals. A Preparatory Committee drafted the ITO Charter and it was approved in 1948 at the conference in Havana, Cuba. The Charter is often referred to as the Havana Charter or the ITO Charter. The content of the ITO Charter was incorporated into the General Agreement, which was signed in 1947. China signed it on 30 October 1947 and was one of the original contracting

---

[1] 'The Historical Background to China's Accession to the WTO' (baidu, 20 November 2009): http://zhidao.baidu.com/ question/122108930.html (last visited 3 January 2014) (available in Chinese only, author's translation).

[2] See Shaoguang Wang, 'The Social and Political Implications of China's WTO Membership', *Journal of Contemporary China*, Vol. 9, No. 25 (2000), pp. 373–405; Thomas Rumbaugh and Nicolas Blancher, *China: International Trade and WTO Accession*, IMF Working Paper, No. WT/04/36 (2004); Karen Halverson Cross, 'China's WTO Accession: Economic, Legal, and Political Implications', *Boston College International and Comparative Law Review (BCICLR)*, Vol. 27, No. 2 (2004), pp. 319–70.

parties. On 21 April 1948 China ratified the Protocol on Provisional Application and formally became one of the original contracting parties.

On 6 March 1950, the Taiwanese authorities, in the name of 'the Republic of China' as the 'Permanent Representative of the United Nations' notified the UN Secretary General of its withdrawal from GATT.[3] In November 1982, China attended the 36th Session of the Contracting Parties to GATT after 32 years of absence. At this conference, issues relating to the participation of China in GATT were discussed. On 31 December 1982, the State Council approved the report on China's participation in GATT.

On 10 July 1986, the Chinese delegation in Geneva submitted a formal application to restore China's status as a GATT contracting party. A year later on 22 October 1987, the Chinese Working Group on GATT held its first meeting in Geneva to determine its working schedule. Subsequently, on 18 and 19 April 1989, the Chinese Working Group held its 7th meeting in Geneva to complete an assessment of China's foreign trade regime.

During the period between 25 and 28 May 1989, in Beijing, China and the US held the 5th round of bilateral negotiations on the restoration of China's status in respect of GATT. Substantial progress was achieved and the negotiations were expected to be concluded by the end of 1989. During 12–14 December 1989, the Chinese Working Group held its 8th meeting in Geneva to resume its deliberations in respect of China's foreign trade regime.

In October 1991, Chinese Premier Li Peng sent a letter to the heads of all the contracting parties and to the Director General of GATT to clarify the position as to the restoration of China's status in relation to GATT and to stress that it was imperative to hold working meetings immediately in order to begin substantive negotiations on the Protocol. On 10 October 1992, China and the US concluded a 'memorandum of market access' and the US committed to firmly support China to obtain the status of a GATT contracting party. However, it is important to note that as a participant at the GATT Marrakesh ministerial conference from 12–15 April 1994, China signed the final Act of the Marrakesh Agreement Establishing the WTO.

At the end of August 1994, China proposed the revised Schedule of Concession on agriculture, non-agriculture and service. From September to October 1994, a delegation from China headed by Wu Jiahuang, the General Secretary of the Customs, held negotiations on market

---

[3]   The legal status of the People's Republic of China was not recognised by the United Nations until 1971.

accession over a period of 50 days in Geneva. Meanwhile, the Chinese Working Group held its 19th conference in Geneva. At this conference, Gu Yongjiang, the head of the Chinese delegation and the Vice Minister of the Ministry of Foreign Trade, strongly condemned the unreasonable obstruction practised by a few contracting parties, as a result of which the parties failed to reach agreement on GATT negotiations at the meeting.

On 28 November 1994, Long Yongtu, then Assistant Director General of the Ministry of Foreign Trade, met with Peter Sutherland, the then Director General of GATT. Meanwhile, Chinese ambassadors to the United States, the European Community and Japan met with senior officers of their host countries and Chinese ambassadors informed senior officers of the decision about the deadline of GATT negotiations.

From 28 November to 19 December 1994, Long Yongtu led the Chinese delegation in the negotiations with the contracting parties in Geneva on market access and protocols, but these negotiations did not result in an agreement. Furthermore, during 11–13 March 1995, Mickey Kantor, the US Trade Representative, visited China. He was able to reach agreement with Minister Wu Yi on eight items relating to China's accession negotiations on a flexible and pragmatic basis, and agreed China's developing country status to resolve this issue in a pragmatic manner on the basis of the Uruguay Round Agreements.

During 7–19 May 1995, at the invitation of the Chairman of the Working Group on China's GATT issue, Long Yongtu and his delegation participated in informal bilateral consultations, in Geneva, with the contracting parties on the subject of China's restoration as a member of GATT. These were dubbed 'test the water' negotiations by the Western media.

On 3 June 1995, China became an observer of the WTO.

In November 1995, the Chinese government notified WTO Director General Renato Ruggiero of the change of name of the Chinese GATT working group to China's 'accession to the WTO' working group.

On 28 November 1995, the US submitted to the Chinese government an informal document, a so-called 'road map', on China's accession to the WTO, listing 28 requirements relating to China's accession.

On 12 February 1996, China and the US held their 10th bilateral consultations on China's accession. China responded to the US on each individual point listed on its road map.

On 22 March 1996, the first formal conference on China's WTO accession was held. Long Yongtu and his delegation attended the conference and held bilateral consultations with WTO members before and after it.

On 6 August 1997, China and New Zealand reached a bilateral agreement on China's accession in Beijing.

On 26 August 1997, China and South Korea reached a bilateral agreement on China's accession issue in Seoul.

From 13–24 October 1997, Long Yongtu, now Vice Minister of the Ministry of Foreign Trade and Economic Cooperation (MOFTEC), leading a Chinese delegation as Chief Representative for Trade Negotiations of MOFTEC in Geneva, held bilateral consultations with the European Union (EU), Australia, Norway, Brazil, India, Mexico, Chile and 30 other WTO members, and signed bilateral market accession agreements with Hungary, the Czech Republic, Slovakia and Pakistan, and almost concluded negotiations with Chile, Colombia, Argentina and India on China's bilateral market accession.

From 26 October to 2 November 1997, Chinese President Jiang Zemin visited the US. In a joint statement with President Clinton he reaffirmed the aim of accelerating China's 'accession' negotiations to achieve an early conclusion.

From 1–16 November 1997, Chinese Premier Li Peng visited Japan with Vice Minister and chief negotiator Long Yongtu, and issued a joint statement on China's accession to the WTO with Koichi Haraguchi, the Japanese Deputy Foreign Minister. Both sides reaffirmed that they had made significant progress on market access negotiations in respect of the service sector, thus indicating that China and Japan had almost concluded China's bilateral market access negotiations.

On 2 November 1997, high-level Chinese and American trade officials attending the Asia-Pacific Economic Cooperation Organization (APEC) Ministerial Conference exchanged views on China's WTO accession and agreed that the two delegations should intensify their efforts to expeditiously implement the China–US summit joint statement on clarifying the purpose of these negotiations.

From 1–12 December 1997, Long Yongtu attended the sixth conference of the WTO China Working Group in Geneva, reached an understanding on the Protocol and most of the contents of the report and held bilateral consultations with the US, the EU, Japan, Australia, Brazil, Mexico and other countries.

From 28 March to 9 April 1998, the Chinese delegation to the 7th WTO Working Group meeting submitted a tariff concessions table consisting of almost 6000 HS codes, which received a positive assessment from some major players.

On 17 June 1998, during an interview with an American journalist, Jiang Zemin proposed the following three principles for China's accession to the WTO: (1) the WTO is incomplete without China's participation; (2) China will undoubtedly join the WTO as a developing country; (3) balancing rights against obligations is a principle of China's WTO accession.

On 16 November 1998, Jiang Zemin met US Vice President Al Gore at the APEC conference in Kuala Lumpur, where both sides expressed the hope that China and the US could conclude bilateral negotiation in early December. On 27 November 1998, the *People's Daily* published China's chief negotiator Long Yongtu's talk. Long said some people thought that the Chinese government no longer treated the accession to the WTO as a priority, but that this was a misunderstanding. He said that China's accession to the WTO was a case of the sooner the better. On 3 March 1999, Sino-American high-level trade delegations stayed up late negotiating tariff reductions and the further opening of the agriculture, telecommunications, financial and insurance sectors.

On 15 March 1999, at a press conference, Chinese Premier Zhu Rongji noted that China had been engaged in GATT and WTO negotiations for over 13 years and that black hair had turned to grey during that period. He expressed the view that it was time for the negotiations to be concluded and that the opportunity existed to achieve this. Firstly, WTO members acknowledged that there was no representation in the WTO without China's participation, which means it neglected the potentially largest market, China. Secondly, the deepening of China's reform and opening-up policy and its accumulation of experience had brought about understanding of the likely monitoring capacity and affordability in the event of China's accession to the WTO. Consequently, China would make the biggest concessions necessary in order to join the WTO.

From 6–13 April 1999, Premier Zhu Rongji visited the US. On 10 April he signed the Sino-US Agricultural Cooperation Agreement and issued a joint statement on China's accession to the WTO. The US committed to firmly support China's accession to the WTO in 1999.

Furthermore, on 13 April 1999, Premier Zhu Rongji and President Clinton agreed over the phone that the two sides should conduct intensive negotiations to resolve the remaining issues relating to China's accession to the WTO. At the end of April 1999, the US chief negotiator led a delegation to China to continue negotiations on the outstanding issues.

However, because of the accidental bombing of the Chinese Embassy in Yugoslavia on 8 May 1999 by US-led NATO forces, the government of China decided to suspend the negotiations on its WTO accession. This suspension was only short-lived, as China and the US resumed the accession negotiations on 6 September 1999.

Similarly, during the same month in Australia, Jiang Zeming reiterated the three principles of China's accession to the WTO. He stated that negotiations between the two sides should be based on the principles of equality and mutual benefit.

On 11 September 1999, Jiang Zemin and Bill Clinton formally met to discuss China's accession to the WTO at the seventh conference of APEC. Jiang stated that the Chinese government had a positive attitude towards China's accession to the WTO, which was not only a requirement in relation to China's economic development and opening-up policy, but also in relation to the need to build a completely open international trading system. He continued by saying that the Chinese government hoped to conduct negotiations on the basis of equality and mutual benefit and to conclude the agreement as soon as possible. President Clinton explained that the US supported China's early accession to the WTO and that he wished to reach agreement as soon as possible with China. Therefore, he expected that the two sides could make further efforts to this end.

Eventually, on 15 November 1999, the two sides reached an agreement on China's accession. This meant that China and the US had finally concluded their bilateral negotiations. Subsequent bilateral negotiations on China's accession were reached on the following dates with key WTO members:

On 12 April 2000, China and Malaysia reached an agreement on China's accession.

On 16 May 2000, China and Latvia reached an agreement on China's accession.

On 19 May 2000, China and the EU reached an agreement on China's accession.

On 29 May 2000, after friendly and constructive negotiations, China and Switzerland ended their bilateral negotiations on China's accession to the WTO and signed the Sino-Switzerland on China's Accession to WTO Bilateral Agreements.

On 5 June 2001, at a press conference in Shanghai, US Trade Representative Robert Zoellick said China's accession to the WTO was beneficial both to China and to the international trade system. Subsequently that month, the US and China reached a comprehensive agreement to resolve the outstanding issues relating to China's accession to the WTO.

With regard to the bilateral negotiations with the EU, on 20 June 2001, the EU reached a comprehensive agreement with the Chinese government on China's accession to the WTO.

Subsequently in July 2001, Long Yongtu, head of the Chinese delegation, stated that all the major issues concerning China's accession to the WTO had been resolved, and that the WTO members would officially consent to China's WTO accession in November. Thus, China would join the WTO after a 15-year application process.

The only remaining country with substantial issues to negotiate with China was Mexico. However, all these were resolved and on 13 September 2001, China and Mexico concluded their bilateral negotiation on China's accession to the WTO, meaning that China had completed all bilateral negotiations on market accession with WTO members.

From 12–17 September 2001, the 18th conference of the WTO China Working Group held in Geneva adopted multilateral documents on China's accession to the WTO, which had been submitted to the Council for consideration, and finally announced that the work of the Chinese Working Group was at an end.

Consequently, on 10 November 2001, the WTO's Fourth Ministerial Conference held in Doha reviewed and voted on China's accession to the WTO. In this regard, on 11 November 2001, in Doha, the Minister of Ministry of Foreign Trade Shi Guangsheng signed China's WTO Accession Protocol, which specifies China's rights and obligations as a WTO member.[4]

On 20 November 2001, WTO Director General Michael Moore sent letters to the members of the WTO stating that the Chinese government had announced its acceptance of the Protocol on China's Accession to the WTO on 11 November 2001, when the Protocol entered into force and China finally became the 143rd member of the WTO.

6.2 AN ASSESSMENT OF CHINA'S ACCESSION TO THE WTO

6.2.1 Response from International and National Media

After China's accession to the WTO, the global media and political elite, as well as authoritative Chinese publications, gave a positive assessment of China's accession to the WTO. For instance, the *Los Angeles Times* pointed out that China's accession would accelerate its development into an increasingly powerful economic power. It also injected new vitality into the WTO. In a period of global economic slowdown, China was one of the few countries to maintain rapid economic growth and its low-cost labour had made it a major world exporter and trade competitor. The US Trade Representative (USTR) pointed out that China's accession would strengthen the global economy and international trade rules, which was good for American workers, consumers, farmers and exporters alike.[5]

---

[4]   See Karen Halverson Cross, 'China's WTO Accession: Economic, Legal and Political Implication', *BCICLR* (2004), China and the WTO at https://www.wto.org/english/thewto_e/countries_e/china_e.htm (last visited 12 May 2015).

[5]   'European and American media highly valued China's accession to the WTO' (sina, 11 November 2001): http://news.sina.com.cn/w/2001-11-11/397000 htm (accessed 10 January 2014) (available in Chinese only, author's translation).

Spain's *Periòdico Razòn* newspaper stated that China had finally joined the WTO after 15 years, which would not only change the course of the development of China's economy, but would also have an unprecedented impact on the world economy. The paper went on to say that it was a historic milestone which would change the world economy. Spain's *ABC* newspaper published an article stating that China's accession to the WTO would have a profound impact on the global economic outlook since it meant that 1.3 billion people had joined on the same day. *El Pais* expressed the view that China had a huge market to contribute to the WTO and that this would help revitalise the world economy following the 11 September 2001 terrorist attacks.[6]

Swedish morning paper *Dagens Nyheter* said that China's accession would bring about tremendous change to China, to other WTO members and to the WTO, and that this was therefore an event of great historical significance. Another Swedish newspaper, *Svenska Dagbladet*, pointed out that after the 'Long March', China's accession to the WTO had finally achieved a historic goal.[7]

Italian national television and a number of local television stations broadcast the news about China's accession to the WTO in evening news programmes. On 11 November, the Italian newspapers published head-lines in prominent places on their front pages to this effect. These media reports said that when WTO Director General Mike Moore announced China's accession to the WTO at the podium, long and warm applause and cheers broke out around the meeting room. The applause, the cheers and the scenario not only showed how much the WTO needs China, but also how popular China's accession was.[8]

British newspaper the *Independent* pointed out that China's accession would change China's mode of operation in world trade. All countries welcomed this huge step. The BBC stated that China's accession to the WTO marked the end of 15 years of negotiations by China. It noted that this was a victory following the successful bid for the 2008 Olympics and a milestone event in terms of China's integration into the world.[9]

The *European Times* published an editorial characterising China's accession to the WTO as an opportunity to improve the competitiveness of its industries, attract more international investment and promote sustainable economic development, and that this could be achieved by the

---

[6]   Ibid.
[7]   Ibid.
[8]   Ibid.
[9]   Ibid.

Chinese people themselves relying on their own wisdom and diligence. The editorial stated that healthy growth in the Chinese economy would benefit neighbouring countries and promote the economy of the Asia-Pacific region and the world at large. French economic daily *Les Echos* said that China had officially become a WTO member, which marked it out as a great success in terms of diplomacy and economy.[10]

On 9 November 2001, Agence France-Presse (AFP) reported from Doha that after 15 years of struggle, China had finally become a WTO member state and that this was a historic moment. This would not only strengthen world trade, but also bring about changes in China. AFP also reported French Finance Minister Laurent Fabius, who just concluded a visit to China, as having said that France congratulated China on its accession to the WTO and that the decision to accept its accession was a greatly meaningful one, not only for China but also for the world.[11]

German Chancellor Gerhard Schroeder considered that China's accession to the WTO fulfilled one of Germany's long-cherished desires, and would promote trade in goods and services worldwide.[12]

The then EU Trade Commissioner Pascal Lamy said that against a background of a difficult period for a challenging multilateral trading system, the conclusion of China's accession to the WTO brought 'much-needed confidence' and hope.[13]

Albania's main daily, *Century News*, published an article entitled: 'The world's 142 countries and territories welcome China's accession to the WTO'. The article stated that China's accession to the WTO was the result of 15 years of effort and potentially opened the largest possible market to the world. Thus 142 members simultaneously congratulated China on its accession. WTO Director General Mike Moore expressed the view that it was a historically great event.[14]

The *People's Daily* of China published an article entitled 'WTO as an opportunity to further expand opening up', which pointed out that China's reform, opening-up policy and modernisation is inevitable. It went on to say that it provides an important opportunity to further promote

---

[10]   Ibid.

[11]   Ibid.

[12]   'Commentary: China's Integration into the World through Accession to the WTO' (sina, 11 November 2001): http://news.sina.com.cn/c/2001-11-11/396793.html (accessed 10 January 2014) (available in Chinese only, author's translation).

[13]   Ibid.

[14]   'European and American media highly valued China's accession to the WTO' (sina, 11 November 2001): http://news.sina.com.cn/w/2001-11-11/397000.htm (accessed 10 January 2014) (available in Chinese only, author's translation).

all-round, multi-level and wide-ranging opening-up in order to boost China's economic development, and that this would have a profound impact. After joining the WTO, China would participate in a greater range and depth of economic globalisation issues. Therefore, accession to the WTO was an opportunity to further accelerate the opening-up process, which was an important part of China's economic future. The article urged all localities, departments and sectors to unify their thinking by reference to the plan laid down by the central government in accordance with the relevant regulations of the WTO. It also noted China's commitment to carefully study and analyse the various impacts accession would have on the country and to propose appropriate measures to seek to open up the markets as well as to protect itself.[15]

The article considered that cadres, especially leading cadres at all levels, must first learn and become familiar with the WTO's basic principles and relevant regulations, as well as China's actual situation, in order to speed up adjusting policies, put in order and amend and abolish some foreign laws and regulations which were both in compliance with WTO rules and in line with the Chinese situation during the transitional period. The article went on to say that it was necessary to change the way in which economic management was conducted by governments in order to enhance the coherence and transparency of policies and to improve competences by reference to international rules. It was necessary to establish an industrial security system in order to speed up the revision and improvement of market access standards relating to quality, sanitation, the prevention of epidemics, environmental protection, security and other matters, and to make full use of antidumping, countervailing and safeguard measures. Companies should develop an increased sense of urgency and competition by accelerating technological innovation and product development, improving quality, improving services and expanding market share during the transition period. It was a requirement to strengthen the popularisation and dissemination of knowledge relating to the WTO and the relevant WTO regulations and to train a team specialising in international economy and law.[16]

It was regarded as important to increase efforts to open as a new starting-point for WTO accession. It was essential to take full advantage of the favourable conditions for accession to the WTO to implement a

---

[15]   'People's Daily Commentator: the WTO as an opportunity to further open up' (sina, 11 November 2001): http://news.sina.com.cn/c/2001-12-11 /416837.html (accessed 10 January 2014) (available in Chinese only, author's translation).
[16]   Ibid.

diversification strategy and increase exports. As well as ensuring that traditional export markets were maintained, it was seen as crucial to actively explore new export markets and vigorously promote market diversification. Continuing to conduct in-depth reform of foreign trade, cultivating new areas of growth for exports and promoting diversification of foreign trade entities were also regarded as being important. This entailed continuing to promote the 'going out' strategy and encouraging qualified domestic companies to invest in overseas projects, engineering projects designed to stimulate the export of domestic equipment, and in materials and labour through foreign investment in order to diversify export mode. Furthermore, it was seen as essential to strengthen energy cooperation with foreign countries and gradually diversify import channels in respect of important strategic materials in accordance with WTO rules and to improve and perfect the system of import management.[17]

In addition, it was felt that China must improve its utilisation of foreign capital following its accession to the WTO. The need to attract foreign capital was linked with domestic industrial upgrading, coordination of local economic development, reformation and reconstruction of state-owned companies and expansion of export. Further improvement of the investment environment, especially the soft environment, was also seen as necessary in order to maintain stability and continuity in investment policy with a view to attracting foreign companies, strengthening intellectual property protection and enhancing China's attractiveness for foreign investment. Active promotion of the flow of foreign high-tech industries was also regarded as necessary, as was encouraging multinational corporations to set up research and development centres and regional headquarters and progressively extending market access in finance, insurance, commerce, tourism, intermediary services and other service sectors. It appeared crucial to study the new situation at hand following the opening-up of the markets, and to solve the new problems that had arisen, in order to achieve healthy and orderly development. China, as a new member of the WTO, would work together with other WTO members to promote the development of the world economy and trade and to establish and improve the multilateral trading system, and would play an active and constructive role.[18]

Accession to the WTO is an opportunity as well as a challenge. China has the confidence, determination and the positive outlook needed to grasp the opportunity before it while calmly dealing with the challenges

---

[17]   Ibid.
[18]   Ibid.

that present themselves. It aims to greet the arrival of a new stage of opening-up, to promote sustainable, healthy and rapid development and to make its own contribution to the development of world trade and economy.[19]

Shi Guangsheng, the head of the Chinese government delegation and Minister of Foreign Trade, considered that full participation in the multilateral trading system and accession to the WTO represented a strategic decision by Chinese leaders in response to the accelerated process of economic globalisation. China had made unremitting efforts in respect of the restoration of the legal status of GATT and its accession to the WTO, which fully demonstrated its determination to deepen its reforms and expand the process of opening-up, as well as its confidence in its ability to achieve this.[20]

In sum, a large number of domestic and international media outlets gave a great deal of positive response to China's 15 years of arduous effort in order to gain accession to the WTO.

6.3   COMMITMENTS OF THE CHINESE GOVERNMENT TO FULFIL CHINA'S OBLIGATIONS[21]

On 1 December 2001 the State Council issued the 'Management of Import and Export Regulations on Goods of the People's Republic of China' and 'Import and Export Ordinance on Technology of the People's Republic of China'. These entered into force on 1 January 2002.

On 9 December 2001, the 'Notice of Related Issues about People's Bank of China on Market Accession for Foreign Financial Institutions' was released. From 11 December 2001, Chinese banks began to fulfil China's accession commitments to the WTO, which involved the full liberalisation of foreign exchange to foreign banks. Similarly, on the same day, the 'Protocol on China's Accession to the WTO' entered into force and China officially became a WTO member.

---

[19]   Ibid.

[20]   'Commentary: China's Integration into the World through Accession to the WTO' (sina, 11 November 2001): http://news.sina.com.cn/c/2001-11-11/396793. html (accessed 10 January 2014) (available in Chinese only, author's translation).

[21]   'A Memorandum on a Decade since China's Accession to the WTO' (mofcom, 22 August 2013): http://sms.mofcom.gov.cn/article/zt_tenth/dsj/2013 08/20130800261406.shtml (accessed 13 January 2014) (available in Chinese only, author's translation).

On 1 January 2002, the Customs Tariff Commission of the State Council promulgated the new Customs Tariff. And later that month, the Textiles Monitoring Body (TMB) of the WTO held its 86th meeting to consider a notice on textile and apparel imports to retain the use of transitional safeguard measures submitted by China. The participating members had no objection to this notice.

On 1 February 2002, the Regulation on Foreign Financial Institutions in China and the Regulation on Chinese Financial Institutions entered into force.

As a consequence of its accession, on 30 June 2002, China opened its markets for trade in services to the US, Canada, Japan, the EU and 23 other WTO members. In order to ensure efficient implementation of WTO commitments, the Ministry of Trade and Economic Cooperation was formally replaced with the Ministry of Commerce in March 2003.

On 1 July 2004, 'Foreign Trade Law Amendments' and 'Registration Measures for Foreign Trade Operators' were officially announced six months ahead of schedule. And as from 11 December 2004, foreign investment into basic telecommunication services was permitted. The retail market for refined oil was opened to foreign investment.

On 1 January 2005, Chinese agricultural tariffs were reduced from the pre-accession level of 23.2 per cent to 15.35 per cent, which fulfilled its WTO commitment. On the same day, China abolished the quota licensing system for imported cars and implemented an automatic import licence administration for automotive products, while the level of tariffs on imported cars dropped to 30 per cent. Therefore, Chinese commitments on the abolition of non-tariff measures were fulfilled.

In November 2006, China released revised 'Regulations of Foreign Banks in the PRC'. As from 11 December 2006 foreign banks were granted national treatment.

On 29 November 2007, China formally submitted to the WTO 'the ratification of the Modification of the Agreement on Trade-Related Intellectual Property Rights' in order to obtain rights to copy and export patented medicines.

On 28 December 2007, the Chinese government signed 'the Application of China's Accession to the Agreement on Government Procurement (GPA) of the WTO'.

During 21–23 May 2008, the second trade policy review for China was held at the WTO headquarters in Geneva, Switzerland.

On 1 January 2010, after reducing import tariffs on fresh strawberries and six other goods, China fulfilled all its concessional obligations on import tariffs.

7. China and the WTO dispute settlement system

Following China's accession to the WTO, most expected that there would be a great number of disputes involving China. In the first few years of joining the WTO, China's participation in disputes was mostly as a third party/participant. It was not until 2008 that China started participating effectively in the WTO dispute settlement process. This chapter, therefore, discusses the practice of China in the WTO dispute settlement system in line with China's approach to the discourse on international rules compliance.

7.1 CHINESE PRACTICE WITHIN THE WTO DISPUTE SETTLEMENT FRAMEWORK

This section addresses China's status and performance in relation to the dispute settlement mechanism through empirical analysis. Official WTO statistics show that as of 31 December 2014, China was involved in 12 cases as a complainant, 32 cases as a defendant and 114 cases as a third party. Case analyses related to China reflect improvement in Chinese practice and attitudes within the WTO dispute settlement framework. Background information indicates how China faced the challenge of compliance from legal, political and economic perspectives.

7.1.1 An Astonishing Beginning as a Complainant

China, as an ancient civilised nation in East Asia, has always been characterised by subtle and restrained features which are known to the world. It had been predicted that China would be a defendant in the first case in which it was involved following its accession to the WTO, but the result was arguably surprising.

In June 2001, US President George W. Bush, prompted by the US steel industry, asked the United States International Trade Commission (USITC) to investigate imports of steel products by reference to Section 201 of the Trade Act of 1974. On 28 June 2001, the USITC decided to hear this case after the investigation had been concluded. The Chinese government expressed serious concern, made an effort to safeguard the legitimate rights and interests of the Chinese steel industry, and paid close attention to the progress of events. On 24 July 2001, China hired an American lawyer on behalf of the Chinese Iron and Steel Association and the Chinese Import and Export Chamber of Commerce on Minmetals Chemicals. This lawyer submitted to the USITC an application in respect of the investigation under Section 201 as well as an application to secure the confidentiality of production data belonging to the companies involved. These applications were submitted on time to ensure that the steel industry could fully participate in the subsequent proceedings and effectively defend their legitimate rights and interests in these proceedings. The USITC's decision in this matter was released in October 2001, and confirmed that a total of 16 imported steel products had caused serious damage to US companies. Pursuant to Section 201 of the Trade Act of 1974, it recommended raising import tariffs on steel in order to protect the US steel industry. On 26 February 2002, the US President announced that the US would be taking safeguard measures in respect of 10 items of imported steel over a three-year period. Tariffs of up to 30 per cent were levied. The Chinese government issued a statement to the effect that the US government's decision would have a serious impact on normal exports made by China's steel companies to the US and would cause them to suffer huge losses. The Chinese government expressed its strong dissatisfaction, and stated that the problems faced by the US steel industry at that time should not be attributed to foreign imports. It argued that the export of Chinese steel products to the US was not enough to constitute injury or threat thereof to US steel companies, and opined that the US government's decision was not consistent with WTO rules. The Chinese government went on to say that it reserved the right to file a complaint under the WTO's dispute settlement mechanism.[1]

On 7, 20 and 26 March, 3 and 4 April, and 14 and 21 May 2002, the EU, Japan, Korea, China, Switzerland, Norway, New Zealand and Brazil requested consultations with the US.[2]

On 14 March 2002, the Chinese government, in line with the relevant

---

[1] 'China's First Case in front of the WTO – Safeguard Measures on Imports from the US' (china, 23 June 2003): http://www.china.com.cn/zhuanti2005/txt/2003-06/23/content_5351822.htm (accessed 18 January 2014) (available in Chinese only, author's translation).

[2] 'WT/DS252, United States – Definitive Safeguard Measures on Imports of Certain Steel Products' (WTO, 24 February 2010): http://www.wto.org/english/tratop_e/dispu_e/cases_e/ds252_e.htm (accessed 28 January 2014).

provisions of WTO safeguard measures, consulted with the US regarding the Section 201 steel safeguard measures. The Chinese government issued a statement that the US, as one of the world's major trading nations, bore a heavy responsibility for the maintenance of the international trade order and should fully take into account the significant damage it had caused to the international trade order. The statement continued by saying that the problems faced by the US steel industry could not be attributed to foreign imports, but were caused by the irrational structure of the industry. Protectionist measures would only hinder the beneficial adjustment of this structure rather than solve the problem. Moreover, the Chinese steel products involved accounted for a small proportion of the US imports of similar products, and no serious damage had been caused to the US steel industry. China demanded that the US should become fully aware of the specific situation in China and properly resolve the issue, stating that China and the US are important trade partners and that the two countries have great economic complementarity. China hoped to resolve the problem through bilateral consultations as soon as possible so as to avoid damaging China–US economic and trade relations.[3]

On 22 March 2002, China and the US engaged in consultations in Washington. The Chinese delegation stated that the US was in violation of a solemn statement in respect of the WTO Agreement and asked the US government to face the fact that China is a developing country. In addition, the Chinese delegation raised trade compensation requirements and reserved the right to take further measures under the WTO Agreement.[4]

On 11 and 12 April 2002, China, the EU, Japan, South Korea, Switzerland and Norway consulted with the US under the DSU with regard to the steel safeguard measures in Geneva. The six parties expressed regret that the US had violated the relevant WTO provisions, imposed protectionist safeguard measures and required the US to terminate its measures immediately. The Chinese delegation expounded China's position, focusing on Chinese interests. Following the consultation, the six parties issued a joint press statement.[5]

---

[3]   'China's First Case in front of the WTO – Safeguard Measures on Imports from the US' (china, 23 June 2003): http://www.china.com.cn/zhuanti2005/txt/2003-06/23/content_5351822.htm (accessed 18 January 2014) (available in Chinese only, author's translation).

[4]   Ibid. See also 'WT/DS252 United States – Definitive Safeguard Measures on Imports of Certain Steel Products' (WTO, 24 February 2010): http://www.wto.org/english/tratop_e/dispu_e/cases_e/ds252_e.htm (accessed 28 January 2014).

[5]   'Chinese First Case in front of the WTO – Safeguard Measures on Imports from the US' (china, 23 June 2003): http://www.china.com.cn/zhuanti2005/

The Chinese government had already undertaken formal bilateral consultation with the US under the dispute settlement mechanism on safeguard measures in accordance with the relevant provisions of the WTO, but the US did not give a clear answer with regard to Chinese requirements relating to compensation and exclusion. In line with the WTO procedure, on 17 May 2003, the Chinese delegation submitted to the WTO Council of Trade in Goods a list of products exported by the US in respect of which concessions were to be suspended, including waste oil, soybean oil and electric compressors. After the Dispute Settlement Body (DSB) eventually ruled that the US had violated the relevant WTO agreements, China imposed an additional 24 per cent tariff, amounting in total to a sum of $94 million.[6]

Because the consultation did not resolve the dispute, on 25 July 2002 the DSB agreed to establish a panel to hear the case and appointed the panellists. On 11 July 2003 the panel report, which contained the finding that the US safeguard measures were inconsistent with WTO agreements, was circulated. On 11 August the US filed an appeal and China also subsequently filed a conditional appeal. On 10 November the Appellate Body's report supported the plaintiffs' claims. On 4 December, the US President signed a presidential decree which announced the termination of safeguard measures as from 5 December. On 10 December the DSB adopted the panel and Appellate Body reports.[7]

China successfully participated in the whole process. The EU and Japan were also involved in this case as complainants, along with five other longstanding member states. China completed all the work necessary to cooperate with various parties in the process of the dispute. During the trial stage of the panel, the written submissions amounted to 2500 pages with 3500 pages of attachments. The complainants held several meetings to clarify their position and views, and were represented by a cast of over 100 at the first hearing. Interestingly, EU officials noted that China had learned from the EU in filing this case, and would therefore know how to deal with the EU in future. Chinese officials from the Ministry of Commerce also admitted that learning by doing and gaining experience had sharpened their talents.[8]

As the first case was brought by China, it was predicted that China

---

txt/2003-06/23/content_5351822.htm (accessed 18 January 2014) (available in Chinese only, author's translation).

[6] Ibid.

[7] 'WTO/DS252, United States – Definitive Safeguard Measures on Imports of Certain Steel Products' (WTO, 24 February 2010): http://www.wto.org/english/tratop_e/dispu_e/cases_e/ds252_e.htm (accessed 28 January 2014).

[8] Zhenyu Sun (oral), GuohuaYang and Xiaoli Shi (organise), *Geneva Time*

would file more and more cases against other member states as well as be the subject of proceedings brought by them.

7.1.2   A Diplomat Within the First Five Years

It has always been predicted that there would be many cases against China as a member of the WTO, especially because of the size of its market. More importantly here is also the fact that China is a centrally planned economy with businesses inextricably linked to the state.[9]

7.1.2.1   A predictable dispute
The *Value-Added Tax on Integrated Circuits* case was the first case featuring China as a respondent after it joined the WTO. On 24 June 2000 the State Council issued No. 18 Document entitled 'A Number of Policies to Encourage the Development of Software Industry and Integrated Circuit Industry'. Its purpose was to motivate general payers of value-added tax (VAT) to sell their integrated circuit products with silicon wafers included. Prior to 2010, when the statutory VAT rate was 17 per cent, the Chinese government's practice was to refund the tax once the actual tax burden had reached more than 6 per cent for researching, developing new integrated circuits and expanding reproduction. In order to encourage production in China, the government refunded 14 per cent of the tax (China imposed 17 per cent VAT for all semiconductor products) to manufacturers designing and producing chips in China, but imports could not benefit from this preferential policy.[10] US chip makers expressed the view that the semiconductor industry had always been a very competitive and price-sensitive field. The Chinese government adopted policies to refund domestic chip manufacturers, giving them a tremendous advantage in international competition. US officials claimed that this violated the WTO rules on the prohibition of preferential treatment of domestic manufacturers and thus constituted discrimination.[11]

Flies – Oral Record from First Ambassador of China to the WTO Sun Zhenyu (People Press, 2011), pp. 41–2 (available in Chinese only, author's translation).

[9]   See Paolo David Farah, 'Five Years of China WTO Membership: EU and US Perspectives about China's Compliance with Transparency Commitments and the Transitional Review Mechanism', *Legal Issues of Economic Integration (LIEI)*, Vol. 33, No. 3 (2006) pp. 263–304.

[10]   'DS309 China – Value-Added Tax on Integrated Circuits' (Chinalawinfo, 6 October 2005): http://www.chinalawinfo.com/wto/wtojdaldetail.asp?jdalid=26 (accessed 17 February 2014).

[11]   'The US Launched an Attack on VAT Levied on Semiconductors after China's Accession to the WTO' (sina, 20 March 2004): http://news.sina.com.

Formal consultations between China and the US began in 2003. USTR Robert Zoellick repeatedly brought up the problem of chip rebates during the assessment procedure in respect of China's accession to the WTO. This attracted the attention of the Chinese government. The Ministry of Finance, the Internal Revenue Service, the Ministry of Commerce and six other ministries set up a research group to study mechanisms for the protection of the chip industry without violating WTO rules.[12]

In 2003, China's trade surplus against the US stood at a record \$124 billion. The Bush administration faced continuous pressure from Congress and players in the domestic industry, who asked the US government to respond to what they perceived as unfair trade practices on the part of China.[13]

On 18 March 2004 the US suddenly filed a claim with the WTO, accusing China of imposing discriminatory tariffs on imported semiconductors in a manner inconsistent with WTO rules and which undermined the interests of the US semiconductor industry. The US focused particularly on six documents of the State Council and ministries. The US argued that these measures violated obligations under the Chinese Protocol of Accession, Articles I and III of GATT 1994, and Article 17 of the General Agreement on Trade in Services (GATS) in violation of the most favoured nation (MFN) principle and national treatment under the WTO.[14]

China's ambassador to the WTO, Sun Zhenyu, disclosed that the relevant agencies of the two countries had been negotiating on the matter and had made some progress. While such negotiation was still ongoing between the two countries, the US made a request for consultations. In respect of the treatment of rebates China initially proposed that Chinese and American companies enjoyed equal treatment and the same export

---

cn/o/2004-03-20/09102095221s.shtml (accessed 17 February 2014) (available in Chinese only, author's translation).

[12] 'Sino-US Chip Dispute: A Litigation without Suspense' (sina, 30 July 2004): http://finance.sina.com.cn/b/20040730/1114913974.shtml (accessed 17 February 2014) (available in Chinese only, author's translation).

[13] 'The US Initiated a Complaint against China to the WTO on Discussing National Treatment' (sina, 23 March 2004): http://finance.sina.com. cn/g/20040323/1046683555.shtml (accessed 17 February 2014) (available in Chinese only, author's translation).

[14] 'WT/DS309 China – Value-Added Tax on Integrated Circuits' (WTO, 24 February 2010): http://www.wto.org/english/tratop_e/dispu_e/cases_e/ds3 09_e.htm; and 'The US Initiated a Complaint against China to the WTO on Discussing National Treatment' (sina, 23 March 2004): http://finance.sina. com.cn/g/20040323/1046683555.shtml (accessed 17 February 2014) (available in Chinese only, author's translation).

policy on tax rebates. However, this concession did not satisfy the US, which insisted that American chip suppliers should also have the opportunity to enjoy the same treatment. For this reason, the US finally decided to submit the dispute to the WTO.[15]

Robert Zoellick characterised China as a sustainable and rapidly growing market with great potential with respect to the consumption of electronics, personal computers, automobiles, mobile phones and refrigerators, so uninterrupted access to the Chinese market was essential for American semiconductor suppliers. The US had hoped to use this dispute to signal to China that it should not take advantage of non-reciprocal tax rates to protect local industries. The rapid development of the Chinese economy has opened up many opportunities to American companies. Nevertheless, before seizing the opportunity, the US wished to ensure that it was a fair market, while the US government sought to promote the creation of a fair market through all possible means.[16]

The chairman of the US Semiconductor Industry Association, George Scalse, stated that the US had held over 50 per cent of the global semiconductor market for a long time and should continue to maintain and enhance its leadership in this field. The Chinese chip market was worth $25 billion and was expanding rapidly at a rate of 25 per cent compound annual growth. The US integrated circuit manufacturers had the largest share among all exporting countries of this growing market, and since more new equipment was being purchased, further opportunities for US companies lay ahead.[17]

On 26 March 2004, China agreed to negotiate with the Ministry of Commerce (MOFCOM), the Development and Reform Commission, the Ministry of Finance, the Ministry of Information Industry, the General Administration of Customs, the State Administration of Taxation and other units to set up a working group in consultation with the US. On 27 April, China and the US held consultations in Geneva, which the EU, Japan and Mexico joined as third parties. On 27 May, 15 June and

---

[15] 'The United States Wanted to Suppress the Chinese Chip Industry' (people, 22 March 2004): http://www.people.com.cn/GB/paper68/11635/1048799. html; and 'The American Semiconductor Industry Demanded a Share of the $25 billion Chinese Chip Market' (sina, 17 July 2004): http://it.sohu.com/20040717/ n221050121.shtml (accessed 18 February 2014) (available in Chinese only, author's translation).

[16] 'The American Semiconductor Industry Demanded a Share of the $25 billion Chinese Chip Market' (sina, 17 July 2004): http://it.sohu.com/20040717/ n221050121.shtml (accessed 18 February 2014) (available in Chinese only, author's translation).

[17] Ibid.

1–2 July, China and the US held three rounds of consultations to reach a consensus in Beijing and Washington respectively.[18]

On 14 July China and the US signed the 'Sino-US Memorandum of Understanding concerning Chinese integrated circuit VAT'. The main content of this was to the effect that from 1 April 2005 China was to discontinue its policy of granting VAT refunds to semiconductor companies. The US and China fulfilled the WTO notification obligation. The US withdrew the complaint under the WTO dispute settlement mechanism. China was granted an adjusting period of 10 months to adopt the new policy.[19]

A MOFCOM official stated that consultation with the US to resolve the dispute had been chosen because China lacked deep understanding of the WTO dispute settlement mechanism, as well as litigation experience and appropriate professionals. However, negotiations to settle the dispute by no means represented a purely expedient measure, but were the result of careful consideration and assessment. Once the dispute was the subject of WTO legal proceedings, it was quite possible that China would lose the case.[20]

On 25 October 2005, the Ministry of Finance and State Administration of Taxation issued a 'Notice Concerning Ministry of Finance and the State Administration of Taxation on Stopping Integrated Circuit VAT Refund Policy' (Cai Shui [2004] No.174).[21] On 5 October 2005, China and the US informed the DSB that they had successfully implemented the content of the Memorandum.[22]

When the US complained to the WTO, the then WTO Director General persuaded it to resolve the dispute through negotiations and to withdraw the allegation against China. The Director General made it clear that he did not want to see the dispute expanding between the major countries and hoped there was room for the two sides to negotiate.[23]

---

[18]   Ibid.

[19]   Ibid.

[20]   Guohua Yang, 'Case Analysis on Integrated Circuit against China' in Chenggang Li (ed.), *Game of WTO Rules—A Decade of Legal Practices of China's Participation in WTO Dispute Settlement* (Beijing: Commercial Press, 2011), p. 285 (available in Chinese only, author's translation).

[21]   'DS309 China – Value-Added Tax on Integrated Circuits' (Chinalawinfo, 6 October 2005): http://www.chinalawinfo.com/wto/wtojdaldetail.asp?jdalid=26 (accessed 18 February 2014).

[22]   'WT/DS309 China – Value-Added Tax on Integrated Circuits' (WTO, 24 February 2010): http://www.wto.org/english/tratop_e/dispu_e/cases_e/ds309_e. htm (accessed 18 February 2014).

[23]   'The WTO urged the US not to Submit the Allegation against the

China failed to achieve actual VAT rebate incentives to encourage the development of the software industry and integrated circuit industry as in fact only a few companies could obtain the benefit of such rebates. The cumbersome and complex application process stipulated in the No. 18 Document and related supporting documents also led to companies enjoying fewer benefits. The Ministry of Information was in fact aware of these problems and there had been for some time an intention to improve the relevant provisions. The filing of a claim on behalf of the US integrated circuit industry prompted China to make amendments.[24]

Although China agreed to discontinue the VAT refund policy, the industry it had developed as an area of focus still needed some support. The key point here is that when China formulates policies, it fully encourages and supports its key developing industries. The challenge here is to ensure such policies are within the WTO rules in order to avoid potential WTO cases.[25]

After China had signed the Memorandum, all Chinese semiconductor companies were fully informed. Some companies pointed out that the No. 18 Document had already played a positive role in the development of the integrated circuit industry in China. The government had introduced this policy during a tough period for the industry, and it had undergone rapid development since then.[26]

Some companies gave nuanced responses. The general manager of Japan's Renesas company, Ito, thought that after China's accession to the WTO, Chinese and international companies should compete under equal conditions. Renesas planned to invest in China for reasons not connected with the preferential policy and its plans would therefore not change in the light of changes made by China to its preferential policy on VAT. Renesas had already established Renesas Stone Co., Ltd. in Beijing, Renesas Semiconductor Co., Ltd. in Suzhou (which was engaged in packaging

Chinese Chip Rebate' (sohu, 19 March 2004): http://it.sohu.com/2004/03/19/32/article219513222.shtml (accessed 19 February 2014) (available in Chinese only, author's translation).

24   'China Chip Tax is Focused and No. 18 Document will be Adjusted?' (people net, 12 May 2004): http://www.people.com.cn/GB/it/1066/2492564.html (accessed 19 February 2014) (available in Chinese only, author's translation).

25   'Reflections on the IC VAT Case' (China Trade Remedy Information): http://www.cacs.gov.cn/cacs/webzine/webzinedetails.aspx?webzineid=541 (accessed 3 February 2012).

26   'The IC Industry Faced Policy Adjustments and Chinese Manufacturers were more Worried than Happy' (*Electronic & Engineering Times*, 14 August 2004): http://www.eet-china.com/ART_8800344681_480101_NT_0da45061.HTM (accessed 19 February 2014).

the integrated circuit chips) and Renesas Semiconductor Design Co. Ltd. in Shanghai. In 2007 Renesas Stone expanded its production capacity from $20–25 million per month to $50 million per month and became the world's largest chip packaging plant. Renesas Suzhou also doubled its capacity in 2007 from $4–5 million per month to $10 million per month. Ito announced its plan to continuously increase investment in the Chinese market.[27]

Semiconductor Manufacturing International Corporation (SMIC) is currently the most advanced integrated circuit manufacturing company in China. It operates three foundries to produce 8-inch chips in Shanghai. SMIC acquired a fourth 8-inch foundry, which was located in Tianjin, and built a 12-inch foundry in Beijing. Marketing Manager Huang Guimei took the view that the success of China's SMIC factories is based on a number of factors, including huge market demand, cost advantages, an abundant talent pool of engineers, geographical proximity to the fast-growing Chinese market, as well as an attractive investment environment for the semiconductor industry. The termination of the VAT refund would not have a fundamental impact on its financial performance or on the competitiveness of the global semiconductor market.[28]

The sales manager of Shougang NEC Electronics Co., Ltd., Zhou Liang, stated that the change in the VAT policy did not have much impact on business. The company could still take advantage of the output portion of the VAT relief treatment as a joint venture. However, local sales had been affected by the change of policy since the cost of entering the market would increase. Nonetheless, because 70 per cent of Shougang NEC Company's business is accounted for by export and only 20 per cent in terms of local sales, the impact is small. It might have an impact on the eagerness of international companies to enter China, while international capital providers tend to prefer a wholly owned operation because many issues of business operation have to be handled in a different way in a joint venture.[29]

Shanghai Belling Co., Ltd. considered that the change of VAT policy had had an impact on the long-term strategy of some Chinese chip companies. The marketing director noted that the change of VAT policy in China was unfavourable to chip companies and that export business, in particular, would be affected. Chinese chip products were exported to less developed areas, which are very price-sensitive. The new policy would

---

[27] Ibid.
[28] Ibid.
[29] Ibid.

increase the amount of VAT added to the cost of the products and would therefore be likely to affect competitiveness. However, the change of policy would also hit some unofficial vendors who avoid tax to export fake products, and all companies stood on the same starting line, which is conducive to the development of the Chinese market. Since the output portion of the VAT in respect of the product was not large, there would not be a big impact even after the tax was increased. However, the company's long-term strategy was to increase its exports and this would inevitably be affected by the change of policy.[30]

Various government departments worked together closely in response to the case, completed negotiations with the US and introduced alternative measures and other tasks for the implementation of the Memorandum. This working model constitutes a prototype for cross-sectors in response to the WTO dispute.[31]

The MOFCOM official stressed that the case had been disposed of properly and that harm had been turned into good. There were obvious flaws in the drafting of the documents involved. These had swiftly been modified so that the parts that allegedly violated the WTO rules were removed, and at the same time a number of supporting measures that would not violate the rules had been added. The result was that support for the development of the integrated circuit industry had been enhanced rather than diminished and the dispute was resolved smoothly by means of consultations with the US.[32]

Thus the first case that the US brought against China ended at the level of consultations. Overall, China was not ready to engage in legal proceedings with the US and the domestic loss did not involve further measures being taken. The reaction of the US was a reasonably positive one, rather than it pursuing the case relentlessly in the hope of giving China a scare, so finally China and the US shook hands on the matter. In addition, achieving dispute settlement is not a matter of looking simply at the end result – gaining time to make an adjustment can be regarded as positive, as can achieving a certain result that a party wished for.

---

[30]   'The IC Industry Faced Policy Adjustments and Chinese Manufacturers were more Worried than Happy' (*Electronic & Engineering Times*, 14 August 2004): http://www.eet-china.com/ART_8800344681_480101_NT_0da45061.HTM (accessed 19 February 2014).

[31]   Chenggang Li (ed.), *Game of WTO Rules— A Decade of Legal Practices of China's Participation in WTO Dispute Settlement* (Beijing: Commercial Press, 2011), p. 18 (available in Chinese only, author's translation).

[32]   Ibid., at p. 46.

7.1.2.2   First outing as a respondent

China – Measures Affecting Imports of Automobile Parts[33] was the first case after its accession to the WTO in which China initiated the arbitration proceedings. It was also the first case in which China, as a respondent, experienced all the WTO dispute settlement procedures.

In 2005 China issued the Administrative Measures on the Import of the Auto Parts with Features of Complete Vehicle, which contained strict provisions on imported complete knocked down (CKD) and semi knocked down (SKD) assembling cars. It provided that where the sum of imported components exceeded 60 per cent of the total price of the vehicle, the same tariff as applicable to a complete vehicle (25 per cent) would be imposed. The import tariff rate in respect of auto parts was 10 per cent. The EU and the US considered the Chinese mechanism in relation to the importing of auto parts to be in breach of WTO rules, and planned to use the WTO and other trading tools to further open up the Chinese auto market. In recent years, American and European car makers had lost ground in their local markets to Japanese companies. As a result, the expanding Chinese market was an important new target.[34]

A MOFCOM official explained that China's intention was to prevent the smuggling of luxury cars through the introduction of relevant measures and to eliminate the practice followed by some companies of importing low-tariff auto parts and then assembling these parts into a complete vehicle. The Administrative Measures sought to prevent the use of tax difference between complete vehicles and auto parts to avoid customs supervision. The other motive for introducing them was that foreign auto companies blocked access to high-technology auto parts, so this initiative aimed at inducing foreign companies to set up production lines or joint ventures with domestic companies in China. Since joining the WTO, China as other WTO members, has an aim of meeting its commitments. In this regard, it has reduced tariffs on automobiles and auto parts. Similar practices have been carried out in other WTO members, especially developing ones. However, because China seems to arguably have a strong aptitude for digesting technical information, foreign companies worry that

---

[33]   Appellate Body Reports, *China – Measures Affecting Imports of Automobile Parts*, WT/DS339,340,342/AB/R (adopted 12 January 2009), as reported in China, see http://www.wto.org/english/tratop_e/dispu_e/cases_e/ds339_e.htm (accessed 20 February 2014) (available in Chinese only, author's translation).

[34]   'The US, EU and Canada Jointly Complained to the WTO and Dispute on Imported Auto Parts Upgraded' (xinhua net, 18 September 2006): http://news.xin huanet.com/auto/2006-09/18/content_5102627.htm (accessed 20 February 2014) (available in Chinese only, author's translation).

setting up production lines in China will give rise to disclosure of technical information. Therefore, they strongly resisted Chinese practices.[35]

On 30 March 2006, the EU and the US submitted a request for consultation to the WTO on the Chinese auto parts import measures on the basis that they constituted discrimination. The USTR complained that China's newly enacted laws and regulations did the opposite of what was required under the commitments to which China was bound by virtue of its accession to the WTO relating to the reduction and limitation of import tariffs on auto parts and the abolition of all 'local content' requirements. The EU claimed that China levied tariffs where the value of the auto parts was equal to or in excess of 60 per cent of the value of a complete vehicle, which was in effect the provision of the parts 'localisation ratio' in violation of WTO rules. China argued that this provision was to prevent 'disguised tax evasion' on the part of some foreign car manufacturers. Some foreign car manufacturers imported split vehicles and then assembled them in China to avoid paying the higher import duty applicable to complete vehicles.[36] On 13 April 2006, Canada proposed consultations on the same issue.[37]

In July 2006, an announcement was posted on the websites of China's General Administration of Customs and the MOFCOM on the original schedule for implementation, which was postponed from 1 July 2006 to 1 July 2008. However, the EU and the US were not satisfied with this compromise and, together with Canada, asked China to cancel the approved standards on vehicle features in their entirety.[38]

On 15 September 2006, the US, the EU and Canada requested the establishment of a panel. A MOFCOM spokesman expressed regret in relation to the situation and reiterated that Chinese import regulations on auto parts were designed to prevent the practice of seeking a tax advantage by avoiding customs supervision and tariffs, to combat illegal assembly and to protect consumers' profits in a manner consistent with WTO rules.

---

[35] 'The AB Supported Chinese Import Tariffs on Car Parts' (xinhua net, 17 December 2008): http://news.xinhuanet.com/auto/2008-12/17/content_10515664.htm (accessed 20 February 2014) (available in Chinese only, author's translation).

[36] 'The Whole Story of the Dispute on the Chinese Auto Parts Tariff' (sohu, 15 February 2008): http://auto.sohu.com/2008 0215/n255175868_2.shtml (accessed 21 February 2014) (available in Chinese only, author's translation).

[37] 'WT/DS342 China – Measures Affecting Imports of Automobile Parts' (WTO, 24 February 2010): http://www.wto.org/english/tratop_e/dispu_e/cases_e/ds342_e.htm (accessed 21 February 2014).

[38] 'The Whole Story of the Dispute on the Chinese Auto Parts Tariff' (sohu, 15 February 2008): http://auto.sohu.com/2008 0215/n255175868_2.shtml (accessed 21 February 2014) (available in Chinese only, author's translation).

China had demonstrated good faith in its consultations with the EU, the US and Canada and expressed regret that the complainants had requested the establishment of a panel.[39]

On 9 January 2007, the Director General of the WTO, Pascal Lamy, designated the members of the panel. On 23 and 24 May and 12 July the panel held two hearings in Geneva. On 18 July 2008 the panel reports were circulated to the WTO members. These contained the finding that China had violated Article III of GATT 1994 and the commitment in paragraph 93 of China's Accession Working Party Report. On 15 September 2008, China notified its decision to appeal. On 15 December 2008, the Appellate Body (AB) reports were circulated to members. These upheld the panel's finding that the measures at issue were inconsistent with Article III of the GATT 1994, but found that the panel had erred in finding the measures at issue to be inconsistent with the commitment in paragraph 93 of China's Accession Working Party Report.[40]

A MOFCOM spokesman noted that the AB supported China's appeal in respect of the imported tariff treatment on car kits and SKD kits to the extent that it corrected the errors made by the panel in its ruling. China welcomed this correction, but regretted the fact that the AB upheld the other parts of the panel's decision.[41]

On 28 August 2009, the Ministry of Industry and Information Technology and National Development and Reform Commission jointly issued the No. 10 Decree on the revision of the import administration in the Development Policy of the Automobile Industry. This entered into force on 1 September 2009 and repealed the Administrative Measures on the Import of the Auto Parts with Features of Complete Vehicle which had been in force since 1 April 2005. To this extent, China purported to be in full compliance with the decision of the DSB.[42]

Although China lost the *Automobile Parts* case, the three-year course of litigation made many domestic auto parts manufacturers grow up. The Chinese government stated that since the final ruling had been made,

---

[39]   Ibid.

[40]   'WT/DS342 China – Measures Affecting Imports of Automobile Parts' (WTO, 24 February 2010): http://www.wto.org/english/tratop_e/dispu_e/cases_e/ds342_e.htm (accessed 21 February 2014).

[41]   'Ministry of Commerce Spokesman Issued a Statement' (people, 18 December 2008): http://paper.people.com.cn/rmrbhwb/html/2008-12/18/content_159870.htm (accessed 21 February 2014) (available in Chinese only, author's translation).

[42]   'China – Measures Affecting Imports of Automobile Parts' (Chinalawinfo, 28 August 2008): http://www.chinalawinfo.com/wto/wtojdaldetail.asp?jdalid=32 (accessed 21 February 2014) (available in Chinese only, author's translation).

domestic auto parts companies should improve their competitiveness and strive to occupy the domestic and foreign market share.[43]

The Vice-President of the China Machinery Industry Federation, Zhang Xiaoyu, considered that even though the original policy had been discontinued, this would not have a big impact on domestic car producers, which had a relatively high degree of localisation. The vast majority of domestic companies had introduced technology and could meet the requirement of 40 per cent localisation. Only a few luxury car manufacturers would be affected, rather than general manufacturers. However, the outlook was good for those luxury car companies which had strengthened their local production due to the tariff reduction, but would not import parts and assemble in China.[44]

A manager from BMW's public relations department in China stated that 3 Series and 5 Series models already met the 40 per cent of local production requirement and a 10 per cent tariff on imported parts and components was imposed on BMW in accordance with the standard as opposed to the 25 per cent tariff levied on imported vehicles. As a result, BMW was not greatly affected. The company would follow domestic laws and regulations and was committed to continue deepening and improving the localisation process. It aimed to increase local procurement with a view to enhancing competitiveness and reducing costs.[45]

A high-level employee from Daimler Northeast Asia Investment Co. stated that Mercedes-Benz had been working to improve localisation and that the main reason for this was to reduce costs. The company expected to reach 40 per cent of local production in 2009, on the basis of steady implementation over a period of time. Since it had commenced its operations in China later than certain other luxury car manufacturers, it had experienced some difficulties in finding parts suppliers. However, localisation is not an easy job. Because luxury car manufacturers produce only a small quantity of cars, suppliers might find it costly to develop a mould for a part. In addition, the important core technology also involves intellectual property rights and Mercedes-Benz suppliers in Germany were reluctant to transfer technology to China as this would be likely to help competitors. There are thousands of parts in a car and bringing them

---

[43]   'Automobile Trade Dispute: WTO Final Ruling against China' (people, 18 December 2008): http://paper.people.com.cn/jhsb/html/2008-12/17/content_159428.htm (accessed 21 February 2014) (available in Chinese only, author's translation).

[44]   Ibid.

[45]   Ibid.

together represents a huge project in terms of consultation, negotiation and implementation.[46]

Southwest Securities auto analyst Dong Jianhua said that allowing a luxury car company to import parts and assemble them in China would harm the domestic parts industry, especially in respect of luxury cars. It is impossible to achieve full localisation in the luxury car industry. Abolishing import management policies was not good for joint ventures because imported parts could increase car prices, which in turn was bad for consumers. Mercedes-Benz, BMW and other luxury car companies set up factories in China at a late stage and their ancillary facilities did not complete the localisation and quality certification in China. Therefore, they definitely wanted to import components directly from abroad, which was consistent with the interests of their home countries and promoted employment in those countries. But this would mean a reduction in Chinese employment opportunities and local gross domestic product (GDP).[47]

Auto analyst Zhong Shi said a small number of joint ventures which had a small production scale and output, and produced high-end models, could benefit. Nevertheless, localisation becomes a trend and decreasing tariffs does not mean that competitiveness increases.[48]

Automotive industry analyst Jia Xinguang noted that the implementation of the Administrative Measures was intended to curb tax evasion on the part of certain small domestic businesses that lacked formal production equipment and assembled CKD without permission, but that the issue had escalated from a domestic matter to an international lawsuit.[49]

Long-term thinking dictates that when facing increasingly fierce international competition, a state should actively learn to adapt to the rules of the game with a view to switching from policy protection to policy assistance and continuing to improve production levels.

Losing the case had some impact on the development of the Chinese auto parts industry. First, it posed a threat to its development. The ruling was undoubtedly good news for European and American auto parts manufacturers. In the prevailing economic climate, component export offered Western companies an important means of boosting their profits.

---

[46] 'Automobile Trade Dispute: WTO Final Ruling against China' (people, 18 December 2008): http://paper.people.com.cn/jhsb/html/2008-12/17/content_159428.htm (accessed 21 February 014) (available in Chinese only, author's translation).

[47] Ibid.

[48] Ibid.

[49] Ibid.

But this ruling had some direct impact on Chinese auto parts manufacturers. However, the technological sophistication of Chinese components improved during the process of development. Localisation of production is cheaper than importing the parts in terms of the maximisation of production efficiency and profits and it is not necessary for foreign-owned companies to bypass localisation. Although the WTO ruling has had some impact, it should not change the current market structure in respect of domestic parts. If the Chinese auto parts industry is diligent and does more to promote localisation, it will be able to withstand the pressure and catch up.[50]

Second, the core technology remains in the hands of foreign car companies. American and European car companies may make use of a lower threshold in respect of imported cars and export more core components to China rather than establishing a joint venture in China, which may encourage the production of a complete car because the car parts import tax rate is 10 per cent.

Third, the price of luxury cars has fallen, thus benefitting owners of high-end models, but the process of localisation has slowed down. The biggest impact of this has been felt in the luxury car market. With the termination of the localisation threshold, the import tariff in respect of all auto parts is 10 per cent for luxury car producers, which is conducive to reducing costs and lowering vehicle prices. Because Mercedes-Benz, BMW and certain other manufacturers of high-end models found it difficult to achieve a localisation rate of 40 per cent, duties were previously imposed upon these companies on the basis of the complete vehicle. Since the ruling entered into force, it became possible to import many luxury car components, thus improving the 'pedigree' of the luxury car brand in China and satisfying entrenched local tastes for a purely imported car, which was good news for some high-end car owners.[51]

Fourth, China must develop additional policies to eliminate 'disguised smuggling'. Pursuant to the entry into force of the WTO ruling, the tax threshold for localisation vanished as the tax difference between the vehicle and parts was no longer allowed. Therefore, there are loopholes in the tax system and disguised smuggling might occur: high tariffs applicable to complete vehicle sales may be avoided by importing auto parts and simply assembling them in China. This phenomenon of disguised

---

[50] 'Chinese Auto Parts Lost and High-end Car Companies Benefit' (sina, 24 December 2008): http://news.sohu.com/20081224/n261384116.shtml (accessed 23 February 2014) (available in Chinese only, author's translation).
[51] Ibid.

tax evasion occurred in 2004, when many car components were imported and assembled into complete vehicles that were much cheaper but lacked safety and quality guarantees. This had a bad influence on the state tax and automotive markets. It is necessary to develop a series of policies and guidelines to plug the loophole in respect of the tax differential restriction and to strengthen supervision in order to minimise the adverse effect of the WTO ruling.[52]

With this in mind, China purportedly implemented the decision of the WTO dispute settlement mechanism, stopped the execution and implementation of related policies and resolved the auto parts dispute, which caused great concern domestically.

7.1.2.3 Revisiting the issue of subsidies

On 2 February 2007, USTR Susan Schwab announced that the US had requested consultations with China concerning measures granting refunds, reductions or exemptions from taxes and other payments. On the same day, the US ambassador to the WTO wrote to Sun Zhenyu, China's ambassador to the WTO, on the subject of Chinese subsidy measures.[53]

The US considered the measures in question to be inconsistent with Article 3 of the Subsidies and Countervailing Measures (SCM) Agreement, Article III of GATT 1994 and Article 2 of the Trade-Related Investment Measures (TRIMs) Agreement. The request for consultations identified that China provided refunds, reductions or exemptions to companies in China. The US provided a description that listed the available evidence for the subsidy involved, including 18 measures. The US took the view that these measures offered Chinese companies tax reimbursements or relief if they met certain criteria. These involved the completion of certain export sales or the purchase of domestic goods rather than imported goods. In addition, it was argued that the measures accorded imported products treatment less favourable than that accorded to like domestic products.[54]

The US accused China of granting preferential tax reductions and exemptions for certain export companies. This is usually prohibited by

---

[52] Ibid.

[53] '*China – Certain Measures Granting Refunds, Reductions or Exemptions from Taxes and Other Payments*' (chinalawinfo, 7 February 2008): http://www.chinalawinfo.com/wto/wtojdaldetail.asp?jdalid=20 (accessed 23 February 2014) (available in Chinese only, author's translation).

[54] 'WT/DS58 China – Certain Measures Granting Refunds, Reductions or Exemptions from Taxes and Other Payments' (WTO, 24 February 2010): http://www.wto.org/english/tratop_e/dispu_e/cases_e/ds358_e.htm (accessed 23 February 2014).

the WTO under the rules on government subsidies supporting export for a specific industry. Susan Schwab noted that these controversially preferential tax and other policies made Chinese products cheaper and thus played a role in stimulating exports of wood products, computers, steel and a wide range of other goods. The US claimed that small and medium-sized businesses in the US were impacted by the competition they faced from Chinese goods.[55]

On 3 February 2007, a MOFCOM spokesman pointed out the US was required to consult with China under the WTO while the two states maintained bilateral communication on subsidy measures. In this regard, China somehow felt the US did not follow the right procedure. On 26 February, Mexico requested consultations with China on the same issue as the US had done. China, the US and Mexico subsequently held two rounds of consultations in Geneva. The MOFCOM spokesman stated that China was serious about consultations. However, the US and Mexico seemed to have paid little attention to the progress made in the consultations and twice requested the establishment of a panel.[56]

On 31 August, the DSB established a panel. The US and Mexico focused on two issues. The first of these involved accusing China of granting tax deductions, reductions and exemptions in respect of purchases made by certain domestic goods companies that led to companies preferring to purchase domestic goods instead of imported goods. The second was to allege that China granted tax deductions, reductions and exemptions to some Chinese export companies. The US and Mexico considered that such measures were inconsistent with WTO rules. The MOFCOM spokesman replied that the US and Mexico had broken off consultations with China, but required the establishment of a panel to resolve the dispute. China expressed regret as to this and stated that it did not understand the reasons for it. In recent years, China had been taking positive and proactive steps to reform its corporate tax system. Most of the controversial laws, regulations and policies raised by the US and Mexico were in the

---

[55] 'MOFCOM Researches on the Request for Consultations from the US and the Dispute may Take Two Years' (Chinanews, 6 February 2007): http://www.chi nanews.com/cj/gncj/news/2007/02-06/868895.shtml (accessed 23 February 2014) (available in Chinese only, author's translation).

[56] 'China – Certain Measures Granting Refunds, Reductions or Exemptions from Taxes and Other Payments' (chinalawinfo, 7 February 2008): http://www. chinalawinfo.com/wto/wtojdaldetail.asp?jdalid=20; and 'MOFCOM Spokesman Issued a Statement on the Establishment of a Panel to Hear WTO Subsidy Dispute' (MOFCOM, 5 September 2007): http://www.mofcom.gov.cn/aarticle/difang/ hunan/200709/20070905064019.html (accessed 23 February 2014) (available in Chinese only, author's translation).

process of being abandoned or repealed. The rule providing that 'income tax was halved for foreign exports with a total output of more than 70 per cent' had actually been repealed in the new Income Tax Law. The complainants were attempting to 'improve' Chinese tax law by means of recourse to the WTO dispute settlement mechanism. China was adamant that the complainants' course of action would not change its economic laws and regulations, including tax policies, which it was in the course of improving in step with social and economic development. The request for the establishment of a panel related, *inter alia*, to a number of measures that had already been repealed. Moreover, with the introduction of the Chinese Enterprise Income Tax Law and its forthcoming entry into force on 1 January 2008, Chinese policies and measures had been fully in compliance with WTO rules. According to China, it seems to be that the proceedings brought by the US and Mexico against China were based on domestic political needs and misunderstanding of China's relevant policies, and ignored the progress and reality of Chinese economic reform.[57]

On 29 November, the Chinese ambassador to the WTO, Sun Zhenyu, signed a 'Memorandum of Understanding concerning Consultations to Resolve Trade Subsidies' with the ambassadors of the US and Mexico respectively. This marked the resolution, through negotiations, of this 10-month dispute. In the Memorandum, China clarified that the policy on the VAT refund applicable in respect of the purchase of domestic equipment did not constitute prohibited subsidies in the WTO and the preferential tax policies had been or would soon be abolished with the entry into force of the new Enterprise Income Tax Law.[58]

The MOFCOM spokesman commented that most of the measures challenged by the complainants were implemented before China's accession to the WTO, and some dated back to the 1980s and 1990s. There was serious misunderstanding of, and prejudice against, Chinese policies, as shown in the belief that Chinese measures were subsidies put in place to encourage export. In response to hundreds of questions raised by the complainants, China explained in detail during the consultation process that some measures had been repealed and that others would not have the

---

[57]   'MOFCOM Spokesman Issued a Statement on the Establishment of a Panel to Hear WTO Subsidy Dispute' (MOFCOM, 5 September 2007): http://www. mofcom.gov.cn/aarticle/difang/hunan/200709/20070905064019.html (accessed 23 February 2014) (available in Chinese only, author's translation).

[58]   'China, the US and Mexico Signed a Memorandum of Understanding on WTO Subsidies Dispute' (MOFCOM, 30 November 2007): http://www.mofcom. gov.cn/aarticle/ae/ai/200711/20071105257413.html (accessed 24 February 2014) (available in Chinese only, author's translation).

results the complainants claimed they would, because of certain restrictions upon them. These explanations eventually succeeded in correcting the complainants' misunderstandings and laid the foundation for consultations to resolve the dispute. China argued on the basis of reason during the consultation process, made the complainants abandon their challenge to the VAT refund policy and the new Enterprise Income Tax Law, and upheld the validity of the new law.[59]

This case leads to reflections on the steps which should be taken. The first of these is that the tax incentives system should be redesigned. China had committed to removing all subsidies prohibited by the SCM Agreement on its accession to the WTO, and this commitment covered all levels of government. The current situation is that some provincial governments give a certain level of subsidy to improve local economic growth and employment through credit, taxes, electricity price, freight price and other measures. Governments at all levels should determine different incentives by reference to the development of industry in China. Companies operating in the same industrial sector, whether domestic or foreign, should enjoy the same preferential policies. The first level of priority should cover infrastructure and high-tech industries, while agriculture should be given a greater degree of preferential treatment. Industries whose markets are basically saturated or whose production capacity has become excessive in China should not benefit from preferential policies. Finally, negative preferential tax policies should be applied to a restricted number of industries, such as tobacco, liquor and polluting industries, in order to limit their growth. When provincial governments formulate preferential policies to attract foreign investment, they must comply strictly with the laws made by the Chinese central government to ensure compliance with WTO rules. On 1 December 2007, on the basis of objections raised by the US and Mexico, China repealed Part XIII of the 'Catalogue for the Guidance of Foreign Investment Industries (2004 Revision)'. The catalogue is designed to encourage foreign companies to invest in certain industries. Thus when foreign companies and foreign-invested companies engage in the direct export of those products, they cannot obtain tax incentives, which has connection with export subsidies.[60]

The second point is that export and import substitution subsidies must

---

59   Yonghui Zhang, 'Comments on Tax Subsidy Case Filed by the US and Mexico' in Chenggang Li (ed.), *Game of WTO Rules— A Decade of Legal Practices of China's Participation in WTO Dispute Settlement* (Beijing: Commercial Press, 2011), p. 318 (available in Chinese only, author's translation).

60   'System of Tax Incentives and Subsidies under the WTO Rules – Status Quo Reflections on China Subsidies' (Department of Commerce Zhejiang Province):

be eliminated and the export tax rebate system needs to be improved. WTO subsidy rules require members to abolish prohibited subsidies. Therefore, China must completely abolish export and import substitution subsidies, adjust tax reductions, exemptions and other incentives and further improve and standardise the export tax rebate system. China should adopt internationally accepted practices, improve the relevant system and methods of granting export tax rebates and establish a stable tax rebate system. In this way, export tax rebates will be based on science and proper standards. The principle of 'how much imposes how much refunds' and 'who levies who rebates' should be applied; the wrongful use of tax rebates should be eliminated through the use of modern management tools; the supervision of the whole process including taxation of exports and the export tax rebate should be strengthened; and a scientific monitoring system to enable mutual restraint and mutual supervision among tax authorities, competent authorities of economy and trade, export companies and relevant departments should be put in place.[61]

The third point is that the control of tax relief should be bolstered and the focus of tax incentives should be shifted. Developed countries treat reductions and exemptions carefully and apply a relatively narrow range of targeted tax incentives. Germany, Canada, the US, Japan and other countries use tax incentives in order to promote high-tech industries as well as taking into account environmental protection, energy conservation and increasing employment opportunities. China has a relatively wide range of tax incentives, mainly for various regions and foreign companies, but not for specific scientific research, development, activities and projects. Developing a wide range of foreign tax incentives should be a priority of foreign tax law. China's accession to the WTO pointed out the direction for the future development of Chinese foreign tax law, which is that it should gradually die out. WTO rules on the requirement of national treatment only differentiate between tariffs and domestic taxes, but make no differentiation as to whether the tax law of its member states is divided into foreign and non-foreign, since all tax should be treated as a domestic tax. Moreover, from the perspective of specific practices in other countries, there is no so-called foreign tax law: tax law is of general application and makes no distinction between foreign and non-foreign taxpayers. In terms of the optimisation of the economic environment, the key focus of tax incentives should be to improve the structure of foreign investment and

---

http://www.Zcom.gov.cn/zcom/zwfb/zwdt/T256013.shtml (accessed 7 February 2012) (available in Chinese only, author's translation).
   [61]   Ibid.

promote the development of high-tech industries. The Enterprise Income Tax Law came into force in 2008, and grants tax incentives in respect of high-tech industry, agriculture, forestry, animal husbandry, fishery and the environmental protection industry, all of which are supported and encouraged by the Chinese government.[62]

The fourth point is that indirect tax incentives should primarily be used, involving a variety of tax incentives. Tax incentives in their various forms each have many pros and cons, and each can play a unique role to encourage certain industries under certain conditions. China could learn from other countries how best to use different forms of preferential tax to achieve predetermined objectives without violating WTO rules. Incentives based on income tax and circulation tax should be coordinated to form a set of scientific, rational and mutually compatible preferential tax incentives in a manner that optimises the effectiveness of such incentives. Direct tax incentives focus on direct reduction and exemption, while indirect tax incentives seek to reduce tax burden by accelerating depreciation, extracting reserves, increasing allowable deductions, permitting the deduction of investments, and so on. Traditional Chinese tax incentives focus on direct tax incentives that have an increasingly negative effect. By contrast, indirect tax incentives are primarily enabling incentives that aim to facilitate industrial restructuring and can be adapted to fit China's current economic development needs.[63]

China has now revised the relevant provisions. In fact, controversial opinions were expressed domestically on the abolition of tax incentives by reference to export performance. Some Chinese officials expressed the criticism that the presence of a large number of foreign export companies as processing bases in China merely brought some nice numbers, a huge surplus and the pressure of trade friction, which placed Chinese companies in a disadvantaged competitive position. In respect of Chinese foreign trade and economic development, the approach of combining two different tax incentive methods could partially solve this problem. China is in a transition period in terms of its foreign trade and the absorption of foreign investment, which means that prohibited subsidies such as deductions, refunds, reductions and exemptions related to export performance and import substitution will have to be discontinued sooner or later. In order to achieve a smooth policy transition, China needs time as a buffer. The

---

[62] 'System of Tax Incentives and Subsidies under the WTO Rules – Status Quo Reflections on China Subsidies' (Department of Commerce Zhejiang Province): http://www.Zcom.gov.cn/zcom/zwfb/zwdt/T256013.shtml (accessed 7 February 2012) (available in Chinese only, author's translation).
[63] Ibid.

WTO dispute outlined above accelerated the introduction of new policies that are harmless to China.[64]

The first five years after China's accession to the WTO was a honeymoon period, although the first case was filed by China as a free-rider. In summary, China mainly acted as a diplomat in the international arena, following Chinese traditional values of non-litigation. The *Automobile Parts* case was an exception to this because the car industry is among China's key industries and cars are among the fastest growing goods in China.

On the one hand, China, as a beginner in the WTO dispute settlement system, has faced many difficulties. On the other hand, the WTO dispute settlement mechanism has resolved some difficulties which had not been resolved domestically for a long time. In the *Value-Added Tax on Integrated Circuits* case, different governmental departments worked together and therefore solved the problem of fragmentation over a period of years. In the *Measures Affecting Imports of Automobile Parts* case, Customs had to improve its supervisory abilities in respect of car smuggling in order to avoid national loss of tax revenue. In the *Value-Added Tax on Integrated Circuits* case, a large number of laws, regulations and policies had to be abandoned and the Enterprise Income Tax Law was introduced, which helped the Chinese central government and provincial governments to put unhelpful laws into order. Thus, by doing all these, China sought to comply with WTO laws faithfully.

Given that China is highly focused on its increasingly potent technology and economic power, its earlier, purely domestic-oriented laws and policies have come under intense review by other WTO members. The *China – Grants, Loans and Other Incentives* case[65] involved more than 100 laws and policies of 15 provinces and three cities with independent planning policies in China, which demonstrates that WTO members' concern about Chinese policies is not limited to policies established by the central government, but also includes a large number of local policies. In the future China is likely to continue to face a number of WTO disputes related to subsidy measures. Therefore, it needs to familiarise itself with the relevant WTO rules and actively discontinue or amend subsidy measures inconsistent with them. At the same time, it seems China would actively defend its policies where they are consistent with WTO rules.[66]

---

[64] Ibid.
[65] 'China – Grants, Loans and Other Incentives' (WTO, 24 February 2010): http://www.wto.org/english/tratop_e/dispu_e/cases_e/ds387_e.htm (accessed 5 March 2014).
[66] 'China – Certain Measures Granting Refunds, Reductions or Exemptions

In the *Grants, Loans and Other Incentives* case, the complainants raised objections against a wide range of existing measures, including those taken both by the central state organs and by provincial governments. Chinese provincial governments had introduced these measures to encourage brand-building, promote the protection of intellectual property and to create a favourable environment for business development. However, because these measures were closely linked to export performance and coupled with supporting measures, the complainants took the view that they constituted export subsidies aimed at encouraging and supporting exports. Measures taken by Chinese provincial governments at all levels included prohibited subsidy elements, comprising import substitution subsidies, export subsidies and other types of subsidy that could be challenged by other WTO members. As a 'concerned' WTO member, China should formulate policies and measures compliant with WTO rules to promote economic development.[67] This case was almost the same as the *China – Certain Measures Granting Refunds, Reductions or Exemptions from Taxes and Other Payments* case.

However, after the *Grants, Loans and Other Incentives* dispute took place, in order to maintain the overall status of national interests, provincial governments quickly reviewed, revised and repealed the relevant documents. Local WTO advisory centres provided a detailed list of queries and related information in English translation for provincial governments. In addition, other relevant departments and bureaux actively coordinated with the MOFCOM, dealt with the dispute and safeguarded national interests.[68]

The three disputes discussed above were resolved and the decisions resulting from them were purportedly implemented by China. China made efforts to negotiate with all complainants with a view to eliminating differences in this way. Although the *Measures Affecting Imports of Automobile Parts* case was resolved through litigation, the Chinese government exhausted all possible avenues open to it in terms of consultations. Furthermore, China seems to have brought its measures into conformity with the DSB recommendations and rulings within a reasonable period of time.[69]

---

from Taxes and Other Payments' (chinalawinfo, 7 February 2008): http://www.chinalawinfo.com/wto/wtojdaldetail.asp?jdalid=20 (available in Chinese only, author's translation).

[67]   Ibid.

[68]   Yonghui Zhang, 'Comments on Grants, Loans and Other Incentives Case' in Chenggang Li (ed.), *Game of WTO Rules— A Decade of Legal Practices of China's Participation in WTO Dispute Settlement* (Beijing: Commercial Press, 2011) p. 378 (available in Chinese only, author's translation).

[69]   For information on implementation status, please refer to DS 309 at http://

7.1.2.4 WTO Chinese years

Statistics from the WTO website[70] indicate that up to 31 December 2014 China had initiated 12 disputes as a complainant and was involved in 20 further disputes as a defendant, among which only three disputes were filed before the end of 2006. In 2007, a total of 13 disputes were initiated in the WTO, of which five involved China. In 2008, China was involved in one-third of WTO disputes. In 2009, it was involved in half the disputes, and therefore 2009 was called the 'WTO Chinese Year'.[71] In 2010, there were 17 disputes, of which five involved China. In 2011, although there were only eight disputes, three involved China. In 2012, there were 27 disputes, of which 10 involved China. These six years were all WTO Chinese years and seemed to have given China chances to understand what the WTO dispute settlement mechanism meant.

1. To be or not to be   Before 2006, European financial service providers applied for licences to operate in China and to develop business based on an exchange letter between Xinhua News Agency[72] and the European Commission of 10 November 1997. This letter stated that Xinhua News Agency Information Management Center should not interfere in the transaction between EU financial information providers and their customers, but should ensure the confidentiality of all information submitted. Furthermore, it should not require financial information providers to submit detailed information on financial transactions between them and their customers, but should commit to approve the licence application within 20 working days after receiving the financial information provider's business presentation documents in China.[73]

On 10 September 2006, Xinhua News Agency laid down a strict requirement for foreign news agencies, entitled 'the Management Rules

---

www.wto.org/english/tratop_e/dispu_e/cases_e/ds309_e.htm; DS 358 at http://www.wto.org/english/tratop_e/dispu_e/cases_e/ds358_e.htm; and DS387 at http://www.wto.org/english/tratop_e/dispu_e/cases_e/ds387_e.htm (accessed 6 January 2015).

[70]   Table of disputes by member, World Trade Organization: http://www.wto.org/english/tratop_e/dispu_e/dispu_ by_country_e.htm (accessed 6 January 2015).

[71]   Naigeng Zhang (ed.) *Dispute Settlement of WTO: the Year of China (2009)* (Shanghai: People Press, 2010) (available in Chinese only, author's translation).

[72]   The Xinhua News Agency is China's state news agency under the State Council.

[73]   'China – Measures Affecting Financial Information Services and Foreign Financial Information Suppliers' (Chinalawinfo, 4 December 2008): http://www.chinalawinfo.com/wto/wtojdaldetail.asp?jdalid=34 (accessed 4 March 2014) (available in Chinese only, author's translation).

for Foreign News Agencies Publishing News and Information in China'. These rules stipulate that foreign financial information providers need approval from the Xinhua News Agency to operate, and must follow further operational requirements including those relating to change of business scope and means of dissemination of information. They must also submit annual reports on their operational activities to the Xinhua News Agency. In the annual review process China required foreign financial information providers to submit confidential information about the service they provided and about their customers' commercial value to the Xinhua News Agency Foreign Information Management Center. Likewise, their customers were required to submit all relevant information to the Center when signing the contract to provide financial information services.[74]

On 20 June 2007, Xinhua News Agency launched 'Xinhua 08', which provides financial information services on a commercial basis to directly compete with other service providers. However, neither 'Xinhua 08' nor other Chinese financial information providers were required to provide services through designated agencies or comply with other requirements. Meanwhile, the relevant regulations provide for Xinhua News Agency to supervise foreign news agencies and financial information providers.[75]

In October 2007, China promulgated the 'Guiding Catalog of Industries for Foreign Investment', in which foreign financial information providers were treated as news agencies and other financial information services were prohibited in the service category of foreign investment, so that foreign financial information providers in China could only establish representative offices that did not allow the establishment of normal forms of commercial presence. These measures undoubtedly limited foreign financial information service providers' opportunities to compete in the Chinese market, which produced a major conflict of interests.[76]

After the Xinhua News Agency had announced the above measures, the EU and the US conducted talks with the Chinese government at different levels. The then EU Trade Commissioner Peter Mandelson held several talks with China, including with the Deputy Prime Minister and with

---

[74] 'China – Measures Affecting Financial Information Services and Foreign Financial Information Suppliers' (Chinalawinfo, 4 December 2008): http://www.chinalawinfo.com/wto/wtojdaldetail.asp?jdalid=34 (accessed 4 March 2014) (available in Chinese only, author's translation).
[75] Ibid.
[76] Ibid.

ministers, as well as with the leaders of the Xinhua News Agency. This issue was also discussed in November 2007 at the EU–China summit.[77]

On 3 March 2008, the EU and the US requested consultations with China with respect to measures affecting financial information services and foreign financial information services suppliers in China. They considered that the measures at issue were inconsistent with various provisions of the GATS and China's Protocol of Accession.[78]

On 3 July, China promised that the Xinhua News Agency would no longer manage the financial information. It clarified that the existing laws and regulations did not prohibit foreign financial information service providers from establishing a commercial presence. The new regulatory body would protect foreign financial information service providers' business secrets under Chinese laws.[79]

On 20 June 2008, Canada had requested consultation on the same matter. It held consultations with China in Geneva on 20 August, followed by a second round of consultations in Geneva on 25 September. Through negotiations they reached an understanding on the issue.[80]

On 4 December 2008, China, the EU, the US and Canada informed the DSB that they had reached an agreement in relation to this dispute in the form of the Memorandum of Understanding on the Impact of Foreign Financial Information Service Provider Measures.[81]

On the same date, the Bloomberg agency commented that this dispute resolution process embodied the great value of the WTO rules and dispute settlement mechanism model.[82]

MOFCOM officials explained that the major adjustment made by China related to the fact that the Xinhua News Agency, which was in charge of financial services supervision, was originally appointed by the

---

[77]   Ibid.

[78]   'China – Measures Affecting Financial Information Services and Foreign Financial Information Suppliers' (WTO, 24 February 2010) http://www.wto.org/english/tratop_e/dispu_e/cases_e/ds372_e.htm (accessed 4 March 2014).

[79]   Hao Zhang, 'Comments on Financial Information Case' in Chenggang Li (ed.), *Game of WTO Rules— A Decade of Legal Practices of China's Participation in WTO Dispute Settlement* (Beijing: Commercial Press, 2011), pp. 369–71 (available in Chinese only, author's translation).

[80]   'China – Measures Affecting Financial Information Services and Foreign Financial Information Suppliers' (WTO, 24 February 2010): http://www.wto.org/english/tratop_e/dispu_e/cases_e/ds378_e.htm (accessed 4 March 2014).

[81]   Ibid.

[82]   'China – Measures Affecting Financial Information Services and Foreign Financial Information Suppliers' (Chinalawinfo, 4 December 2008): http://www.chinalawinfo.com/wto/wtojdaldetail.asp?jdalid=34 (accessed 4 March 2014).

State Council Information Office. However, the Xinhua News Agency was not an administrative department and therefore its management could not be achieved by means of an administrative licence. Pursuant to the negotiations with the US, the EU and Canada, the State Council Information Office can carry out administration. As compared with the previous situation, with the exception of the fact that certain functions have changed in Chinese departments, the management system has been rationalised, the management tools and methods used are more rigorous and uniform and the actual regulatory effect has been improved. In essence, Chinese interests have not been affected negatively except that certain costs have been involved in adjusting policies. The impact on Chinese interests is negligible and some adjustments even help serve China's long-term interests.[83]

This case, resolved through consultations, was the result of the consideration of many factors and the careful assessment of pros and cons by the Chinese government. Chinese respondent groups thought it was feasible to formulate alternative measures in line with WTO rules within a short period, and negotiations to settle the case would not affect management efforts that continue to strengthen foreign news agencies' ability to provide financial information services in China. Following negotiations to resolve the case, the relevant departments formulated 'Regulations on Foreign Institutions Providing Financial Information Services in China'. These regulations do not weaken administration, but further strengthen and improve management. At the same time, China's reputation as a country that complies with WTO rules and helps create a harmonious international environment for development has been maintained.[84]

Objectively speaking, from the perspective of the way in which world finance is run and the state of development of the Chinese financial industry, the requirements put forward by the EU and the US were reasonable. Transparency of financial information can help the healthy development of the financial market. The Memorandum provides that foreign financial information providers are allowed to set up in China. As a consequence, several industry giants in Europe and America that monopolise financial information services are free to extend their tentacles towards the Chinese market. Therefore, the Chinese government should strengthen the

[83]   Chenggang Li (ed.), *Game of WTO Rules— A Decade of Legal Practices of China's Participation in WTO Dispute Settlement* (Beijing: Commercial Press, 2011), pp. 46–7 (available in Chinese only, author's translation).

[84]   Hao Zhang, 'Comments on Financial Information Case' in Chenggang Li (ed.), *Game of WTO Rules— A Decade of Legal Practices of China's Participation in WTO Dispute Settlement* (Beijing: Commercial Press, 2011), p. 365 (available in Chinese only, author's translation).

regulation of the industry. After experiencing many years of competition, the international financial information services market has shown a high degree of market concentration which continues to grow. In respect of the market share of the various global financial information services providers, since 2007 Bloomberg (US), Reuters (UK) and Thomson (Canada) have dominated the market. Thomson's acquisition of Reuters Group turned the industry into a duopoly. The Chinese government should rely on the expertise and information superiority of financial authorities and make full use of the financial antitrust system in order to effectively deal with the threat posed by these developments.[85]

The financial sectors have deficiencies and financial information services have just begun operating in China. It seems to be from all these that if China completely opens up the financial information services market, its financial security will face competition and the stable development of the Chinese economy will face enormous challenges, particularly given the current situation of increasing uncertainty as regards the structure of the international financial market and global financial markets. China seems to be concerned that such a move may even hinder the solid pace of Chinese economic development. Therefore, the Chinese government needs to strengthen its regulatory work, in particular with regard to the implementation of an anti-monopoly mechanism. The Memorandum states that China has agreed to transfer the regulatory power in respect of foreign financial information suppliers from the Xinhua News Agency to an independent regulatory body.[86]

The Chinese financial information services market is in a developmental stage and its potential is not unknown to competitors. Consequently, it has been a key target for the world's major financial information service providers. It plays a critical role in China's overall economic development. If China cannot introduce an effective monitoring mechanism, this might not only hurt the financial sector.[87]

2. A war over resources in the context of an economic crisis   On 23 June 2009 the US and the EU requested consultations with China. They claimed that China had adopted export quotas, export duties and other

---

[85]   'China – Measures Affecting Financial Information Services and Foreign Financial Information Suppliers' (Chinalawinfo, 4 December 2008): http://www.chinalawinfo.com/wto/wtojdaldetail.asp?jdalid=34 (accessed 4 March 2014).

[86]   Ibid.

[87]   Wanyang Xie, 'Comments on Financial Information Service Measures' (sina, 9 December 2009): http://blog.sina.com.cn/s/blog_4a87beef0100g7fs.html (accessed 5 March 2014) (available in Chinese only, author's translation).

price and volume control measures in respect of nine raw materials, including bauxite, coke, fluorite, magnesium, manganese, silicon metal, silicon carbide, yellow phosphorus and zinc, in violation of its WTO accession commitments. They argued that this put other countries at a disadvantage in relation to the production and export of steel, aluminium and other chemical products, while Chinese domestic manufacturers gained an unfair competitive advantage.[88]

Mexico subsequently consulted with China in August 2009 with regard to the same measures. In July and September 2009, China, the US, the EU and Mexico held two rounds of constructive consultations on the export of raw materials which did not, however, result in a satisfactory solution.[89]

China clarified the relevant export management measures during the consultations and specified that the main purpose of these measures was to protect the environment and natural resources. During the consultations, China expressed willingness to communicate with the member states involved in order to resolve the dispute, and stressed that it always respects and complies with WTO rules and its own commitments and that it believed that its export-related measures were in line with WTO principles and rules.[90]

EU Trade Commissioner Karel De Gucht noted that export quotas, export taxes and other export restrictions imposed on raw materials by China had distorted competition and raised the price on the international market so that EU companies had to face a more difficult situation in the circumstances of the current economic crisis.[91]

The European Commission claimed that over the past few years the EU had negotiated with China on many occasions but had been unsuccessful. Therefore, it had resorted to the WTO dispute settlement mechanism to find a satisfactory solution. The EU requested consultations on specific issues, including quantitative restrictions on the export of bauxite, coke, silicon carbide and zinc; export taxes on phosphorus, bauxite, coke, silicon metal, magnesium, manganese and zinc; and minimum export prices, an

---

[88] 'China – Measures Related to the Exportation of Various Raw Materials' (Chinalawinfo, 30 January 2012): http://www.chinalawinfo.com/wto/wtojdaldetail.asp?jdalid=25 (accessed 5 March 2014).

[89] Ibid.

[90] 'China Rejected the US, EU and Mexico WTO Panel Request on Export of Raw Materials' (xinhua net, 20 November 2009): http://news.xinhuanet.com/world/2009-11/20/content_12499532.htm (accessed 5 March 2014) (available in Chinese only, author's translation).

[91] 'Resorting to the WTO and the US and EU's Fight for Scarce Chinese Resources' (people, 25 June 2009): http://finance.people.com.cn/GB/9537958.html (accessed 5 March 2014) (available in Chinese only, author's translation).

approval process in respect of export contracts; as well as other unreasonable demands related to raw materials.[92]

The European Commission put the total value of EU imports of raw materials from China in 2008 at 4.5 billion euros. These materials are widely used in the steel, aluminium and chemical industries. The restrictive policies applied by China in respect of exports may reduce the value of the EU's total industrial output by up to 4 per cent and involve about 500,000 members of the working population. From the EU's perspective, Chinese export restrictions on raw materials are akin to pinching the neck of European companies, many of which rely heavily on imports of raw materials. China is a major global supplier of some of these raw materials, which means the EU has little choice.[93]

The EU believed that because of Chinese restrictions on the export of raw materials applied through the use of minimum prices and export taxes, the price of raw materials sold on the international market had been artificially increased and the competitiveness of downstream industries in the EU had been directly damaged. In one particular case, key investment in an EU industry had been completely cut off. This led to unfair competition between these European companies and their Chinese counterparts.[94]

The US stated that the raw materials involved are widely used in steel, chips, aircraft and many other industries. The US officials disclosed that the relevant trade volume reached billions of dollars.[95]

China argued that its intention in limiting the export of materials associated with high energy consumption and pollution was to protect the environment and resources. Moreover, according to the Protocol, China still has the right to implement restrictions on the export of nearly a hundred raw materials. The EU argued that the restrictions actually imposed went beyond the permitted scope.[96]

On 21 December 2009, the DSB established a single panel to examine the dispute. China stated that the relevant export control measures in respect of raw materials had been clearly explained and that China had expected to resolve the issue through dialogue, but the insistence of the US, the EU and Mexico on the establishment of a panel was a disappointment to China. Since the establishment of a panel had become inevitable, China would seek to protect its rights and interests during the

---

[92] Ibid.
[93] Ibid.
[94] Ibid.
[95] Ibid.
[96] Ibid.

panel stage.[97] However, it was unable to explain why the price of related resources for production and consumption differed between China and foreign countries. Furthermore, related resources did not reduce production because of protective measures.[98]

On 5 July 2011, the report of the panel was circulated to members. The panel agreed with China on the scope of the review, allocation and management of the export quota and the grant of export licences, found that it had repealed the measures imposing an export price limit and recognised comprehensive management measures in respect of refractory clay and fluorite. However, the panel ruled that Chinese export duties and export quotas were inconsistent with China's WTO commitments and the relevant WTO rules, and did not comply with the exception clause in respect of the conservation of exhaustible natural resources and protection of human life and health, and so on.[99]

On 31 August 2011, China notified its decision to appeal, and on 6 September 2011 the US appealed the panel report. On 30 January 2012, the AB report was circulated to members. The AB upheld most of the panel's recommendations, except: (1) it reversed the panel's recommendations as to claims related to export licensing requirements, minimum export price requirements, Chinese administration and allocation of export quotas, and fees and formalities in connection with exportation; (2) it held that the panel had erred in its interpretation of the phrase 'made effective in conjunction with' in Article XX(g) of GATT 1994.[100]

An official from the Treaty and Law Department of the MOFCOM stated that China welcomed the fact that the AB had agreed with China on several important issues and had corrected the panel's ruling. However, China expressed regret that the AB had upheld the panel's ruling that Article XX of the GATT did not apply to export tariffs, etc. In order to protect the environment and avoid exhausting natural resources, the Chinese government has in recent years improved, and continues to improve, the management of certain resource products, especially those associated with high

---

[97] 'WTO Established a Panel to Investigate Chinese Restrictions on the Export of Raw Materials' (xinhua net, 22 December 2009): http://news.xinhuanet.com/fortune/2009-12/22/content_12686189.htm (accessed 6 March 2014) (available in Chinese only, author's translation).

[98] 'Precautions should be Taken in Rare Earth Policy' (ifeng, 2 February 2012): http://finance.ifeng.com/roll/20120202/5523093.shtml (accessed 6 March 2014) (available in Chinese only, author's translation).

[99] 'China – Measures Related to the Exportation of Various Raw Materials' (WTO, 6 May 2013): http://www.wto.org/english/tratop_e/dispu_e/cases_e/ds394_e.htm (accessed 6 March 2014).

[100] Ibid.

pollution, high energy consumption and high resource consumption. China was concerned that WTO rules both emphasise freedom of trade and allow members to take the necessary steps to protect resources and the environment. China stated that it would carefully evaluate the WTO rulings and achieve sustainable development in accordance with them with a view to implementing scientific management of resource products.[101]

At the DSB meeting on 28 January 2013, China reported that on 28 December 2012 the General Administration of Customs had promulgated the 2013 Tariff Implementation Program. On 31 December 2012, the MOFCOM and the General Administration of Customs had jointly promulgated the 2013 Catalogue of Goods Subject to Export Licensing Administration. Under these notices, both of which entered into force on 1 January 2013, export duties and export quotas no longer applied to certain raw materials. Thus China had fully implemented the DSB's recommendations and rulings in these disputes.[102]

The WTO verdict had various impacts on domestic industry. Dong Chunming, a magnesium researcher from Sunlight Metal Consulting Co. Ltd, commented that the WTO ruling met the interests of upstream raw material suppliers, and in 2011 several Chinese People's Political Consultative Conference (CPPCC) members proposed the abolition of export duties. China is an exporter of magnesium and meets 85 per cent of the global demand for magnesium. It had set a 10 per cent export tariff on magnesium exports mainly due to the high energy consumption involved: production of one ton of magnesium requires about 5 tons of coal and 1.1 tons of ferrosilicon. Magnesium resources are relatively abundant compared with bauxite and zinc. Dong Chunming predicted that once China had reduced or eliminated its export tariffs on magnesium, the EU would increase magnesium imports. This is good news for upstream raw material producers, but will undermine the cost advantages on the domestic demand side. A representative of Shanxi Huasheng Aluminum Company stated that bauxite faces the same situation as magnesium. Although more than 50 per cent of the Chinese aluminium industry's bauxite needs are met by imports, there are still a great deal of low-priced exports.[103]

---

[101] 'The WTO Ruled on the Violation of Chinese Export Restrictions in Respect of Nine Raw Materials' (xinhua net, 1 February 2012): http://news.xin huanet.com/fortune/2012-02/01/c_111475447.htm (accessed 8 March 2014) (available in Chinese only, author's translation).

[102] 'China – Measures Related to the Exportation of Various Raw Materials' (WTO, 6 May 2013): http://www.wto.org/english/tratop_e/dispu_e/cases_e/ds394_e.htm (accessed 6 March 2014).

[103] 'A Chain Reaction of the WTO Ruling: Will Rare Earth be the Next

At the beginning of this century, the US and the EU implemented antidumping measures in respect of bauxite, magnesium, manganese, coke, fluorite and other raw materials. For example, since 2006, a number of international refractory material providers have sued on the basis of Chinese dumping measures relating to magnesium and bauxite. As a result, most Chinese companies were ruled to impose high antidumping duties. Ironically, given the current shortage of raw materials and the increase in the cost of raw materials, the US and the EU filed a case complaining of restrictions on the export of raw materials.[104]

In fact, applying restrictions on the export of resource products is a consistent practice of almost all WTO members and many developed countries take good care of domestic resources with strategic significance. The US has abundant oil resources, but depends on imports instead of exploiting local resources. It also sealed its largest rare earth mine, in Mountain Pass, and made a clear decision that the vast majority of timber cannot be felled for export. Japan shut down all coal production and, in order to conserve resources, merely retained Kushiro coal mine in Hokkaido in order to preserve the relevant technology. In 2007 Japanese annual coal production was only 600,000 tons and the rest of the coal used was imported.[105]

The WTO ruling was undoubtedly a huge challenge to China's export policy on raw materials. However, the industry was worried that although this case did not involve rare earth products, the US and the EU would set their sights on rare earth.[106]

Certain strategies were available to China. Firstly, export volume needs to be determined by reference to domestic production and the remaining amount of the product. Secondly, governance starts from the source of the production. If China integrates and regulates on the basis of upstream production and strictly implements environmental laws and regulations, the elimination of export control will not have too much impact on the industry and the environment. At present the phenomenon of excessive mining and digging is out of control in China and substandard mines and smelters are still operating, which ultimately is because China does not

---

One?' (China Net on Aluminum, 1 February 2012): http://news.cnal.com/industry/2012/02-01/1328062609264010.shtml (accessed 9 March 2014) (available in Chinese only, author's translation).
[104]   Ibid.
[105]   'The WTO Ruled as to a Chinese Violation in the Raw Materials Case' (xinhua net, 22 February 2011): http://news.xinhuanet.com/fortune/2011--02/22/c_121106802.htm (accessed 9 March 2014) (available in Chinese only, author's translation).
[106]   Ibid.

strictly implement the relevant laws and regulations. If the required environmental standard can be strictly enforced, the natural environment will not be devastated. Thirdly, China can enhance the environmental threshold and industry standard. If China proceeds in strict accordance with standardised plans for the approval of mines and for their exploration and exploitation across the whole country, it will naturally have a reliable guarantee for the protection of raw materials. Fourthly, the government can impose a resource tax.[107]

However, the contradiction between the need for energy conservation and the need to prevent environmental pollution caused by the production process cannot be resolved within the trade sector. The relevant Chinese governments need to change their ways of thinking so that instead of placing excessive reliance on trade control, the regulation of resource products is achieved by regulating the production process. Controlling the source is an effective means of controlling what emanates from it.[108]

Every person and business should put the interests of the country and the people before the interests of a company or an individual in China. Then, on the basis that the interests of the nation and the people are not being undermined, it is permissible to seek to maximise the interests of a company or an individual. The Chinese as individuals should not excessively mine or smuggle but should seek to establish a solid industrial platform so that businesses and individuals can develop better. Failure to do so will lead to contentious cases before international dispute settlement mechanisms such as the WTO DSB. Therefore, it is important for China to put the protection of the environment and resources first, and in a way that will not violate its international obligations.[109]

The Chinese media focused a great deal of attention on the *Measures Related to the Exportation of Various Raw Materials* case from its beginning to its end because of the claim of its links to national security. The Chinese government and relevant companies invited experts and scholars to discuss and publish their insights. They unanimously denounced the sinister motivations of what they saw as predator states. From a Chinese perspective, this may seem a reasonable conclusion, but everyone is equal before the national interest: China has its national interest, the US has American national interest, while the EU represents the Union's interests.

---

[107] Hui Wang, 'Correctly Understand and Deal with the WTO Ruling on Raw Materials Dispute' (China non-ferrous metals net, 2 February 2012): http://www.cnmn.com.cn/ShowNews1.aspx?id=228664 (accessed 9 March 2014) (available in Chinese only, author's translation).
[108] Ibid.
[109] Ibid.

In view of Chinese traditional thinking with regard to the notion of compliance, the mature party to a dispute should abandon simple 'right and wrong' judgements. China should be able to afford to be a loser as well as to be a winner. Excessive criticism is futile and meaningless. Of course, in the international arena China should express its innocence, in support of the national interest, but at the same time it needs to do more in-depth thinking.

China should focus on what there is to be learned from its failures. In this case, it again cited the GATT 1994 Article XX exception, which it had relied on successfully only in the shrimp/turtle case,[110] although the US needed to modify the measure in question. The AB supported American views on the Article XX exceptions. This ruling led to a lot of criticism and accusations, as a result of which the panel and AB take a very cautious approach to cases in which Article XX is invoked as a defence. As the WTO is an international trade organisation, it is easy to understand why it favours trade over criticism of its limitations – it is beyond its remit to protect non-trade issues. But this does not mean that environmental issues do not concern the WTO at all or that Article XX of GATT is a forbidden zone. In the *Brazil – Retreaded Tyres* case,[111] the panel and AB partially supported Brazil's reliance on the exceptional clause. Other countries' successes can be learned from in order to win under Article XX of GATT.

Chinese investment policies, industrial policies and environmental supervision should play an important role in resolving the environmental problem. The lesson learned from it is that it is not a good idea to simply rely on a single export control. One of the problems exposed by this case is that there is a lack of experience in managing trade in China. It is imperative to make advances in learning the 'WTO language' and in mastering WTO rules. Moreover, external pressures and obstacles should not hinder China's overall development, but this should occur at China's own pace.[112]

Chinese policymakers should not hastily formulate and implement policies that clearly contravene international trade rules. As a major exporter, China itself is a major target of international trade litigation. If it formulates policies that will result in it losing cases easily, it is simply looking for trouble. Many measures can be used to achieve the desired outcome while

---

[110]   DS 58, 61 *United States – Import Prohibition of Certain Shrimp and Shrimp Products*.

[111]   DS 332, *Brazil – Measures Affecting Imports of Retreaded Tyres*.

[112]   'To Safeguard Economic Sovereignty One should Speak Good "WTO Language"' (xinhua net, 2 February 2012): http://news.xinhuanet.com/fortune/2012-02/02/c_122647388.htm (accessed 10 March 2014) (available in Chinese only, author's translation).

still complying with the WTO rules. These include governance of the way in which sources are explored, the improvement of environmental standards and the technical qualification requirements applied to mining companies, gradual reduction of production leading to price increases and the governance of disorderly development and cheap consumption. Governance of the mining market is one important governmental task. China does not make an effort to standardise production processes, but uses the method of limiting lower price exports through the trade aspect, which is equivalent to violating international trade rules and exports bad domestic governance practices to the world. It reflects a lack of responsibility in Chinese administrative governance and the use of opportunistic policies. Such reckless behaviour will cause trouble during a period of trade protectionism.[113]

In addition, there is a gap between China and other countries as to the way in which WTO norms are understood. China should not choose WTO standards on the basis of its own demands, nor should it focus purely on the protection of resources on the basis of superficially plausible reasons, since neither will help resolve trade disputes.[114]

3. A tough negotiation in the renewable energy generation sector   Two EU member states, Italy and Greece, decided that if the main components of renewable energy generation originated from the EU or the European Economic Area, the electricity produced could benefit from a certain amount or percentage of subsidies. The Deputy Director of the Treaty and Law Division of the Chinese Ministry of Commerce stated that many European countries have implemented electricity price subsidies for renewable energy without distinguishing the origin of the renewable energy generated. However, on this basis Italy and Greece gave extra electricity subsidies for renewable energy generation so that local EU manufacturers gained favourable competition. For example, in 2010 China exported cells and modules to Italy of a value of $4.8 billion. In 2011, Italy issued its subsidy measure, causing the value of Chinese exports to fall to $3.88 billion. For the first nine months of 2012, the value of Chinese exports was only $760 million – a decrease of 78.8 per cent.[115]

---

[113]   'Precautions should be Taken in Rare Earth Policy' (ifeng, 2 February 2012): http://finance.ifeng.com/roll/20120202/5523093.shtml (accessed 10 March 2014) (available in Chinese only, author's translation).

[114]   'The Dangerous Situation of Rare Earth May Change Export Policy and it is Imperative to Extend the Industrial Chain' (China non-ferrous metals net, 6 February 2012): http://www.cnmn.com.cn/ShowNews1.aspx?id=228946 (accessed 10 March 2014) (available in Chinese only, author's translation).

[115]   'China Filed a Case on Renewable Energy Generation Subsidy Measures

In September 2012, the European Commission insisted on launching antidumping investigations into Chinese renewable energy generation regardless of the fact that China had repeatedly called for trade frictions to be resolved through consultations. The dispute, involving a value of nearly 130 billion RMB (about $20.9 billion), is the largest case China has been involved in over the years. After the antidumping investigation, the EU countervailing investigation started. One group, known as EU ProSun, comprising many EU companies, had complained to the European regulatory authorities in September that Chinese solar companies received illegal subsidies.[116]

Since 2011, the US and the EU have separately launched 'double anti' measures. Given that the market was deteriorating, Chinese solar companies faced poor conditions and serious losses. A US investment institute, Maxim Group, released data in August 2012 that showed that the debt of China's 10 largest solar companies was as much as $17.5 billion. In response to the export disruption caused by the US and the EU, since 2011 Chinese solar companies have accelerated the pace of development in south-east Asia, India, Africa, the Middle East and other emerging markets. However, progress has been slow and subject to market size, as a consequence of which some companies have turned their sights to the domestic market, although even that is still difficult.[117]

On 1 November 2012, the Chinese Ministry of Commerce announced its decision with immediate effect on the antidumping and countervailing investigation of solar-grade polysilicon instigated by the EU.[118] On 5 November 2012, China requested consultations with the EU regarding the feed-in tariff programmes.[119] A Ministry of Commerce spokesman expressed the view that the tariff subsidies violated the principles of national treatment and MFN under the WTO Agreement, constituted import substitution subsidies prohibited under the WTO Agreement, seriously affected the exports of Chinese solar products and damaged

against the EU to the WTO' (xinhua net, 6 November 2012): http://news.xinhua net.com/fortune/2012-11/06/c_123917427.htm (accessed 13 February 2014) (available in Chinese only, author's translation).

[116]   Ibid.

[117]   'Chinese Solar Companies Seek to Break Through' (xinhua net, 6 November 2012): http://news.xinhuanet.com/fortune/2012-11/06/c_113622651.htm (accessed 13 February 2014) (available in Chinese only, author's translation).

[118]   Ibid.

[119]   'WT/DS452 European Union and certain Member States – Certain Measures Affecting the Renewable Energy Generation Sector' (WTO, 18 December 2012): http://www.wto.org/english/tratop_e/dispu_e/cases_e/ds452_e.htm (accessed 13 February 2014).

China's legitimate rights as a WTO member. The Chinese government has the right and responsibility for its own solar companies fighting for a fair international trade environment. Developing solar photovoltaic and other renewable energy can help solve the problems of energy security and climate change in line with the common interest of every country. Each state should take a long-term perspective, strengthen industrial coopera-tion and open up international trade, instead of seeking short-term benefit via trade protectionism measures. China has repeatedly stated that it will resolutely oppose all forms of trade protectionism and will firmly exercise the right to safeguard its legitimate rights.[120]

Some relevant Chinese figures did not hesitate to make their views known. Wang Zhixin, the Head of Media at Yingli Group, thought it was encouraging for the industry as a whole. These were some of the efforts at the national level that showed the importance of the solar industry. Companies were actively responding to the EU's investigation and had established a union called CASE, which included Chinese solar companies and European upstream and downstream companies. Shi Limin, the Deputy Secretary of the New Energy Chamber in All-China Federation of Industry and Commerce, considered some of the EU laws and practices to be contrary to the principles of the WTO and that Chinese litigation on this matter would create a fair international trade environment.[121]

The EU would file a solar subsidy case against China soon and China brought a case against the EU in the WTO. From the Chinese point of view, this made the EU realise that it should not simply hold up the mirror to others, but should also look at itself. WTO rules divide prohibited sub-sidies into import substitution and export subsidies. Italy and Greece were using import substitution subsidies by reference to the material origin. This amounted to the use of prohibited subsidies and also violated the principle of national treatment. A Chinese Ministry of Commerce researcher noted that China had begun to strike back with a portfolio of diversified methods of dealing with trade protection behaviour on the part of the US and the

---

[120] 'Ministry of Commerce Spokesman Shen Danyang Issued a Statement on the Chinese Solar Subsidies Case against the EU in the WTO' (MOFCOM, 5 November 2012): http://www.mofcom.gov.cn/aarticle/ae/ag/201211/2012110 8419302.html (accessed 13 February 2014) (available in Chinese only, author's translation).
[121] 'China Filed a Case on Renewable Energy Generation Subsidy Measures against the EU to the WTO' (xinhua net, 6 November 2012): http://news.xin huanet.com/fortune/2012-11/06/c_123917427.htm (accessed 13 February 2014) (available in Chinese only, author's translation).

EU. While facing measures of trade protection, it is necessary to choose a real and proper means of fighting back. In addition, in order to deal with international trade externally, China should accelerate the development of the domestic market and promote the balancing development of domestic and international markets. Insiders took the view that in fact the development of new industries should be encouraged and supported. Every state is supportive. The investigation of Chinese solar products was jointly launched by the EU and the US, making support measures for emerging industry a controversial issue worldwide and triggering a trade mêlée. Trade protection behaviour, and even a trade war, has no winner and both sides will suffer loss. The trade war regarding solar products was not a simple economic problem, but rose to a political and national strategic level.[122]

While the Chinese government resolved this trade dispute through the WTO mechanism and proposed new policies to support the development of the solar industry, solar companies also actively sought to help themselves. LDK solar company signed an agreement with Henrui, a new energy company, on a restructuring issue. As the first to take steps towards restructuring, LDK's actions had implications for other solar companies suffering 'winter'. Li Hejun, President of the New Energy Chamber in the All-China Federation of Industry and Commerce, stated that this was a good time to expand. His reasoning was that since the whole industry was facing difficulties and many overseas companies were on the verge of bankruptcy, Chinese companies could spend less money than would usually be the case to acquire some well-known companies and advanced technology in order to achieve a dominant position for the next round of competition. On 20 March 2013, Suntech, a company located in the city of Wuxi, announced its bankruptcy and reorganisation.[123]

Germany was the first to take steps to ease tensions with the Chinese Ministry of Commerce. On 30 August 2012, at a critical moment of uncertainty as to whether the EU would file an antidumping case in respect of Chinese solar products in not less than 10 days, Angela Merkel visited China for the sixth time in four years and the second in 2012. The delegation included almost half of the German cabinet. Contrary to the impression given to the outside world that Merkel said nothing about solar energy, good news finally came. China and Germany agreed to resolve the issue relating to the solar industry through negotiation to

---

[122]   'China Filed a Case on Renewable Energy Generation Subsidy Measures against the EU to the WTO' (xinhua net, 6 November 2012): http://news.xinhua net.com/fortune/2012-11/06/c_123917427.htm (accessed 13 February 2014) (available in Chinese only, author's translation).

[123]   Ibid.

avoid antidumping litigation and thereby strengthen cooperation. During the visit, Merkel made it clear in her meeting with reporters that she hoped the European Commission, relevant companies and China would seek to eliminate and resolve the problem through communication or consultations rather than through antidumping proceedings.[124]

The Chinese government seems to have paid a great deal of attention to this event and it is purported that Prime Minister Li Keqiang personally carried out a lot of critical work. To the outside world, Premier Li clarified on different occasions that the solar products case benefits nobody but harms others. If handled improperly, it might lead to a trade war where there would be no winner. He therefore hoped that the two sides in the overall situation would be able to resolve the dispute through consultations. Internally, Premier Li himself learned about the difficulties faced by domestic solar companies, sought ways forward for them, encouraged them and exhorted the whole industry to work together with the Chinese government to overcome difficulties.[125]

On 4 June 2013, the European Commission announced that from 6 June it would impose temporary punitive duties of 11.8 per cent in respect of Chinese solar cells and key components despite opposition from 18 member states of the EU. This was the first stage of the preliminary ruling. The tax rate decreased compared with the rate of 47.6 per cent proposed by the European Commission. But after two months, if the two sides failed to achieve a solution, the rate would rise to 47.6 per cent within the next four months, which was the second phase of the preliminary ruling. After a preliminary implementation period, if the two parties were still unable to reach a solution by the end of the year, the EU would make the final decision. As long as this was supported by the majority of member states, higher duties would be applied in the next five years.[126]

China initiated counter-measures. After the EU had announced the antidumping result of the preliminary ruling on Chinese solar products, the Chinese government immediately launched investigation procedures in respect of wine from the EU. Then it was said that China was preparing to start an antidumping investigation focusing on luxury cars from the EU. The immediate counter-measure launched by China seems to

---

[124] 'Solar Event' (ifeng, 4 September 2012): http://finance.ifeng.com/news/industry/20120904/6985516.shtml (accessed 14 February 2014) (available in Chinese only, author's translation).

[125] 'EU-China Trade War: Prime Minister's Public Relations' (xinhua net, 18 June 2013): http://news.xinhuanet.com/fortune/2013-06/18/c_124870820.htm (accessed 14 February 2014) (available in Chinese only, author's translation).

[126] Ibid.

have produced an instant result. Three of the EU's major exporters of wine – Italy, France and Spain – suggested to the European Commission that a special summit of EU leaders should be held. This was rejected by Commission President José Manuel Barroso.[127]

Meanwhile, the Chinese solar industry also actively responded and matured during the process. The China Chamber of Commerce for Machine and Electricity (CCCME) organised the collection of data from companies to prepare the legal defence, promoted China–EU cooperation between industries to resolve friction, actively conducted effective public relations and lobbying, and so on. The CCCME principally tackled two issues: first, it put together further legal defences; and second, it communicated closely with companies to prepare plans for negotiations. In fact, the companies' response was not just an emergency policy. Artes, Yingli and other solar companies had started researching and implementing a strategy to shift to global emerging markets, and a proportion of leading companies had moved away from over-reliance on the EU market. The Asia-Pacific region comprising Japan, Thailand and India, where large populations are concentrated, became the market targeted for exploration.[128]

On 14 June 2013 Premier Li proposed six measures: the promotion of rational distribution, improvement of grid security, development of a solar electricity subsidy, promotion of financial support, strengthening of industry standards and encouraging mergers and acquisitions. All of these were aimed at supporting the solar industry.[129]

After tough and delicate negotiations between China and the EU, the European Commission and the Chinese solar industry agreed a price guarantee in respect of their trade dispute over solar products. This agreement entered into force on 6 August 2013 and was unanimously supported by the 28 EU member states. The price seems to have reflected the wishes of the vast majority of Chinese companies. Chinese solar products continued to be exported to the EU and maintained a reasonable market share on the basis of trade arrangements between the parties.[130]

European and American media and experts gave positive comments

[127] Ibid.

[128] Ibid.

[129] 'Chinese Solar Products Expand Domestic Demand (Hot Dialysis)' (People, 16 July 2013): http://paper.people.com.cn/gjjrb/html/2013-07/16/content_1269025. htm (accessed 14 February 2014) (available in Chinese only, author's translation).

[130] 'Price Joint Statement on Trade Dispute in respect of the Export of Chinese Solar Products to the EU' (the Central People's Government of the PRC, 27 July 2013): http://www.gov.cn/gzdt/2013-07/27/content_2456534.htm (accessed 14 February 2014) (available in Chinese only, author's translation).

on this trade dispute. The Associated Press pointed out that Chinese Premier Li Keqiang had played a decisive role in the successful negotiations concerning the friction between the EU and China over this matter. Five Chinese industry organisations, comprising CCCME, the China Renewable Energy Society, the Trans Union New Energy Chamber of Commerce, the Renewable Energy Professional Committee of China Association of Resources Comprehensive Utilization, and the China Solar Industry Alliance issued a joint statement expressing gratitude to Premier Li. Many European companies were also grateful to him because he not only helped Chinese solar companies to achieve a great victory through negotiations, but also objectively saved the EU. If the EU entered into a full trade war with China, it would be a disaster for European businesses.[131]

EU Trade Commissioner De Gucht told the BBC that the success of the negotiations between China and the EU over this matter lay in the fact that it met the common interest of both sides, and that he was pleased with the outcome of the negotiations. The China–EU friendship agreement would stabilise the European solar panel market.[132]

The *Financial Times* commented that if the EU imposed high tariffs in respect of Chinese solar panels, the price of solar panels would rise significantly, which was not conducive to the growth of solar panel installation and would harm the interests of both European consumers and installers. Fortunately, Mr Li Keqiang had promoted the success of China–EU negotiations and saved EU solar panel installers' livelihood.[133]

An Asia expert from the European Council on Foreign Relations told the US *Wall Street Journal* that many EU member states had no intention of starting a trade war against China because it would damage their trade interests with China. During negotiations between China and the EU, the EU's largest economy, Germany, opposed the levying of huge duties on China. In the past five years, Germany and China had increasingly strengthened their trade relations in a manner which benefited German exporters, which increasingly relied on the huge domestic demand in China.[134]

Deutsche Welle commented that the negotiations conducted by both sides were fair and impartial and the success of negotiations meant that the EU would avoid an expensive trade war. During the course of the

---

[131] 'Foreign Media: Li Keqiang Promoted China-EU Solar Negotiations to Achieve Success' (China Daily, 5 August 2013): http://caijing.chinadaily.com.cn/2013-08/05/content_16870071.htm (accessed 15 February 2014) (available in Chinese only, author's translation).

[132] Ibid.

[133] Ibid.

[134] Ibid.

solar negotiations, Chinese Premier Li Keqiang and German Chancellor Angela Merkel advocated the resolution of their differences through dialogue and consultations.[135] There would be no benefit to either side if the EU imposed permanent duties on Chinese solar products. Before the European Commission released its preliminary ruling, Li Keqiang talked to the European Commission President José Manuel Barroso on the phone. Premier Li was concerned that this case involved China's core economic interests and hoped to resolve trade disputes through dialogue and consultations in lieu of a trade war. This positive and clear attitude finally resulted in successful EU–China negotiations.[136]

The following four conclusions can be drawn from the entire process and the outcome of the case. Firstly, the leaders of China and the EU played an important and decisive role in resolving the issue. Secondly, the parties were able to quickly resolve the dispute because of effective consultations and negotiations at all levels, both within China and the EU, including the Chinese State Council, the Chinese Ministry of Commerce, business associations and many companies that were involved. These actors communicated on the basis of the principle of mutual respect and followed the rules of the game. Thirdly, the outcome was the result of common trade needs and competition between powers. If the EU tried to have its own way, this would certainly lead to China seeking revenge in relation to the EU's products. The threat of retaliation by China becomes increasingly potent as China's economic power increases, but neither side would benefit from this happening. Finally, from the perspective of the trend of world economic recovery and trade disputes, most major economies follow the WTO's free trade principle. The fact that two large global trading entities were able to resolve a dispute involving such a large amount of money is good news and sets a good example for other major economies to follow. But achieving a price commitment in respect of solar products does not mean that the dispute has been resolved, since there may be difficulties in implementing the price, service life, market

---

[135]   It is important to note that this approach is very much in line with Confucianism. See Mo Zhang, 'The Socialist Legal System with Chinese Characteristics: China's Discourse for the Rule of Law and a Bitter Experience', *Temple International & Comparative Law Journal*, Vol. 24 (2010), pp. 1–64; Teemu Ruskola, 'Law Without Law, or is "Chinese Law" an Oxymoron?', *William & Mary Bill of Rights Journal*, Vol. 11 (2003), pp. 655–69.

[136]   'Foreign Media: Li Keqiang Promoted China-EU Solar Negotiations to Achieve Success' (China Daily, 5 August 2013): http://caijing.chinadaily.com.cn/2013-08/05/content_16870071.htm (accessed 15 February 2014) (available in Chinese only, author's translation).

share, and sanctions. Reaching a price commitment achieved an initial result between China and the EU, but the parties need to continue to work together and implement the commitment.

As mentioned earlier, since China acceded to the WTO it has been involved in 32 disputes. In 12 of these it has been the complainant, and in the other 20 it has been the respondent. Of the 24 disputes it was involved in between 2007 and 2012, it was the complainant in 10 and the respondent in 15. From a Chinese perspective, China has withstood the test of being involved in many cases both as a complainant and respondent. It has learned a lot from the WTO dispute settlement mechanism and at the same time has sought to fulfil its responsibility as a large trading state. Consequently, Chinese officials have repeatedly noted that the Chinese government has consistently complied with WTO laws and engages in consultations or litigation to solve disputes. Although critics have accused the WTO of being a tool used by developed countries to control developing countries, from the Chinese experience one can conclude that the WTO is a means of somehow accelerating national economies and ensuring a level playing field in international trade.

7.1.2.5   The challenge of compliance for China

Like other WTO members, China faces many difficulties relating to implementation and compliance. During the WTO Chinese years, several hard cases appeared of a kind which had never been seen before in the history of the WTO. Yet China's own practice involves interpreting how to implement and comply with WTO rules.

1. The amendment of Chinese copyright law   In early 2002, the US International Intellectual Property Alliance (IIPA) submitted material to the USTR and stated that piracy rates in the Chinese market were as high as 90 per cent which caused staggering loss to both American and Chinese creators and companies. It went on to say that China is a WTO member and should publicly acknowledge it has not complied with the WTO obligation to take enforcement measures against piracy on a commercial scale. The 'Special 301' report released by the USTR mentioned that Chinese administrative penalties did not curb further infringement and the threshold was too high to start a criminal case. The USTR urged China to modify its judicial interpretation so as to deal with cases more efficiently and to implement deterrent penalties.[137]

---

[137]   Guohua Yang, 'Careful Preparation for Four Years, but for Once All Bets are Off – the Whole Story of the Chinese IPR Case' (Chinalawinfo, 20 March

In 2004, the IIPA made a further proposal to the USTR that amendment of Chinese criminal law should be sought. In 2005 the USTR issued the 'Special 301' report that serious infringement by China was not acceptable, and put China on the 'Priority Watch List'. It regarded China as a country that did not provide adequate protection or enforcement in respect of intellectual property rights. The US government would work with industry and other interested parties to initiate the WTO procedure to push China to comply with its obligations under Trade-Related Aspects of Intellectual Property Rights (TRIPS), and in particular push it to adopt a criminal enforcement system with deterrent force.[138]

On 28 April 2006, the USTR publicly announced the intention to consider the use of the WTO dispute settlement mechanism because China had not given the US proper intellectual property protection in respect of copyright, inventions, brands and trade secrets and little progress had been made in respect of solving the deficiencies in the law enforcement mechanisms. Subsequently, in various speeches, testimony and interviews, USTR officials constantly declared the intention to bring WTO proceedings against China.[139]

On 5 October 2006, the US–China Economic and Security Review Committee, which is a consulting agency for the US Congress, wrote a letter to members of Congress urging that the US should use the WTO dispute settlement mechanism to resolve the intellectual property right (IPR) issue in China. It recommended that Congress ask the Administration to resort to the WTO on Chinese IPR infringement and lack of enforcement. On 11 October 2006, 13 Democrats from the Ways and Means Committee in the House of Representatives, led by Nancy Pelosi, wrote a joint letter to President Bush recommending the filing of a complaint with the WTO as to flagrant violation of IPR international rules in China. They wrote that no other country infringes American IPR to the extent that occurs in China: piracy, counterfeiting and theft of patents were very serious; American software piracy rate was up to 90 per cent, resulting in an annual loss of $2 billion to the US; annual copyright loss was more than $2.5 billion; and the loss to the US auto industry due to counterfeit parts reached $12 billion a year, in respect of which China is a major offender.[140]

On 10 April 2007, the US sought consultations with China under the

---

2009): http://www.chinalawinfo.com/wto/wtojdaldetail.asp?jdalid=28 (accessed 26 February 2014) (available in Chinese only, author's translation).
    138   Ibid.
    139   Ibid.
    140   Ibid.

WTO dispute settlement mechanism relating to measures affecting the protection and enforcement of IPR and certain publications and audio-visual entertainment products' trading rights and distribution services. A MOFCOM spokesman expressed strong dissatisfaction with this development, on the basis that it would seriously undermine established cooperation between the two sides. He said that the Chinese government's attitude towards the protection of IPR has always been firm and its achievement is clear to all. In respect of market access for publications, the two sides engaged in good communication and consultation. The US had referred two cases to the WTO, which went against the spirit of the consensus on the vigorous development of bilateral economic and trade relations and the proper treatment of economic and trade issues.[141]

On 24 April, at the 2007 China IPR Forum, Vice Premier Wu Yi stressed that on the issue of IPR protection the two governments should adhere to the principle that dialogue is better than confrontation and cooperation is better than a fight. On the subject of intellectual property protection, China had made a great contribution within 30 years of a kind which developed countries had taken a century to complete. China had passed the WTO annual review and the development of the IPR protection was recognised by the majority of countries in the world, as well as by domestic and foreign companies. However, in referring two cases to the WTO on the same day, which had never before occurred in the history of the WTO, the USTR was not convinced by the seriousness of the Chinese government to implement IPR rules. The Chinese government was therefore strongly dissatisfied and was determined to respond actively in accordance with WTO rules.[142] A China Copyright Bureau spokesman pointed out that China and the US have a routinely institutionalised consultation mechanism on the issue of IPR. The Sino-US IPR dispute could be resolved by way of communication between the two countries. The US government's referral of the dispute to the WTO would not contribute to bilateral cooperation in respect of intellectual property.[143] Tian Lipu, the Director of the China

---

[141] 'America Filed Two Cases against China in the WTO' (xinhua net, 10 April 2007): http://news.xinhuanet.com/world/2007-04/10/content_5957297.htm (accessed 26 February 2014) (available in Chinese only, author's translation).

[142] 'Wu Yi Attended and Spoke at a High-Level Forum on the Protection of IPR' (xinhua net, 24 April 2007): http://news.xinhuanet.com/politics/2007-04/24/content_6020185.htm (accessed 26 February 2014) (available in Chinese only, author's translation).

[143] 'Copyright Bureau Spokesman: Piracy is a Global Problem' (xinhua net, 17 April 2007): http://news.xinhuanet.com/politics/2007-04/17/content_5988900.htm (accessed 26 February 2014) (available in Chinese only, author's translation).

Intellectual Property Office, said that the Chinese government had made enormous efforts to combat piracy and strengthen IPR protection. Thus, it did not make sense for the US to file a case on IPR against China with the WTO and it should withdraw.[144]

On 7 and 8 June 2007, China and the US held consultations in Geneva. China emphasised that efforts in the area of IPR protection had been made, including significantly reducing the threshold in respect of piracy. It pointed out that in April 2007 the Supreme People's Court and the Supreme People's Procuratorate of the People's Republic of China (PRC) had issued 'Judicial Interpretation on Criminal Cases of IPR Infringement' and the threshold for criminal liability in respect of piracy had been reduced from 1000 copies under the '2004 Judicial Interpretation' to 500 copies. In addition, China had enhanced anti-piracy enforcement. In July 2007 the Ministry of Public Security and the American Federal Bureau of Investigation had jointly launched the 'Summer Solstice' action, successfully cracked two big criminal cases on transnational production and sale of pirated software, arrested 25 suspects, seized pirated CDs and security labels totalling 360 000 items, and had frozen or sequestered funds, vehicles and real estate involved in the criminal activity that had a value of more than 60 million yuan.[145] On 16 July the US proposed the launching of further negotiations relating to the copying issue about which the US was concerned.

On 13 August 2007, the US requested the establishment of a panel. American complaints focused on the following four points: firstly, the threshold issue on Chinese law for wilful acts of trademark counterfeiting or copyright piracy to be subject to criminal procedures and penalties; secondly, the disposal issue that infringing goods were confiscated by Chinese customs authorities; thirdly, the scope of coverage of criminal procedures and penalties for unauthorised reproduction or unauthorised distribution of copyrighted works; fourthly, the denial of copyright and related rights protection and enforcement to creative works of authorship, sound recordings and performances that had not been authorised for publication or distribution within China.[146]

A MOFCOM spokesman stated that China regretted that the US had

---

[144]   'SIPO Director: The US should Withdraw its WTO Complaint' (the Central People's Government of the PRC, 3 July 2007): http://www.gov.cn/jrzg/2007-07/03/content_671831.htm (accessed 26 February 2014) (available in Chinese only, author's translation).

[145]   'Sino-US consultations on Chinese Intellectual Property Protection' (xinhua net, 9 June 2007): http://news.xinhuanet.com/world/2007-06/09/content_6220032.htm (accessed 26 February 2014) (available in Chinese only, author's translation).

[146]   'DS362 China – Measures Affecting the Protection and Enforcement of

resorted to the WTO on the IPR issue. Gao Huncheng, Vice-Minister of the MOFCOM, disclosed that China had held bilateral consultations in accordance with the relevant WTO provisions and had discussed China's relevant laws with the US with the utmost sincerity. China argued that the laws and regulations adopted in recent years fully complied with the TRIPS Agreement administered by the WTO, but unfortunately the US had still requested the establishment of a panel. China adhered to the position as always.[147]

Nicholas Lardy, a famous American expert on Chinese issues and a Senior Fellow at the Institute of International Economics, clarified that the US itself is very lax on piracy control but nonetheless required China to do better. There was a suspicion of double standards regardless of the fact that the two countries were at different stages of economic and social development. American corporate giants including Microsoft agreed that China had made great progress in clamping down on piracy.[148] The German government and media commented that a cooperative approach's prospects of success were better where intellectual property was concerned.[149]

On 26 January 2009 the panel circulated its final report, which dismissed most of the allegations by the US and broadly upheld the Chinese intellectual property system. On the threshold of criminal rules, the panel concluded that the US had failed to prove that the relevant provisions of the Chinese criminal law did not meet the requirements of the TRIPS Agreement. With respect to the Chinese Copyright Law, the panel found that China had the right to prohibit the circulation and exhibition of works, although China had failed to protect copyright in prohibited works (i.e. works banned because of their illegal content), inconsistent with the Berne Convention and the TRIPS Agreement.[150]

Intellectual Property Rights' (WTO, 26 May 2010): http://www.wto.org/english/tratop_e/dispu_e/cases_e/ds362_e.htm (accessed 27 February 2014).

[147] 'MOFCOM Expressed Regret that the IPR Case had been Referred to the WTO' (xinhua net, 16 August 2007): http://news.xinhuanet.com/newscenter/2007-08/16/content_6544019.htm (accessed 27 February 2014) (available in Chinese only, author's translation).

[148] 'Expert: China Probably Won the Sino-US IPR cases' (*Chinese Economy*, 5 June 2007): http://www.ce.cn/xwzx/gnsz/gdxw/200706/05/t20070605_11601360.shtml (accessed 27 February 2014) (available in Chinese only, author's translation).

[149] 'The German Government and Media Thought that the Prospect of Mutual Cooperation is Better in the IPR Case' (China Trade Remedy Information, 17 April 2007): http://www.cacs.gov.cn/cacs/newcommon/details.aspx?articleId=30795 (accessed 27 February 2014) (available in Chinese only, author's translation).

[150] 'DS362 China – Measures Affecting the Protection and Enforcement of

The USTR considered that the US had won on the core issue.[151] A MOFCOM spokesman expressed regret as to the panel's ruling against China on customs measures and the Chinese Copyright Law, while China welcomed that the panel had found that China did not violate the TRIPS Agreement at the criminal threshold in respect of intellectual property crime.[152]

An article published by the Third World Network, a pro-developing-country think-tank, entitled 'Case Ruling Favorable to China' pointed out that the US had made a total of 11 claims, but won only two outright and three-fifths of the third.[153] Michael Geist, a Canadian law professor and intellectual property expert, wrote an article entitled 'Why the US Lost Its WTO IP Complaint against China Badly', which related the exotic phenomenon of Reuters claiming 'America Win' as compared with the mild Chinese attitude. He noted that anyone who bothered to work through the 147-page decision would find that the headlines of the American newspaper got it wrong. China was required to amend elements of its copyright law. On this issue, the US clearly won, but this particular concern was certainly the least important of the three issues at stake. But on the big issues of this case – border measures and IP enforcement – almost all of the contested laws were upheld as valid. However, as is always the case, both sides seemed to have been claiming victory in this case.[154]

Forbes published an article entitled 'WTO's China Piracy Ruling: All Bark and No Bite', which stated mockingly that 'the proclamation of victory was empty or premature, or both'. Steve Dickinson, a China-based lawyer and partner at Harris Moure, commented as follows: 'The US claim was trivial and hyper technical. They won on the hyper technical issue. The only serious issue was the criminal sanctions issue and they lost

---

Intellectual Property Rights' (WTO, 26 May 2010): http://www.wto.org/english/tratop_e/dispu_e/cases_e/ds362_e.htm (accessed 27 February 2014).

[151] 'Snapshot of WTO Cases Involving the United States' (USTR, 8 August 2012): http://www.ustr.gov/sites/default/files/Snapshot%20Aug8.fin_.pdf (accessed 28 February 2014).

[152] 'China Regretted Part of Panel Ruling on Intellectual Property Dispute' (China news, 27 January 2009): http://www.chinanews.com/cj/gncj/news/2009/01-27/1542340.shtml (accessed 28 February 2014) (available in Chinese only, author's translation).

[153] Wenhua Ji, 'Sino-US IPR Dispute: Who is the Winner?' (sohu, 21 May 2010): http://2010ipb828.blog.sohu.com/152134204.html (accessed 28 February 2014) (available in Chinese only, author's translation).

[154] Michael Geist, 'Why the US Lost Its WTO IP Complaint against China Badly' (michaelgeist, 27 January 2009): http://www.michaelgeist.ca/content/view/3645/125/ (accessed 28 February 2014).

on that one. So what this means is exactly nothing.'[155] He also stated, in a separate article, that 'the US did this to appease US media companies who want to see some action on the issue of market access (not piracy)'.[156]

On 26 February 2010, China adopted an amendment to the Copyright Law which modified the provisions concerned.[157] As Vice Premier Wu Yi stated, protecting IPR is an inevitable choice to improve international competitiveness and is an established strategy for China, which will not be easily changed. According to the '2007 Action Plan on IPR Protection in China', China's current priorities are to continue to improve IP laws and regulations, including enacting and amending laws, rules and regulations on the protection of trademarks, patents and copyright through the introduction of relevant judicial interpretations by the Supreme People's Court of the PRC, strengthening the construction platform on the protection of IP and intensifying the clampdown on infringement such as piracy. These efforts are to continue on a step-by-step basis without interference. Some IP protection steps on an operational level, such as general education, information and consulting services, would be adjusted according to demand. In general China's IPR protection follows set steps.[158]

The IP issue has occupied a central position in Sino-US economic and trade relations for a long time. This explains why it has become a bit political in nature. China and the US have clashed several times over IPR protection and have been on the verge of a trade war a few times. The Sino-US IPR disputes escalated this battle to a new level. Compared with other WTO cases, it more clearly reflected the ups and downs of the Sino-US economic and trade relationship: it echoed historical grievances and highlighted the different interests of the two countries, and represented a conceptual conflict that relates to the fact that they are at different stages of development.[159]

---

[155] Tina Wang, 'WTO's China Piracy Ruling: All Bark and No Bite' (Forbes, 27 January 2009): http://www.forbes.com/2009/01/27/china-wto-piracy-markets-equity-0127_markets2.html (accessed 28 February 2014).

[156] Steve Dickinson, 'The WTO, China's Media, Copyrights and Other IP. It's a Control Thing' (chinalawblog, 9 February 2009): http://www.chinalawblog.com/2009/02/the_wto_chinas_media_copyright.html (accessed 28 February 2014).

[157] Panel Report, *China – Measures Affecting the Protection and Enforcement of Intellectual Property Rights*, WT/DS362/R (adopted 20 March 2009).

[158] 'Wu Yi: Protection of IP is an Inevitable Choice to Improve International Competitiveness' (xinhua net, 24 April 2007): http://news.xinhuanet.com/politics/2007-04/24/content_6019055.htm (accessed 28 February 2014) (available in Chinese only, author's translation).

[159] Wenhua Ji, 'Sino-US IPR Dispute: Who is the Winner' (sohu, 21 May 2010): http://2010ipb828.blog.sohu.com/152134204.html (accessed 28 February 2014) (available in Chinese only, author's translation).

From the viewpoint of the Chinese, this case should indicate to the US that it cannot play the WTO dispute settlement mechanism like an organ and that China's determination and positive attitude towards IP protection cannot be easily denied. People can have faith that no matter how small the problem is, China will take serious steps to correct it. Moreover, strengthening IPR protection is in China's own interests. At the same time, China also clearly recognises that it has a long way to go on both domestic protection and, increasingly, on overseas protection. The Sino-US IP game goes far beyond the specific areas involved in this case and has more than bilateral scope or even WTO scope. In fact, it is a typical reflection of the institutional conflict on IP maintenance and application between developed and developing countries. With the rapid development of the Chinese economy, this game will constantly test Chinese wisdom.[160]

2. A threat to Chinese cultural industries   On 10 April 2007, the US requested consultations with China concerning (1) certain measures that restrict trading rights with respect to imported films for theatrical release, audio-visual home entertainment products (e.g. video cassettes and DVDs), sound recordings and publications (e.g. books, magazines, newspapers and electronic publications); and (2) certain measures that restrict market access for, or discriminate against, foreign suppliers of distribution services for publications and foreign suppliers of audio-visual services (including distribution services) for audio-visual home entertainment products.[161] The US claimed that China's distribution rights for the above products were only granted to Chinese state-owned enterprises (SOEs). In addition, it claimed that certain provisions for the review of audio-visual products and other publications were aimed purely at foreign companies and that this affected the interests of Hollywood studios, Apple's online music store iTunes and other US media content providers.[162] The total revenue of American films overseas amounted to $7 billion, in relation to which the annual rental income China obtained was about $30 million.

---

[160]   Ibid.

[161]   'DS363 China – Measures Affecting Trading Rights and Distribution Services for Certain Publications and Audio-visual Entertainment Products' (WTO, 12 October 2012): http://www.wto.org/english/tratop_e/dispu_e/cases_e/ds363_e.htm (accessed 28 February 2014).

[162]   'The US Complaint to the WTO about China's Restrictions on Foreign Publications' (China IPR Protection net, 12 October 2007): http://www.ipr.gov.cn/alxdarticle/alxd/alxdqt/alxdqtgjal/200710/128664_1.html (accessed 28 February 2014) (available in Chinese only, author's translation).

Only China Film Group was entitled to import foreign films, and film distribution rights were monopolised by China Film Group and Huaxia Film Distribution Company.[163]

On 5 and 6 June 2009, the two parties held consultations in Geneva, but no result was achieved. During the consultations, China explained it had conscientiously fulfilled its commitments following its accession to the WTO. It promised to import 20 movies annually and about 500 000 copies of publications and numerous types of audio and video products from different origins, which offered a very good chance for such products produced by WTO members to find their way into the Chinese market. On 10 October 2007, the US requested the establishment of a panel.[164]

On 12 August 2009, the panel report was circulated to members. The panel concluded: (1) that a number of Chinese measures were inconsistent with China's obligations under the Accession Protocol on the basis that they restricted the rights of companies in China, and in some cases of foreign companies not registered in China and of foreign individuals, to import reading materials, films for theatrical release, audio-visual home entertainment (AVHE) products and sound recordings; (2) because there was at least one other reasonably available alternative, China's measures concerned reading materials and finished audio-visual products were not 'necessary' within the meaning of Article XX(a); (3) Chinese measures limiting commercial presence for the distribution of videocassettes, DVDs, etc., to joint ventures with Chinese majority ownership, and measures limiting the operating term for joint ventures, but not for wholly Chinese-owned companies, were inconsistent with China's market access commitments under Article XVI of GATS and its national treatment commitments under Article XVII.[165]

On 13 August 2009, a MOFCOM spokesman pointed out that China respected and supported the panel's ruling on proper management of the transmission mode of cultural products as a particularity, but regretted,

---

[163] Haizhi Zhang, 'China Appeals Sino-US WTO Market Access for Publications Case' (China Intellectual Property News, 19 August 2009): http://www.cipnews.com.cn/showArticle.asp?Articleid=13025 (accessed 2 March 2014) (available in Chinese only, author's translation).

[164] 'The US Proposed to Establish a Panel in the WTO on Market Access for Publications' (xinhua net, 22 October 2007): http://news.xinhuanet.com/newscenter/2007-10/22/content_6925727.htm (accessed 2 February 2014) (available in Chinese only, author's translation).

[165] 'DS363 China – Measures Affecting Trading Rights and Distribution Services for Certain Publications and Audiovisual Entertainment Products' (WTO, 12 October 2012): http://www.wto.org/english/tratop_e/dispu_e/cases_e/ds363_e.htm (accessed 3 March 2014).

without rejecting, the American claim relating to the import and distribution of Chinese publications, films and audio-visual products. China would carefully assess the report and would not exclude the possibility of making an appeal. It stressed that the application of management measures in respect of cultural products was justified. Furthermore, there was a lack of Chinese cultural products on the international markets and their competitiveness was still weak. In the theatrical performances market, the income ratio between import and export was 10:1; in the publishing market it was 6.84:1; in copyright trade, it was 10.3:1; and in the film market it was 30:1.[166]

On 22 September 2009, China notified its intention to appeal to the AB on certain issues of law covered in the panel report and certain legal interpretations developed by the panel. On 5 October, the US also notified its intention to appeal.[167]

On 21 December 2009, the AB report was circulated to members. The AB upheld most of the panel's ruling, but stated that China could invoke Article XX of GATT. The MOFCOM spokesman clarified that in terms of market access in respect of publication, China fulfilled its obligations under the WTO Agreement. The channel for foreign publications, films and audio-visual products into the Chinese market is smooth. During the proceedings of the AB, China clarified its views and reminded the AB to pay attention to the particularity of cultural products and to respect members' service commitment. China welcomed the AB's ruling on the restrictive clarifications contained in the panel's decision and its confirmation that Article XX could be invoked in this case. China regretted some of the findings of the AB. It was of the view that cultural products have both commercial and cultural value, which should be distinguished from the management of the general trade in goods.[168]

On 19 March 2011, the State Council adopted 'Decision on Amending Regulations of Publication Administration'. At the DSB meeting on 23

---

[166] 'MOFCOM Spokesman Made Speech on the Panel Report on the US Publication Market Access Case (MOFCOM, 13 August 2009): http://www. mofcom.gov.cn/aarticle/ae/ag/200908/20090806455664.html (accessed 3 March 2014) (available in Chinese only, author's translation).

[167] 'DS363 China – Measures Affecting Trading Rights and Distribution Services for Certain Publications and Audiovisual Entertainment Products' (WTO, 12 October 2012): http://www.wto.org/english/tratop_e/dispu_e/cases_e/ ds363_e.htm (accessed 3 March 2014).

[168] 'MOFCOM Spokesman Issued a Statement on the AB Ruling on the Publication Market Accession Dispute' (MOFCOM, 22 December 2009): http:// www.mofcom.gov.cn/aarticle/ae/ag/200912/20091206689022.html (accessed 3 March 2014) (available in Chinese only, author's translation).

March 2012, China stated that it had ensured full implementation of the DSB's recommendations and rulings except for those concerning films for theatrical release. On 9 May 2012, China and the US informed the DSB of key elements relating to films for theatrical release as set forth in the Memorandum of Understanding mentioned at the DSB meeting on 22 February 2012. The Memorandum included the fact that China had agreed to allow 14 additional special films, namely 3D, IMAX and IMAX 3D, in addition to the 20-film a year limit, and to increase the split sales proportion of its box office from the previous level of 13 per cent to the current level of 25 per cent.[169]

This was the first case relating to a service trade dispute in which China had been involved in the WTO, and it mainly related to the interpretation of trade in services in China's WTO commitments.

This judgment was regarded as the biggest defeat China had experienced as a WTO member since joining in 2001. The WTO ruling meant that China had to adjust its import policies in respect of American movies, audio and video products and book products. The AB ruling allowed China to retain import rights in respect of two state-owned film distribution companies and to protect the Chinese government's right to review foreign films. In addition to this, China need not increase the import limit set at 20 foreign films per year. However, it had to allow the US and other foreign companies to import movies, music and books into China and to allow joint ventures to distribute music over the Internet.[170]

Market participants believed that audio-visual products suffered more directly from this ruling, but that the change of policy would not have a significant impact on the recording industry in China. It would facilitate the future market for performance. As the market opens, there will be more importers and costs will fall, leading to healthy competition.[171]

The ruling could have an impact on the book publishing industry and

---

[169] 'DS363 China – Measures Affecting Trading Rights and Distribution Services for Certain Publications and Audiovisual Entertainment Products' (WTO, 12 October 2012): http://www.wto.org/english/tratop_e/dispu_e/cases_e/ds363_e.htm; and 'Sino-American Film Agreement: Domestic movies "Dance with Wolves" and only the Strong will Survive"' (sohu, 20 February 2012): http://yule.sohu.com/20120220/n335246842.shtml (accessed 3 March 2014) (available in Chinese only, author's translation).
[170] 'China Accepts the WTO Ruling and Further Opens the Market for Entertainment Products' (China Business, 16 July 2010): http://www.cb.com.cn/economy/2010_0716/139080.html (accessed 3 March 2014) (available in Chinese only, author's translation).
[171] 'China Accepts the WTO Ruling and will Open up the Entertainment Market Next Year' (Sinovision net, 16 July 2010): http://www.sinovision.net/

may lead to changes in the distribution system. Previously, imported books entered China subject to distribution by China Publishing Group. Foreign publishers were unable to export directly to Chinese booksellers. Following this case, foreign publications may enter China through distribution channels. According to Chinese officials, this will not affect the overall structure of the market because cultural publications have both economic and social value. China will not change its practice of reviewing foreign publications.[172]

The negative impact of the ruling on industries associated with Chinese cultural products is reflected in the film industry. From 2003 onwards for a period of six consecutive years, sales of domestic films exceeded those of imported films. The ruling meant that foreign film companies can distribute films directly to Chinese cinemas instead of this being done by China Film Group Corporation.[173]

It is well known that the global proliferation of American books, audio and video products has triggered a sense of cultural crisis in many countries. France, Japan and South Korea have all taken different measures to restrict the free import of American books, audio and video products and have provided many subsidies for domestic cultural industries in order to resist cultural penetration.[174]

When a cultural industry is in its infancy, the government offers an 'incubator' to help it grow. In the late 1970s Japan opened up its cultural market under pressure from the US. At one point, Hollywood movies had more than an 80 per cent share of the Japanese film market. But after the 1990s, Japanese movies regained 50 per cent of the market from Hollywood. Moreover, Japanese films also occupy a strong position in Asia and are exported overseas. On the other hand, Chinese lifestyles, values, language and culture are very different from those of the West, and these give Chinese books and its audio-visual industry unique advantages.[175]

China faced up rationally to this defeat. On the one hand, its domestic

---

portal.php?mod=view&aid=141517 (accessed 3 March 2014) (available in Chinese only, author's translation).

[172] 'The Sino-US Market Access for Publications Case Settled' (sina, 24 December 2009): http://finance.sina.com.cn/roll/20091224/00017145931.shtml (accessed 3 March 2014) (available in Chinese only, author's translation).

[173] Ibid.

[174] 'Expect to See some Reflections After Losing the Publication Case' (ifeng, 28 September 2009): http://finance.ifeng.com/roll/20090928/1290212.shtml (accessed 3 March 2014) (available in Chinese only, author's translation).

[175] Ibid.

book and audio-visual industries continued to grow. On the other hand, it opened up the market to American books, audio and video products so as to test the domestic industry. The Chinese government and its relevant industries must reflect on how to open the market while retaining a competitive edge.[176]

China needs to examine the relevant domestic legal provisions. Some may be inconsistent with WTO commitments, but may not in fact achieve the desired intention. Anachronistic provisions should be repealed. In terms of linguistic issues, if the legal text and working language of negotiation are non-Chinese, care should be taken to note the context in which such language is used, use professional terms and consult appropriate specialists to avoid semantic errors being made by either side. As a well-known English adage has it, the devil is in the detail.[177]

In order to help China increase its soft power, it should take advantage of the opportunities offered by American publications as a prime means of broadcasting content. The export of publications offers an extremely effective channel for a country to export value and achieve cultural penetration. China is a socialist country and also a big East Asian country imbued with the heritage of Eastern civilisation and Confucian values. As such, there is a conflict of ideology and civilisation with the US, which represents capitalism and Western civilisation. Therefore, in terms of cultural security due to the change in the international situation brought about by the end of the Cold War, China's security strategy has undergone major change. The status of non-military security has become increasingly prominent and cultural security seems to have become a very important aspect of this. In terms of the need to safeguard national interests, China cannot fully open its publishing markets and fundamental concessions on this issue are proceeding very slowly. However, the US has never given up on cultural penetration, so dispute between the two countries over market access in respect of this area was inevitable.[178]

In view of the foregoing, one could posit that China would gradually and steadily open up, especially where the publishing market is concerned. Subject to the precondition of ensuring national security, China can

---

[176]   Ibid.

[177]   Yougen Wang and Baihua Gong, 'Comments on the Publication Dispute' (sina blog, 11 February 2010): http://blog.sina.com.cn/s/blog_4c0f444d0100gz24. html (accessed 3 March 2014) (available in Chinese only, author's translation).

[178]   Yifang Zhang, 'Chinese Publication Market under the WTO Framework: From the Perspective of the Sino-US Game' (blogbus, 10 December 2010): http:// yifan-cheung.blogbus.com/ (accessed 3 March 2014) (available in Chinese only, author's translation).

gradually enlarge market access for publications. This will play an important role in eliminating backward and uncompetitive domestic industries and in promoting the development of internationally competitive emerging industries. In summary, in this area, safeguarding national security and preventing cultural invasion by other countries cannot be ignored. On this basis in the future, and for a long period of time, the Chinese believe that they must adhere to a strategy of gradually opening up, promoting domestic industrial upgrading and economic restructuring, and enhancing international competitiveness.[179]

3. Not just for a credit card logo   In March 2010 Visa, American Express and MasterCard discussed a protest on the restriction of their business development in China through the USTR. However, this went no further than a discussion with lawyers and no formal complaint was made, perhaps because these three large credit card organisations failed to agree on the way forward.[180]

Upon China's accession to the WTO in 2001, it promised to open up the market in respect of credit card and other financial transaction services before the end of 2006. The US criticised the fact that China still did not allow foreign companies to issue credit cards for RMB settlement in China and China established a network to support the credit card or transacted through the inter-bank sales network.[181]

In 2010, MasterCard released a research report which stated that in 10 years' time China would have 900 million credit cards in use, meaning that it would overtake the US and become the world's largest credit card market. It also predicted that by 2025 Chinese credit card business income would grow by a factor of 20 and profits by a factor of 30, meaning approximately $105 billion and $34 billion respectively.[182]

Usually a banking card can only be linked to one banking card organisation, but in recent years China has issued a number of dual-currency cards. These so-called dual-currency credit cards are banking cards issued by two banking card organisations in cooperation. For instance, many Chinese banking cards have both the Chinese UnionPay logo and the American

[179]   Ibid.
[180]   'Visa Filed a Case against UnionPay to the WTO' (sina, 20 September 2010): http://finance.sina.com.cn/money/bank/bank_card/20100920/14128687311.shtml (accessed 12 March 2014) (available in Chinese only, author's translation).
[181]   'The US Filed Two Complaints against China in the WTO' (sina, 17 September 2010): http://finance.sina.com.cn/j/20100917/08268673850.shtml (accessed 12 March 2014) (available in Chinese only, author's translation).
[182]   Ibid.

Visa or MasterCard logo on them. Because Visa and MasterCard were unable to conduct RMB business in China while UnionPay conducted little overseas business, they cooperated to issue dual-currency cards.[183]

UnionPay has been developing its overseas business since 2004, and by 2011 its card was accepted in 130 countries and regions. A total of 13 million UnionPay cards had been issued by nearly 90 institutions in more than 20 countries and regions (the card numbers begin with 62 and the card face bears the UnionPay logo). UnionPay extended its cooperation with nearly 200 overseas institutions and the value of its overseas transactions totalled 297.98 billion yuan by 2011.[184]

In 2010 Visa sent a letter to its global member banks stating that as from 1 August of that year, once the bank accepted the dual-currency credit card with a Visa logo outside mainland China, regardless of whether consumers paid by credit card or withdrew cash from an ATM, the funds could not go through the Chinese UnionPay liquidation channel. Visa threatened to punish the acquiring banks by means of a fine of $50,000 if they disobeyed. Further breaches would be met by a fine of $25,000 per month. Visa argued that the aim of this move was to ensure that all participants in the payment system and interested parties would be able to enjoy the same level of convenience, standard services and protection of rights for global cardholders. The purpose was to ensure that Visa cardholders were able to enjoy a safe, convenient and reliable payment experience and service guarantee (including risk management, the treatment of transactions, etc.) provided by the Visa payment system. Visa stressed that if a cardholder used a dual-currency credit card beginning with the digit '4', this meant that the transaction would be processed through Visa's payment network. However, it also said that it would not block transactions conducted using UnionPay cards beginning with the digits '62' from being processed through its channel outside of China.[185]

Chinese UnionPay responded by stating that the dual-currency cards marked with the logos of UnionPay and Visa were not pure single-brand

---

[183] 'It is Better not to Use the Dual Currency Card when Going Abroad As Visa will Separate from UnionPay' (sina, 2 June 2010): http://finance.sina.com.cn/money/bank/bank_hydt/20100602/08258043750.shtml (accessed 12 March 2014) (available in Chinese only, author's translation).

[184] 'UnionPay Speeds up Internationalization' (xinhua net, 25 July 2012): http://news.xinhuanet.com/2012-07/25/c_112529998.htm (accessed 12 March 2014) (available in Chinese only, author's translation).

[185] 'RMB payment services: UnionPay or Visa?' (ifeng, 25 July 2012): http://news.ifeng.com/gundong/detail_2012_07/25/16293424_0.shtml (accessed 12 March 2014) (available in Chinese only, author's translation).

banking cards. Both parties had the obligation to provide overseas services for cardholders, and this was directly related to cardholders' interests and the issuing banks' commitments towards cardholders. No party had the right to prevent the cardholder from choosing overseas payment channels individually and cardholders are entitled to choose overseas payment channels.[186]

Since Visa usually settles in US dollars, cardholders have to pay a 1–2 per cent currency conversion fee and will bear foreign exchange loss. Visa had repeatedly asked China to open bank clearing channels to earn the channel fee being captured by the Bank of China. Competing interests according to the Chinese is the main reason why Visa blocked UnionPay's overseas channels so as to force China to open Chinese banking card channels.[187]

On 15 September 2010, the US made two requests in the WTO for consultations with China. The first of these related to measures imposing countervailing and antidumping duties on grain-oriented flat-rolled electrical steel and the second was about electronic payment services. The US alleged that China only permitted a Chinese entity (UnionPay) to supply electronic payment services (EPS) for payment card transactions denominated and paid in RMB in China. Service suppliers from other member states could only supply these services for payment card transactions paid in foreign currency. China also required all payment card processing devices to be compatible with that entity's system and that payment cards must bear its logo. It further argued that the Chinese entity had guaranteed access to all merchants in China that accept payment cards, while services suppliers from other member states had to negotiate for access to merchants.[188]

The MOFCOM responded that the measures relating to electronic payment cards were consistent with WTO rules. The Chinese ambassador to the US told the media that China's WTO commitments, including banking-related commitments, had been fulfilled.[189]

---

[186] 'Visa and UnionPay: Former Partners and Now Enemies' (xinhua net, 3 June 2012): http://news.xinhuanet.com/fortune/2010-06/03/c_12174197.htm (accessed 12 March 2014) (available in Chinese only, author's translation).

[187] 'Visa Blocked UnionPay's Overseas Channels' (ifeng, 21 September 2010): http://finance.ifeng.com/bank/special/visayinl/ (accessed 12 March 2014) (available in Chinese only, author's translation).

[188] 'China – Certain Measures Affecting Electronic Payment Services' (WTO, 30 September 2013): http://www.wto.org/english/tratop_e/dispu_e/cases_e/ds413_e.htm (accessed 12 March 2014).

[189] Shaohua Sun, 'The WTO will Establish a Panel on Electronic Payment Services' (xinhua net, 15 February 2011): http://jjckb.xinhuanet.com/2011-02/15/

On 11 February 2011, the US requested the establishment of a panel. China pointed out that China and the US had consulted in accordance with WTO rules, but that the negotiations had not led to a mutually satisfactory solution. The US insisted on going through with the panel procedure, at which China expressed great regret. Meanwhile the MOFCOM replied that China always respects WTO rules. China would examine the request filed by the US and would resolve the two disputes in accordance with WTO procedures.[190]

The *Washington Post* reported that the US's main aim was to prompt China to open up the market to foreign companies by means of promoting the WTO procedure, while expressing the concern that existed in the US about the Chinese exchange rate issue.[191]

On 16 July 2012, the panel's report was circulated to members. The panel agreed with China's views on 13 claims and the US's views on 11 claims. It concluded that the electronic payment services involved fell within the ambit of Chinese commitments in respect of all payment and money transmission services, and dismissed the US's claim that UnionPay's market position allowed foreign EPS suppliers to provide services through a commercial presence in China only if they meet certain qualification requirements related to local (RMB) currency business. Furthermore, it also dismissed, on the basis of insufficient evidence, the US's claim that China maintained UnionPay as an across-the-board monopoly supplier for the processing of all domestic RMB payment card transactions. However, it found that the fact that China required all payment cards issued in China to bear the UnionPay logo was inconsistent with Article XVII of the GATS. This meant that, contrary to its commitments, China had failed to provide national treatment to EPS suppliers from other WTO member states. A MOFCOM spokesman commented that China welcomed the panel's rulings on some contentious issues, while expressing reservations on certain other issues that had been decided in favour of the US. China would carefully evaluate the panel report and carry out proper follow-up work in accordance with WTO dispute settlement procedures.[192]

---

content_287623.htm (accessed 12 March 2014) (available in Chinese only, author's translation).

[190] Ibid.

[191] 'The US Requested to Establish a Panel against China in the WTO' (ifeng, 13 February 2011): http://news.ifeng.com/world/detail_2011_02/13/4647907_0. shtml (accessed 13 March 2014) (available in Chinese only, author's translation).

[192] 'China – Certain Measures Affecting Electronic Payment Services' (WTO, 30 September 2013): http://www.wto.org/english/tratop_e/dispu_e/cases_e/ds413_e. htm (accessed 12 March 2014); 'MOFCOM Spokesman Issued a Statement on the

The US officials shouted for joy on 16 July when the preliminary ruling of the WTO was given, with White House spokesman Jay Carney telling reporters that it was a victory for the US. The USTR General Counsel agreed, calling it a decisive victory which would create about 6000 jobs in America. USTR General Counsel Tim Reif also noted that the WTO's ruling could open up a market of a value of $1 trillion for US companies. However, other US experts believed that the ruling involved gains and losses for both sides.[193]

However one analyses the matter, although the US was successful, this belated win, according to the Chinese, was unhelpful. Accordingly, China had succeeded in seizing a large market in competition with US companies such as Visa and MasterCard. According to British media reports, the total issuance of UnionPay cards had reached 2 billion pieces, making UnionPay one of the largest banking card companies globally. Moreover, UnionPay cards are not only widely used in China. They are in use in 130 countries and regions and accepted by more than 7 million foreign merchants.[194]

An official for UnionPay disclosed that its internationalisation is necessary for China's economic development and 'go global' strategy, the facilitation of cross-border financial services, the provision of a corporate response to global competition, improvement of capabilities and brand establishment. UnionPay's aim is to build a global network with an international brand. This calls for further expansion in the acceptance of UnionPay outside of China in order to support Chinese activities overseas and increase efforts to issue offshore UnionPay cards so as to provide convenient, safe and efficient UnionPay card payment services for daily and overseas payment by local residents.[195]

Because of the late commencement of its internationalisation drive,

---

Panel Report of the US Electronic Payment Dispute' (MOFCOM, 16 July 2012): http://www.mofcom.gov.cn/aarticle/ae/ag/201207/20120708234210.html (accessed 14 March 2014) (available in Chinese only, author's translation).

[193] 'The WTO Rejected Some of the US's Allegations about China UnionPay' (xinhua net, 18 July 2012): http://news.xinhuanet.com/world/2012--07/18/c_123425783.htm (accessed 14 March 2014) (available in Chinese only, author's translation).

[194] 'The WTO Ruling on the UnionPay Dispute: the US is Happy and China is not Angry' (xinhua net, 18 July 2012): http://news.xinhuanet.com/fortune/2012--07/18/c_123426446.htm (accessed 14 March 2014) (available in Chinese only, author's translation).

[195] 'Acceleration of UnionPay Internationalization' (xinhua net, 25 July 2012): http://news.xinhuanet.com/fortune/2012-07/25/c_112529998.htm (accessed 14 March 2014) (available in Chinese only, author's translation).

UnionPay was in a weak position in the international market. Visa and MasterCard used to have almost 80 per cent of the global market for banking cards, with China's UnionPay, Japan's JCB, American Express and South Korea's BC Card sharing the remaining approximately 22 per cent of the market. UnionPay seems to be accelerating the pace of internationalisation, which may change the structure of the global banking card industry. In terms of banking card rates, the Chinese believe that UnionPay currently has an absolutely dominant position and its settlement services are available in more than 130 countries and regions around the world without a currency conversion fee. Visa charges 1–2 per cent or an even higher currency conversion fee when providing services in more than 200 countries and territories. In addition, Chinese consumers using RMB settlement can avoid multiple exchange loss. The internationalisation of UnionPay is a strategic consideration in terms of building an independent RMB clearing payment system, safeguarding Chinese financial security and promoting the internationalisation of RMB.[196]

However, a UnionPay official admitted that the current volume of card issuance abroad is still small, and is mainly for people who study, travel and do business overseas. He pointed out that taking into account differences in culture, geography, language and habits, UnionPay creates win–win cooperation with institutions from different parts of the world and participates in and influences the formulation of international standards for the banking card industry. The key challenge for UnionPay in terms of its internationalisation drive is to balance cooperation against competition with organisations that provide the same type of cards.[197]

In concrete terms, UnionPay's market penetration is increasing in various overseas markets. It has more than 95 per cent of the market in Hong Kong, more than 70 per cent in Singapore, more than 60 per cent in Taiwan and more than 50 per cent in France, Germany, Switzerland and other European markets.[198] Central Bank data shows that up to the end of 2011, China had issued a total of 2949 billion banking cards. This amounted to an increase of 22.1 per cent compared with 2010, while the cumulative amount issued through credit cards had reached 285 million, which represents an increase of 24.3 per cent compared with 2010.[199]

---

[196]   Ibid.

[197]   'Acceleration of UnionPay's Internationalization' (xinhua net, 25 July 2012): http://news.xinhuanet.com/fortune/2012-07/25/c_112529998.htm (accessed 14 March 2014) (available in Chinese only, author's translation).

[198]   Ibid.

[199]   'At the End of Last Year China Issued a Total of 2,949 Billion Bank Cards' (xinhua net, 19 March 2012): http://news.xinhuanet.com/fortune/

A 2010 Retail Banking Research Institute report indicated that UnionPay had issued 2336 billion cards, which accounted for 29.2 per cent of global card volume over and above Visa's market share (28.6 per cent). This made it the world's largest credit card issuer. However, Visa still has far more than UnionPay in terms of usage, transaction amount and overseas market share.[200]

At its meeting on 31 August 2012, the DSB adopted the panel report.[201] This required China to gradually open up its electronic payment services market and allowed other card providers (such as Visa) to issue RMB payment cards in China.[202]

Mei Xinyu, a researcher from the MOFCOM International Trade and Economic Cooperation Research Institute, considered that UnionPay has a bigger market size and its market position and share in China has been fairly stable, and that therefore it is not worried about overseas card issuers affecting its market dominance. The accession of foreign credit card issuers would not bring about a foreign monopoly over the market. In addition, the accession of foreign credit card issuers would stimulate UnionPay to improve its services and innovate products in order to provide a better service. This would also help bring about favourable conditions for UnionPay to enter the US market.[203]

A member of UnionPay's senior management expressed the view that China had not made a commitment on RMB clearing and settlement services under the WTO. Even if China accepts the WTO ruling, opening up the RMB clearing and settlement market will be a gradual process. Guo Tianyong, the director of the Banking Research Center at the Central University of Finance pointed out that opening up the domestic banking card clearing business was related to financial security, so China should control the process itself. It will not happen overnight. The director of

---

2012-03/19/c_111675221.htm (accessed 14 March 2014) (available in Chinese only, author's translation).

[200] Minhui Jiang, 'The Spanish Media Reported that UnionPay Exceeded Visa' (MOFCOM, 2 November 2011): http://www.mofcom.gov.cn/aarticle/i/jyjl/m/201111/20111107809623.html (accessed 14 March 2014) (available in Chinese only, author's translation).

[201] Panel Report, China – Certain Measures Affecting Electronic Payment Services, WT/DS413/R (adopted 31 August 2012).

[202] 'China Abstained UnionPay Appeals' (xinhua net, 9 September 2012): http://news.xinhuanet.com/fortune/2012-09/09/c_123691035.htm (accessed 14 March 2014) (available in Chinese only, author's translation).

[203] 'Admission to Visa and MasterCard' (China net, 6 September 2012): http://finance.china.com.cn/roll/20120906/1002065.shtml (accessed 14 March 2014) (available in Chinese only, author's translation).

Treaty and Law Department at the MOFCOM noted the ruling concluded that the electronic payment service concerned falls under the Chinese GATS schedule in respect of all payment and money transmission services to which China is committed, and that some of the measures involved violate the principle of national treatment. China had reserved the ruling on the service classification.[204]

On 22 November 2012, China and the US informed the DSB that they had agreed that a reasonable period of time was 11 months. Accordingly, the reasonable period of time expired on 31 July 2013. At the DSB meeting on 23 July 2013, China reported that it had fully implemented the DSB's recommendations and rulings. The US disagreed with this assertion.[205] It argued that China had not fully implemented the WTO ruling, but did not at that point require the establishment of a compliance panel.

Going forward, the Chinese may consider the following five issues:

First, it could adjust UnionPay's development strategy. The transaction volume of UnionPay cards ranks it in third place globally, and it is fully equipped and has sufficient capacity to compete with other banking cards in the international market without government support. Moreover, whether the use of UnionPay cards is to be determined by market forces of supply and demand, as and when the regulatory authority formulates regulatory standards it needs to avoid covertly defining or limiting the use of UnionPay.[206]

Second, private capital should be introduced in an orderly manner. At present China is actively encouraging and guiding the healthy development of private investment, and the introduction of private capital into the financial sector has become a hot topic both at home and abroad. The banking card industry is an important part of modern finance and is dominated by a small number of companies as compared with the wider banking sector. Visa has almost a 70 per cent market share in respect of international banking cards. When China opens up its banking card market to foreign institutions in order to effectively implement its WTO

---

[204] Xun Yang, 'UnionPay: No Commitment to Open RMB Clearing' (Chinadaily, 6 September 2012): http://www.chinadaily.com.cn/hqgj/jryw/2012-09-06/content_6925870.html (accessed 14 March 2014).

[205] 'China – Certain Measures Affecting Electronic Payment Services' (WTO, 30 September 2013): http://www.wto.org/english/tratop_e/dispu_e/cases_e/ds413_e.htm (accessed 14 March 2014).

[206] Zhen Li, 'The WTO Ruling Boosts the Reform of UnionPay' (legal daily, 9 October 2012): http://www.legaldaily.com.cn/international/content/2012-10/09/content_3886163.htm?node=34031 (accessed 16 March 2014).

commitments, it will also need to prudently open the market to domestic qualified private capital.[207]

Third, rapid research needs to be done in order to establish a financial competition regime. The modern economy is an institutional economy, and finance must be able to rely on the system so as to develop in a healthy and stable manner. Visa used exactly the same mode of operation with foreign financial information providers to enter the Chinese market in 2008 when it filed a case against China through the WTO platform relating to lack of research into competition systems in China. The establishment of a financial competition system is urgently needed in order to ensure compliance with international standards while taking account of the factual circumstances of the Chinese market, with the main aim of preventing the formation of a monopoly.[208]

Fourth, a Chinese defence system in relation to national financial strategic security should be developed. In the near future, since international banking card organisations have now accessed the Chinese market, China's economic and financial security may be subject to some degree of threat. Although banking cards belong to the second tier of financial services compared with banking, securities and insurance, once foreign financial institutions have a share in the banking card market, it is possible that economic and financial information that has an impact on national security will be controlled by other countries. It is therefore vital to design a defence system covering national financial strategic security.[209]

Fifthly, the legitimate interests of financial consumers should be protected. Boosting domestic demand and promoting consumption are at the heart of the national strategy for transforming the mode of economic growth. Given the recent trend of financialisation, protecting consumers' financial interests plays an important role. Visa and other institutions were recently hit with $7.2 billion in antitrust fines, the highest amount imposed in US history, as punishment for implementing monopolistic strategies. UnionPay should learn a lesson from this in terms of the protection of consumer rights, including the right to know, the right to choose, the right to privacy, the right to security and the right to fair dealing, etc.[210]

4. A hard case to implement Oriented electrical steel, also known as cold-rolled grain-oriented silicon steel, is an indispensable soft magnetic

---

[207] Ibid.
[208] Ibid.
[209] Ibid.
[210] Ibid.

material used in the power generation industry and is mainly used in transformers, rectifiers, reactors, large motors and other products.[211]

Because of the highly technological nature of oriented electrical steel production and the complexity of the process, most Chinese steel factories, except Wuhan steel factory and Baoshan steel factory, have no ability to produce oriented electrical steel. Rising prices of raw material such as iron ore and coal, plus the high cost of technology in China, have led to sale prices for foreign oriented electrical steel being lower than domestic prices by about 1000 yuan per ton and, at the end of 2009, the difference was as much as 2000 yuan per ton. Oriented electrical steel produced overseas is generally regarded as being of low-end quality. Baoshan and Wuhan steel factories proposed investigating the possibility of producing oriented electrical steel in order to maintain the normal market order and have a positive impact on the business of the two factories.[212]

On 10 December 2009, the MOFCOM issued a preliminary ruling in respect of Notice No. 99 (2009) concerning antidumping and countervailing investigation in respect of oriented electrical steel from the US and an antidumping investigation in respect of oriented electrical steel from Russia. This was the first time that China had conducted a countervailing investigation relating to imported products and was the first time it had conducted the antidumping and countervailing duty investigations simultaneously in relation to one country; i.e. a dual investigation.[213] On 15 April 2010, the MOFCOM issued a final ruling on Notice No. 21 (2010), under which it was to impose antidumping duties in respect of the oriented electrical steel from the US and Russia and countervailing duty on the US.[214]

---

[211] 'The WTO Releases the Final Ruling on "Oriented Electrical Steel Double Reverse" Case' (xinhua net, 19 October 2012): http://jjckb.xinhuanet.com/2012-10/19/content_407276.htm (accessed 16 March 2014) (available in Chinese only, author's translation).

[212] 'China Showed Double-Anti Sword: Levy Heavy Duties on Oriented Electrical Steel' (Yicainews, 14 April 2010): http://www.yicai.com/news/2010/04/337228.html (accessed 18 November 2014) (available in Chinese only, author's translation).

[213] 'MOFCOM: Dual Investigations on Oriented Electrical Steel from the US and Russia' (Chinanews, 10 December 2009): http://www.chinanews.com/cj/cj-cyzh/news/2009/12-10/2010595.shtml (accessed 17 March 2014) (available in Chinese only, author's translation).

[214] 'MOFCOM Notice No. 21 of 2010: Final Determination of Anti-dumping Investigation in respect of Oriented Electrical Steel Originating in the US and Russia and of Countervailing Investigation Originating in the US' (MOFCOM, 13 April 2010): http://www.mofcom.gov.cn/aarticle/b/c/201004/20100406864469.html (accessed 17 March 2014) (available in Chinese only, author's translation).

On 15 September 2010, the US requested consultations with China, and on 11 February 2011 it requested the establishment of a panel. On 15 June 2012, the panel report was circulated to members.[215] On 16 June 2012, the director of the MOFCOM's Treaty and Law Department noted that the panel had decided a number of contentious issues in China's favour, which the Chinese government welcomed. China would carefully evaluate the other decisions made by the panel and reserved the right to appeal.[216]

On 20 July 2012, China notified the DSB of its intention to appeal. On 18 October 2012, the AB's report, which upheld all the panel's decisions, was circulated to members.[217] The director of the MOFCOM's Treaty and Law Department stated that although the AB had not rejected the panel's main conclusions, it supported some of China's claims. In particular, it agreed that in respect of the price impact assessment the investigating authority was not required to prove a causal relationship between the impact on price and the dumping or import subsidy, and it pointed out that the panel's interpretation and application of the law was inconsistent with the common intentions of the WTO members. WTO members had different understandings of some of the provisions of the Anti-Dumping Agreement and Agreement on SCM, so the AB clarified the meaning of these terms in order to help members' investigating authorities correctly apply antidumping and countervailing rules. China stated that it would carefully evaluate the AB and panel reports and properly handle the implementation in accordance with WTO rules.[218]

At the DSB meeting of 30 November 2012 China stated that it intended to implement the DSB recommendations in a manner that respected its WTO obligations. On 8 February 2013, the US requested that the reasonable period of time be determined through binding arbitration pursuant to Article 21.3(c) of the DSU. The arbitrator determined that the reasonable period of time for China to implement the rulings of the DSB in this dispute was 8 months and 15 days; i.e. by 31 July 2013. On 13 January

---

[215] 'China-Countervailing and Anti-Dumping Duties on Grain Oriented Flat-rolled Electrical Steel from the US' (WTO, 3 March 2014): http://www.wto.org/english/tratop_e/dispu_e/cases_e/ds414_e.htm (accessed 17 March 2014).

[216] 'The WTO Releases the Ruling on Oriented Electrical Steel' (xinhua net, 16 June 2012): http://news.xinhuanet.com/fortune/2012-06/16/c_112229067.htm (accessed 17 March 2014) (available in Chinese only, author's translation).

[217] 'China-Countervailing and Anti-Dumping Duties on Grain Oriented Flat-rolled Electrical Steel from the US' (WTO, 3 March 2014): http://www.wto.org/english/tratop_e/dispu_e/cases_e/ds414_e.htm (accessed 17 March 2014).

[218] 'China Appeal Failed on Electrical Steel Case under the WTO' (xinhua net, 20 October 2012): http://news.xinhuanet.com/fortune/2012-10/20/c_123848183.htm (accessed 17 March 2014) (available in Chinese only, author's translation).

2014, the US requested consultations pursuant to Article 21.5 of the DSU, and on 13 February 2014, it requested the establishment of DSU Article 21.5 compliance panel. Accordingly, the compliance panel will issue its final report to the parties in the second quarter of 2015.[219]

The director of the MOFCOM's Treaty and Law Department issued a statement stating that China expressed regret. China respected the WTO ruling. China implemented the decision in the case in full within a reasonable period of time, including the revision of related measures and issuance of the Provisional Rule on Enforcement of WTO Trade Remedy Dispute Rulings. The Rule laid a good foundation for a working institutionalisation of the WTO trade remedy dispute ruling. According to China, this fully demonstrated the sincerity of the Chinese government in implementing the WTO ruling. China would deal with the subsequent issues in accordance with the relevant provisions of the WTO.[220]

The US and the EU initiated many antidumping and countervailing investigations in respect of China. Therefore, when acting as a complainant, China pursues antidumping, countervailing and safeguard measures against its major trading partners, and is ready to move out of its traditional Confucianism culture of negotiations to defend its interest at the WTO DSB.

This case and the China steel safeguard measure case formed attack-defensive transformation, involving demands related to different interests which have the aim of making the other party open up its markets. The changing roles of the complainant and the respondent explain the continuous deepening of international trade exchange between two countries and shows that Sino-US friction may sometimes be inevitable. Cooperation and dispute will coexist for a long time, which continuously tests the wisdom and charm of these two great powers in international trade.

A considerable number of difficult cases are challenging, and will continue to challenge in the future, the Chinese government's ability to implement and comply with WTO DSB rulings and recommendations. In the intellectual property rights case, the required amendment was arguably minor. However, it took China almost three years to implement the

---

[219] 'China-Countervailing and Anti-Dumping Duties on Grain Oriented Flat-rolled Electrical Steel from the US' (WTO, 8 October 2014): http://www.wto.org/english/tratop_e/dispu_e/cases_e/ds414_e.htm (accessed 18 November 2014).

[220] 'The Director of Treaty and Law Department in MOFCOM Made a Speech on the Oriented Electrical Steel Case under the WTO Dispute Settlement Mechanism' (MOFCOM, 14 January 2014): http://www.mofcom.gov.cn/article/ae/ai/201401/20140100459536.shtml (accessed 17 March 2014) (available in Chinese only, author's translation).

ruling in the *Publications and Audio-visual Entertainment Product* dispute. The US believes that China has not yet implemented the ruling in the *Electronic Payment* case. This was the first time that the US had initiated a compliance procedure against China on oriented electrical steel. Although China implemented the ruling in the *Raw Material* dispute, it is still uncertain that it will comply with the ruling made in the *Rare Earth* case, since rare earth is an important strategic resource of a non-renewable nature. As is often the way, China will keep on searching above and below, as in the famous poem by Chinese poet Qu Yuan.

7.2   PERSPECTIVES ON CHINA AND THE WTO DISPUTE SETTLEMENT SYSTEM

This section offers a summary of the use China has made of the WTO dispute settlement mechanism, both from the practical perspective of the Chinese government (MOFCOM) and the academic perspective of Chinese researchers. The reason for analysing these two views is because of the diverse contributions they offer to the Chinese thinking with regard to compliance with WTO rules. While academics in China are a force for good in terms of their inputs to Chinese trade policymaking, government officials sometimes fail to understand the strict legalistic views of academic scholarships.

7.2.1   The Chinese Government's Perspective[221]

As early as 2000, before China's accession to the WTO, its government began to participate in the preparatory work of the dispute settlement mechanism. In June 2000, the Law Division of the former Ministry of Foreign Trade arranged for officials from major domestic economic ministries and legislative branches, as well as various academics and lawyers, amounting to a total of 23 people to attend a two-week WTO seminar at the Georgetown University Law Center located in Washington, DC. The US seminar organiser was John H. Jackson, who is regarded as the father of GATT and the WTO. He invited 23 US officials, academics, lawyers, WTO secretariat staff and dispute resolution experts and systematically

---

221   Guohua Yang, 'China's Course of Participation in the WTO Dispute Settlement Mechanism' (Chinalawinfo, 2011): http://article.chinalawinfo.com/ Article_Detail.asp?ArticleID=64388&Type=mod (accessed 7 April 2014) (available in Chinese only, author's translation).

introduced the history of the WTO, some relevant WTO agreements and a number of WTO cases.

At that time learning about the WTO was popular in China as people regarded understanding WTO rules as being fashionable. But the majority of seminar lecturers criticised the WTO's defects and conducted brainstorming exercises on how it might be developed. Chinese participants felt that there was a big gap between China and the West in terms of knowledge and understanding of the WTO. This seminar gave Chinese participants a clear signal: there would be a long way to go if China truly wanted to participate in WTO affairs, especially in the field of professional legal dispute resolution work.

In October 2000 the Law Department of what was then the Ministry of Foreign Trade held a large WTO seminar in Beijing. Experts from the US, Europe, Australia and the WTO Secretariat, including Professor Jackson, presented views on the main WTO agreements. More than 100 people, including domestic officials, academics and lawyers, attended the seminar.

Furthermore, in September 2001 the Law Department of the Ministry of Foreign Trade invited Gaetan Verhoosel from the Legal Department of the WTO Secretariat and senior US trade law attorney Chris Parlin to hold a five-day seminar on WTO cases in Beijing. The aim of the seminar was to introduce the procedures used in the WTO's dispute settlement mechanism and it focused on three WTO cases. Domestic officials, academics and lawyers participated in the discussion. The seminar marked a switch from general study of the WTO to specific study of the WTO's dispute settlement mechanism.

In November 2001, the Law Department of the Ministry of Foreign Trade established a WTO law section, which was transferred from the WTO Legal Work Group Office in the former Ministry of Foreign Trade. By the end of 1999, after China and the US had signed a bilateral agreement on China's accession to the WTO, it was widely believed that China's accession was just around the corner. It became an urgent matter for China to modify its laws and regulations to comply with WTO rules. The major ministries set up the Clean-up Regulations Office. Because the laws and regulations relating to foreign trade and economy were those principally affected and because the Ministry of Foreign Trade, as it then was, was responsible for the negotiation work in respect of WTO accession, the WTO law section was a specific institution. It was only in charge of the clean-up work relating to the laws and regulations concerning foreign trade and economy, but was also required to provide advice to other ministries. Its work involved understanding domestic policies, regulations and WTO rules. This professional requirement forced its officers to learn by doing and to conduct research in relation to the WTO agreements and cases at the early stage. This laid a preliminary foundation for the later work that was required to be done in relation to WTO dispute settlement. Now that China is a WTO member, the WTO law section and the newly established WTO department jointly handle WTO matters in China.

In 2002 China participated in the US steel safeguard measures case and some third-party cases, which meant that it acquired some direct experience of the operation of the WTO dispute settlement mechanism. The case in question took nearly 21 months, from 5 March 2002 when the US President announced the US's intention to take measures, to 10 November 2003 when the AB made its final decision to the effect that the US measures were inconsistent with WTO provisions. China was involved in the whole process of the case as one of the complainants. This gave the Chinese government an enhanced understanding of the WTO's mode of operation, particularly with respect to the characteristics of the dispute settlement mechanism. This experience stood it in good stead to take full advantage of this mechanism to resolve future disputes.

China's involvement as a third party is important. Firstly, it is a big trading country with extensive trade interests. Secondly, as a third party China can obtain a lot of information on international trade. Thirdly, as a third party it participates in the formulation and development of rules. Fourthly, involvement as a third party allows it to train a professional team. China has been extensively involved as a third party in WTO dispute settlement cases. The Treaty and Law Department is responsible for specific work and hires domestic lawyers to draft the relevant legal documents. The Ministry of Foreign Trade worked closely with the major Chinese ministries involved with economic issues, as well as the import and export chambers of commerce, trade associations and large companies, to determine China's stance in respect of these cases. It also tracked the latest developments in the international trading system. For each case, the Ministry of Foreign Trade drafted a written statement in its third party capacity, participated in WTO hearings and answered the panel's written questions. Since the parties have to submit a large amount of written materials covering a wide range of subject matter and the WTO sets strict time limits, carrying out this work is challenging for a newcomer.

In addition to holding seminars, the Treaty and Law Department has extensive contact with foreign lawyers in order to prepare for cases that may occur in the future. Besides hosting visiting foreign lawyers as part of its daily work and taking their views and perspectives into account, representatives of the department visited Washington during the consultations with the US on the *Steel Safeguard Measures* case and paid calls to a number of American law firms. The degree to which these firms were involved in WTO issues was assessed, along with practical issues, such as the fees they charged. In March 2002, Zhang Yuqing, the director of the Treaty and Law Department, led a delegation to Washington specifically to visit US law firms and to meet with Charlene Barshefsky. Ms Barshefsky was a USTR during the time of the Clinton administration. She handled the 1996 Sino-US IPR negotiations and the 1999 Sino-US negotiations on Chinese accession to the WTO, and is therefore well known in China. She is now an attorney in a Washington law firm and remains quite interested in Chinese business matters. Her meeting with director Zhang to some extent indicated that foreign law firms took a positive view on China's role in the WTO. In fact, China's role in the future of the WTO dispute settlement mechanism was the subject of a seminar that took place in Washington in August 2002.

Because WTO adjudication involves strong litigation skills, in January 2004 the Treaty and Law Department of the MOFCOM[222] held a three-day WTO litigation strategies and techniques seminar in Beijing. Domestic officials, academics and lawyers conducted discussions with John Jackson, who has many years' experience in WTO litigation; and Olivier Prost, an attorney who acted on China's behalf in the *US Steel Safeguard Measures* case. The theme of this seminar indicated that learning WTO rules involved a further technical and operational level.

In order to participate more effectively in the WTO dispute settlement mechanism, in addition to the general preparations, the Treaty and Law Department also studied various key issues thoroughly. In March 2003 it collaborated with a law firm to complete the 'Legal Research Report on American Specific Product Safeguard Legislation and Practice', which contains full reasoning on the relationship between the general safeguard measures and special safeguard measures and offers legal analysis on the first *US Special Safeguard Measures* case. In April 2004 it cooperated with a law firm to produce the 'Research Report on Textile Safeguard Measures and the US Textile Safeguard Measures Legislation', which analysed the relationship between textile safeguard measures, general safeguard measures and the WTO Agreement on Textiles and Clothing. In April 2004 it collaborated with another law firm to produce the 'Research Report on American WTO Anti-dumping Cases', which focused on the US as a defendant in WTO antidumping cases.

Moreover, in 2002 and 2004 respectively the Treaty and Law Department's WTO Law Office completed the 'Research on the Consultation Procedure in the WTO Dispute Settlement Mechanism'

---

[222]　In March 2003 the Ministry of Foreign Trade was disbanded and the Ministry of Commerce was established.

and 'Research on the Panel Procedure in the WTO Dispute Settlement Mechanism', which drew on the experience gained from participation in WTO dispute settlement cases. These two reports were the product of comprehensive research into two procedures and also drew on WTO cases. Ji Wenhua at the WTO Law Office wrote the 'Overview of WTO New Round Negotiations on the Dispute Settlement Mechanism' on the basis of his own experience of participation in the negotiations. This included an introduction and evaluation of the parties' positions and reasons. Yang Guohua and Li Yongsha at the WTO Law Office cooperated to publish a book called *Explanation of WTO Dispute Settlement Procedures* in March 2004. This was a practical guide, which cited 105 WTO reports and provided a comprehensive study of previous cases under the WTO dispute settlement rules and procedures. After reading the English version, Professor Jackson wrote a preface for the book. In April 2004, Yang Guohua published a book entitled *Study on the US Steel Safeguard Measures Case*, which provided a comprehensive introduction to China's first case.

On 10 December 2003, China won the *Steel Safeguard Measures* case. On 6 October 2005, China reached a mutual agreement through consultation on the integrated VAT case. This was the first occasion on which China had appeared as a respondent following its accession to the WTO. On 30 March 2006, the *Auto Parts Imports Measures* case was the first case in which China experienced a full WTO dispute settlement procedure as a defendant. The case ended with the AB ruling against China on 15 December 2008.[223]

After five years' preparation and training, China's WTO litigation hit a peak. Of 12 cases in which it was the complainant, 11 were filed after 2007. Meanwhile, it was the respondent in 19 cases, of which 17 were filed after 2007.

With the increase in its caseload, China experienced more 'firsts'. When the *Poultry Import Measures* case (DS392) was still in progress, the US made substantive changes to the relevant legislation. Meanwhile, China for the first time made adjustments to the relevant practice following the ruling in the *Auto Parts Import Measures* case (DS339), and it for the first time amended the relevant law and regulations based on the ruling in the *Intellectual Property* case (DS362).

The statistics show that in 2009, half of the cases brought in the WTO involved China, which had only been an official WTO member for eight and a half years. The first week of June 2010, in which three cases

---

[223] Appellate Body Reports, *China – Measures Affecting Imports of Automobile Parts*, WT/DS339, 340, 342/AB/R (adopted 12 January 2009).

involving China were heard in Geneva, was dubbed 'Chinese Cases Week'. On Tuesday and Wednesday the first hearing of the *Tire Special Safeguard Measures* case against the US (DS309) took place, while on Wednesday and Thursday the second trial of the *Fastener Anti-dumping* case against the EU (DS397) went ahead. The first consultation in the *Fastener Anti-dumping* case against China (DS407) happened on Friday. A Chinese delegation numbering more than 20 people shuttled between the various conference rooms. No wonder people think that China has become one of the most active members in the WTO dispute settlement mechanism, just after the US and the EU.

As a result of being involved in so many cases, the Chinese government has come to feel very much at home at the WTO. Furthermore, many of the cases have dealt with familiar problems. Issues such as antidumping and safeguard measures are closely related to matters with which Chinese companies are familiar, including dumping, injury causation, dumping and injury, import growth, substantial damage and so on. Consequently, the Commerce Department staff have many contacts from previous cases.

China has now had a great deal of experience of the whole WTO procedure, as well as the substantive issues. For example, antidumping and safeguard measures are matters of importance for Chinese companies and the MOC staff have encountered such issues as dumping, injury, causation of dumping and injury, import growth, substantial damage and so on in previous cases. Furthermore, they are familiar with the operation of WTO litigation because they have had extensive and long-term contact with the WTO Secretariat staff. Furthermore, Chinese citizens have served as panellists (e.g. Zhang Yuqing in the *EU – Bananas* case), work in the WTO's Legal Affairs Department under the Secretariat, which is in charge of cases. They have also served on the AB (Zhang Yuejiao is the former director of the Treaty and Law Department) and work in the AB Secretariat. At the same time, the Chinese government extensively cooperates with the highest level of international law firms, extensively communicates with the best WTO experts, such as the AB's former chairman James Bacchus, and constantly improves the working level of government officials.

The MOFCOM has created a distinctive and highly efficient litigation mechanism called 'four-body interaction'. This involves governmental officials, domestic lawyers, foreign lawyers and related industry sectors. The MOFCOM hires lawyers in Washington to deal with cases involving the US and has recruited lawyers in Brussels to handle cases against the EU. They often organise a legal group of three to four lawyers, from senior lawyers to paralegals, and from the senior adviser to leading counsel, who work together to provide a high-quality legal service to the Chinese government.

More importantly China as a full member of the WTO participates in the creation of rules, including reform negotiations on the dispute settlement mechanism as well as a new round of negotiations on other issues. In order to better participate in the WTO dispute settlement mechanism, the MOFCOM also works on the following three matters.

The first of these is to recommend the Chinese WTO panel members. On 17 February 2004, the DSB's regular meeting admitted only three panellists nominated by China, which led to widespread concern in Chinese society. By 31 December 2013, there were 19 Chinese panellists on the WTO dispute settlement panel list. It is of great significance that Chinese panellists are included in the WTO panel list so that China may participate in WTO matters in a wider range of areas and at a deeper level. First, according to the provisions of the DSU, WTO dispute settlement panellists should be senior governmental and non-governmental individuals. The presence of 19 Chinese WTO panellists means that Chinese expertise in the WTO professional field has been recognised by the WTO. This also reflects deepening Chinese participation in WTO affairs. Second, the panellists on the WTO Secretariat panel list are currently drawn from 43 countries. Two years after China's accession to the WTO, there were only three Chinese panellists. Third, it is important for the Chinese government's ability to promote its dispute settlement work that Chinese panellists are successful in that role. If Chinese panellists hear the case, they can accumulate more experience in dispute resolution and can better serve Chinese interests in WTO affairs.

The second matter is the legal research on the new round of negotiations. The WTO negotiations concerning new issues and rules are in progress. It is important to follow up these issues and it is helpful for China to prospectively and creatively participate in the WTO dispute settlement mechanism. All the personnel of the MOFCOM's Treaty and Law Department were involved in studying and analysing the legal issues involved in the new WTO round, and the results of their research were published.

The third matter is the editing of booklets entitled the *WTO Dispute Settlement Dynamic*. In order to track the development of WTO dispute settlement and provide a reference for the relevant companies, the Treaty and Law Department's WTO law section edits the *WTO Dispute Settlement Dynamic*, which includes summaries of the latest WTO cases, explanations of the nature of Chinese participation in dispute resolution and dispute settlement negotiation, case statistics and other information. It has won praise for its up-to-date information and large data support.

The Chinese government has come to realise that the WTO dispute settlement mechanism is an important platform that can be used to support the country's trade and economic interests. Along with its increasing participation in the WTO dispute settlement mechanism, China has developed an increasingly rational and pragmatic approach to understanding WTO litigation. The 2005 White Paper on China's Peaceful Development Road noted that in economic international relations trade friction between different countries is completely normal. China complies with WTO rules and international practice, enters into dialogue on the basis of equality and uses the WTO dispute settlement mechanism to deal with trade frictions.[224]

If there is room for argument in any given case, the Chinese government enters into WTO proceedings where the rulings of the panel and the AB distinguish the rights and wrongs of the case and safeguard national interests. If the measures involved have obvious flaws and the negative impact of altering a policy can be controlled, the Chinese government may opt to resolve the case through consultations. Whether consultations resolve the case satisfactorily or a DSB ruling goes against China, the Chinese government properly fulfils its commitments, implements the ruling, upholds its image as a responsible trading nation and safeguards the legal authority of the WTO multilateral trading system.[225]

In deciding whether or not to initiate a WTO dispute settlement procedure, the Chinese government often considers two factors.[226] These are whether the disputed measures significantly damage national interests and whether they violate WTO rules. In practice, if these two conditions are deemed pursuant to a preliminary assessment to be fulfilled, the Chinese government will enter into a WTO dispute settlement procedure.[227]

The MOFCOM has become accustomed to using the WTO dispute settlement mechanism to resolve trade disputes between countries rather than to express anger. This indicates progress on the part of the government and the country, which is an important symbol of its integration into the international system of rules. More importantly, it lays a good foundation for China to participate in the formulation of international rules, thus allowing its voice to be heard more loudly. China should not only be

---

[224] Chenggang Li (ed.), *Game of WTO Rules— A Decade of Legal Practices of China's Participation in WTO Dispute Settlement* (Beijing: Commercial Press, 2011, p. 23) (available in Chinese only, author's translation).

[225] Ibid., at p. 31.

[226] See Liyu H. and Gao H., 'China's Experience in Utilizing the WTO Dispute Settlement Mechanism', in Gregory C. Shaffer and Ricardo Melendez-Ortiz (eds), *Dispute Settlement at the WTO: The Developing Country Experience* (Cambridge University Press, 2010).

[227] Chenggang Li (ed.), at p. 32.

an economic power, but also uphold and develop the rule of law. China itself will benefit from the rule of law and the international community will benefit from what China brings to international rules.

7.2.2   Academic Scholarship

The Chinese government needs a stable support team of experts and scholars to study the WTO dispute settlement mechanism. Apart from Zhang Yuejiao, who is an AB member, there are 19 Chinese WTO panellists: Zeng Lingliang from Wuhan University, Zhu Lanye from East China University of Politics and Law, Dong Shizhong from Fudan University, Han Liyu from Renmin University, Gong Baihua from Fudan University, Huang Dongli from Chinese Academy of Social Sciences, Shi Xiaoli from China University of Political Science and Law, Zhang Naigen from Fudan University, Zhang Yuqing, Li Enheng, Li Zhong-zhou, Yang Guohua, E. Defeng, Zhang Liping, Li Yongsha, Chen Yusong, Hong Xiaodong, Suo Bicheng and Zhang Xiangchen from MOFCOM. These academic experts and scholars perform a dual role. They are practitioners in their capacity as judges and researchers as members of a think-tank.

Chinese scholars researching the GATT/WTO dispute settlement mechanism on a chronological basis can divide the system's history into the following phases: the first phase is the introductory phase in respect of the DSU (1986–2001), the second is the DSU deep study phase (2002–07), and the third is the Chinese cases deep study phase (2008–). The sections below will provide some analyses of these phases with a view to demonstrating how the discourse on compliance with international trade rules has evolved over the years among scholars in China.

7.2.2.1   The DSU introductory phase

Chinese study of the GATT/WTO dispute settlement mechanism began from the middle of the 1980s. Chinese scholars hoped to learn the latest rules of the game in the international arena of dispute resolution through such research. Their motivation to do so was that they regarded the GATT/WTO dispute settlement system as representing the most advanced system on the international level, and they wished to push the Chinese legal system to adapt to it and achieve consistency with international rules, as well as enable China to absorb such rules as soon as possible. Their research aimed to improve Chinese trade competitiveness and to gain more benefit from international trade.

Although before December 2001 China was not a WTO member, on the international stage it was a real foreign judicial participant and often played the role of a respondent. The US and the EU had frequently raised dumping investigations domestically against China, and other GATT/ WTO members had also initiated dumping investigations against China. The Chinese government hoped that China could join the WTO in order to protect its legal rights and trade interests. Chinese scholars tended to take an eclectic attitude towards the resolution of disputes, which meant they welcomed rule-oriented resolution but did not reject the use of diplomatic channels to achieve the same purpose. This reflects Chinese values and the deep-rooted culture of Confucianism.[228]

Chinese scholars researching on the WTO and its core normative framework frequently refer to Adam Smith's free trade theory[229] and David Ricardo's comparative advantage theory.[230] Even legal researchers often mention these two theories together with the related economic and legal theory of Marxism, because they believe that the goal of the WTO is to promote the free flow of trade which has a close relationship with the economy. In order to conduct effective and persuasive judicial interpretation, they argue that the WTO can no longer isolate itself from key economic and political science theories. In this regard, constructivism and reputation costs discussed in Chapter 4 of this book are central to the understanding of interpretation and compliance with WTO rules.

However, at that time, Chinese WTO experts predicted that China would soon encounter a great deal of trade friction and that it was necessary to conduct research immediately to avoid being unprepared for situations that might arise in the future. The WTO differs from other international organisations because of its quasi-judicial nature. If one member requests consultation under the DSU, the procedure starts automatically, regardless of whether the counterpart is willing to participate or not. This made research into the dispute settlement mechanism essential and urgent.

At this stage, such research focused on statutes and case studies. Chinese

---

[228]   Guohua Yang, 'Accession to the WTO: What Does It Mean to China?' (Chinalawinfo, 3 July 2002): http://article.chinalawinfo.com/Article_Detail. asp?ArticleID=2822&Type=mod; Weitian Zhao, 'WTO and International Law' (Chinalawinfo, 3 July 2002): http://article.chinalawinfo.com/Article_Detail. asp?Article ID=2063; Yan Zou, 'WTO and Regional Economic Integration' (Chinalawinfo, 3 July 2002): http://article.chinalawinfo.com/Article_Detail. asp?ArticleID=792; Qingjiang Kong, 'Will China Behave in the WTO Dispute Settlement Mechanism?: The Law and Practice of the Chinese Approach to Trade Disputes' (Chinalawinfo, 3 July 2002): http://article.chinalawinfo.com/ Article_Detail.asp?ArticleID=1197 (accessed 14 April 2014) (available in Chinese only, author's translation).

[229]   Adam Smith, *The Wealth of Nations* (Penguin, 1999).

[230]   David Ricardo, *Principles of Political Economy and Taxation* (first published 1817, Prometheus 1996).

scholars hoped that by studying the dispute settlement mechanism they would be able to help the government to understand that China could fully integrate into the international economic system without violating international trade rules, and that the GATT/WTO dispute resolution mechanism provided an effective means of protecting Chinese legitimate interests. Academic scholarship in this domain focused on introducing and analysing cases, laws and GATT/WTO principles.[231]

As with other WTO members, when the Chinese government formulates its policies in respect of specific matters, it must take into account international and domestic interests. In the collision between thousands of years of China's traditional Confucian values and the Western approach to economy and law, the biggest shock lay in the way in which China has transformed itself to adapt to the reality of globalisation and thereafter altered its trade policy.

Although at this stage China had not joined the WTO, and therefore Chinese voices and perspectives were not being heard, Chinese scholars regarded it as an important matter and conducted research on the GATT/WTO dispute settlement mechanism.

7.2.2.2   The DSU deep study phase
Deng Xiaoping's reform and opening-up policy seems to have injected vitality into the Chinese economy, which ushered in a new era in which China experienced rapid economic growth during the 1990s. Accession to the WTO was a means of boosting this development, and study of the WTO became a field of key importance for international economic lawyers.

Experts anticipated that immediately following China's accession to the WTO, a large number of Chinese cases would arise. However, this did not actually occur. Following its accession to the WTO, China had to comply with WTO rules, but it had a five-year transitional period before the full implementation of the rules. This period from 2002 to 2006 was therefore labelled a 'honeymoon period' by foreign media.[232]

---

[231]   Yaotian Wang and Hanmin Zhou, *Comprehensive Study on General Agreement on Tariffs and Trade* (1st ed., China Foreign Trade and Economic Press, 1992); Minyou Yu, Haizong Zuo and Zhixiong Huang, *Comprehensive Study on the WTO Dispute Settlement Mechanism* (Shanghai People Press, 2001); Lanye Zhu, *GATT International Trade Dispute Casebook* (Law Press, 1992); Lanye Zhu, *Case Analysis on WTO international Trade Dispute* (Law Press, 2000) (available in Chinese only, author's translation).

[232]   'The Associated Press: China and the WTO Honeymoon Period Ends' (Finance, 11 December 2006): http://finance.icxo.com/htmlnews/2006/12/11/978181.htm (accessed 14 April 2014).

Of course at this stage the Chinese government did not accomplish very much and in its first WTO case it was in fact the complainant. Research on every aspect of the first Chinese WTO case was carried out by Chinese scholars.[233] A large number of Chinese experts and scholars began to research the WTO dispute settlement mechanism, and study of the WTO became a core part of international law scholarship in China. This was not only in the area of general international law *par excellence*, as many experts in other fields of international law also focused on this area.

In 2004 legal scholars' enthusiasm for this topic was reinvigorated by the filing of a case by the US against China on integrated circuits. Although the case was eventually settled through consultations, Chinese experts began to think, analyse and make in-depth recommendations in respect of existing situations. They conducted their research from different perspectives, including the relationships between tax policy (VAT and income tax were involved in this case) and the influence of the Chinese WTO Accession Protocol on this policy, as well as the formulation and adjustment of industrial policy, industrial competitiveness, industrial reconstruction, domestic tax issues, actionable and non-actionable subsidies and R&D subsidies.[234]

The *Measures Affecting Imports of Automobile Parts* case represented the culmination of the research done in respect of the WTO dispute settlement mechanism, and from 30 March 2006 to 12 January 2009 this case held many scholars' attention.

---

[233] Guohua Yang, 'The Research on the US Steel Safeguard Measures Case' (Chinalawinfo, 14 March): http://article.chinalawinfo.com/Article_Detail. asp?ArticleID=22746&Type=mod; Weitian Zhao, 'Evaluation of the US Steel Safeguard Measures Case' (CNKI, 10 December 2003): http://cpfd.cnki.com.cn/ Article/CPFDTOTAL-FSMZ200312001022.htm; Yanli Jiang, 'The DSU Dispute Settlement Mechanism: from the Perspective of the US Steel Safeguard Measures Case' (CNKI, 23 October 2005): http://cdmd.cnki.com.cn/Article/CDMD-10183-2005-108977.htm (accessed 14 April 2014) (available in Chinese only, author's translation).

[234] Ya Qin, 'WTO Subsidy Rules and Chinese Industrial Policy: Reflections on the Chinese IC Case' (CNKI, 1 March 2004): http://www.cnki.com.cn/ Article/CJFDTotal-GJJF200403016.htm; Chen Wang, 'WTO Legal Analysis on Sino-US IC Dispute' (CNKI, 21 April 2005): http://mall.cnki.net/magazine/article/SJMY200504008.htm; Yingfeng Long, 'Reflections on the Chinese IC Case' (CNKI, 14 April 2007): http://www.cnki.com.cn/Article/CJFDTotal-SWSW200704016.htm; Ying Yu, 'The Use of Science and Technology Industrial Policy under the WTO Framework: IC Case Analysis' (CNKI, 6 July 2007): http://mall.cnki.net/magazine/Article/KJJB200707004.htm (accessed 14 April 2014) (available in Chinese only, author's translation).

Chinese scholars generally believe that China needs to use the WTO dispute settlement mechanism, which is a legal weapon for the protection of international trade liberalisation, in order to safeguard Chinese legitimate rights and interests. A search of the Chinese Journal Database reveals nearly 100 000 articles on this matter, including articles on the impact of China's accession to the WTO, the existing problems and coping strategies, the impact on the industry, analysis of antidumping cases, analysis of US and EU policy towards China, subsidy issues, suggestions regarding legislation, analysis of compatibility with WTO principles, the relationship between WTO agreements and the dispute settlement mechanism, analysis of the dispute settlement mechanism reform, inspiration drawn by China from other trade disputes, discussion of the legal system in the light of Chinese characteristics, the transformation of governmental functions, research on new trends, and so on.

In short, this database has rich content that ranges from substantive law to all aspects of procedural law. The material that can be found there basically reveals an affirmative and positive attitude towards the WTO dispute settlement mechanism and suggests that the government should seek to adapt to the WTO laws. They also put forward strategies to be adopted once China is involved in a WTO case. If consultations can settle the dispute, China should actively cooperate with its counterpart. If proceedings cannot be avoided, China should still have a positive attitude. On the one hand, it should safeguard its legitimate rights and interests, but on the other it should implement the WTO ruling and comply with the WTO rules. China should accept victory or defeat with equal magnanimity.

Because the case China was at that time involved in was limited in terms of its scope and field, the considerable number of articles written about it cannot truly reflect their value. They covered specific issues, such as a piece of paper, a dish, a piece of coal, a battery, a pair of shoes, textiles, pharmaceuticals, IT, private companies, multinationals, logistics, technology industry, accounting, taxation, customs, banking, education, personnel, the environment, party building, trial mode, cross-strait relations, sovereignty, etc. Almost everything was included and studies were made from different perspectives.

In short, during the second stage Chinese experts and scholars comprehensively reviewed and summarised almost all the relevant laws and the actual situation of most industries, proposed regulations and pointed out operations that did not comply with WTO law, predicted the future possibility of friction and its possible consequences, figured out the impact of WTO accession on specific products, departments, fields and industries and provided insights with reference to trade disputes in which other WTO member states were involved.

In the same way as the government, which actively participated as a third party in the WTO dispute settlement mechanism, Chinese scholars and experts actively prepared and continuously reinforced the foundations for future disputes: they believed in the truth of the proverb: 'don't have thy cloak to make when it begins to rain'.

7.2.2.3   The Chinese cases deep study phase

After 2007 more and more cases involving China were brought before the WTO dispute settlement system. So far the cases in which China is involved have covered the three pillars, namely goods, services and intellectual property rights. They have also involved antidumping, countervailing and safeguard measures, tax policy, market access, import substitution, customs measures, Agreement on the Application of Sanitary and Phytosanitary Measures (SPS), criminal threshold, double remedy, export quotas and management measures, financial transaction service (e-payment), financial information services and regulatory issues related to non-market economy countries, and export subsidies and tax incentives subsidies to the famous brand. Some of these issues have previously arisen in the history of WTO dispute settlement and some have Chinese characteristics. The emergence of these problems and situations expands the subject matter of WTO dispute settlement and the emergence of new issues involves applying the relevant substantive laws in ways which have never been done before.

Chinese scholars have begun considering the problems involved in the WTO's substantive laws and proposing ideas in this respect, rather than simply predicting what decisions the panel and AB might make. They focus on issues such as analysis of the WTO's legality of particular measures, countermeasures involved in the WTO dispute settlement mechanism as well as review of the past performance of the dispute resolution mechanism and its future prospects. Some of the academic scholarship focused on experiences and lessons to be learned in respect of the WTO dispute settlement system following China's accession to the WTO, evaluation of specific industrial performance some years after accession, the nexus between trade and the environment, labour standards and human rights, and so on. Chinese scholars started out as spectators but are now active participants, and have begun to question the judgments made by the panel and the AB as well as certain provisions of the WTO agreements. They have come to realise that the WTO legal provisions contain certain defects, and that the panel and AB have provided a number of unclear or incorrect explanations, as well as some questionable and ambiguous judgments. These matters indicate to some extent that Chinese scholars are now eager to move from the role of participant to that of policymaker.

As the saying goes, Rome was not built in a day. By dint of a large number of analyses of China-related disputes, Chinese scholars have gradually deepened their understanding of the WTO's substantive laws and have comprehensively grasped the WTO dispute settlement mechanism. Since 2008, two prestigious journals dealing with WTO law, the *Journal of International Economic Law* and the *Journal of World Trade*, have published many articles by Chinese scholars, which display their unique Chinese views and discoveries. A few articles also appeared in these two journals before 2008. A search through Baidu or Google in respect of any given case involving China will produce hundreds of thousands of results relating to articles and books written by Chinese scholars. The number of books and articles that have appeared from 2003, when China first used the WTO dispute settlement mechanism, to 2014 is staggering. The emergence of these Chinese cases enhances the research level of Chinese scholars, thus allowing these Chinese unique views to find their way into mainstream scholarships. This in turn provides an incentive to present more views and thoughts at the domestic level.

Both governmental and academic circles have a positive attitude towards Chinese implementation of the rulings made in WTO cases. They comment that China should properly implement and comply with WTO rulings. This approach both demonstrates the style that should be adopted by a responsible big country and is an important aspect of occupying the moral high ground.[235] Zhang Yuqing, the former director of the Treaty and Law Department in the MOFCOM, has expressed the view that China's proper implementation of WTO rulings reflects China's image as a responsible trading nation, benefits its future development and upgrades its international status in the long run. Zeng Huaqun, the President of the China Association of International Economics, is of the opinion that China's performance in implementing DSB rulings should be affirmed and that exemplary behaviour regarding implementation on China's part could prompt other WTO members to follow suit, which would help underline China's reputation for international responsibility. Therefore, the notion of reputation cost and not necessarily existing WTO remedies have been key to ensuring compliance with WTO rules by China. Professor Zuo Haicong from Nankai University offers the analysis that strong execution can be expected because the National People's Congress and the State Council are able to reach consensus without undue difficulty, so that the

---

[235]   Zhenyu Sun, *A Pressing Time in Geneva: Oral Record by China's First Ambassador of the Mission to the WTO, Sun Zhenyu* (collated by Guanhua Yang and Xiaoli Shi, People Press 2011) (available in Chinese only, author's translation).

amendment and repeal of laws, administrative regulations, departmental rules and local rules and regulations can be achieved without fuss. Prompt and definitive execution is an attribute that derives from the traditional Chinese culture of Confucianism and trustworthiness and its legal tradition of abiding by international obligations, supported by the premise of China's respect for DSB rulings and its support for the WTO system.[236]

---

[236] Minyang Wang, 'China Has the Best Performance in the WTO Ruling' (China net, 29 October 2013): http://news.china.com.cn/live/2013-10/29/content_23135413.htm (accessed 16 April 2014) (available in Chinese only, author's translation).

8. Chinese Confucianism and compliance

Ann Kent has argued that by virtue of its history, cultural traditions and power, China's compliance was in doubt as it historically considered itself to be the Middle Kingdom unconstrained by international society. It has lacked a rule of law tradition and it is powerful enough to ignore its international obligations.[1] The question is: does China, with its brand of Confucianism, have a bad reputation for non-compliance or not?

8.1 CHINESE CONFUCIANISM IN CONTEXT[2]

In China, Confucianism is a deep-rooted tradition. When talking about Chinese civilisation, almost everyone mentions Confucianism, including the virtues of sincerity or honesty, although there was no concept of compliance in ancient times.

The concept of sincerity and/or compliance can be traced back to the spring and autumn periods. God helps people who obey, and the moral person helps those who are trustworthy.[3] God blesses people who are honest, trustworthy, who comply with the laws of nature and its good ways, and God gives fortune and luck to such people.[4] Gentlemen promote ethics and build achievements.[5] Sincerity is the law of Heaven;

---

[1] Ann Kent, *China, the United Nations and Human Rights: the Limits of Compliance* (University of Pennsylvania Press, 1999), p. 2; and Ann Kent, *Beyond Compliance: China, International Organizations and Global Security* (Stanford University Press, 2007), p. 3.

[2] Juying Wang, 'Chinese Traditional Honesty View' in Shourong Lan (ed.), *Ethics and Social Honesty of the Legal Analysis* (Huazhong University of Science and Technology Press, 2010), pp. 57–82 (available in Chinese only, author's translation).

[3] 'The Copulative' in *Yi* (gushiwen): http://so.gushiwen.org/guwen/bookv_423.aspx (accessed 10 July 2014) (available in Chinese only, author's translation).

[4] Ibid.

[5] 'Stem Classic' in *Zhou Yi* (baidu, 2 September 2006): http://zhidao.baidu.

to be an honest person is the law of humanity.[6] Confucius said that if a man lacks sincerity, we do not know what will happen.[7] At home one obeys one's parents and at school one respects one's teachers. One should be cautious, sincere, merciful and kind.[8] Trustworthiness is the foundation of action, and action is the basis of the person. If there is no sincerity, there is no success; and if there is no sincerity, there is no career.[9] What one says should be honest and faithful and what one does should be sincere and serious. Even if one travels to other countries, this approach is feasible. If what one says is fraudulent and hypocritical and what one does is arrogant and frivolous, even if one is in one's native land, does such an approach work?[10] The sincerity that Confucian culture emphasises is a fundamental issue for one who lives in the world, faithfulness is the fundamental principle of a state, and the honesty of a ruler determines the survival of a country. Zeng Zi said that one should treat everyone one meets with sincerity and dedicate oneself to dealing with everything one encounters. Even if the environment is harsh and immoral, one should follow this rule and not be shaken from it.[11] Xun Zi considered that power should be controlled, rules should be followed and sincerity should be established – then one could manage a state.[12] Although the teachings of Confucius, Zeng Zi and Xun Zi are very different in many ways, sincerity is a highly consistent element in their

---

com/question/12104333.html (accessed 10 July 2014) (available in Chinese only, author's translation).

  [6]   *Golden Mean* (51zzl): http://www.51zzl.com/jiaoyu/zhongyong.asp (accessed 10 July 2014) (available in Chinese only, author's translation).

  [7]   *The Analects* (baidu, 19 April 2013): http://wenku.baidu.com/link?url=wnIV4 AczxIJQjTlRuatMVNp-VmA FgxBZeAeXBtURnO1z13sorRVM__IVIZ1GLW8 FF-K4-Wiux7woEAKZN1zpX8lIKIxljfR8M5OhEs8uRYa (accessed 10 July 2014) (available in Chinese only, author's translation).

  [8]   Ibid.

  [9]   Zhou Liu, *Lue Xin, Liu Zi* (sina, 20 May 2009): http://blog.sina.com.cn/s/ blog_4cc28ae00100d31d.html (accessed 10 July 2014) (available in Chinese only, author's translation).

  [10]   *The Analects* (baidu, 19 April 2013): http://wenku.baidu.com/link?url=wnIV4 AczxIJQjTlRuatMVNp-VmA FgxBZeAeXBtURnO1z13sorRVM__IVIZ1GLW8 FF-K4-Wiux7woEAKZN1zpX8lIKIxljfR8M5OhEs8uRYa (accessed 10 July 2014) (available in Chinese only, author's translation).

  [11]   De Dai, 'Zeng Analects' in *Da Dai Rites Record* (baidu, 26 June 2014): http://baike.baidu.com/view/47630.htm?fr=aladdin (accessed 10 July 2014) (available in Chinese only, author's translation).

  [12]   Kuang Xun, 'Power' in *Xun Zi* (chinakongzi, 23 November 2007): http:// www.chinakongzi.org/rjwh/lsjd/xunzi/200711/t20071123_2911783.htm (accessed 10 July 2014) (available in Chinese only, author's translation).

ideology. Guan Zi thought that ancient kings should focus on sincerity to achieve unity and maintain ties with the people.[13] Sincerity is not needed only by the ruling class: all people should be honest so that the whole of society can operate normally. Mo Zi, the founder of Moist, was very honest. He believed that if one has no strong ambition, one's wisdom is therefore not accessible; and if one has no sincerity, things have no result.[14] Only by keeping one's promise can one obtain people's trust and maintain one's reputation. Mo Zi thought that sincerity is doing what one says and stressed that one must keep one's promise, do what one says one is going to do and gain people's trust through action.[15] He first regarded sincerity as a means of managing a state. Three elements are required in order to govern a country: the law, sincerity and power. Sincerity needs to be built up by the king and his courtiers.[16] People across the country obey the king because of his sincerity and virtue.[17] Sincerity also occupied a very important position in the thinking of military strategists. Sun Bin presented the law of war, which is that he who has sincerity wins the war.[18]

During the Tang Dynasty many books mentioned the word of sincerity. Hanyu, a Confucian representative, raised it as the precondition of success in all undertakings.[19] Li Ao, who was Hanyu's student, considered that understanding of and research into all things obtains knowledge. From this starting-point he reasoned that after obtaining knowledge,

---

[13]   Zhong Guan, 'No. 12 Pivot Words' in *Guan Zi* (gushiwen): http://www.gushiwen.org/GuShiWen_9212c060 f1.aspx (accessed 10 July 2014) (available in Chinese only, author's translation).

[14]   Di Mo, 'Cultivation' in *Mo Zi* (gushiwen): http://www.gushiwen.org/gushiwen_38dc49770f.aspx (accessed 10 July 2014) (available in Chinese only, author's translation).

[15]   Di Mo, 'Jiang Shang' in *Mo Zi* (gushiwen): http://www.gushiwen.org/GuShiWen_81d9f4f408.aspx (accessed 14 July 2014) (available in Chinese only, author's translation).

[16]   Lihong Jiang, 'Power' in *Shang Jun Shu Zhui Zhi* (China Press, 1st ed. 1986), p. 75 (available in Chinese only, author's translation).

[17]   Fei Han, 'Perverse' in *Hanist Notes* (gushiwen): http://www.gushiwen.org/gushiwen_c4fa6839a3.aspx (accessed 14 July 2014) (available in Chinese only, author's translation).

[18]   Sun Bin, *Sun Bin's Arts of War* (gushiwen): http://www.gushiwen.org/guwen/sunbin.aspx (accessed 14 July 2014) (available in Chinese only, author's translation).

[19]   Yu Han, *Human Nature* (baidu, 6 December 2011): http://wenku.baidu.com/link?url=UnsgsB4I4KStDFXn1oxoR7zYbYMnP_FAVqmxhsouHpy e51aa-dbMfpszNC7LLck5Dt91a9xpFbJxlS08gqb-8eYmQLs8JnuR2ewTJAPwOG (accessed 14 July 2014) (available in Chinese only, author's translation).

one obtains sincerity; that after obtaining sincerity, one achieves a positive state of mind; that after achieving a positive state of mind, one may improve oneself; that after improving oneself, one can manage one's family; that once one can manage one's family, one can govern a country; and that, finally, after governing the country, the whole world is peaceful.[20] In this way, he guided people to gradually return to the faith of the saints' realm.

The concept of sincerity was refined during the Song Dynasty. Zhu Xi, a master of both Confucian and traditional philosophy during that era, believed that speaking honestly to be sincere, and doing honestly is also to be sincere, and that therefore sincerity is no sooner said than done.[21]

In conclusion we may find that sincerity in Confucian terms has advantages and disadvantages. The social role of Confucian thinking about sincerity is mainly in creating a certain social and moral atmosphere and in helping to form public opinion. As Confucianism is in the mainstream of Chinese traditional culture, it has far-reaching influence on other classical types of thinking about sincerity. However, the disadvantage of Confucian sincerity is that it is limited to the moral level rather than being extended to the institutional level, and is limited to being a facet of the cultivation of morals rather than being a strong mechanism of social control. Therefore there is no concept of 'compliance' but only that of sincerity or honesty. Chinese traditional culture holds that sincerity is the natural expression of the inherent virtue of benevolence. It is the main content of external social ethics, indicates a high degree of confidence, is a basic sign of a perfect personality and the noble realm, and is an important safeguard of a successful life.

8.2   CONTEMPORARY CHINA AND COMPLIANCE

What about contemporary China? Do the Chinese comply with international law? And how do others view its record of compliance?

---

[20]   Ao Li, *Reply the Book of Human Nature* (baidu, 14 August 2010): http://wenku.baidu.com/link?url=zAKtzY_Joi6yXB0sxVHYdSxENpNBGYrhz2Yle_83kpipCOj Z1SouwEGA12uNz5_MRT6VbkHRr8ODZ9eSvO8PKBwHQUwCNpMauO0y7ta W5JC (accessed 14 July 2014) (available in Chinese only, author's translation).
[21]   Jingde Li, *Zhuist Words* (baidu, 8 February 2012): http://wenku.baidu.com/link?url=bvXAfA3XnE1ihLXvLaCDgUZUtTSlnc6ABc7Oo5oDJJ49cIDI3u quB41yXAaLPKwROVbkgtqmLdJbYGqnYGqvGa9XmOLJCRFm9EZQstglU 8hm (accessed 14 July 2014) (available in Chinese only, author's translation).

China has traditionally regarded itself as being the centre of the universe and the head of the Confucian family of nations, whose existence long predates the much younger and essentially Western discipline of international law. It is understandable, therefore, that China might feel reluctant to be bound by Western customary law, in the making of which it did not participate. Treaties, on the other hand, as expressions of consent, remain the logical source of international law for China.[22]

8.2.1   From a Bilateral Perspective

China has concluded border treaties with all neighbouring countries, apart from India, through negotiations. Where borders were already well defined, there have been no reports of Chinese aggression. This was true even with respect to areas such as Hong Kong and large parts of Soviet Asia, which China considers as having been wrongfully wrested from it through 'unequal treaties'.[23]

The unanimous opinion of diplomats is that China has an excellent record of compliance with international agreements.[24] The PRC unilaterally withdrew its forces from Korea, which in effect involved compliance with important parts of both the Armistice Agreement and the General Assembly Resolution of 1 February 1951. It has also complied with agreements concluded by parties of unequal strength and primarily for the benefit of Japan, a weaker party, because it lacked effective government protection in the face of Japan's policy of non-recognition towards China.[25] In terms of Chinese compliance with the various trade agreements, it is unanimously agreed that the Chinese have always met their financial obligations promptly.[26]

8.2.2   From a Multilateral Perspective

China has had a bitter and humiliating history. Due to the Opium War, which took place over a period of 60 years during the late Qing Dynasty era, the Chinese government had to sign dozens of unfair international agreements which pushed the Chinese people into an abyss of misery, and compliance with those agreements was a further humiliation for China.

---

[22]   Luke T. Lee, *China and International Agreements: A Study of Compliance* (A.W. Sijthoff Leyden & Rule of Law Press Durham, NC, 1969), p. 16.
[23]   Ibid., at pp. 35–7.
[24]   Ibid., at p. 19.
[25]   Ibid., at p. 59.
[26]   Ibid., at p. 79.

From 1949 to 1971, China was alienated from the international community. After it was finally admitted to the UN in 1971, its initially cautious behaviour bespoke a state whose international policies were still largely overshadowed by its own history and its domestic ideological struggles.[27] Since 1980, China has gradually shown acceptable compliance in the field of arms control and disarmament at all five levels of compliance, including accession to treaties, procedural and substantive compliance and legislative and practical implementation. It has also achieved deep compliance in terms of its preparedness to redefine its interests in line with the norms it had previously rejected, to renegotiate its sovereignty and to accept the benefits offered by international organisations.[28]

China has increasingly complied with its obligations in respect of the World Bank and International Monetary Fund. It has complied deeply, in that it has accepted the constraints on sovereignty consequent upon the restructuring of its economy, has shouldered the costs of participation by making increased contributions and has reassessed many of its interests in terms of the dominant norms of the institutions concerned. The result of these efforts is the impressive growth in the country's GDP.[29]

China's record of compliance with the UN Environment Program is more mixed. In the area of ozone protection, it has complied internationally with its reporting obligations and in setting voluntary targets. It has complied domestically in meeting legal and institutional targets and in the practical implementation of its reduction targets. It accepted the costs of ratifying the London and Copenhagen Amendments, renegotiated its sovereignty and reassessed its interests as being best served by conforming with the norms of the regime. To that extent it has complied deeply at an international level. In respect of climate change, China was not subject to an obligation under the Framework Convention to meet reduction targets, and it sought to avoid the introduction of such targets in the ensuing negotiations because the climate change instruments involved relatively larger domestically economic costs than was the case for other states.[30]

In respect of international human rights, China has demonstrated increasing procedural compliance and has accepted some International Labour Organization (ILO) norms and rules at the level of domestic legislation. However, with a few exceptions, it has failed to comply with the ILO's norms, principles and rules in terms of practical implementation,

---

[27] Ann Kent, *Beyond Compliance: China, International Organizations and Global Security* (Stanford University Press, 2007), p. 34.
[28] Ibid., at p. 100.
[29] Ibid., at p. 140.
[30] Ibid., at pp. 176–80.

which is at a deep level of compliance. Concerning the UN Committee against Torture, China has gradually moved towards compliance at the procedural level in terms of its reporting obligations, and has made some progress in respect of its domestic legislation. However, the Chinese authorities have acknowledged the gap between China's procedural compliance at international level and practical compliance within China.[31]

China has complied with international norms and procedures at the three different international levels: accession to treaties, procedural compliance and substantive compliance.[32]

In terms of both multilateral and bilateral treaties, China has achieved compliance. However, legal scholars have raised arguments as to the quality of such compliance. Achieving full compliance is a controversial topic even for developed countries, which means that it is often a very harsh requirement for developing countries such as China. That said, the advantages of sharp scholarly criticism as to China's compliance outweigh their disadvantages from the perspectives both of theory and of practice.

8.2.3   From the WTO Perspective

China's compliance with international laws is a matter of sovereignty and national interests, as well as its international reputation. It is not desirable for the country to turn a blind eye to international law and regard its obligations as optional. If China loses WTO cases and does not comply with the DSB's rulings and recommendations, this may lead to retaliation, affect Chinese trade interests and cause job losses. Ultimately, compliance with WTO rulings is based on objective needs. Furthermore, consciousness of national image, national interests and business interests is a vital component of compliance. If this was lacking in respect of the implementation of the WTO's rulings, how could the WTO enforce them? And if the WTO could not do so, how could the member states maintain the multilateral system?[33]

China conscientiously implements the DSB's recommendations and rulings. This not only reflects its high degree of trust in and respect for the WTO Dispute Settlement Mechanism, but also the fact that China is

---

[31]   Ibid., at pp. 216–19.
[32]   Ibid., at p. 227.
[33]   Xiaogie Lue, Liyu Han, Dongli Huang, Xiaoli Shi and Guohua Yang (eds), *The Rule of Law in China a Decade After its Accession to the WTO: A Series of Interviews to Commemorate the Tenth Anniversary of China's Accession to the WTO* (People Press, 2011), p. 20 (available in Chinese only, author's translation).

a responsible large country that faithfully fulfils the international obligations embodied in WTO global trade governance. In addition, China's compliant approach contributes to the peaceful settlement of international disputes, which is a basic principle of international law.[34]

---

[34] Minyou Yu and Heng Liu, *China's Performance in a Decade of the WTO* (MOFCOM, November 2010): http://images.mofcom.gov.cn/cwto/accessory/201011/1289262759181.pdf (accessed 7 May 2014) (available in Chinese only, author's translation).

9. Conclusion

I have endeavored rather to show exactly what is the meaning of the question and what difficulties must be faced in answering it, than to prove that any particular answers are true.
George E. Moore[1]

While our analyses in this volume might have raised contemporary academic and policy issues that may be the subject of further research, we have tried to conceptualise the notion of implementation of global trade rules generally as well as in the context of Chinese Confucian theory. As the second largest economy with the largest trade surplus in the world as of 2015, China is endowed with a legal tradition largely grounded on trust and persuasion rather than strict normativity that characterises the civil and common law traditions. In view of this, it was therefore necessary to employ international relations theories such as constructivism and reputation costs to demonstrate why the 161 WTO members would stick or not stick to their international law obligations emanating from WTO rules. The necessity to employ these two theories is because of the nexus between the role of sanctions as instruments to induce compliance with WTO rules in constructivist thinking and reputation cost scholarship on the one hand and the reluctance of Confucianism to root sanctions in a formal international structure. Although constructivism and reputation costs on the one hand and Confucianism on the other hand are rather not comparable concepts, there is no denial that sanctions as remedies for non-compliance with inter-state obligations are neither at the centre of Confucian legal tradition nor at the centre of the discourses on reputation costs and constructivism. In other words, the issue of implementation discussed in this volume has not been grounded on sanctions as defining remedies.

By acceding to the WTO, China joined the family of nations enmeshed in a rule-oriented multilateral structure with limited flexibility to opt out from agreed commitments at will. With persuasion engrained in Chinese Confucian tradition, a rule-oriented multilateral system acceding to the

---

[1]   Quote found in Markus Burgstaller, *Theories of Compliance with International Law* (Martinus Nijhoff Publishers, 2005), p. 191.

WTO means that China would drastically repeal and adapt many of its domestic regulations in order to avoid faltering from its WTO obligations. By using WTO case law, this volume has demonstrated some of the opportunities and challenges China has encountered/is encountering going through this process.[2] As has been discussed in this volume, while it has been challenging for China to uphold its commitments under the WTO, its membership to the WTO has been instrumental in its integration into the global economy and the enhancement of the predictability of the entire trading system.

In spite of the claim made by many observers and, indeed, some academics that the WTO is an integral part of the globalisation project because of 'its intrusion' into sectors that once represented the cornerstones of state sovereignty, it is importance how we perceive reality. While theories can be a linchpin in predicting and providing useful answers to future state behaviour, it is a truism that insofar as nation-states with different histories and traditions cluster to form a multilateral organisation like the WTO, their perspectives on complying with agreed commitments will largely be informed by their histories and traditions. However, insofar as these challenges and the incentives to take measures that are inconsistent with the spirit of the WTO agreements continue to exist, theorising the compliance regime in the context of the founding principles of the legal system of a major WTO member like China remains highly relevant in contemporary debates.

Over the years, informed observers have come up with various critical analyses relating to the debate on implementation in the GATT/WTO system. Some of these writings poignantly paint a picture of a world trade dispute settlement system that sometimes struggles to get WTO members to comply with their international commitments.[3] This volume has to a large extent moved away from a discourse that hinges only on identifying cases where implementation has not happened or has happened half-heartedly to a discourse on the theoretical logic of implementation which at the same time focuses on Confucian theory as the foundation of the Chinese legal tradition. Because Confucian tradition seeks more to persuade than to oblige, this volume has sought to

---

[2]   See Julia Ya Qin, '"WTO-Plus" Obligations and Their Implications for the World Trade Organization Legal System: An Appraisal of the China Accession Protocol', *Journal of World Trade*, Vol. 37, No. 3 (2003), pp. 483–522.

[3]   See David Palmeter and Petros Mavroidis, *Dispute Settlement in the World Trade Organization: Practice and Procedure* (Cambridge University Press, 2004); Petersmann (1997); Jackson, *The World Trade Organization* (1998); and in the context of GATT, see Hudec (1990).

identify the points of potential conflict that may exist between China's legal system and systems founded on Western legal traditions when discussing compliance with WTO treaty norms.[4] While the concept of *pacta sunt servanda* has sometimes been the cornerstone of the discussion on compliance with WTO rules, compliance in the context of the Confucian legal tradition is largely discussed without excessive emphasis on normativity.

Persuasive conceptual arguments have been put forward in recent years in academic scholarship as to the need to ensure that there is sufficient nexus between international obligations of nation-states and the basic social reality in those states.[5] Although specific exceptions may exist, the fashioning of municipal legislation does not usually provide answers to problems relating to societal values or offer means of resolving conflicts.

Although there is arguably a consensus among both critics and admirers of the Uruguay Round project that the ability of the WTO adjudicating body to successfully settle disputes has been impressive, it may be argued that there has been no such consensus when it comes to unilateralism and mercantilism since the advent of the world trading system in 1995. While the Westphalian conception of sovereignty is highly incongruous with many of the reports of the WTO adjudicating body, WTO arbitrators[6] in particular seem to have largely adhered to the notion that from its inception all members of the WTO adhered to the 'underlining principle of "mutual disarmament"'[7] in trade. In this regard, whatever remedy was available for non-compliance in the WTO was intended neither to be a permanent solution nor to be a substitute for implementing an adopted

---

[4]   Gilbert Rozman (ed.), *The East Asian Region: Confucian Heritage and its Modern Adaptation* (Princeton University Press, 1991); Heriyanto Yang and Yogyakarta, 'The History and Legal Position of Confucianism in Post-independence Indonesia', *Marburg Journal of Religion*, Vol. 10, No. 1 (2005); H. Patrick Glenn, *Legal Traditions of the World* (Cambridge University Press, 5th ed., 2014), pp. 319–56.

[5]   From the point of view of this scholarship, this argument supports the idealistic view that international law must not be disconnected from existing international challenges. This approach must also take into consideration the historical context. Koskenniemi, for instance, finds it necessary 'to read the law "backward" in order to reveal the interpretation which it carries of the world we live in'. See Koskenniemi (2005), p. 422 et seq.

[6]   See *EC – Bananas* Arbitration Report, WT/DS27/ARB/ECU, para. 76; and *US – FSC*, WT/DS108/ARB, paras. 5.4–5.7 (Authorization to Suspend Concessions, 7 May 2003).

[7]   See Pascal Lamy, 'The World Trade Organization: New Issues, New Challenges', *En Temps Réel* (4 September 2014), p. 5.

DSB report. On the contrary, it seems to be that because of the inherent defect in this remedial structure, individual domestic interests have largely been stumbling blocks to the realisation of the original objective of remedial functions.

References

ARTICLES AND BOOKS

Alford, Roger P., Reflections on *US – Zeroing*: A Study in Judicial Over-reaching by the WTO Appellate Body, *Columbia Journal of Transnational Law*, Vol. 45 (2006).

Allan, Pierre, *Game Theory and International Relations: Preferences, Information and Empirical Evidence* (Edward Elgar, 1994).

Allott, Philip, *Eunomia: New Order for a New World* (Oxford University Press, 1990).

Allott, Philip, Kant or Won't: Theory and Moral Responsibility (The BISA Lecture, December 1995), *Review of International Studies*, Vol. 23 (1997).

Alvarez-Jimenez, Alberto, The WTO Appellate Body's Decision-Making Process: A Perfect Model For International Adjudication?, *Journal of International Economic Law*, Vol. 12, No. 2 (2009), pp. 289–331.

Alston, Philip, Resisting the Merger and Acquisition of Human Rights by Trade Law: A Reply to Petersmann, *European Journal of International Law*, Vol. 13, No. 4 (2002), pp. 815–44.

Anderson, Kym, Peculiarities of Retaliation in WTO dispute settlement, *World Trade Review*, Vol. 1, No. 2 (2002), pp. 123–34.

Apollis, G., Le règlement de l'affaire du Rainbow Warrior, *Review Gènèrale de Droit International Public*, 91 (1987).

Aust, Anthony, *Modern Treaty Law and Practice* (Cambridge University Press, 2007).

Austin, John, *The Province of Jurisprudence Determined; Cambridge Text in the History of Political Thought* (Cambridge University Press, 1995), edited by Wilfrid E. Rumble.

Axelrod, Robert, *The Evolution of Cooperation* (New York: Basic Books, 1984).

Baldwin, David A., Bargaining with Economic Statecraft, in Edward D. Mansfield (ed.), *International Conflict and the Global Economy* (Edward Elgar Publishing, 2004).

Baldwin, Robert E., Failure of the WTO Conference at Cancun: Reasons and Remedies, *The World Economy*, Vol. 9, No. 10 (2006), pp. 677–96.

Bagwell, Kyle, Petros C. Mavroidis and Robert W. Staiger, The Case for Tradable Remedies in WTO Dispute Settlement, *mimeo* (21 January 2004).

Baird, Douglas G., Robert H. Gertner and Randal C. Picker, *Game Theory and the Law* (Harvard University Press, 1994).

Bartels, Lorand, Applicable Law in WTO Dispute Settlement Proceedings, *Journal of World Trade*, Vol. 35, No. 3 (2001), pp. 499–519.

Bartels, Lorand, The Enabling Clause and Positive Conditionality in the European Community's GSP Program, *Journal of International Economic Law*, Vol. 6, No. 2 (2003), pp. 507–32.

Bartelson, Jens, The Concept of Sovereignty Revisited, *European Journal of International Law*, Vol. 17, No. 2 (2006), pp. 463–74.

Bello, Judith, The WTO Dispute Settlement Understanding: Less Is More, *American Journal of International Law*, Vol. 90, 416 (1996).

Benvenisti, Eyal et al., *The Impact of International Law on International Cooperation: Theoretical Perspectives* (Cambridge University Press, 2011).

Bernhardt, Rudolf, *Encyclopedia of Public International Law*, Volume III, pp. 1097–8 (Max Planck Institute for Comparative Public Law and International Law, 1997).

Bhala, Raj, *International Trade Law Theory and Practice* (Lexis Publications, 2001).

Bhala, Raj, The Power of the Past: Towards *De Jure Stare Decisis* in WTO Adjudication (Part Three of a Trilogy), *George Washington International Law Review*, Vol. 33 (2001), pp. 873–978.

Bhala, Raj, WTO Dispute Settlement and Austin's Positivism: a Primer on the Intersection, *International Trade Law & Regulation*, Vol. 9, No. 1 (2003), pp. 14–25.

Bilder, Richard B. and Beth Stephens, Remedies in International Human Rights Law by Dinah Shelton, Book Review and Note Book Review, *American Journal of International Law*, Vol. 95 (2001).

Bishop, William, The Choice of Remedies for Breach of Contract, *Journal of Legal Studies*, Vol. XIV (1985), pp. 299–320.

Blackhurst, Richard, The Future of the WTO: Some Comments on the Sutherland Report, *World Trade Review*, Vol. 4, No. 3 (2005), pp. 378–89.

Blokker, Niels, International Organisation: the Untouchable, *International Organisation Law Review*, Vol. 10 (2013), pp. 259–75.

Blüthner, Andreas, Has the Appellate Body Erred? An Appraisal and Criticism in the WTO Hormones Case, *Journal of International Economic Law*, Vol. 2, No. 4 (1999), pp. 603–39.

Bodansky, Daniel, John R. Crook and David J. Bederman, The ILC's State Responsibility Articles: Counterintuiting Countermeasures, *American Journal of International Law*, Vol. 96, 817 (October 2002).

von Bogdandy, Armin, Law and Politics in the WTO-Strategies to Cope with a Deficient Relationship, *Max Planck Yearbook of United Nations Law*, Vol. 5 (2001), pp. 609–74.

von Bogdandy, Armin and Markus Wagner, The 'Sutherland Report' on WTO Reform – A Critical Appraisal, *World Trade Review*, Vol. 4, No. 3 (2005), pp. 439–47.

Bolton, John R., Is there Really 'Law' in International Affairs?, *Transnational Law and Contemporary Problems*, Vol. 10, No. 1 (2000).

Bordo, Michael D. and Murshid Antu Panini, Globalization and Changing Patterns in the International Transmission of Shocks in Financial Markets, *Journal of International Money and Finance*, Vol. 25 (2006), pp. 655–74.

Boyle, Alan, Further Development of the Law of the Sea Convention: Mechanisms for Change, *International and Comparative Law Quarterly*, Vol. 54, No. 3 (2005), pp. 563–84.

Bronckers, Marco and Neboth van den Broek, Financial Compensation in the WTO: Improving the Remedies of WTO Dispute Settlement, *Journal of International Economic Law (JIEL)*, Vol. 8, No. 1 (2005), pp. 101–26.

Browne, René E., Revisiting 'National Security' in an Interdependent World: The GATT Article XXI Defense After Helms-Burton, *The Georgetown Law Journal*, Vol. 86 (1997), p. 405.

Brownlie, Ian, *The Rule of Law in International Affairs: International Law at the Fiftieth Anniversary of the United Nations* (Martinus Nijhoff Publishers, 1998).

Brownlie, Ian, *Principles of Public International Law*, 5th edition (Oxford University Press, 1998).

Brownlie, Ian, *Principles of Public International Law*, 6th edition (Oxford University Press, 2003).

Brownlie, Ian, *Principles of International Law*, 7th edition (Oxford University Press, 2008).

Brunnée, Jutta and Stephen Toope, International Law and Constructivism: Elements of an Interactional Theory of International Law, *Columbia Journal of Transnational Law*, Vol. 39 (2000), pp. 19–34.

Burgstaller, Markus, *Theories of Compliance with International Law* (Martinus Nijhoff Publishers, 2005).

Bütler, Monika and Heinz Hauser, The WTO Dispute Settlement System: First Assessment from an Economic Perspective, *Journal of Law, Economics and Organization (JLEO)*, Vol. 16, No. 2 (2000), pp. 503–33.

Byers, Michael, *Custom, Power and the Power of Rules: International Relations and Customary International Law* (Cambridge University Press, 1999).

Calabresi, Guido and A. Douglas Melamed, Property Rules, Liability Rules, and Inalienability: One View of the Cathedral, *Harvard Law Review*, Vol. 85, No. 6 (April 1972), pp. 1089–1128.

Cameron, James and Kevin Gray, Principles of International Law in the WTO Dispute Settlement Body, *International & Comparative Law Quarterly*, Vol. 50 (2001), pp. 248–98.

Carmody, Chios, Remedies and Conformity under the WTO Agreement, *Journal of International Economic Law*, Vol. 5, No. 2 (2002), pp. 307–29.

Carmody, Chios, WTO Obligations as Collective, *European Journal of International Law*, Vol. 17, No. 2 (2006), pp. 419–43.

Carmody, Chios, A Theory of WTO Law, *Journal of International Economic Law*, Vol. 11, No. 3 (2008), pp. 527–57.

Caron, David D., The ILC Articles on State Responsibility: The Paradoxical Relationship Between Form and Authority, *American Journal of International Law (AJIL)*, Vol. 96 (2002), p. 857.

Carr, E.H., *Nationalism and After* (New York, 1945).

Cass, Deborah Z., The 'Constitutionalization' of International Trade Law: Judicial Norm-Generation as the Engine of Constitutional Development in International Trade, *European Journal of International Law*, Vol. 12, No. 1 (2001), pp. 39–75.

Chang, Seung Wha, Taming Unilateralism Under the Multilateral Trading System: Unfinished Job in the WTO Panel Ruling on U.S. Sections 301–310 of the Trade Act of 1974, *Law and Policy in International Business*, Vol. 31, 1151 (2000).

Charney, Jonathan I., Third State Remedies in International Law, *Michigan Journal of International Law (MIJIL)*, Vol. 10, 57 (Winter 1989).

Charnovitz, Steve, Rethinking WTO Trade Sanctions, *American Journal of International Law (AJIL)*, Vol. 95 (2001), pp. 792–832.

Charpentier, J., L'affaire du Rainbow Warrior, *Annuaire Français de Droit International*, Vol. 31 (1985), pp. 210–20.

Chayes, Abram and Antonia Handler Chayes, *The New Sovereignty: Compliance with International Regulatory Agreement* (Harvard University Press, 1995).

Cheng, Bin, *General Principle of Law as Applied by International Courts and Tribunals* (Cambridge University Press, 1953, 2006).

Chinkin, C.M., Third Party Intervention Before the International Court of Justice, *American Journal of International Law*, Vol. 80 (July 1986), pp. 495–531.

Chinkin, Christine, *Third Parties in International Law* (Oxford University Press, 1993).

Choudhry, Sujit, Globalisation in Search of Justification: Toward a

Theory of Constitutional Interpretation, *Indiana Law Journal*, Vol. 74, No. 3 (1999), pp. 819–92.

Christian, Walter, Constitutionalizing (Inter)national Governance – Possibilities for and Limits to the Development of an International Constitutional Law, *German Yearbook of International Law*, Vol. 44 (2001), pp. 172–3.

Coase, Ronald H., *The Firm, the Market and the Law* (Chicago University Press, 1988).

Code of Justinian (527–565), Corpus Juris civilis, *The Attorney's Pocket Dictionary* (Oxford University Press, 2001).

Collier, Paul, Why the WTO is Deadlocked: And What Can Be Done About It, *The World Economy*, Vol. 29, No. 10 (2006) pp. 1177–1201.

Commonwealth Secretariat Publication, *The Cotonou Agreement, a User's Guide* (Commonwealth Secretariat, 2004).

Cooter, Robert and Thomas Ulen, *Law and Economics* (London, 1988).

Cooter, Robert and Thomas Ulen, *Law and Economics*, 2nd edition (New York, 1997).

Cooter, Robert and Thomas Ulen, *Law and Economics*, International edition, 4th edition (London, 2004).

Coron, David D., The ILC Articles on State Responsibility: The Paradoxical Relationship Between Form and Authority, *American Journal of International Law*, Vol. 96 (2002).

Cotterrell, Roger, *The Politics of Jurisprudence: A Critical Introduction to Legal Philosophy*, 2nd edition (London, 2003).

Cottier, Thomas, The Challenge of Regionalization and Preferential Relations in World Trade Law and Policy, *European Foreign Affairs Review*, Vol. 2 (1996), pp. 146–67.

Cottier, Thomas, *Limits of International Trade: The Constitutional Challenge*, paper presented at the 94th Annual Meeting of the American Society of International Law (2000), pp. 220–22.

Cottier, Thomas and Krista N. Schefer, Good Faith and the Protection of Legitimate Expectations in the WTO, in Marco Bronckers and Reinhard Quick (eds), *New Directions in International Economic Law. Essays in Honour of John H. Jackson* (Kluwer Law International, 2000), pp. 47–68.

Covelli, Nick and Rajeev Sharma, Proposals for Reform of the WTO Dispute Settlement Understanding in Respect of Third Parties, *International Trade Law & Regulation*, Vol. 9, No. 1 (January 2003).

Craswell, Richard, Contract Remedies, Renegotiation, and the Theory of Efficient Breach, *Southern California Law Review*, Vol. 61 (1988), pp. 629–70.

Crawford, James, The ILC's Articles on Responsibility of State for

International Wrongful Acts: A Retrospective, *American Journal of International Law*, Vol. 96, 874 (2002).

Crawford, James, *Brownlie's Principles of International Law*, 8th edition (Oxford University Press, 2012).

Cullen, Holly, The Role of History in Thomas Franck's Fairness in International Law and Institution, *European Journal of International Law*, Vol. 13, No. 4 (2002), pp. 927–40.

Curzon, L.B., *Dictionary of Law*, 6th edition (Longman, 2002).

Cuyvers, Ludo and Stijn Verherstraeten, *The Network of Interlocking Directorates between International Economic Organizations*, Department of International Economics, International Management and Diplomacy working paper (University of Antwerp, Issue 024, 2004).

Daillier, Patrick and Alain Pellet, *Droit International Public*, 6th edition (Paris, 1999).

Dam, Kenneth W., *The GATT Law and International Economic Organization* (Chicago, 1970).

Danilenko, Gennady M., International *Jus Cogens*: Issues of Law-Making, *European Journal of International Law*, Vol. 2, No. 1 (1991).

D'Aspremont, Jean and Jörg Kammerhofer (eds), *International Legal Positivism in a Post-Modern World* (Cambridge University Press, 2014).

D'Aspremont, Jean, The Idea of 'Rules' in Sources of International Law, *British Yearbook of International Law*, Vol. 84 (2014), pp. 1–31.

Daoudi, M.S. and M.S. Dajani, *Economic Sanctions: Ideals and Experience* (London, 1983).

Daoudi, M.S. and M.S. Dejani, *Economic Diplomacy: Embargo Leverage and World Politics* (London, 1985).

Davey, William J., Supporting the World Trade Organization Dispute Settlement System, *Journal of World Trade (JWT)*, Vol. 34, No. 1 (2000), pp. 167–70.

Davey, William J., Reforming WTO Dispute Settlement, in Mitsuo Matsushita and Dukgeun Ahn (eds) *New Perspectives of the World Trading System: WTO and East Asia* (London: Cameron May, 2004), Chapter 6.

De Mestral, Armand, NAFTA Dispute Settlement: Creative Experiment or Confusion?, in Bartel et al. (eds) *Regional Trade Agreements and the WTO Legal System* (Oxford University Press, 2006), pp. 359–81.

Diego-Fernandez, Mateo and Roberto Rios Herran, The Reform of the WTO Dispute Settlement Understanding: A Closer Look at the Mexican Proposal, *Manchester Journal of International Economic Law (MJIEL)*, Vol. 1 (2004).

Dixit, Avinash K. and Barry J. Nalebuff, *Thinking Strategically: The Competitive Edge in Business, Politics, and Everyday Life* (W.W. Norton, 1993).

Dixon, Martin et al., *Cases & Materials on International Law*, 4th edition (Oxford University Press, 2003).

Dixon, Martin, *International Law*, 6th edition (Oxford University Press, 2007).

Dunne, Tim, Milja Kurki and Steve Smith (eds), *International Relations Theories: Discipline and Diversity* (Oxford University Press, 2007).

Durling, James P., Deference, But Only When Due: WTO Review of Anti-Dumping Measures, *Journal of International Economic Law*, Vol. 7, No. 1 (2003), pp. 125–53.

Dworkin, Ronald, *Taking Rights Seriously* (Harvard University Press, 1977).

Dworkin, Ronald, *Law's Empire* (Cambridge University Press, 1986).

Ehlermann, Claus-Dieter, Tensions between the Dispute Settlement Process and the Diplomatic and the Treaty-making Activities of the WTO, *World Trade Review*, Vol. 1, No. 3 (2002), pp. 301–8.

Ehlermann, Claus-Dieter and Nicolas Lockhart, Standard of Review in WTO Law, *Journal of International Economic Law*, Vol. 7, No. 3 (2004), pp. 491–521.

Ehlermann, Claus-Dieter, Six Years on the Bench of the 'World Trade Court', in Ortino Federico and Ernst-Ulrich Petersmann (eds), *The WTO Dispute Settlement System 1995–2003* (Kluwer Law International, 2004), pp. 522–3.

Ehlermann, Claus-Dieter and L. Ehring, Decision-Making in the World Trade Organization: Is the Consensus Practice of the World Trade Organization Adequate for Making, Revising and Implementing Rules on International Trade?, *Journal of International Economic Law*, Vol. 8, No. 1 (2005), pp. 51–75.

Emmerson, Andrew, Conceptualizing Security Exceptions: Legal Doctrine or Political Excuse?, *Journal of International Economic Law*, Vol. 11, No. 1 (2008) pp. 135–54.

Espiell, Hector Gros, GATT: Accommodating Generalized Preferences, *Journal of World Trade Law*, Vol. 8 (1974), pp. 341–63.

Fierke, K.M., Constructivism, in Tim Dunne et al. (eds) *International Relations Theories: Discipline and Diversity* (Oxford University Press, 2007).

Fitzmaurice, Gerald, Third Report on the Law of Treaties, UN Document A/CN.4/115, *Yearbook of the International Law Commission* (1958, II).

Flambouras, Dionysios P., The Doctrine of Impossibility of Performance and *Clausula Rebus Sic Stantibus* in the 1980 Convention on Contracts for the International Sales of Goods and the Principles of European Contract Law – A Comparative Analysis, *Pace International Law Review (PILR)*, Vol. XIII, No. I (Spring 2001), pp. 261–93.

Fowler, Michael Ross and Julie Marie Bunck, *Law, Power, and the Sovereign State* (Pennsylvania State University Press, 1995).

Frankel, Susy, Challenging TRIPS-Plus Agreements: The Potential Utility of Non-Violation Disputes, *Journal of International Economic Law*, Vol. 12, No. 4 (2009), pp. 1023–65.

Frank, Thomas M., *Fairness in International Law and Institutions* (Oxford: Clarendon Press, 1995).

Friedmas, Thomas, *The Lexus and the Olive Tree: Understanding Globalization*, 2nd edition (First Anchor Books, 2000).

Fitzmaurice, Gerald, The General Principles of International Law Considered from the Standpoint of the Rule of Law, *Recueil des Cours de l'Academie de la Haye*, Vol. 92, No. 1 (1957).

Fukunaga, Yuka, Securing Compliance through the WTO Dispute Settlement System: Implementation of DSB Recommendations, *Journal of International Economic Law*, Vol. 9, No. 2 (2006), pp. 383–426.

Furtado, Xavier, International Law and the Dispute over the Spratly Islands: Whither UNCLOS?, *Contemporary Southeast Asia*, Vol. 21, No. 3 (1999), pp. 386–404.

Garcia-Rubio, Mariano, *On the Application of Customary Rules of State Responsibility by the WTO Dispute Settlement Organs: A General International Law Perspective* (Geneva: Graduate Institute of International Studies, 2001).

Garner, Bryan A., *Black's Law Dictionary* (West Group, 1999).

Glaser, Charles, Realist as Optimists: Cooperation as Self-Help, in Michael E. Brown (ed.), *The Perils of Anarchy: Contemporary Realism and International Security* (MIT Press, 1995).

Glenn, H. Patrick, *Legal Traditions of the World*, 5th edition (Oxford University Press, 2014).

Goh, Gavin and Andreas R. Ziegler, Retrospective Remedies in the WTO After Automotive Leather, *Journal of International Economic Law (JIEL)*, Vol. 6, No. 3 (2003), pp. 545–64.

Goldsmith, Jack L. and Eric A. Posner, *The Limits of International Law* (Oxford University Press, 2005).

Goldsmith, Jack L. and Eric A. Posner, International Agreements: A Rational Choice Approach, *Virginia Journal of International Law*, Vol. 44, No. 1 (2003), pp. 113–43.

Gomory, Ralph E. and William J. Baumol, *Global Trade and Conflicting National Interests* (Cambridge: MIT Press, 2000).

Goode, Walter, *Dictionary of Trade Policy Terms* (Cambridge University Press, 2003).

Greenwald, John, WTO Dispute Settlement: an Exercise in Trade Law Legislation? *Journal of International Economic Law*, Vol. 7, No. 1 (2003), pp. 113–24.

Grieco, Joseph M., Anarchy and the Limits of Cooperation: A Realist

Critique of the Newest Liberal Institutionalism, *International Organisation*, Vol. 42 (1988), pp. 485–507.

Gros, Espiell Hector, GATT: Accommodating Generalised Preferences, *Journal of World Trade*, Vol. 8 (1974), pp. 341–63.

Grossman, Gene M. and Elhanan Helpman, Trade War and Trade Talks, *Journal of Political Economy*, Vol. 103, No. 4 (1995), pp. 678–708.

Gubbay, A.R., Human Rights in Criminal Justice Proceedings: The Zimbabwean Experience, in Cherif Bassiouni and Ziyad Motala (eds), *The Protection of Human Rights in African Criminal Proceedings* (Kluwer, 1995).

Guzman, Andrew T., A Compliance-Based Theory of International Law, *California Law Review*, Vol. 90 (2002), pp. 1823–87.

Guzman, Andrew T., *How International Law Works: A Rational Choice Theory* (Oxford University Press, 2008).

Haas, Richard N., *Sovereignty: Existing Rights, Evolving Responsibilities*, Remarks at the School of Foreign Service and the Mortara Center for International Studies at Georgetown University in Washington (14 January 2003), available at: http://www.iwar.org.uk/news-archive/2003/01-15.htm (last visited 20 May 2011).

Hahn, Michael J., Vital Interests and the Law of GATT: An Analysis of GATT Security Exception, *Michigan Journal of International Law*, Vol. 12 (1991).

Hall, Peter A. and Rosemary C.R. Taylor, Political Science and the Three New Institutionalisms, *Political Studies*, Vol. XLIV (1996), pp. 936–57.

Hart, H.L.A., *The Concept of Law*, Oxford University Press (first published in 1961 and republished in 1994).

Henkin, Louis, *How Nations Behave: Law and Foreign Policy*, 2nd edition (Columbia University Press, 1979).

Henkin, Louis, International Law: Politics, Values and Functions, *Recueil des Cours*, Vol. 216, No. 9 (1989 IV), p. 278.

Henkin, Louis, *International Law: Cases and Materials* (Dordrecht, 1993).

Hoekman, B. and Petros C. Mavroidis, Competition, Competition Policy and the GATT, *CEPR Discussion Paper* No. 876 (London: Centre for Economic Policy, 1994).

Hoekman, Bernard and Michael Kostecki, *The Political Economy of the World Trading System: From GATT to the WTO* (Oxford University Press, 1995).

Hoekman, Bernard and Petros C. Mavroidis, Policy Externalities and High-Tech Rivalry: Competition and Multilateral Cooperation beyond the WTO, *Leiden Journal of International Law*, Vol. 9 (1996), pp. 273–318.

Holland, James and Julian Webb, *Learning Legal Rules*, 7th edition (Oxford University Press, 2010).

Holning, Lau, Rethinking the Persistent Objector Doctrine in International Human Rights Law, *Chicago Journal of International Law*, Vol. 6 (2005).

Hopf, Ted, The Promise of Constructivism in International Relations Theory, *International Security*, Vol. 23, No. 1 (1998), pp. 171–200.

Horn, Henrik and Petros C. Mavroidis, *Remedies in the WTO Dispute Settlement System and Developing Country Interest*, Institute for International Economic Studies, Stockholm University Centre for Economic Policy Research, mimeo (11 April 1999).

Howse, Robert, Human Rights in the WTO: Whose Rights, What Humanity? Comment on Petersmann, *European Journal of International Law*, Vol. 13, No. 3 (2002), pp. 651–9.

Howse, Robert, in Thomas Cottier, Petros C. Mavroidis and Patrick Blatter, *The Rule of the Judge in International Trade Regulation* (University of Michigan Press, 2003).

Hu, Jiaxiang, The Role of International Law in the Development of the WTO Law, *Journal of International Economic Law*, Vol. 7, No. 1 (2004), pp. 143–67.

Hudec, Robert E., The GATT Legal System: A Diplomat's Jurisprudence, *Journal of World Trade*, Vol. 4 (1970), p. 615.

Hudec, Robert E., *The GATT Legal System and World Trade Diplomacy* (Praeger Publishers, 1975).

Hudec, Robert E., *The GATT Legal System and World Trade Diplomacy* (Minneapolis Quarterly Review, 1990).

Hudec, Robert E., *Enforcing International Trade Law, The Evolution of the Modern GATT Legal System* (Butterworth Legal Publishers, 1993).

Hudec, Robert E., Free Trade, Sovereignty, Democracy: The Future of the World Trade Organization, *World Trade Review*, Vol. 1, No. 2 (2002), pp. 211–22.

Hsieh, Pasha L., China's Development of International Economic Law and WTO Legal Capacity Building, *Journal of International Economic Law (JIEL)*, Vol. 13, No. 4 (2010), pp. 997–1036.

Hutchinson, D.N., Solidarity and Breaches of Multilateral Treaties, *The British Year Book of International Law*, Fifty-Ninth Year of Issue (1988), pp. 150–214.

Jackson, John H., The WTO Dispute Settlement Understanding – Misunderstandings of the Nature of Legal Obligation, *American Journal of International Law*, Vol. 91 (1997).

Jackson, John H., *The World Trading System, Law and Policy of International Economic Relations*, 2nd edition (MIT Press, 1997).

Jackson, John H., The Great 1994 Sovereignty Debate: United States Acceptance and Implementation of the Uruguay Round Results, *Columbia Journal of Transnational Law*, Vol. 36 (1997), pp. 157–88.

Jackson, John H., The World Trade Organization, Constitution and Jurisprudence, *Chatham House working paper*, 85 (1998).

Jackson, John H., Designing and Implementing Effective Dispute Settlement Procedures: WTO Dispute Settlement, Appraisal and Prospects, in Ann O. Krueger (ed.), *The WTO as an International Organization* (Chicago University Press, 1998), pp. 193–213.

Jackson, John H., *The Jurisprudence of GATT and the WTO: Insights of Treaty Law and Economic Relations* (Cambridge University Press, 2000).

Jackson, John H., *The World Trading System: Law and Policy of International Economic Relations* (The MIT Press, 2000).

Jackson, John H., Sovereignty Modern: A New Approach to an Outdated Concept, *American Journal of International Law* (2003), at pp. 782–802.

Jackson, John H., International Law Status of WTO Dispute Settlement Reports: Obligation to Comply or Option to 'Buy Out'?, *American Journal of International Law*, Vol. 98 (2004), pp. 109–25.

Jackson, John H., The State of International Economic Law – 2005: The Changing Fundamentals of International Economic Law and Ten Years of the WTO, *Journal of International Economic Law*, Vol. 8, No. 1 (2005), pp. 3–15.

Jackson, John H., *Sovereignty, the WTO, and Changing Fundamentals of International Law* (Cambridge University Press, 2006).

Jackson, John H., *Sovereignty, the WTO, and Changing Fundamentals of International Law, Lauterpacht Memorial Lectures* (Cambridge University Press, 2009).

Janis, Mark, Nature of *jus cogens*, *Connecticut Journal of International Law*, Vol. 3 (1988), pp. 359–63.

Jiang, Lihong, Power in *Shang Jun Shu Zhui Zhi*, 1st edition (China Press, 1986), p. 75 (available in Chinese only, author's translation).

Kahler, Miles, Conclusion: The Causes and Consequences of Legalization, *International Organization*, Vol. 54, No. 3 (2000), pp. 661–83.

Kaplow, Louise and Steven Shavell, Property Rules Versus Liability Rules: An Economic Analysis, *Harvard Law Review (HLR)*, Vol. 109 (1996), pp. 715–90.

Kazazi, Mojtaba, *Burden of Proof and Related Issues: A Study on Evidence before International Tribunals* (Kluwer Law International, 1996).

Kele, Onyejekwe, International Law of Trade Preferences: Emanations from the European Union and the United States, *St Mary's Journal (SMJ)*, Vol. 26 (1995), p. 425.

Keller, Perry (ed.), *Chinese Law and Legal Theory* (Ashgate, 2001).

Kelley, Claire R., Realist Theory and Real Constraints, *Virginia Journal of International Law*, Vol. 44 (Winter 2004), pp. 545–636.

Kelsen, Hans, *General Theory of Law and State* (Harvard University Press, 1945).

Kelsen, Hans, *Essays in Legal and Moral Philosophy* (translated by Peter Heath) (Kluwer Academic Publisher Series, 1973).

Kelsen, Hans, *General Theory of Law and State* (translated and republished) (Harvard University Press, 1999).

Kent, Ann, *China, the United Nations and Human Rights: the Limits of Compliance* (University of Pennsylvania Press, 1999).

Kent, Ann, *Beyond Compliance: China, International Organizations and Global Security* (Stanford University Press, 2007).

Keohane, Robert O., *After Hegemony: Cooperation and Discord in the World Political Economy* (Princeton University Press, 1984).

Keohane, Robert O., International Institutions: Can Interdependence Work? *Foreign Policy*, Vol. 110 (1998), pp. 82–92.

Keohane, Robert O., International Relations and International Law: Two Optics, *Harvard International Law Journal*, Vol. 38 (1998).

Keohane, Robert O., International Relations and International Law: Interests, Reputation, Institutions, *American Society of International Law*, 375–9 (1999).

Keohane, Robert O., International Liberalism Reconsidered, in John Dunn (ed.), *The Economic Limits to Modern Politics*, Chapter 5 (Cambridge University Press, 1990), pp. 165–94.

Kelly, Claire R., The Value Vacuum: Self-Enforcing Regimes and the Dilution of the Normative Feedback Loop, *Michigan Journal of International Law*, Vol. 22 (2001).

Kelly, Claire R., Realist Theory and Real Constraints, *Virginia Journal of International Law*, Vol. 44, No. 2 (2004), pp. 545–636.

Kessie, Edwini, The 'Early Harvest Negotiations' in 2003, in F. Ortino and E.-U. Petersmann (eds), *The WTO Dispute Settlement System 1995–2003* (Kluwer Law International, 2004), pp. 113–50.

Kingsbury, Benedict, The Concept of Compliance as a Function of Competing Conceptions of International Law, *Michigan Journal of International Law*, Vol. 19, No. 2 (1998), pp. 345–72.

Kingsbury, Benedict, Legal Positivism as Normative Politics: International Society, Balance of Power and Lassa Oppenheim's Positive International Law, *European Journal of International Law*, Vol. 13, No. 2 (2002).

Klabbers, Jan, Clinching the Concept of Sovereignty: Wimbledon Redux, *Austrian Review of International and European Law*, Vol. 3, No. 3 (1999), pp. 345–67.

Klein, Natalie, *Dispute Settlement in the UN Convention on the Law of the Sea* (Cambridge University Press, 2009).

Komuro, Norio and Edwin Vermulst, Anti-Dumping Disputes in the

WTO: Navigating Dire Straits, *Journal of World Trade*, Vol. 31, No. 5 (1997), pp. 5–44.

Koskenniemi, Martti, *From Apology to Utopia, The Structure of International Legal Argument* (Helsinki: Finnish Lawyers' Publishing Company, 1989).

Koskenniemi, Martti, *From Apology to Utopia, The Structure of International Legal Argument, Reissue with New Epilogue* (Cambridge University Press, 2005).

Koskenniemi, Martti, Lauterpacht: The Victorian Tradition in International Law, *European Journal of International Law (EJIL)*, Vol. 2 (1997), pp. 215–63.

Koskenniemi, Martti, Solidarity Measures: State Responsibility as a New International Order? *British Year Book of International Law* (2001).

Koskenniemi, Martti, *The Gentle Civilizer of Nations: The Rise and Fall of International Law, 1870–1960* (Cambridge University Press, 2002).

Koskenniemi, Martti, International Law in Europe: Between Tradition and Renewal, *European Journal of International Law*, Vol. 16, No. 1 (2005), pp. 113–24.

Kramer, Matthew H., The Big Bad Wolf: Legal Positivism and Its Detractors, *The American Journal of Jurisprudence*, Vol. 49 (2004), pp. 1–10.

Krasner, Stephen D., *Sovereignty: Organized Hypocrisy* (Princeton University Press, 1999).

Krasner, Stephen D., What's Wrong with International Law Scholarship? International Law and International Relations: Together, Apart, Together?, *Chicago Journal of International Law*, Vol. 1, No. 93 (2000).

Krasner, Stephen D. (ed.), *Problematic Sovereignty: Contested Rules and Political Possibilities* (Columbia University Press, 2001).

Kreijen, Gerard et al. (eds), *State Sovereignty, and International Governance* (Oxford University Press, 2002).

Kronman, Anthony T., Specific Performance, *The University of Chicago Law Review*, Vol. 45, No. 2 (1978), pp. 351–82.

Kuijper, Pieter Jan, The Law of GATT as a Special Field of International Law, *Netherlands Year Book of International Law* (1994).

Kumm, Mattias, The Legitimacy of International Law: A Constitutionalist Framework of Analysis, *European Journal of International Law*, Vol. 15, No. 5 (2004), pp. 907–31.

Lamy, Pascal, The World Trade Organization: New Issues, New Challenges, *En Temps Réel* (4 September 2014).

Lammers, Johan G., Immunity of International Organisation: The Work of the International Law Commission, *International Organisation Law Review*, Vol. 10 (2013), pp. 276–86.

Lanye, Zhu, The Effects of the WTO Dispute Settlement Panel and Appellate Body Reports: Is the Dispute Settlement Body Resolving Specific Disputes Only or Making Precedent at the Same Time?, *Temple International & Comparative Law Journal*, Vol. 17, No. 1 (2003), pp. 221–36.

Lawrence, Robert Z., *Crimes & Punishments? Retaliation under the WTO* (Washington, DC: Institute for International Economics, October 2003).

Lawrence, Robert Z., China and the Multilateral Trading System, *National Bureau of Economic Research (NBER) Working Paper* No. 12759 (2006).

Lee, Luke T., *China and International Agreements: A Study of Compliance* (Durham, NC: A.W. Sijthoff Leyden & Rule of Law Press, 1969).

Lester, Simon, The Development of Standards of Appellate Review for Factual, Legal and Law Application Questions in WTO Dispute Settlement, *Trade Law & Development*, Vol. 4, No. 1 (2012), pp. 125–49.

Lewis, Jeffrey, Institutional Environment and Everyday EU Decision Making: Rationalist or Constructivist?, *Comparative Political Studies*, Vol. 36, No. 1/2 (February–March 2003).

Li, Chenggang (ed.), *Game of WTO Rules – A Decade of Legal Practices of China's Participation in WTO Dispute Settlement* (Commercial Press, 2011) (available in Chinese only, author's translation).

Linderfalk, Ulf, The Source of *Jus Cogens* Obligations – How Legal Positivism Copes with Peremptory International Law, *Nordic Journal of International Law*, Vol. 82, No. 3 (2013), pp. 369–89.

Lindsay, Peter, The Ambiguity of GATT Article XXI: Subtle Success or Rampant Failure?, *Duke Law Journal*, Vol. 52 (2003).

Lue, Xiaogie et al. (eds), *The Rule of Law in China a Decade After its Accession to the WTO: A Series of Interviews to Commemorate the Tenth Anniversary of China's Accession to the WTO* (People Press, 2011) (available in Chinese only, author's translation).

Ma, Qian, 'Reasonable Period of Time' in the WTO Dispute Settlement System, *Journal of International Economic Law*, Vol. 15, No. 1 (2012), pp. 1–19.

MacCormick, Neil, *Legal Reasoning and Legal Theory* (Oxford University Press, 1994).

Maggi, Giovanni and Robert W. Staiger, The Role of Dispute Settlement Procedures in International Trade Agreement, *Quarterly Journal of Economics*, Vol. 126 (2011).

Maniruzzaman, A.F.M., State Contracts in Contemporary International Law: Monist Versus Dualist Controversies, *European Journal of International Law*, Vol. 12, No. 2 (2001), pp. 309–28.

Mansfield, Edward D. (ed.), *International Conflict and the Global Economy* (Edward Elgar Publishing, 2004).

Marceau, Gabriella and Cornelium Reiman, When and How Is a Regional Trade Agreement Compatible with the WTO?, *Legal Issues of Economic Integration*, Vol. 28, No. 3 (2001), pp. 297–336.

Martin, Will and L. Alan Winters, *The Uruguay Round and the Developing Countries* (Cambridge University Press, 1996).

Matsushita, Mitsuo, Thomas J. Shoenbaum and Petros C. Mavroidis, *The World Trade Organization: Law, Practice and Policy* (Oxford University Press, 2003).

Mavroidis, Petros C., Government Procurement Agreement – The Trondheim Case: The Remedies Issue, *Swiss Review of International Economic Relations/Aussenwirtschaft*, Vol. 48 (1993).

Mavroidis, Petros C., Remedies in the WTO Legal System: Between a Rock and a Hard Place, *European Journal of International Law*, Vol. 11 (2000), pp. 763–813.

Mavroidis, Petros C., No Outsourcing of Law? WTO Law as Practiced by WTO Courts, *American Journal of International Law*, Vol. 102, No. 3 (2008), pp. 421–74.

McKnight, Brian, *Law and Order in Sung China* (Cambridge University Press, 1992).

McRae, Donald, What is the Future of the WTO Dispute Settlement?, *Journal of International Economic Law*, Vol. 7, No. 1 (2004), pp. 3–21.

Meagher, Niall, So far, so good: but what next? The Sutherland Report and WTO dispute settlement, *World Trade Review*, Vol. 4, No. 3 (2005), pp. 409–17.

Mearsheimer, John J., The False Promise of International Institutions, *International Security*, Vol. 19, No. 3 (Winter 1994/1995).

Mearsheimer, John J., Structural Realism, in T. Dunne et al. (eds), *International Relations Theories* (Oxford University Press, 2007), pp. 71–87.

Merills, J.G., *International Dispute Settlement*, 3rd edition (Cambridge University Press, 1998).

Mitchell, Andrew D., Good Faith in WTO Dispute Settlement, *Melbourne Journal of International Law*, Vol. 7, No. 2 (2006), pp. 339–73.

Mitchell, Andrew D., The Legal Basis for Using Principles in WTO Disputes, *Journal of International Economic Law*, Vol. 10, No. 4 (2007), pp. 795–835.

Mitchell, Andrew D., Proportionality and Remedies in the WTO Disputes, *Journal of International Economic Law*, Vol. 17, No. 5 (2007), pp. 985–1008.

Montaguguti, Elisabetta and Maurits Lugard, The GATT 1994 and

Other Annex 1A Agreements: Four Different Relationships? *Journal of International Economic Law* (2000), pp. 473–84.

Morgenthau, Hans J., *In Defence of the National Interest* (Knopf, 1951).

Morgenthau, Hans J., *Politics Among Nations: The Struggle for Power and Peace*, 6th edition (Alfred A. Knopf, 1985).

Mueller, Denis C., *Public Choice III* (Cambridge University Press, 2003).

Naiki, Yoshiko, The Mandatory/Discriminatory Doctrine in WTO Law: The US – Section 301 Case and its Aftermath, *Journal of International Economic Law*, Vol. 7, No. 1 (2004).

Neuhold, Hanspeter, The Foreign Policy 'Cost-Benefit-Analysis' Revisited, *German Yearbook of International Law*, Vol. 42 (1999), pp. 84–124.

Ngangjoh-Hodu, Yenkong and Roberto Rios-Herran, WTO Dispute Settlement System and the Issue of Compliance: Multilaterizing the Enforcement, *Manchester Journal of International Economic Law*, Vol. 2, No. 2 (2004).

Ngangjoh-Hodu, Yenkong, *Pacta sunt servanda* and Complaints in the WTO Dispute Settlement, *Manchester Journal of International Economic Law*, Vol. 1, No. 2 (2004).

Ngangjoh-Hodu, Yenkong, *Theories and Practices of Compliance with WTO Law* (Kluwer, 2012).

Nichols, Philip M., Realism, Liberalism, and the World Trade Organization, *University of Pennsylvania Journal of International Economic Law*, Vol. 25, No. 2 (2004).

Nong, Hong, *UNCLOS and Ocean Dispute Settlement: Law and Politics in the South China Sea* (Routledge, 2012).

North, Douglass C. et al., An Economic Theory of the Growth of the Western World, *The Economic History Review* (April 1970).

North, Douglass C., *Institutions, Institutional Change, and Economic Performance* (Cambridge University Press, 1990).

Nussbaum, Arthur, *A Concise History of the Law of Nations*, 2nd edition (Macmillan Publishers, 1954).

O'Connor, Bernard, Remedies in the WTO Dispute Settlement System: The Bananas and Hormones cases, *Journal of World Trade*, Vol. 38, No. 2 (2004), pp. 245–66.

O'Connor, John F., *Good Faith in International Law* (Dartmouth Publishing Co., 1991).

Odell, John S., Chairing a WTO Negotiation, *Journal of International Economic Law*, Vol. 8, No. 2 (2005), pp. 425–48.

Oesch, Mathias, *Standards of Review in WTO Dispute Settlement Resolution* (Oxford University Press, 2003).

Orakhelashvili, Alexander, The Idea of European International Law,

European Journal of International Law, Vol. 17, No. 2 (2006), pp. 315–47.

Oran, R. Young, Regime Dynamics: The Rise and Fall of International Regimes, in Stephen D. Krasner (ed.), International Regimes, Special Issue of *International Organisation*, Vol. 36, No. 2 (1982).

Palmeter, David and Petros C. Mavroidis, The WTO Legal System: Sources of Law, *American Journal of International Law*, Vol. 92, No. 3 (1998), p. 116.

Palmeter, David and Petros C. Mavroidis, *Dispute Settlement in the World Trade Organization: Practice and Procedure* (Kluwer Law International, 1999).

Paul, You, *Le Préambule des Traités Internationaux* (Fribourg: Librairie de l'Université, 1941).

Pauwelyn, Joost, Evidence, Proof and Persuasion in WTO Dispute Settlement: Who Bears the Burden?, *Journal of International Economic Law* (1998).

Pauwelyn, Joost, Enforcement and Countermeasures in the WTO: Rules are Rules – Toward a More Collective Approach, *American Journal of International Law*, Vol. 94 (April 2000), pp. 335–47.

Pauwelyn, Joost, The Role of Public International Law in the WTO: How Far Can We Go? *American Journal of International Law*, Vol. 95 (2001), pp. 535–78.

Pauwelyn, Joost, *Conflict of Norms in Public International Law: How WTO Law Relates to Other Rules of International Law* (Cambridge University Press, 2004).

Pearsall, Judy, *The Concise Oxford Dictionary*, 10th edition revised (Oxford University Press, 2001).

Peng, Shin-yi, The WTO Legalistic Approach and East Asia: From the Legal Culture Perspective, *Asian-Pacific Law & Policy Journal*, Vol. 1 (2000), p. 13.

Pescatore, Pierre, The GATT Dispute Settlement Mechanism: Its Present Situation and Its Prospect, *Journal of World Trade* (1993), pp. 5–20.

Pescatore, Pierre et al., *Handbook of WTO/GATT Dispute Settlement*, Vol. 1 (Kluwer Law International, 1997).

Petersmann, Ernst-Ulrich, *The New GATT Round of Multilateral Trade Negotiations: Legal and Economic Problems* (Deventer, 1991).

Petersmann, Ernst-Ulrich, International Competition Rules for the GATT/ WTO World Trade and Legal System, *Journal of World Trade*, Vol. 27 (1993).

Petersmann, Ernst-Ulrich, *The GATT/WTO Dispute Settlement System, International Law, International Organizations and Dispute Settlement* (Kluwer Law International, 1997).

Petersmann, Ernst-Ulrich, *International Trade Law and the GATT/WTO Dispute Settlement System*, Vol. II, Studies in Transnational Economic Law (Kluwer Law International, 1999).

Petersmann, Ernst-Ulrich, The WTO Constitution and Human Rights, *Journal of International Economic Law*, Vol. 3, No. 1 (2000).

Petersmann, Ernst-Ulrich, The 'Human Rights Approach' Advocated by the UN High Commissioner for Human Rights and by the International Labour Organization: Is it Relevant for the WTO Law and Policy? *Journal of International Economic Law*, Vol. 7, No. 3 (2004), pp. 605–27.

Petersmann, Ernst-Ulrich, Multilevel Judicial Governance of International Trade Requires a Common Conception of Rule of Law and Justice, *Journal of International Economic Law*, Vol. 10, No. 3 (2007), pp. 529–51.

Pingel-Lenuzza, Isabelle, International Organisation and Immunity from Jurisdiction: To Respect or to Bypass, *International & Comparative Law Quarterly (ICLQ)*, Vol. 51, No. 1 (2002), pp. 1–15.

Polinsky, Mitchell A., Risk Sharing Through Breach of Contract Remedies, *Journal of Legal Studies*, Vol. 12, No. 427 (1983).

Posner, Eric A., Economic Analysis of Contract Law after Three Decades: Success or Failure?, *The Yale Law Journal*, Vol. 112, No. 4 (2003), pp. 829–80.

Posner, Eric A. and Alan O. Sykes, Efficient Breach of International Law: Optimal Remedies, Legalised Noncompliance, and Related Issues, *Michigan Law Review (MLR)*, Vol. 110 (2011), pp. 243–95.

Posner, Richard, Economic Analysis of Law, *University of Chicago Law Review*, Vol. 53 (1986), pp. 117–18.

Powell, Walter W. and Paul J. DiMaggio, *The New Institutionalism in Organizational Analysis* (University of Chicago Press Books, 1991).

Qin, Julia Ya, The Impact of WTO Accession on China's Legal System: Trade, Investment and Beyond, *Wayne State University Law School Research Paper*, No. 07-15 (2007).

Quick, Reinhard and Andreas Blüthner, Has the Appellate Body Erred? An Appraisal and Criticism in the WTO Hormones Case, *Journal of International Economic Law*, Vol. 2, No. 4 (1999), pp. 603–39.

Qureshi, Asif H., *Perspectives in International Economic Law* (Kluwer Law International, 2002).

Quayat, David, The Forest for the Trees: A Roadmap to Canada's Litigation Experience in Lumber IV, *JIEL*, Vol. 12, No. 1 (2009), pp. 115–51.

Raustiala, Kal and Anne-Marie Slaughter, International Law, International Relations and Compliance, in Walter Carlnaes, Thomas Risse and Beth Simmons (eds), *Handbook of International Relations* (SAGE Publications, 2002).

Raustiala, Kal, Rethinking the Sovereignty Debate in International Economic Law, *Journal of International Economic Law*, Vol. 6, No. 4 (2003), pp. 841–78.

Rawls, John, *A Theory of Justice* (Oxford University Press, 1972).

Regan, Donald H., Do World Trade Organization Dispute Settlement Reports Affect the Obligations of Non-Parties? Response to McNelis, *Journal of World Trade (JWT)* (2003), pp. 883–96.

Reinisch, August, The Immunity of International Organisations and the Jurisdiction of their Administrative Tribunals, *Chinese Journal of International Law*, Vol. 7, No. 2 (2008), pp. 285–306.

Ricardo, David, *Principles of Political Economy and Taxation* (first published 1817, Prometheus 1996).

Riphagen, Willem, *Preliminary Report on State Responsibility*, Year Book of the International Law Commission, Vol. II, Part 1 (1980).

Rodrik, Dani, Has Globalization Gone too Far? *Institute of International Economics (IIE)* (1997).

Roessler, Frieder, The Competence of GATT, *Journal of World Trade Law*, Vol. 21, No. 73 (1987).

Roessler, Frieder, The Institutional Balance Between the Judicial and the Political Organs of the WTO, in Marco Bronckers and Reinhard Quick (eds), *New Directives in International Economic Law, Essays in Honour of John H. Jackson* (Kluwer Law International, 2000), pp. 325–45.

Roessler, Frieder and Petina Gappah, A Re-appraisal of Non-Violation Complaints Under the WTO Dispute Settlement Procedures, in Patrick F.J. Macrory et al. (eds), *The World Trade Organization: Legal, Economic and Political Analysis* (Springer, 2005), pp. 1371–87.

Rolland, Sonia E., Redesigning the Negotiation Process at the WTO, *Journal of International Economic Law*, Vol. 13, No. 1 (2010), pp. 65–110.

Root, Elihu, The Outlook for International Law, *American Society of International Law*, Vol. 2 (December 1915), pp. 5–10.

Rosas, Allan, Implementation and Enforcement of WTO Disputes Settlement Finding: An EU Perspective, *Journal of International Economic Law*, Vol. 4, No. 1 (2001), pp. 131–44.

Rose, Gideon, Neoclassical Realism and Theories of Foreign Policy, *World Politics*, Vol. 51 (1998), pp. 144–72.

Rosenne, Shabtai, *Intervention in the International Court of Justice* (Martinus Nijhoff, 1993).

Rosenne, Shabtai, *The World Court: What it is and How it Works* (Martinus Nijhoff, 1995).

Rozman, Gilbert (ed.), *The East Asian Region: Confucian Heritage and its Modern Adaptation* (Princeton University Press, 1991).

Rothwell, Donald and T. Stephens, *The International Law of the Sea* (Hart Publishing, 2010).

Rousseau, Charles, De la Compatibilité des Norme Juridiques Contradictoires dans L'ordre International, *Revue Générale de Droit International Public*, Vol. 39, No. 133 (1932), pp. 150–51.

Ruskola, Teemu, Law Without Law, or is 'Chinese Law' an Oxymoron?, *William & Mary Bill of Rights Journal*, Vol. 11 (2003), pp. 655–69.

Sarcedoti, Giorgio, Precedent in the Settlement of International Economic Disputes: The WTO and Investment Arbitration Models, *Bocconi Legal Research* Paper No.1931560 (2011).

Sarooshi, Dan, Sovereignty, Economic Autonomy, the United States, and International Trading System: Representations of a Relationship, *European Journal of International Law*, Vol. 15, No. 4 (2004), pp. 651–76.

Schaefer, Matthew, Sovereignty, Influence, Realpolitik and the World Trade Organization, *Hastings International and Comparative Law Review*, Vol. 25, No. 3 (2002), pp. 341–69.

Schloemann, Hannes L. and Stefan Ohlhoff, Constitutionalization and Dispute Settlement in the WTO: National Security as an Issue of Competence, *American Journal of International Law*, Vol. 93 (1999).

Schoenbaum, Thomas J., Junji Nakagawa and Linda C. Reif (eds), *Trilateral Perspectives on International Legal Issues: From Theory Into Practice* (Ardsley, New York: Transnational Publishers, 1998).

Schwartz, Warren F. and Alan O. Sykes, Toward a Positive Theory of the Most Favored Nation Obligation and Its Exceptions in the WTO/GATT System, *International Review of Law and Economics*, Vol. 16 (1996), pp. 27–51.

Schwartz, Warren F. and Alan O. Sykes, The Economic Structure of Renegotiation and Dispute Resolution in the World Trade Organization, *Journal of Legal Studies*, Vol. XXXI (2002), pp. 179–204.

Scobbie, Iain G.M., The Theorist as Judge: Hetsch Lauterpacht's Concept of the International Judicial Function, *European Journal of International Law*, Vol. 8, No. 2 (1997), pp. 264–98.

Scobbie, Iain, Tom Franck's Fairness, *European Journal of International Law*, Vol. 13, No. 4 (2002).

Shaffer, Gregory C. and Ricardo Melendez-Ortiz (eds), *Dispute Settlement at the WTO: The Developing Country Experience* (Cambridge University Press, 2010).

Shahabuddeen, Mohamed, *Precedent in the World Court* (Cambridge University Press, 1996).

Shavell, Steven, *Foundation of Economic Analysis of Law* (Harvard University Press, 2004).

Shaw, Malcolm N., *International Law*, 7th edition (Cambridge University Press, 2014).

Shell, Richard G., The Trade Stakeholders Model and Participation and Nonstate Parties in the World Trade Organization, *University of Pennsylvania Journal of International Economic Law*, Vol. 17, No. 1 (1996).

Shelton, Dinah, *Remedies in International Human Rights Law* (Oxford University Press, 1999).

Simma, Bruno, Self Contained Regimes, *Netherlands Year Book of International Law*, Vol. 6 (1985), pp. 111–36.

Simma, Bruno and Andreas Paulus, The Responsibility of Individuals for Human Rights Abuses in Internal Conflicts – A Positivist View, *American Journal of International Law*, Vol. 93, No. 302 (1999).

Simma, Bruno and Dirk Pulkowski, Of Planets and the Universe: Self-contained Regimes in International Law, *European Journal of International Law*, Vol. 17, No. 3 (2006), pp. 483–529.

Simpson, Gerry, The Situation on the International Legal Theory Front: The Power of Rules and the Rule of Power, *European Journal of International Law*, Vol. 11, No. 2 (2000), pp. 439–64.

Sinclair, Ian, *The Vienna Convention on the Law of Treaties* (Melland Schill Monographs in International Law) (Manchester University Press, 1984).

Slaughter, Anne-Marie, International Law and International Relations Theory, A Prospectus for International Lawyers: A Dual Agenda, *American Journal of International Law*, Vol. 87, No. 205 (1993).

Slaughter, Anne-Marie, Andrew S. Tulumello and Stephan Wood, International Law and International Relations Theory: A New Generation of Interdisciplinary Scholarship, *American Journal of International Law*, Vol. 93, No. 3 (1998), pp. 367–97.

Smith, Adam, *The Wealth of Nations* (Penguin, 1999).

Snyder, Jack, *Myth of Empire: Domestic Politics and International Ambition* (Cornell University Press, 1991).

Sobel, Joel, A Theory of Credibility, *Review of Economics Studies*, Vol. 52, No. 4 (1985), pp. 557–73.

Staiger, Robert W., International Rules and Institutions for Trade Policy, in *Handbook of International Economics*, G.M. Grossman and K. Rogoff edition (Amsterdam: Elsevier, 1995), pp. 1495–1551.

Steger, Debra P., The Future of the WTO: The Case for Institutional Reform, *Journal of International Economic Law*, Vol. 12, No. 4 (2009), pp. 803–33.

Stein, Arthur A., Coordination and Collaboration: Regime in an Anarchic World, in Stephen D. Krasner (ed.), International Regimes, *International Organisation*, Vol. 36, No. 115 (1983).

Stewart, Terence P., *GATT Uruguay Round: A Negotiating History (1986–1992)*, Vol. I (Kluwer Law International, 1993).

Stewart, Terence P., *The GATT Uruguay Round: A Negotiating History (1986–1992)*, Vol. II (Kluwer Law International, 1993).

Stiglitz, Joseph, *Globalisation and its Discontents* (Penguin Books, 2002).

Strezhnev, Anton, Using Latent Space Models to Study International Legal Precedent: An Application to the WTO Dispute Settlement Body, *APSA 2014 Annual Meeting Paper* (2014).

Sugden, Robert and Alan Williams, *The Principles of Practical Cost-benefit Analysis* (Oxford University Press, 1981).

Sun, Zhenyu, *A Pressing Time in Geneva: Oral Record by China's First Ambassador of the Mission to the WTO*, Sun Zhenyu (collated by Yang Guanhua and Shi Xiaoli, People Press, 2011) (available in Chinese only, author's translation).

Sunstein, Cass R. and Robert W. Hahn, A New Executive Order for Improving Federal Regulation? Deeper and Wider Cost-Benefit Analysis, *Chicago, John M. Olin Law & Economics Working Paper* No. 150 (2nd series) (2002).

Sykes, Alan O., The Remedy for Breach of Obligation under the WTO Dispute Settlement Understanding: Damages or Specific Performance?, in Marco Bronckers and Reinhard Quick (eds), *New Directions in International Economic Law* (Kluwer Law International, 2000).

Sykes, Alan O., The Safeguards Mess: A Critique of WTO Jurisprudence, *University of Chicago Law & Economics*, Working Paper No. 187 (June 2003).

Tallon, D., Exemptions, in C.M. Bianca and M.J. Bonell (eds), *Commentary on the International Sales Law* (Milan: Guiffrè, 1987).

Tarullo, Daniel K., The Hidden Costs of International Dispute Settlement: WTO Review of Domestic Anti-Dumping Decisions, *Law & Policy in International Business*, Vol. 34, No. 109 (2002), p. 118.

The Legal Texts: *The Results of the Uruguay Round of Multilateral Trade Negotiations* (Cambridge University Press, 2002).

Thirlway, Hugh, *The Sources of International Law* (Oxford University Press, 2014).

Trachtman, Joel P., Trade and . . . Problems, Cost-Benefit Analysis and Subsidiary, *European Journal of International Law*, Vol. 9, No. 1 (1998), pp. 32–85.

Trachtman, Joel P., The Domain of WTO Dispute Resolution, *Harvard International Law Journal*, Vol. 40, No. 2 (Spring 1999), pp. 333–7.

Trachtman, Joel P., Persistent Objectors, Cooperation, and the Utility of Customary International Law, *Duke Journal of Comparative & International Law*, Vol. 21 (2010).

Trebilcock, Michael J. and Robert Howse, *Regulation of International Trade*, 2nd edition (Routledge, 2001).

Trebilcock, Michael J. and Robert Howse, *The Regulation of International Trade*, 3rd edition (Routledge, 2005).

Ulen, Thomas S., The Efficiency of Specific Performance: Toward a Unified Theory of Contract Remedies, *Michigan Law Review*, Vol. 83, No. 2 (1984), pp. 341–403.

Van den Bossche, Peter, World Trade Organization Dispute Settlement in 1997 (Part I), *Journal of International Economic Law*, Vol. 1, No. 1 (1998), pp. 161–71.

Van den Bossche, Peter, WTO Dispute Settlement in 1997 (Part II), *Journal of International Economic Law*, Vol. 1, No. 1 (1998), pp. 479–490.

Van den Bossche, Peter and Iveta Alexovičová, Effective Global Economic Governance by the World Trade Organization, *Journal of International Economic Law*, Vol. 8, No. 3 (2005), pp. 667–90.

Van den Bossche, Peter, *The Law and Policy of the World Trade Organization: Text, Cases and Materials*, 2nd edition (Cambridge University Press, 2008).

Van den Bossche, Peter and Werner Zdouc, *The Law and Policy of the World Trade Organization: Text, Cases and Materials*, 3rd edition (Cambridge University Press, 2013).

van den Broek, Naboth, Power Paradoxes in Enforcement and Implementation of World Trade Organization Dispute Settlement Reports: Interdisciplinary Approaches and New Proposals, *Journal of World Trade*, Vol. 37, No. 1 (2003).

Verdross, Alfred, Forbidden Treaties in International Law, *American Journal of International Law*, Vol. 31 (1937), pp. 571–92.

Villalpando, Santiago M., Attribution of Conduct to the State: How the Rules of State Responsibility may be applied within the WTO Dispute Settlement System, *Journal of International Economic Law* (2002), pp. 393–420.

Voon, Tania and Alan Yanovich, The Facts Aside: The Limitations of WTO Appeals to Issues of Law, *Journal of World Trade*, Vol. 40, No. 2 (2006), pp. 239–58.

Waincymer, Jeff, *WTO Litigation: Procedural Aspect of Formal Dispute Settlement* (Cameron May, 2002).

Waltz, S.M., International Relations: One World, Many Theories, *Foreign Policy*, Vol. 110.

Wang, Guiguo, *Chinese Law* (Kluwer Law International, 1999).

Wang, Guiguo, *Law and Punishment: the Western and the Traditional Chinese 'Legal Mind'* (Clarendon Press, 1986).

Wang, Juying, Chinese Traditional Honesty View, in Lan Shourong (ed.),

Ethics and Social Honesty of the Legal Analysis (Huazhong University of Science and Technology Press, 2010) (available in Chinese only, author's translation).

Wang, Yaotian and Hanmin Zhou, *Comprehensive Study on General Agreement on Tariffs and Trade*, 1st edition (China Foreign Trade and Economic Press, 1992) (available in Chinese only, author's translation).

Weil, Prosper, *Le Droit International Economique, Mythe ou Realité?*, Societé Francaise Pour le Droit International, Aspects du Droit International Economique (Colloque d'Orleans, Paris, eds Pedone, May 1971).

Westlake, John, *Collected Papers* (1914).

Wilhelmsson, Thomas, Good Faith and the Duty of Disclosure in Commercial Contracting – The Nordic Experience, in Roger Brownsword, Norma J. Hird and Geraint Howells (eds), *Good Faith in Contracts* (Ashgate Publishing, 2000).

Williamson, Oliver E., *The Economic Institution of Capitalism: Firms, Market Relational Contracting* (Macmillan Publishers, 1985).

World Trade Organization, *The Legal Texts, The Results of the Uruguay Round of Multilateral Trade Negotiations* (Cambridge University Press, 2002).

Wu, Xiaohui, No Longer Outside, Not Yet Equal: Rethinking China's Membership in the World Trade Organization, *Chinese Journal of International Law (CJIL)*, Vol. 10, No. 2 (2011), pp. 227–70.

Yang, Heriyanto and Yogyakarta, The History and Legal Position of Confucianism in Post-Independence Indonesia, *Marburg Journal of Religion*, Vol. 10, No. 1 (2005).

Yang, Guohua, Case Analysis on Integrated Circuit against China, in Li Chenggang (ed.), *Game of WTO Rules – A Decade of Legal Practices of China's Participation in WTO Dispute Settlement* (Commercial Press, 2011) (available in Chinese only, author's translation).

Young, Oran R., Regime Dynamics: The Rise and Fall of International Regimes, in Stephen D. Krasner (ed.), International Regimes, Special Issue of *International Organisation*, Vol. 36, No. 2 (1982).

Yu, Minyou et al., *Comprehensive Study on the WTO Dispute Settlement Mechanism* (Shanghai People Press, 2001) (available in Chinese only, author's translation).

Yu, Xingzhong, Legal Pragmatism in the People's Republic of China, *Journal of Chinese Law*, Vol. 2 (1989), p. 3.

Yuval, Shany, Toward a General Margin of Appreciation Doctrine in International Law?, *European Journal of International Law*, Vol. 16 (2005).

Zehfuss, Maja, *Constructivism in International Relations: The Politics of Reality* (Cambridge University Press, 2002).

Zeitler, Helge Elisabeth, 'Good Faith' in the WTO Jurisprudence: Necessary Balancing Element or an Open Door To Judicial Activism?, *Journal of International Economic Law*, Vol. 8, No. 3 (2005), pp. 721–58.

Zhang, Hao, Comments on Financial Information Case, in Li Chenggang (ed.), *Game of WTO Rules – A Decade of Legal Practices of China's Participation in WTO Dispute Settlement* (Commercial Press, 2011) (available in Chinese only, author's translation).

Zhang, Mo, The Socialist Legal System with Chinese Characteristics: China's Discourse for the Rule of Law and a Bitter Experience, *Temple International & Comparative Law Journal*, Vol. 24 (2010), pp. 1–64.

Zhang, Naigeng (ed.), *Dispute Settlement of WTO: the Year of China (2009)* (Shanghai People Press, 2010) (available in Chinese only, author's translation).

Zhang, Yonghui, Comments on Tax Subsidy Case Filed by the US and Mexico, in Li Chenggang (ed.), *Game of WTO Rules – A Decade of Legal Practices of China's Participation in WTO Dispute Settlement* (Commercial Press, 2011) (available in Chinese only, author's translation).

Zhu, Lanye, *GATT International Trade Dispute Casebook* (Law Press, 1992) (available in Chinese only, author's translation).

Zhu, Lanye, *Case Analysis on WTO International Trade Dispute* (Law Press, 2000) (available in Chinese only, author's translation).

Zoller, Elisabeth, *La Bonne Foi en Droit International Public* (Paris: Pedone, 1977).

Zonnekeyn, Geert A., EC Liability for Non-Implementation of WTO Dispute Settlement Decisions – Are the Dice Cast? *Journal of International Economic Law*, Vol. 7, No. 2 (2004), pp. 483–90.

OFFICIAL SOURCES

Draft Articles on State Responsibility adopted by the International Law Commission on first reading, 'Report of the International Law Commission on the work of its forty-eighth session (6 May–26 July 1996)', *Official Records of the General Assembly, Fifty-first Session, Supplement No. 10* (A/51/10), pp. 144–5.

Draft Articles on Responsibility of States for Internationally Wrongful Acts, adopted by the International Law Commission (ILC) at its fifty-third Session (November 2001). Official Records of the UN General Assembly, Supplement No. 10(A/56/10), chap. IV .E.1

EC Council Regulation No. 2501/2001 on 'Drug Arrangement', of December 10, 2001.

EC Council Regulation; 2193/2003 (OJ L 328 p.3).

European Commission, 'WTO challenge against EU sugar will hurt developing countries', in document DN:IP/03/993, Brussels (10 July 2003).

EU Regulation No 2038/1999 on the Common Organisation of the Market in Sugar.

GATT Contracting Parties Decision of November 28th 1979 in document L/4903, BISD 26S/203.

GATT Council Minutes of the Meeting held on 3 November 1981, C/M/152 (dated 21 December 1981).

GATT Council Minutes of the Meeting held on 14 May 1987, in C/M/209, 29 May 1987.

Permanent Court of International Justice Publications, Series A Judgments, Vol. 1, Nos. 1–8 (1923–1927) Kraus Reprint, Liechtenstein (1970).

Report by the Director-General of GATT, in GATT, *The Tokyo Round of Multilateral Trade Negotiations* (1979), Vol. I, p. 99.

Report of the Study Group on the Fragmentation of International Law: Difficulties Arising from the Diversification and Expansion of International Law, International Law Commission, Fifty-sixth session, UN General Assembly, A/CN.4/L.663/Rev.1 (28 July 2004).

United States: Executive Order No. 12,291, 3 C.F.R. 127 (1981).

United States: Executive Order No. 12,866, 3 C.F.R. 638, 639 (1993).

United States: Unfunded Mandates Reform Act of 1995, Pub. L. No. 104-4, 109 Stat. 48 (2 USC. § 1501)

WTO Dispute Settlement Body Minutes, Special Session, TN/DS/W/17 (9 October 2002).

WTO Dispute Settlement Body Minutes, Special Session, TN/DS/W/M/6 (13–14 November 2002).

WTO Document WT/DS265/21, WT/DS266/21 and WT/DS283/2 of 11 July 2003.

WTO Document, TN/AG/W/1/Rev.1.

WTO General Council Meeting, WT/GC/M/60 (23 January 2001).

WTO Dispute Settlement Body Minutes, Special Session, TN/DN/DS/9 (28 May 2003).

Working Procedure of the WTO Appellate Body, WT/AB/WP/1 (15 February 1996).

Working Procedure of the WTO Appellate Body, WT/AB/WP/7 (1 May 2003).

Working Procedure of the WTO Appellate Body, WT/AB/WP/7 (2004).

WTO Decision Adopted by the General Council on Doha Work Programme, WT/L/579 (2 August 2004).

WTO Dispute Settlement Body (DSB) Special Session, Proposal to the Trade Negotiations Committee (TNC) (Report Obtained from Edwini Kessie, Counsellor, Council & TNC Division WTO) (28 May 2004).

WTO Dispute Settlement Body (DSB) Special Session, Report by the Chairman, Ambassador David Spencer, to the TNC to the Trade Negotiations Committee (TNC), TN/DS/10 (12 June 2004).

Yearbook of the International Law Commission (YBILC), Volume I, Summary Records of the sixteenth session United Nations Publication, A/CN.4/SER.A/1964 (11 May–24 July 1964).

Yearbook of the International Law Commission (YBILC), Volume II, Documents of the sixteenth session including the reports of the Commission to the General Assembly, United Nations Publication, Third Report on the Law of Treaties, by Sir Humphrey Wedlock, Special Rapporteur, A/CN.4/167 and Add.1–3 (3 March, 9 and 12 June and 7 July 1964).

Yearbook of the International Law Commission (YBILC), Volume II, Documents of the Second Part of the Seventeenth session and of the eighteenth session including the reports of the Commission to the General Assembly, United Nations Publication, Fifth Report on the Law of Treaties, by Sir Humphrey Wedlock, Special Rapporteur, A/CN.4/SER.A/1966/Add.1 (3 and 18 January 1966).

ONLINE SOURCES

Acceleration of UnionPay Internationalization (25 July 2012), obtainable at http://news.xinhuanet.com/fortune/2012-07/25/c_112529998.htm (last visited 14 March 2014) (available in Chinese only, author's translation).

A Chain Reaction of the WTO Ruling: Will Rare Earth be the Next One? (1 February 2012), obtainable at http://news.cnal.com/industry/2012/02-01/1328062609264010.shtml (last visited 9 March 2014) (available in Chinese only, author's translation).

Act Concerning the Conditions of Accession and the Adjustment to the EC Treaty of 22 January 1972, obtainable at http://www.eurotreaties.com/ukaccessionact.pdf (last visited 10 September 2004).

Admission to Visa and MasterCard (6 September 2012), obtainable at http://finance.china.com.cn/roll/20120906/1002065.shtml (last visited 14 March 2014) (available in Chinese only, author's translation).

Alain Pellet: State sovereignty and the protection of fundamental human rights: An international law perspective, Pugwash Occasional Paper,

February (2000), obtainable from http://www.pugwash.org/reports/rc/pellet.htm (last visited 17 April 2012).

A Memorandum on a Decade since China's Accession to the WTO (22 August 2013), obtainable at http://sms.mofcom.gov.cn/article/zt_tenth/dsj/201308/20130800261406.shtml (last visited 13 January 2014) (available in Chinese only, author's translation).

America Filed Two Cases against China in the WTO (10 April 2007), obtainable at http://news.xinhuanet.com/world/2007-04/10/content_5957297.htm (last visited 26 February 2014) (available in Chinese only, author's translation).

At the End of Last Year China Issued a Total of 2,949 Billion Bank Cards (19 March 2012), obtainable at http://news.xinhuanet.com/fortune/2012-03/19/c_111675221.htm (last visited 14 March 2014) (available in Chinese only, author's translation).

Automobile Trade Dispute: WTO Final Ruling Against China (18 December 2008), obtainable at http://paper.people.com.cn/jhsb/html/2008-12/17/content_159428.htm (last visited 21 February 2014) (available in Chinese only, author's translation).

BNA, Daily Report for Executive (17 June 2004), 'Brazilian Farmers Eye Retaliatory Options if US Fails to Comply with Cotton Ruling'.

China Abstained UnionPay Appeals (9 September 2012), obtainable at http://news.xinhuanet.com/fortune/2012-09/09/c_123691035.htm (last visited 14 March 2014) (available in Chinese only, author's translation).

China Accepts the WTO Ruling and Further Opens the Market for Entertainment Products (16 July 2010), obtainable at http://www.cb.com.cn/economy/2010_0716/139080.html (last visited 3 March 2014) (available in Chinese only, author's translation).

China Accepts the WTO Ruling and will Open up the Entertainment Market Next Year (16 July 2010), obtainable at http://www.sinovision.net/portal.php?mod=view&aid=141517 (last visited 3 March 2014) (available in Chinese only, author's translation).

China Appeal Failed on Electrical Steel Case under the WTO (20 October 2012), obtainable at http://news.xinhuanet.com/fortune/2012--10/20/c_123848183.htm (last visited 17 March 2014) (available in Chinese only, author's translation).

China – Certain Measures Granting Refunds, Reductions or Exemptions from Taxes and Other Payments (7 February 2008), obtainable at http://www.chinalawinfo.com/wto/wtojdaldetail.asp?jdalid=20 (last visited 23 February 2014) (available in Chinese only, author's translation).

China Chip Tax is Focused and No. 18 Document will be Adjusted? (12 May 2004), obtainable at http://www.people.com.cn/GB/it/1066/2492564.

html (last visited 19 February 2014) (available in Chinese only, author's translation).

China Filed a Case on Renewable Energy Generation Subsidy Measures against the EU to the WTO (6 November 2012), obtained at http://news.xinhuanet.com/fortune/2012-11/06/c_123917427.htm (last visited 13 February 2014) (available in Chinese only, author's translation).

China Measures Affecting Financial Information Services and Foreign Financial Information Suppliers (4 December 2008), obtainable at http://www.chinalawinfo.com/wto/wtojdaldetail.asp?jdalid=34 (last visited 4 March 2014) (available in Chinese only, author's translation).

China Measures Affecting Imports of Automobile Parts (28 August 2008), obtainable at http://www.chinalawinfo.com/wto/wtojdaldetail.asp?jdalid=32 (last visited 21 February 2014) (available in Chinese only, author's translation).

China – Measures Related to the Exportation of Various Raw Materials (30 January 2012), obtainable at http://www.chinalawinfo.com/wto/wto-jdaldetail.asp?jdalid=25 (last visited 5 March 2014) (available in Chinese only, author's translation).

China Regretted Part of Panel Ruling on Intellectual Property Dispute (27 January 2009), obtainable at http://www.chinanews.com/cj/gncj/news/2009/01-27/1542340.shtml (last visited 28 February 2014) (available in Chinese only, author's translation).

China Rejected the US, EU and Mexico WTO Panel Request on Export of Raw Materials (20 November 2009), obtainable at http://news.xinhuanet.com/world/2009-11/20/content_12499532.htm (last visited 5 March 2014) (available in Chinese only, author's translation).

China's First Case in front of the WTO – Safeguard Measures on Imports from the US (23 June 2003), obtainable at http://www.china.com.cn/zhuanti2005/txt/2003-06/23/content_5351822.htm (last visited 18 January 2014) (available in Chinese only, author's translation).

China Showed Double-Anti Sword: Levy Heavy Duties on Oriented Electrical Steel (14 April 2010), obtainable at http://www.yicai.com/news/2010/04/337228.html (last visited 18 November 2014) (available in Chinese only, author's translation).

China, the US and Mexico Signed a Memorandum of Understanding on WTO Subsidies Dispute (30 November 2007), obtainable at http://www.mofcom.gov.cn/aarticle/ae/ai/200711/2007110525 7413.html (last visited 24 February 2014) (available in Chinese only, author's translation).

Chinese Auto Parts Lost and High-end Car Companies Benefit (24 December 2008), obtainable at http://news.sohu.com/20081224/n261384116.shtml (last visited 23 February 2014) (available in Chinese only, author's translation).

Chinese Solar Companies Seek to Break Through (6 November 2012), obtainable at http://news.xinhuanet.com/fortune/2012-11/06/c_113622 651.htm (last visited 13 February 2014) (available in Chinese only, author's translation).

Chinese Solar Products Expand Domestic Demand (Hot Dialysis) (16 July 2013), obtainable at http://paper.people.com.cn/gjjrb/html/2013-07/16/content_1269025.htm (last visited 14 February 2014) (available in Chinese only, author's translation).

Commentary: China's Integration into the World through Accession to the WTO (11 November 2001), obtainable at http://news.sina.com.cn/c/2001-11-11/396793.html (last visited 10 January 2014) (available in Chinese only, author's translation).

Confucius (ed.), *Analects* (ancient poetry website), obtainable at http://www.gushiwen.org/guwen/lunyu.aspx (last visited 29 November 2014) (available in Chinese only, author's translation).

Copyright Bureau Spokesman: Piracy is a Global Problem (17 April 2007), obtainable at http://news.xinhuanet.com/politics/2007-04/17/content_5988900.htm (last visited 26 February 2014) (available in Chinese only, author's translation).

Cross, Karen Halverson, China's WTO Accession: Economic, Legal and Political Implication, *BCICLR* (2004), China and the WTO at https://www.wto.org/english/thewto_e/countries_e/china_e.htm (last visited 12 May 2015).

Dai, De, Zeng Analects in *Da Dai Rites Record* (26 June 2014), obtainable at http://baike.baidu.com/view/47630.htm?fr=aladdin (last visited 10 July 2014) (available in Chinese only, author's translation).

Dickinson, Steve, The WTO, China's Media, Copyrights and Other IP. It's a Control Thing (9 February 2009), obtainable at http://www.chinalawblog.com/2009/02/the_wto_chinas_media_copyright.html (last visited 28 February 2014).

DS309 China – Value-Added Tax on Integrated Circuits (6 October 2005), obtainable at http://www.chinalawinfo.com/wto/wtojdaldetail.asp?jdalid=26 (last visited 17 February 2014) (available in Chinese only, author's translation).

Elliott, Kimberly Ann and Gary Clyde Hufbauer, Sanctions, The Concise Encyclopedia of Economics, obtainable at http://www.econlib.org/library/Enc/Sanctions.html (last visited 25 June 2003).

EU–China Trade War: Prime Minister's Public Relations (18 June 2013), obtainable at http://news.xinhuanet.com/fortune/2013-06/18/c_1248708 20.htm (last visited 14 February 2014) (available in Chinese only, author's translation).

European and American media highly valued China's accession to the WTO (11 November 2001), obtainable at http://news.sina.com. cn/w/2001-11-11/397000.htm (last visited 10 January 2014) (available in Chinese only, author's translation).

Expect to See some Reflections After Losing the Publication Case (28 September 2009), obtainable at http://finance.ifeng.com/ roll/20090928/1290212.shtml (last visited 3 March 2014) (available in Chinese only, author's translation).

Expert: China Probably Won the Sino–US IPR cases (5 June 2007), obtainable at http://www.ce.cn/xwzx/gnsz/gdxw/200706/05/t20070605_ 11601360.shtml (last visited 27 February 2014) (available in Chinese only, author's translation).

Foreign Media: Li Keqiang Promoted China–EU Solar Negotiations to Achieve Success (5 August 2013), obtainable at http://caijing.chinadaily. com.cn/2013-08/05/content_16870071.htm (last visited 15 February 2014) (available in Chinese only, author's translation).

Geist, Michael, Why the U.S. Lost Its WTO IP Complaint Against China. Badly (27 January 2009), obtainable at http://www.michaelgeist.ca/ content/view/3645/125/ (last visited 28 February 2014).

Golden Mean, obtainable at http://www.51zzl.com/jiaoyu/zhongyong. asp (last visited 10 July 2014) (available in Chinese only, author's translation).

Guan, Zhong, No. 12 Pivot Words in *Guan Zi* (gushiwen), obtainable at http://www.gushiwen.org/GuShiWen_9212c060f1.aspx (last visited 10 July 2014) (available in Chinese only, author's translation).

Han, Fei, Perverse in *Hanist Notes* (gushiwen), obtainable at http:// www.gushiwen.org/gushiwe_c4fa6839a3.aspx (last visited 14 July 2014) (available in Chinese only, author's translation).

Han, Yu, Human Nature (6 December 2011), obtainable at http:// wenku.baidu.com/link?url=UnsgsB4I4KStDFXn1oxoR7zYbYMnP_F AVqmxhsouHpye51aa-dbMfpszNC7LLck5Dt91a9xpFbJxlS08gqb-8e YmQLs8JnuR2ewTJAPwOG (last visited 14 July 2014) (available in Chinese only, author's translation).

It is Better not to Use the Dual Currency Card when Going Abroad As Visa will Separate from UnionPay (2 June 2010), obtainable at http: //finance.sina.com.cn/money/bank/bank_hydt/20100602/08258043750. shtml (last visited 12 March 2014) (available in Chinese only, author's translation).

Ji, Wenhua, Sino–US IPR Dispute: Who is the Winner? (21 May 2010), obtainable at http://2010ipb828.blog.sohu.com/152134204.html (last visited 28 February 2014) (available in Chinese only, author's translation).

Jiang, Minhui, The Spanish Media Reported that UnionPay Exceeded Visa (2 November 2011), obtainable at http://www.mofcom.gov.cn/

aarticle/i/jyjl/m/201111/20111107809623.html (last visited 14 March 2014) (available in Chinese only, author's translation).

Jiang, Yanli, The DSU Dispute Settlement Mechanism: from the Perspective of the US Steel Safeguard Measures Case (23 October 2005), obtainable at http://cdmd.cnki.com.cn/Article/CD MD-10183-2005108977. htm (last visited 14 April 2014) (available in Chinese only, author's translation).

Kong, Qingjiang, Will China Behave in the WTO Dispute Settlement Mechanism?: The Law and Practice of the Chinese Approach to Trade Disputes (3 July 2002), obtainable at http://article.chinalawinfo.com/ Article_Detail.asp?ArticleID=1197 (last visited 14 April 2014) (available in Chinese only, author's translation).

Li, Ao, Reply the Book of Human Nature (14 August 2010), obtainable at http://wenku.baidu.com/link?url=zAKtzY_Joi6yXB0sxVHYdSxENpN BGYrhz2Yle_83kpipCOjZ1SouwEGA12uNz5_MRT6VbkHRr8ODZ9 eSvO8PKBwHQUwCNpMauO0y7taW5JC (last visited 14 July 2014) (available in Chinese only, author's translation).

Li, Jingde, Zhuist Words (8 February 2012), obtainable at http:// wenku.baidu.com/link?url=bvXAfA3XnE1ihLXvLaCDgUZUtTSlnc6 ABc7Oo5oDJJ49cIDI3uquB41yXAaLPKwROVbkgtqmLdJbYGqnYG qvGa9XmOLJCRFm9EZQstglU8hm (last visited 14 July 2014) (available in Chinese only, author's translation).

Li, Zhen, The WTO Ruling Boosts the Reform of UnionPay (9 October 2012), obtainable at http://www.legaldaily.com.cn/international/content/ 2012-10/09/content_3886163.htm?node=34031 (last visited 16 March 2014) (available in Chinese only, author's translation).

Liu, Zhou, Lue Xin in *Liu Zi* (20 May 2009), obtainable at http://blog.sina. com.cn/s/blog_4cc 28ae00100d31d.html (last visited 10 July 2014) (available in Chinese only, author's translation).

Long, Yingfeng, Reflections on the Chinese IC Case (14 April 2007), obtainable at http://www.cnki.com.cn/Article/CJFDTotal-SWSW200704016. htm (last visited 14 April 2014) (available in Chinese only, author's translation).

Ministry of Commerce Spokesman Issued a Statement (18 December 2008), obtainable at http://paper.people.com.cn/rmrbhwb/html/2008-12/18/content_159870.htm (last visited 21 February 2014) (available in Chinese only, author's translation).

Ministry of Commerce Spokesman Shen Danyang Issued a Statement on the Chinese Solar Subsidies Case Against the EU in the WTO (5 November 2012), obtainable at http://www.mofcom.gov.cn/aarticle/ae/ ag/201211/2012110 8419302.html (last visited 13 February 2014) (available in Chinese only, author's translation).

MOFCOM Dual Investigations on Oriented Electrical Steel from the US and Russia (10 December 2009), obtainable at http://www.chinanews.com/cj/cj-cyzh/news/2009/12-10/2010595.shtml (last visited 17 March 2014) (available in Chinese only, author's translation).

MOFCOM Expressed Regret that the IPR Case had been Referred to the WTO (16 August 2007), obtainable at http://news.xinhuanet.com/newscenter/2007-08/16/content_6544019.htm (last visited 27 February 2014) (available in Chinese only, author's translation).

MOFCOM Notice No. 21 of 2010: Final Determination of Anti-dumping Investigation in respect of Oriented Electrical Steel Originating in the US and Russia and of Countervailing Investigation Originating in the US (13 April 2010), obtainable at http://www.mofcom.gov.cn/aarticle/b/c/2010 04/20100406864469.html (last visited 17 March 2014) (available in Chinese only, author's translation).

MOFCOM Researches on the Request for Consultations from the US and the Dispute may Take Two Years (6 February 2007), obtainable at http://www.chinanews.com/cj/gncj/news/2007/02-06/86 8895.shtml (last visited 23 February 2014) (available in Chinese only, author's translation).

MOFCOM Spokesman Issued a Statement on the AB Ruling on the Publication Market Accession Dispute (22 December 2009), obtainable at http://www.mofcom.gov.cn/aarticle/ae/ag/200912/20091206689022.html (last visited 3 March 2014) (available in Chinese only, author's translation).

MOFCOM Spokesman Issued a Statement on the Establishment of a Panel to Hear WTO Subsidy Dispute (5 September 2007), obtainable at http://www.mofcom.gov.cn/aarticle/difang/hunan/200709/2007 0905064019.html (last visited 23 February 2014) (available in Chinese only, author's translation).

MOFCOM Spokesman Issued a Statement on the Panel Report of the US Electronic Payment Dispute (16 July 2012), obtainable at http://www.mofcom.gov.cn/aarticle/ae/ag/201207/20120708234210.html (last visited 14 March 2014) (available in Chinese only, author's translation).

MOFCOM Spokesman Made Speech on the Panel Report on the US Publication Market Access Case (13 August 2009), obtainable at http://www.mofcom.gov.cn/aarticle/ae/ag/200908/20090806455664.html (last visited 3 March 2014) (available in Chinese only, author's translation).

Mo, Di, Cultivation in *Mo Zi* (gushiwen), obtainable at http://www.gushiwen.org/gushiwen_38dc 49770f.aspx (last visited 10 July 2014) (available in Chinese only, author's translation).

Mo, Di, Jiang Shang in Mo Zi (gushiwen), obtainable at http://www.gushiwen.org/GuShiWen_81d9f4f408.aspx (last visited 14 July 2014) (available in Chinese only, author's translation).

Official Journal (OJ) of the European Communities, 30 June 2001, COUNCIL REGULATION (EC) No 1260/2001 of 19 June 2001 on the common organisation of the markets in the sugar sector.

Pauwelyn, Joost, The Nature of WTO Obligations, Jean Monnet Working Paper 1/02 2002, obtainable from the web site of European Union Jean Monnet Center at http://www.jeanmonnetprogram.org/papers/papers02. html (last visited 30 May 2003).

People's Daily Commentator: the WTO as an opportunity to further open up (11 November 2001), obtainable at http://news.sina.com.cn/c/2001-12-11/416837.html (last visited 10 January 2014) (available in Chinese only, author's translation).

Powell, Jim, Why Trade Retaliation Closes Markets and Impoverishes People, Cato Policy Analysis No. 143 (20 November 1990), www.cato. org/pubs/pas/pa-143.html (last visited 7 June 2004).

Precautions should be Taken in Rare Earth Policy (2 February 2012), obtainable at http://finance.ifeng.com/roll/20120202/5523093. shtml (last visited 6 March 2014) (available in Chinese only, author's translation).

Price, Joint Statement on Trade Dispute in respect of the Export of Chinese Solar Products to the EU (27 July 2013), obtainable at http://www.gov. cn/gzdt/2013-07/27/content_2456534.htm (last visited 14 February 2014) (available in Chinese only, author's translation).

Qin, Ya, WTO Subsidy Rules and Chinese Industrial Policy: Reflections on the Chinese IC Case (1 March 2004), obtainable at http://www.cnki.com. cn/Article/CJFDTotal-GJJF200403016.htm (last visited 14 April 2014) (available in Chinese only, author's translation).

Reflections on the IC VAT Case, obtainable at http://www.cacs.gov.cn/cacs/ webzine/webzine details.aspx?webzineid=541 (last visited 3 February 2012) (available in Chinese only, author's translation).

Resorting to the WTO and the US and EU's Fight for Scarce Chinese Resources (25 June 2009), obtainable at http://finance.people.com.cn/ GB/9537958.html (last visited 5 March 2014) (available in Chinese only, author's translation).

RMB payment services: UnionPay or Visa? (25 July 2012), obtainable at http://news.ifeng.com/gundong/detail_2012_07/25/16293424_0. shtml (last visited 12 March 2014) (available in Chinese only, author's translation).

Stem Classic in *Zhou Yi* (2 September 2006), obtainable at http://zhidao. baidu.com/question/12104333.html (last visited 10 July 2014) (available in Chinese only, author's translation).

Sino-American Film Agreement: Domestic movies 'Dances with Wolves' and 'Only the Strong will Survive' (20 February 2012), obtainable at http://yule.sohu.com/20120220/n335246842.shtml (last visited 3 March 2014) (available in Chinese only, author's translation).

Sino-US Chip Dispute: A Litigation without Suspense (30 July 2004), obtainable at http://finance.sina.com.cn/b/20040730/1114913974.shtml (last visited 17 February 2014) (available in Chinese only, author's translation).

Sino-US consultations on Chinese Intellectual Property Protection (9 June 2007), obtainable at http://news.xinhuanet.com/world/2007-06/09/content_6220032.htm (last visited 26 February 2014) (available in Chinese only, author's translation).

SIPO Director: The US should Withdraw its WTO Complaint (3 July 2007), obtainable at http://www.gov.cn/jrzg/2007-07/03/content_671831.htm (last visited 26 February 2014) (available in Chinese only, author's translation).

Snapshot of WTO Cases Involving the United States (8 August 2012), obtainable at http://www.ustr.gov/sites/default/files/Snapshot%20Aug8.fin_.pdf (last visited 28 February 2014).

Solar Event (4 September 2012), obtainable at http://finance.ifeng.com/news/industry/20120904/6985516.shtml (last visited 14 February 2014) (available in Chinese only, author's translation).

Sun, Bin, Sun Bin's *Arts of War* (gushiwen), obtainable at http://www.gushiwen.org/guwen/sun bin.aspx (last visited 14 July 2014) (available in Chinese only, author's translation).

Sun, Shaohua Sun, The WTO will Establish a Panel on Electronic Payment Services (15 February 2011), obtainable at http://jjckb.xinhua-net.com/2011-02/15/content_287623.htm (last visited 12 March 2014) (available in Chinese only, author's translation).

System of Tax Incentives and Subsidies under the WTO Rules – Status Quo Reflections on China Subsidies, obtainable at http://www.Zcom.gov.cn/zcom/zwfb/zwdt/T256013.shtml (last visited 7 February 2012) (available in Chinese only, author's translation).

The AB Supported Chinese Import Tariffs on Car Parts (17 December 2008), obtainable at http://news.xinhuanet.com/auto/2008-12/17/content_10515664.htm (last visited 20 February 2014) (available in Chinese only, author's translation).

The Analects (19 April 2013), obtainable at http://wenku.baidu.com/link?url=wnIV4AczxIJQjTlRuatMVNp-VmAFgxBZeAeXBtURnO1z13sorRVM__IVIZ1GLW8FF-K4-Wiux7woEAKZN1zpX8lKIxljfR8M5OhEs8uRYa (last visited 10 July 2014) (available in Chinese only, author's translation).

The American Semiconductor Industry Demanded a Share of the $25 billion Chinese Chip Market (17 July 2004), obtainable at http://it.sohu.

com/20040717/n221050121.shtml (last visited 18 February 2014) (available in Chinese only, author's translation).

The Associated Press, China and the WTO Honeymoon Period Ends (11 December 2006), obtainable at http://finance.icxo.com/html-news/2006/12/11/978181.htm (last visited 14 April 2014).

The Copulative in *Yi* (gushiwen), obtainable at http://so.gushiwen.org/guwen/bookv_423.aspx (last visited 10 July 2014) (available in Chinese only, author's translation).

The Dangerous Situation of Rare Earth May Change Export Policy and it is Imperative to Extend the Industrial Chain (6 February 2012), obtainable at http://www.cnmn.com.cn/ShowNews1.aspx?id=228946 (last visited 10 March 2014) (available in Chinese only, author's translation).

The Director of Treaty and Law Department in MOC Made a Speech on the Oriented Electrical Steel Case under the WTO Dispute Settlement Mechanism (14 January 2014), obtainable at http://www.mofcom.gov.cn/article/ae/ai/201401/20140100459536.shtml (last visited 17 March 2014) (available in Chinese only, author's translation).

The German Government and Media Thought that the Prospect of Mutual Cooperation is Better in the IPR Case (17 April 2007), obtainable at http://www.cacs.gov.cn/cacs/newcommon/details.aspx?articleId=30795 (last visited 27 February 2014) (available in Chinese only, author's translation).

The Historical Background to China's Accession to the WTO (20 November 2009), obtainable at http://zhidao.baidu.com/question/122108930.html, last visited 3 January 2014) (available in Chinese only, author's translation).

The IC Industry Faced Policy Adjustments and Chinese Manufacturers were more Worried than Happy (14 August 2004), obtainable at http://www.eet-china.com/ART_8800344681_480101_NT_0da45061.HTM (last visited 19 February 2014) (available in Chinese only, author's translation).

The Sino-US Market Access for Publications Case Settled (24 December 2009), obtainable at http://finance.sina.com.cn/roll/20091224/00017145931.shtml (last visited 3 March 2014) (available in Chinese only, author's translation).

The United States Wanted to Suppress the Chinese Chip Industry (22 March 2004), obtainable at http://www.people.com.cn/GB/paper68/11635/1048799.html (last visited 18 February 2014) (available in Chinese only, author's translation).

The US Complaint to the WTO about China's Restrictions on Foreign Publications (12 October 2007), obtainable at http://www.ipr.gov.cn/alxdarticle/alxd/alxdqt/alxdqtgjal/200710/128664_1.html (last visited 28 February 2014) (available in Chinese only, author's translation).

The US, EU and Canada Jointly Complained to the WTO and Dispute
on Imported Auto Parts Upgraded (18 September 2006), obtainable
at   http://news.xinhuanet.com/auto/2006-09/18/content_5102627.htm
(last visited 20 February 2014) (available in Chinese only, author's
translation).

The US Filed Two Complaints Against China in the WTO (17 September
2010), obtainable at http://finance.sina.com.cn/j/20100917/08268673850.
shtml (last visited 12 March 2014) (available in Chinese only, author's
translation).

The US Initiated a Complaint Against China to the WTO on Discussing
National Treatment (23 March 2004), obtainable at http://finance.sina.
com.cn/g/20040323/1046683555.shtml (last visited 17 February 2014)
(available in Chinese only, author's translation).

The US Launched an Attack on VAT Levied on Semiconductors After
China's Accession to the WTO (20 March 2004), obtainable at http://
news.sina.com.cn/o/2004-03-20/09102095221s.shtml (last visited 17
February 2014) (available in Chinese only, author's translation).

The US Proposed to Establish a Panel in the WTO on Market Access
for Publications (22 October 2007), obtainable at http://news.xinhua-
net.com/newscenter/2007-10/22/content_6925727.htm (last visited 2
February 2014) (available in Chinese only, author's translation).

The US Requested to Establish a Panel Against China in the WTO
(13   February   2011),   obtainable   at   http://news.ifeng.com/world/
detail_2011_02/13/4647907_0.shtml (last visited 13 March 2014) (available in Chinese only, author's translation).

The Whole Story of the Dispute on the Chinese Auto Parts Tariff
(15   February   2008),   obtainable   at   http://auto.sohu.com/20080215/
n255175868_2.shtml (last visited 21 February 2014) (available in Chinese
only, author's translation).

The WTO Releases the Final Ruling on 'Oriented Electrical Steel Double
Reverse' Case (19 October 2012), obtainable at http://jjckb.xinhuanet.
com/2012-10/19/content_407276.htm (last visited 16 March 2014) (available in Chinese only, author's translation).

The WTO Releases the Ruling on Oriented Electrical Steel (16 June
2012),   obtainable   at   http://news.xinhuanet.com/fortune/2012-06/16/
c_112229067.htm (last visited 17 March 2014) (available in Chinese only,
author's translation).

The WTO Rejected Some of the US's Allegations about China UnionPay
(18 July 2012), obtainable at http://news.xinhuanet.com/world/2012-07/
18/c_123425783.htm (last visited 14 March 2014) (available in Chinese
only, author's translation).

The WTO Ruled as to a Chinese Violation in the Raw Materials Case (22

February 2011), obtainable at http://news.xinhuanet.com/fortune/2011--02/22/c_121106802.htm (last visited 9 March 2014) (available in Chinese only, author's translation).

The WTO Ruled on the Violation of Chinese Export Restrictions in Respect of Nine Raw Materials (1 February 2012), obtainable at http://news.xinhuanet.com/fortune/2012-02/01/c_111475447.htm (last visited 8 March 2014) (available in Chinese only, author's translation).

The WTO Ruling on the UnionPay Dispute: the US is Happy and China is not Angry (18 July 2012), obtainable at http://news.xinhuanet.com/fortune/2012-07/18/c_123426446.htm (last visited 14 March 2014) (available in Chinese only, author's translation).

The WTO urged the US not to Submit the Allegation against the Chinese Chip Rebate (19 March 2004), obtainable at http://it.sohu.com/2004/03/19/32/article219513222.shtml (last visited 19 February 2014) (available in Chinese only, author's translation).

UnionPay Speeds up Internationalization (25 July 2012), obtainable at http://news.xinhuanet.com/2012-07/25/c_112529998.htm (last visited 12 March 2014) (available in Chinese only, author's translation).

Visa and UnionPay: Former Partners and Now Enemies (3 June 2012), obtainable at http://news.xinhuanet.com/fortune/2010-06/03/c_12174197.htm (last visited 12 March 2014) (available in Chinese only, author's translation).

Visa Blocked UnionPay's Overseas Channels (21 September 2010), obtainable at http://finance.ifeng.com/bank/special/visayinl/ (last visited 12 March 2014) (available in Chinese only, author's translation).

Visa Filed a Case against UnionPay to the WTO (20 September 2010), obtainable at http://finance.sina.com.cn/money/bank/bank_card/20100920/14128687311.shtml (last visited 12 March 2014) (available in Chinese only, author's translation).

Wang, Hui, Correctly Understand and Deal with the WTO Ruling on Raw Materials Dispute (2 February 2012), obtained at http://www.cnmn.com.cn/ShowNews1.aspx?id=228664 (last visited 9 March 2014) (available in Chinese only, author's translation).

Wang, Chen, WTO Legal Analysis on Sino-US IC Dispute (21 April 2005), obtainable at http://mall.cnki.net/magazine/article/SJMY200504008.htm (last visited 14 April 2014) (available in Chinese only, author's translation).

Wang, Minyang, China Has the Best Performance in the WTO Ruling (29 October 2013), obtainable at http://news.china.com.cn/live/2013-10/29/content_23135413.htm (last visited 16 April 2014) (available in Chinese only, author's translation).

Wang, Tina, WTO's China Piracy Ruling: All Bark and No Bite (27

January 2009), obtainable at http://www.forbes.com/2009/01/27/china-wto-piracy-markets-equity-0127_markets2.html (last visited 28 February 2014).

Wang, Yougen and Gong, Baihua, Comments on the Publication Dispute (11 February 2010), obtainable at http://blog.sina.com.cn/s/blog_4c0f444d0100gz24.html (last visited 3 March 2014) (available in Chinese only, author's translation).

World Centrifugal Sugar Production, 1996–2001, obtainable at http://www.fas.usda.gov/htp/sugar/2000/May/b&csi.pdf (last visited 12 October 2004).

WTO Notification on Preferential Trade Agreement, www.wto.org/english/tratop_e/region_e/region_e.htm.

WTO Established a Panel to Investigate Chinese Restrictions on the Export of Raw Materials (22 December 2009), obtainable at http://news.xinhua-net.com/fortune/2009-12/22/content_12686189.htm (last visited 6 March 2014) (available in Chinese only, author's translation).

Wu Yi Attended and Spoke at a High-Level Forum on the Protection of IPR (24 April 2007), obtainable at http://news.xinhuanet.com/politics/2007-04/24/content_6020185.htm (last visited 26 February 2014) (available in Chinese only, author's translation).

Wu, Yi, Protection of IP is an Inevitable Choice to Improve International Competitiveness (24 April 2007), obtainable at http://news.xinhuanet.com/politics/2007-04/24/content_6019055.htm (last visited 28 February 2014) (available in Chinese only, author's translation).

Xie, Wanyang, Comments on Financial Information Service Measures (9 December 2009), obtainable at http://blog.sina.com.cn/s/blog_4a87beef0100g7fs.html (last visited 5 March 2014) (available in Chinese only, author's translation).

Xun, Kuang, Power in *Xun Zi* (23 November 2007), obtainable at http://www.chinakongzi.org/rjwh/lsjd/xunzi/200711/t20071123_2911783.htm (last visited 10 July 2014) (available in Chinese only, author's translation).

Yang, Guohua, Accession to the WTO: What Does It Mean to China? (3 July 2002), obtainable at http://article.chinalawinfo.com/Article_Detail.asp?ArticleID=2822&Type=mod (last visited 7 April 2014) (available in Chinese only, author's translation).

Yang, Guohua, Careful Preparation for Four Years, but for Once All Bets are Off – the Whole Story of the Chinese IPR Case (20 March 2009), obtainable at http://www.chinalawinfo.com/wto/wtojdaldetail.asp?jdalid=28 (last visited 26 February 2014) (available in Chinese only, author's translation).

Yang, Guohua, China's Course of Participation in the WTO Dispute Settlement Mechanism (2011), obtainable at http://article.chinalawinfo.

com/Article_Detail.asp?ArticleID=64388&Type=mod (last visited 7 April 2014) (available in Chinese only, author's translation).

Yang, Guohua, The Research on the US Steel Safeguard Measures Case (14 March 2004), obtainable at http://article.chinalawinfo.com/Article_Detail.asp?ArticleID=22746&Type=mod (last visited 14 April 2014) (available in Chinese only, author's translation).

Yang, Xun, UnionPay: No Commitment to Open RMB Clearing (6 September 2012), obtainable at http://www.chinadaily.com.cn/hqgj/jryw/2012-09-06/content_6925870.html (last visited 14 March 2014) (available in Chinese only, author's translation).

Yu, Minyou and Liu Heng, China's Performance in a Decade of the WTO (11 November 2010), obtainable at http://images.mofcom.gov.cn/cwto/accessory/201011/1289262759181.pdf (last visited 7 May 2014) (available in Chinese only, author's translation).

Yu, Ying, The Use of Science and Technology Industrial Policy under the WTO Framework: IC Case Analysis (6 July 2007), obtainable at http://mall.cnki.net/magazine/Article/KJJB200707004.htm (last visited 14 April 2014) (available in Chinese only, author's translation).

Zhang, Haizhi, China Appeals Sino-US WTO Market Access for Publications Case (19 August 2009), obtainable at http://www.cipnews.com.cn/showArticle.asp?Articleid=13025 (last visited 2 March 2014) (available in Chinese only, author's translation).

Zhang, Yifang, Chinese Publication Market under the WTO Framework: From the Perspective of the Sino-US Game (10 December 2010), obtainable at http://yifan-cheung.blogbus.com/ (last visited 3 March 2014) (available in Chinese only, author's translation).

Zhao, Weitian, Evaluation of the US Steel Safeguard Measures Case (10 December 2003), obtainable at http://cpfd.cnki.com.cn/Article/CPFDTOTAL-FSMZ200312001022.htm (last visited 14 April 2014) (available in Chinese only, author's translation).

Zhao, Weitian, WTO and International Law (3 July 2002), obtainable at http://article.chinalawinfo.com/Article_Detail.asp?ArticleID=2063 (last visited 7 April 2014) (available in Chinese only, author's translation).

Zou, Yan, WTO and Regional Economic Integration (3 July 2002), obtainable at http://article.chinalawinfo.com/Article_Detail.asp?ArticleID=792 (last visited 7 April 2014) (available in Chinese only, author's translation).

TREATIES AND CONVENTIONS

African, Caribbean and Pacific States (ACP)-European Economic Community (EEC) (Lomé Convention) Lomé, 28 February 1975 as modified by the Cotonou Agreement (signed 23 June 2000), obtainable at http://europa.eu.int/comm/development/body/cotonou/pdf/agr01_en.pdf (last visited 20 June 2004).

Charter of the United Nations, 26 June 1945, San Francisco, UNTS Vol. 402, page 71.

Covenant of the League of Nations, 28 June 1919, Versailles, Treaty of Peace between the Allied and Associated Powers and Germany (Treaty of Versailles), Consolidated Treaty Series Vol. 225.

Convention for the Protection of Human Rights and Fundamental Freedoms, 4 November 1950, Rome, UNTS Vol. 87.

Free Trade Area of the Americas, December, 1994 Miami, obtainable at http://www.ftaa-alca.org/View_e.asp (last visited 2 July 2003).

General Agreement on Tariffs and Trade (GATT), 30 October 1947, Geneva. UNTS Vol. 55 P. 187 (also known as GATT 1947).

International Convention on Civil and Political Rights, 16 December 1966, New York. UNTS Vol. 999 P. 57.

Marrakesh Agreement Establishing the World Trade Organization, 15 April 1994, Marrakesh.

ANNEX 1

Annex 1A: Multilateral Agreements on Trade in Goods
  General Agreement on Tariffs and Trade 1994
  Agreement on Agriculture
  Agreement on the Application of Sanitary and Phytosanitary Measures
  Agreement on Textiles and Clothing
  Agreement on Technical Barriers to Trade
  Agreement on Trade Related Investment Measures
  Agreement on the Implementation of Article VI of the General Agreement on Tariffs and Trade 1994
  Agreement on the Implementation of Article VII of the General Agreement on Tariffs and Trade 1994
  Agreement on Preshipment Inspection
  Agreement on Rules of Origin
  Agreement on Import Licensing Procedures
  Agreement on Subsidies and Countervailing Measures
  Agreement on Safeguards

Annex 1B: General Agreement on Trade in Services and Annexes
Annex 1C: Agreement on Trade-Related Aspects of Intellectual Property
Rights

ANNEX 2

Understanding on Rules and Procedures Governing the Settlement of
Disputes

ANNEX 3

Trade Policy Review Mechanism

ANNEX 4

Plurilateral Trade Agreements
Agreement on Trade in Civil Aircraft
Agreement on Government Procurement
International Dairy Agreement
International Bovine Meat Agreement
Available at official WTO website at http://www.wto.org/english/docs_e/
legal_e/legal_e.htm (last visited 2 July 2003).
North American Free Trade Area (NAFTA), December 1992, obtainable at
http://www.itcilo.it/english/actrav/telearn/global/ilo/blokit/nafta.htm#
Introduction (last visited 2 July 2003).
Rio Declaration on Environment and Development (Rio Declaration
on Environment and Development, 3–14 August 1992, UN General
Assembly Doc. A/CONF.151/26 Vol. I).
Statute of the International Court of Justice, 26 June 1945, San Francisco
(Part of the United Nations Charter).
Treaty Establishing the European Communities (EC Treaty) OJ C 340 (10
November 1997) p. 173.
Treaty Establishing the European Economic Community, 25 March
1957, Rome UNTS Vol. 298 p. 11.
Treaty Establishing a Single Council and a Single Commission of the
European Communities, 8 April 1965, Brussels, OJ 152 (13 June
1967).
Treaty on European Union, 7 February 1992, Maastricht, OJ C 191 (29
July 1992).

United Nations Charter of Economic Rights and Duties of States of 17 December 1984, Chapter I, UN General Assembly Resolution 3281(XXIX), UN Document A/RES/39/163, available at http://www.un.org/documents/ga/res/29/ares29.htm (last visited 17 March 2004).

Vienna Convention on the Law of Treaties, 22 May 1969, Vienna, UNTS Vol. 1155, p. 331.

Index

academic scholarship
China cases deep study phase 191–3
DSU deep study phase 188–91
DSU introductory phase 186–8
amicus briefs 11
Sutherland Report on 13
Appellate Body (AB)
appeals process in DSU 31–2
applicable law *see* applicable law
before WTO disputes settlement
body
burden of proof, inconsistences in
allocating 18–19
deference 13
economic reasons to appeal 34
factual findings not subject to review
33
greater use of dispute mechanism by
broader WTO membership
32–5, 36
issues of law, appeals on 33, 35
jurisdiction 33
competence de la competence
principle 60–61
length of time for appeals 33–4
member's confidence in 33, 35
numbers of appeals 32
references to international law
practices 13–14
applicable law before WTO disputes
settlement body 41–62
applicable law in dispute settlement
47–9
jurisdiction of DSU 48–9, 64
consent as key element in formation
of WTO law 41–2
customary international law as
source of WTO law 53–7
customary international law
central to interpreting WTO
agreements 55

other customary international law
rules 56–7
remedies and customary
international law 56
treaty interpretation 53, 55
WTO law and international law
56
general principles of law 57–61
AB and panels, and 59–60
estoppel 58–9
risk of over-reliance on 58–9
secondary source of law, as 57–8
sources of law, as 57, 60
sources of WTO law, as 60
weaknesses 60
when applied 58
purposes of WTO dispute settlement
system 43–6
sources of public international law/
trade law 41–3, 47
conflict rules 43
determining existence of dispute,
importance of 44
ICJ, and 47, 48
no clear specification of sources
of WTO law 42
state consent 43
text of WTO covered agreements:
straightforward sources 49–53
covered agreements as primary
source of WTO law 49,
51–3
international law, panels and AB
considering 50–51, 64
primary obligations, AB/panels
determining if measures
consistent with 51–2
Association of South East Asian
Countries (ASEAN) 17
audio-visual products 160–66
automobile parts imports 119–25, 131

Bali 2013 Package (trade facilitation/
    food security) 9, 10
Bank of International Settlement
    63
BRICS economies 1, 15
burden of proof 18–19

China
  climate change 199
  compliance *see* Confucianism and
      compliance
  Confucianism *see* Confucianism
  DSU *see* China and WTO dispute
      settlement system
  economy, size of 202
  foreign exchange reserves, holding
      world's largest 2
  GDP, growth in 199
  globalisation, implications of 91
  history 198–9
  human rights 199–200
  internal economic liberalisation 2
  law, approach to 91–4
    Confucianism, and *see*
        Confucianism
    civil codes 92
    criminal codes 92, 93
    disputes
      disruptive to harmony 93–4
      informal settlements preferred
          93–4
      resolved by mutual concessions
          93
    idea of law, origins of 92
    instrument of last resort, as 93
    perception of law as evil 93
    purpose of law as punishment 92,
        94
    reluctance to be bound by Western
        customary law 198
    rule of law 2, 91, 93, 94, 185–6
  perception of itself 198
  regulatory and institutional
      reforms 2
  world trade, increased share of 2
  WTO, joining 1, 2
    accession negotiation to current
        commitments 95–107
    assessment of China's accession to
        WTO 101–6

commitment of Chinese
    government to fulfil
    obligations 106–7
  history of China's accession 1, 2,
      95–101
  positive response from
      international/national media
      101–6
China and WTO dispute settlement
    system 2, 94, 108–93
  Chinese practice within WTO
      dispute settlement framework
      108–78
    astonishing beginning as a
        complainant: steel industry
        safeguards 108–12
    diplomat within first five years
        112–78
  compliance, challenge of 153–78
    Chinese cultural industries, threat
        to 160–66
    compliance panel 11
    copyright law, amendment of
        153–60
    credit cards/logos 166–74
    hard case to implement: oriented
        electrical steel 174–8
  compliance with DSB's
      recommendation 200–201
  diplomat within first five years,
      China as 112–78
    challenge of compliance 153–78
    difficulties faced by China 131,
        153
    first outing as respondent:
        automobile parts imports
        119–25, 131
    predictable dispute: value-added
        tax on integrated circuits
        112–18, 131
    revisiting issue of subsidies
        125–32
    WTO Chinese years 133–53
  DSU rule-oriented system
      challenging traditional Chinese
      beliefs 91
  factors in initiating dispute
      settlement procedure 185
  number of cases 1, 15, 108, 133, 153,
      182–3

perspectives on China and WTO
    dispute settlement system
    178–93
    academic scholarship: China cases
      deep study phase 191–3
    academic scholarship: DSU
      introductory phase 186–8
    academic scholarship: DSU deep
      study phase 188–91
    Chinese Government's perspective
      178–86
    recognition of importance of
      dispute settlement mechanism
      184–6
preparatory work on dispute
    settlement system
    acquiring knowledge about the
      system 178–83
    cases, participating in 180,
      182–3
    litigation skills, developing 181,
      182, 183, 185
    rule-creation, participation in 180,
      184, 185–6
    third party, involvement as 180
WTO Chinese years 133–53
    to be or not to be: financial
      information services 133–7
    tough negotiation in renewable
      energy generation sector
      145–53
    war over resources in economic
      crisis: export of raw materials
      137–45
China and WTO law: accession
    negotiation to current
    commitments 95–107
    assessment of China's accession to
      WTO 101–6
    positive response from
      international/national media
      101–6
    commitment of Chinese government
      to fulfil obligations 106–7
    history of China's accession to WTO
      1, 2, 95–101
    GATT, application to restore
      membership of 96–7
    ITO, and 95–6
    WTO, accession to 1, 97–101

membership of WTO key to China's
    economic success 2
climate change 199
competence de la competence principle
    60–61
compliance
    China, by *see* compliance: China
    Chinese Confucianism, and *see*
      Confucianism and compliance
    compliance with WTO rulings based
      on objective need 200
    GATT, compliance responsibilities
      resting with parties under 23–4
    good faith 45, 59
    national image, interests and
      business interests as vital
      components of 200
    non-compliance 11–12, 204–5
    remedies, and 36, 71–2
    non-compliance, remedies for 8,
      12, 35–40
    world trade law 8
    discourse and constructivism, and
      72–81
    WTO Dispute Settlement
      Understanding/System 70
    constructivism, and 72–81
    major issue of concern, as 64–5
    pacta sunt servanda 40, 49, 70
    reputation costs, and 3, 40, 81–7
compliance: China
    challenge of compliance 153–78
    Chinese cultural industries, threat
      to 160–66
    compliance panel 11
    copyright law, amendment of
      153–60
    credit cards/logos 166–74
    hard case to implement: oriented
      electrical steel 174–8
Confucianism and compliance 70,
    194–201
    advantages and disadvantages of
      sincerity 197
    Chinese Confucianism in context
      194–7
    importance of sincerity 195–7
    meaning of sincerity 196, 197
    no concept of compliance 197
    sincerity as fundamental issue 195

contemporary China and
    compliance 197–201
  bilateral perspective, from 198
  multilateral perspective, from
    198–200
  WTO perspective, from 200–201
DSB's recommendations,
    compliance with 200–201
international agreements, China's
    compliance with 198
international organisations, China's
    compliance with
    International Monetary Fund 199
    United Nations Committee
      against Torture 200
    UN Environment Program 199
    World Bank 199
    WTO dispute settlement system
      200–201
Confucianism 2, 91
  Analects 92
  compliance, and *see* Confucianism
    and compliance
  deep-rooted tradition in China 194
  education, effective management
    through 93
  forbearance, importance of 92–3
  greatest source of normativity, as 88
  harmony as political goal 92, 93
  law necessary for uneducated people
    92–3
  notion of law in Confucian
    tradition/need to adapt 3, 15, 91
  origins 92
  persuasion and negotiations as
    central tenets 2–3, 70, 91, 177,
    202–3, 203–4
  rule of law, and 3
  sanctions 202
  sincerity and/or compliance, concept
    of 194–7
  values as foundation of China's
    cultural/legal tradition 2, 15, 70,
    91, 92
    basis for norms of Chinese
      behaviour 92
Confucianism and compliance 70,
    194–201
  Chinese Confucianism in context
    194–7

advantages and disadvantages of
    sincerity 197
  importance of sincerity 195–7
  meaning of sincerity 196, 197
  no concept of compliance 197
  sincerity as fundamental issue 195
contemporary China and
    compliance 197–201
  bilateral perspective, from 198
  multilateral perspective, from
    198–200
  WTO perspective, from 200–201
constructivism 3, 72–81, 202
  balancing approach determining
    rights and duties of states 77–81
  collective legitimisation of behaviour
    73–4
  ideas and norms influencing
    international relations 74–7
  identity of actors as guiding
    principle of inter-state
    interactions 73, 74
  international institutional regimes as
    important forums 72
  law, nature of 74
  nature of world trading system 73
  world trade law compliance
    discourse, and 72–81
copyright law, Chinese
  amendments to 159
  intellectual property rights
    protection, inadequacy of 146
  piracy rates 145, 156
  WTO dispute settlement system, and
    153–60
credit cards 166–74
  dual-currency/Union Pay credit
    cards 166–8
cultural industries, threat to Chinese
    160–66
  conflict of ideology between China/
    US 165
  cultural security, importance of
    165
  global proliferation of US books/
    audio-visual products, effects of
    164
customary international law
  application in WTO case law
    undeveloped 57

China reluctant to be bound by Western customary law 198
codification 52–3
few customs clearly operating in area of trade law 55
international norms, ingredients for creation of 53–4
persistent objector principle 54, 57
remedies, and 56
source of WTO law, as 53–7
  customary international law central to interpreting WTO agreements 55
  other customary international law rules 56–7
  WTO law and international law 56
treaty interpretation 53, 55
deference 13
dispute settlement mechanisms
applicable law in dispute settlement 47–9
DSU *see* Dispute Settlement Understanding/System (DSU)
GATT *see under* GATT
good faith compliance 45, 59
importance of 22–3
inter-state cooperation, and 17, 43
dispute settlement in inter-state agreements 17–18, 20
  purpose of dispute settlement 18, 20, 22–3
importance of peaceful settlement of disputes 16, 44, 201
procedural rules 20–21
  right to veto dispute resolution bodies/reports 21
purpose of 45
  future role of dispute settlement system, debate over 45–6
  international/trade agreements 19–20, 22–3
relevance in international/trade agreements 16–20
activism 19
diplomatic resolution of disputes 20, 22
dispute, meaning of 16, 44
inconsistencies in interpretation of international treaties 18–19

peaceful settlement of disputes, endorsing 16, 44
proliferation of dispute settlement facilities 17
purpose of dispute settlement 19–20, 22–3
reasons for disputes 19
role/future role of dispute settlement 17–18, 20
remedies *see* remedies
Dispute Settlement Understanding/System (DSU) 2, 3, 20, 29, 71
activism/making sense of agreements 19
jurisprudential progressivism 55
agreement on importance of 12
amicus briefs 11
  Sutherland Report on 13
Appellate Body *see* Appellate Body (AB)
applicable law *see* applicable law
  before WTO disputes settlement body
arbitration procedures 11
China, and *see* China and WTO dispute settlement system
collective countermeasures 12
compliance 70
  constructivism, and 72–81
  major issue of concern, as 64–5
  pacta sunt servanda 40, 49
  reputation costs, and 3, 40, 81–7
deference
  panels and AB, and 13
  standard of review, and 13
  Sutherland Report on 13
disputes, meaning of 44
emerging economies participating in 1
establishment of 11
estoppel 58–9
evolution of *see* evolution of GATT/WTO dispute settlement system
GATT Art XX, inconsistencies in interpreting 18
good faith in initiating complaints/in procedures 59, 60
greater use by broader WTO membership 32–5, 36
numbers of disputes 44

jurisdiction 47–50
    no adjudication on non-WTO
        issues 47, 64
    'non-violation' and 'situation'
        complaints 47–8
    over any dispute from any WTO
        agreement 29–30, 48–9
non-compliance with report 11–12
panels
    appeals from 31–2
    applicable law *see* applicable law
        before WTO disputes
        settlement body
    automatic right to resort to,
        members' 31
    competence de la competence
        principle 60–61
    obligations under Art 11
        interpreted broadly 34
    rulings/recommendations,
        adoption of 31–2
    terms of reference 50
precedent 11, 19
    Sutherland Report on 13
preventive measures 12
promised reforms not moving
        forward 10–13
    constructive ambiguity impeding
        progress 12
    issues of potential concern 10, 11
    questions over how two-tier
        system would operate 11
purposes of 30–31, 43–6
    future role of dispute settlement
        system, debate over 45–6
    role of dispute settlement system
        45
remand 11
remedies 11, 12, 32
    compensation 36–7
    compliance, and 36, 71–2
    divisions among members 12
    meaningful incentives to comply,
        absence of 40
    MFN basis, compensation
        awarded on basis of 36
    negotiable remedies 12
    non-compliance for 12
        controversies on remedies for
            non-compliance 35–40

non-retroactive 34, 39–40, 82
    remedy *ex nunc* outside *acquis* of
        WTO 40
    retaliation 37
    remedies regime as *lex specialis* 14
    reputation costs 3, 40, 81–7
    sanctions, need for threat of 39
    suspension of concessions/other
        obligations 36, 37
    Sutherland report on 14
review of DSU, agreement for 11, 12
role/scope of 18–19
rule-based system, DSU as 30–32,
        91
    appeal stage of process 31–2
    automatic right to resort to panel
        process, members' 31
    compulsory nature of DSU 30
    DSU guided by GATT 1994
        provisions 31
    'institutionalised bargaining',
        move away from 30
    preserving balance of rights/
        obligations of WTO members
        31
    rule of law, DSU based on 91
sequencing 11–12
standards of review
    de novo review 13
    Sutherland Report on 13
    total deference 13
two-tier system 17, 43–4
Doha Development Round/trade talks
        9, 10
    decision-making by consensus 10
    lack of progress 15
Doha Ministerial Conference 12
Doha Ministerial Declaration 12
dubio mitius 60

economic crisis *see* financial/economic
        crisis
electrical steel, oriented 174–8
electronic payments 166–74
estoppel 58–9
evolution of GATT/WTO dispute
        settlement system 16–40
    constructing more legalistic dispute
        settlement method under GATT
        22–7

compliance responsibilities resting
  with parties 23–4
shift from diplomacy to more
  legalistic system 24–5, 30
shortcomings in GATT system,
  need to remedy 26–7
suspension of concessions regime
  25–6
trade protectionist policies, effect
  of 23
types of approach 22
controversies on remedies for non-
  compliance with DSB rulings
  35–40
DSU as rule-based system 30–32
greater use of DSU by broader
  WTO membership 32–5, 36
relevance of dispute settlement
  mechanisms in trade agreements
  16–20
resolving disputes 'the GATT way'
  20–22
procedural rules 20–21
Uruguay Round package as agreed
  by WTO members 27–30
see also dispute settlement
  mechanisms; Dispute Settlement
  Understanding/System (DSU)
export of raw materials 137–45

financial/economic crisis (2008) 2
resources in context of economic
  crisis 137–45
financial information services 133–7
Fuller, Lon 74

GATT (1948–1994) 9
concerns about future of GATT
  26–7
contracting parties appointing
  experts 9
dispute settlement structure 11, 17
  codification of 'customary
    practice' 25
  compliance as responsibility of
    contracting parties 23–4
  consultations between contracting
    parties 23
  diplomatic resolution of disputes
    20, 22, 24–5, 30, 91

evolution of *see* evolution of
  GATT/WTO dispute
  settlement system
ICJ, and 21
legal proceedings, aversion to 23–4
more legalistic method,
  constructing 24–7, 30
'non-violation' and 'situation'
  complaints 47–8
'nullification or impairment' 23,
  25
pragmatism/avoidance of legalism
  21
problems with lack of proper/
  reliable structure 22
procedural uncertainty, early 21–2
resolving disputes 'the GATT way'
  20–22
shortcomings in GATT system,
  need to remedy 26–7
inconsistencies in interpreting Art
  XX 18
nature of 28
remedies 20–21, 22, 25–6
  flawed system of 36
  remedy of last resort 25
  retaliation 37
  suspension of concessions 25–6
  unilateral suspension of
    concessions 26
trade protectionist interest groups,
  and 23
violations of contracting parties'
  rights and obligation 23
general principles of law 57–61
AB and panels, and 59–60
estoppel 58–9
risk of over-reliance on 58–9
secondary source of law, as 57–8
sources of law, as 57, 60
sources of WTO law, as 60
weaknesses 60
when applied 58
global governance 7
globalisation 7, 63
China, implications for 91
economic globalisation, effects/
  meaning of 8
influence on international trade rules
  7, 8

meaning 7–8
trade liberalisation *see* trade
　liberalisation
WTO as integral part of 8, 203
good faith
　DSU, and 59, 60
　dispute settlement mechanisms, and
　　45, 59
　initiating complaints/in procedures
　　59, 60
　WTO treaty obligations and 37,
　　49

Haberler, Professor Gottfreid 9
human rights, China's compliance with
　199–200
　International Labour Organization
　　norms/rules 199–200

ICSID
　length of time for appeals 34
intellectual property *see* copyright law,
　Chinese
International Court of Justice 32
　dispute, definition of 44
　GATT disputes, and 21
　length of time for appeals 33–4
　sources of public international law
　　(Art 38(1) Statute) 47, 48, 50
international economic law 3, 7
　national legal systems, enmeshed
　　in 8
　respect for international norms
　　linked to economic incentives
　　38–9
　Sutherland Report, and 13
　see also applicable law before WTO
　　disputes settlement body
International Labour Organization
　(ILO) 199–200
International Monetary Fund 28, 63
　China's compliance with obligations
　　198
international trade law *see* world trade
　law
International Trade Organization
　(ITO) 95
　ITO Charter 95–6
International Tribunal for the Law of
　the Sea (ITLOS) 48

Jackson, John 12
jura novit curia 14, 56
jus cogens 42, 50

Kant, Immanuel 38

legitimate expectation, loss of 20
less developed countries
　trade, development of 9
Leutwiler, Fritz 9
lex specialis, remedies regime as 14
locus standi 14, 56

mercantilism 71, 204
most favoured nation (MFN)
　compensation awarded on basis of
　　36
　customary law, and 55
　'mutual disarmament' principle 71, 204
North American Free Trade
　Agreement (NAFTA)
　dispute settlement 17
　length of time for appeals 34

pacta sunt servanda 40, 49, 70, 204
panels
　appeals from 31–2
　applicable law *see* applicable law
　　before WTO disputes settlement
　　body
　automatic right to resort to,
　　members' 31
　competence de la competence
　　principle 60–61
　deference 13
　general principles of law, and 59–60
　international law, considering 50–51,
　　64
　obligations under Art 11 interpreted
　　broadly 34
　primary obligations, panels
　　determining if measures
　　consistent with 51–2
　rulings/recommendations, adoption
　　of 31–2
　terms of reference 50
peaceful settlement of disputes
　importance of 16, 44, 201
　international agreements endorsing
　　16, 44

persistent objector principle 54, 57
precautionary principle 14, 56
precedent 11, 19
  Sutherland Report on 13
protectionist market policies 23

remedies 20–21, 22
  customary international law 56
  DSU, under 11, 12, 32
    compensation 36–7
    compliance, and 36, 71–2
    divisions among members 12
    meaningful incentives to comply,
      absence of 40
    MFN basis, compensation
      awarded on basis of 36
    negotiable remedies 12
    non-compliance for 12
      controversies on remedies for
        non-compliance 35–40
    non-retroactive 34, 39–40, 82
    remedies regime as *lex specialis* 14
    remedy *ex nunc* outside *acquis* of
      WTO 40
    reputation costs 3, 40, 81–7
    retaliation 37
    sanctions, need for threat of 39
    suspension of concessions/other
      obligations 36, 37
    Sutherland report on 14
  functions of 35
  GATT, under 20–21, 22, 25–6
    flawed system of 36
    remedy of last resort 25
    retaliation 37
    suspension of concessions 25–6
    unilateral suspension of
      concessions 26
  notion of reparation in international
    law 39–40
  sanctions, need for threat of 38
  scepticism as to effectiveness of 81
renewable energy generation sector
  145–53
reputation costs 3, 202
  diminishing 40
  essential tool to enhance compliance
    with trade rules, as 81–7
  importance of 82
  rational choice theory 81

reliability and reputation costs
  83–4
reputation at level of world trade
  law, factors in 84–7
  nature of treaties, and 87–8
  domestic audiences 87, 88
  reputation costs enhancing
    compliance with WTO law
    87–8
res judicata 60
restitutio in integrum 14
Ricardo, David 38
Rousseau, Charles 41
rule of law
  China, and 2, 91, 93, 94, 185–6
  Confucianism, and 3
  DSU based on 91

Seattle Ministerial Conference 11
sincerity
  concept of 194–7
  fundamental issue, as 195
  importance of 195–7
  meaning of 196, 197
Smith, Adam 38
Sobel, Joel 83–4
sources of public international/trade
  law 41–3, 47
  conflict rules 43
  customary international law as
    source of WTO law 53–7
  customary international law central
    to interpreting WTO
    agreements 55
  general principles of law 60
  ICJ, and 47, 48
  no clear specification of sources of
    WTO law 42
  state consent 43
  text of GATT/WTO as primary
    source of WTO law 49–53
  treaty interpretation 53, 55
  WTO covered agreements as
    primary source of WTO law 49,
    51–3
sovereignty
  China
    accepting constraints on 199
    compliance, and 200
    debates on meaning of 65, 66–7

definitions of 66–7
evolving concept, as 66
intrusion by WTO into 203
rights and duties of states
　determining extent of 80–81
trade openness putting state
　sovereignty at risk 65
traditional notion of concept 65–6,
　71, 204
　no longer tenable 67–8
WTO, and 69
state responsibility, law of 14
steel, oriented electrical 174–8
Stiglitz, Joseph 7
subsidies 125–32
Sutherland Report
composition of consultative board 8, 9
criticisms of 12, 13–14
DSU remedies regime as *lex specialis*
　14
failure to implement
　recommendations 10
publication of 9–10
reasons for establishing consultative
　board 10–11
role of consultative board 8–9
useful comments on relevant issues
　13

theorising WTO implementation
　regime 63–88
nature of treaties and reputation
　costs 87–8
reputation costs as essential tool to
　enhance compliance with trade
　rules 81–7
trade liberalisation as limitation of
　power of nation-state 63–72
world trade law compliance
　discourse and constructivism
　72–81
Tokyo Round/Code 25
trade agreements
dispute settlement mechanisms in *see
　under* dispute settlement
　mechanisms
proliferation of 16
trade liberalisation
limitation of power of nation-state,
　as 63–72

WTO as engine for 7, 36, 37
Trade-Related Aspects of Intellectual
　Property Rights (TRIPS) 146,
　157
treaties
dispute settlement
　inter-state agreements, in 17–18,
　　20
　purpose of 18, 20, 22–3
interpretation under customary law
　53, 55
logical source of international law
　for China 198
manifest error in formation of 14,
　57
no retroactive application of 14,
　56–7
reputation costs, nature of treaties
　and 87–8
successive treaties 56

ubi jus, ibi remedium 14
unilateral actions/unilateralism 68–9,
　204
United Nations 28
United Nations Committee against
　Torture 200
United Nations Conference on Trade
　and Development 63
United Nations Convention on the
　Law of the Sea (UNCLOS) 48, 49
United Nations Economic and Social
　Council (ECOSOC) 95
United Nations Environment Program
　199
Uruguay Round 11, 27–30, 71, 204
utilitarianism 73

value-added tax on integrated circuits
　112–18, 131
Vienna Convention on the Law of
　Treaties
Art 60/multilateral retaliation 26
interpretation of treaties 55

Wendell Holmes Jr, Chief Justice
　Oliver 35
World Bank 28, 63
China's compliance with obligations
　198

world trade law
  changing fundamentals in global
    architecture, and 7–15
  compliance
    discourse and constructivism, and
      72–81
    international law obligations, with
      8
    remedies for non-compliance 8
    see also compliance
  consent as key element in formation
    of WTO law 41–2
  customary international law as
    source of WTO law 53–7
    few customs clearly operating in
      area of trade law 55
    market opening as customary
      practice in international
      economic relations 54–5
  globalisation, influence on
    international trade rules of 7, 8
  growing intercourse between WTO
    rules/other international law
    rules 13–14
  hard and soft law in international
    trade norm-making 8
  importance of 8
  international law, and 56
    international law's place in WTO's
      acquis 13–14
  reputation costs *see* reputation
    costs
  sources of trade law 41–3, 47
    conflict rules 43
    customary international law as
      source of WTO law 53–7
    customary international law
      central to interpreting WTO
      agreements 55
    general principles of law 60
    ICJ, and 47, 48
    no clear specification of sources
      of WTO law 42
    state consent 43
    text of GATT/WTO as primary
      source of WTO law 49–53
    treaty interpretation 53, 55
    WTO covered agreements as
      primary source of WTO law
      49, 51–3

  see also applicable law before WTO
    disputes settlement body
World Trade Organization (WTO)
  applicable law *see* applicable law
    before WTO disputes settlement
    body
  challenges facing world trading
    system 8–15
    consultative board examining *see*
      Sutherland Report
    Haberler Report 9
    Leutwiler Report 9
  Charter and Annexes, WTO 29
    Agreement on Agriculture (AG)
      29
    Civil Aircraft, Agreement on
      Trade in 30
    DSU 29–30
    GATS 29
    Government Procurement,
      Agreement on 30
    trade in goods agreements/GATT
      29
    Trade Policy Review Mechanism
      (TPRM) 30
    TRIPS 29
  China *see* China
  common intentions of members 18
  consensus and single undertaking
    principles 10
  'constructive ambiguity' in trade
    negotiations 10
  criticisms of 69
  dispute settlement mechanism *see*
    Dispute Settlement
    Understanding/System (DSU)
  emerging economies, and 15
  equal treatment 51
  establishment of 17, 18, 27
  globalisation, and 7
  good faith principle, WTO treaty
    obligations and 37, 49
  Headquarters Agreement, WTO 28
  implementation regime, theorising
    63–88
    nature of treaties and reputation
      costs 87–8
    reputation costs as essential tool
      to enhance compliance with
      trade rules 81–7

trade liberalisation as limitation of
    power of nation-state 63–72
world trade law compliance
    discourse and constructivism
    72–81
law *see* world trade law
legalism, trend towards 91–2
Marrakesh Agreement establishing
    18, 28
members/member-based
    organisation 1, 2, 15, 28–9, 41
nature of
    immunity for WTO/staff from
    municipal courts' jurisdiction
    28

legal personality 28
multilateral institution, as 1, 2, 15,
    27–9
rule-based trading system, as
    2, 3
WTO Agreement as an
    'interpendence' regime 54
reputation costs, and 82–7
reservations not permitted 38
trade liberalisation/economic
    growth, WTO as engine for 7,
    36, 37
trade-related agreements, based on
    15
unilateral actions 68–9